JOURNAL FOR THE STUDY OF THE NEW TESTAMENT SUPPLEMENT SERIES
122

Executive Editor
Stanley E. Porter

Editorial Board
Richard Bauckham, David Catchpole, R. Alan Culpepper,
Margaret Davies, James D.G. Dunn, Craig A. Evans, Stephen Fowl,
Robert Fowler, Robert Jewett, Elizabeth Struthers Malbon

Sheffield Academic Press

Matthew's Transfiguration Story and Jewish-Christian Controversy

A.D.A. Moses

Journal for the Study of the New Testament
Supplement Series 122

Published by Sheffield Academic Press Ltd
Mansion House
19 Kingfield Road
Sheffield, S11 9AS
England

Printed on acid-free paper in Great Britain
by Bookcraft Ltd
Midsomer Norton, Bath

British Library Cataloguing in Publication Data

A catalogue record for this book is available
from the British Library

ISBN 1-85075-576-0

CONTENTS

Preface   9
Abbreviations   10

Chapter 1
INTRODUCTION   13
  1. Statement of Purpose   14
  2. Method   14
  3. Working Assumptions   16

Chapter 2
A CRITICAL SURVEY OF SCHOLARSHIP ON THE
TRANSFIGURATION   20
  1. The Transfiguration, the Resurrection, Ascension and
     Parousia   20
  2. The Transfiguration and the Theme of Suffering   25
  3. The Transfiguration Viewed within Jewish and Hellenistic
     Categories   32
  4. The Transfiguration and the Function of Moses and Elijah   36
  5. The Transfiguration and Moses-Sinai Symbolism   42

Chapter 3
A SURVEY OF MOSES-SINAI AND TRANSFIGURATION THEMES
IN SECOND TEMPLE JUDAISM   50
  1. Moses-Sinai and Moses-Transfiguration Language and
     Themes in Philo   50
  2. Moses-Sinai and Transfiguration Motifs in Josephus   57
  3. Moses-Sinai and Transformation Motifs in Qumran
     Literature   61
  4. Moses-Sinai and Moses-Transfiguration Themes in
     Samaritan Literature   66
  5. Moses-Sinai and Transfiguration Motifs in the Apocrypha
     and Pseudepigrapha   74

6. A Survey of Moses-Sinai and other Moses Motifs in
        Rabbinic *halakah* and *haggada*   77
7. A Survey of Moses-Sinai Motifs in the Fragments of Lost
        Judeo-Hellenistic Works   80

Chapter 4
MATTHEW 17.1-13 IN THE LIGHT OF LITERARY PARALLELS
AND DANIEL 7-SINAI CONSIDERATIONS   85
1. The Transfiguration in the Light of Parallels in Graeco-
        Hellenistic Literature   85
2. The Transfiguration in the Light of Parallels in Apocalyptic
        Literature   87
3. The 'Vision-Form', Matthew's Use of τὸ ὅραμα and
        Danielic Motifs   89
4. The Sinai-Daniel 7 Conceptual Setting: The Relationship
        between Matthew's Presentation of the 'Coming of the
        Son of Man' (16.27-28), the 'Coming of God' at Sinai,
        Daniel 7 and Matthew 17.1-13   103

Chapter 5
AN EXEGESIS OF MATTHEW 17.1-13 IN THE LIGHT OF SOURCE
AND REDACTION CRITICAL ISSUES   114
1. Matthew 17.1 and Mark 9.2a   114
2. Matthew 17.2 and Mark 9.2b-3   120
3. Matthew 17.3 and Mark 9.4   127
4. Matthew 17.4 and Mark 9.5   130
5. Matthew 17.5 and Mark 9.7   135
6. Matthew 17.6-7   148
7. Matthew 17.8 and Mark 9.8   150
8. Matthew 17.9; 17.10-13 in the Light of Mark 9.9-10 and
        9.11-13   150

Chapter 6
MATTHEW'S TRANSFIGURATION PERICOPE (17.1-13) IN THE
LIGHT OF THE JESUS-MOSES AND EXODUS-SINAI PARALLELISM
ELSEWHERE IN THE FIRST GOSPEL   161
1. Moses and Matthew's Infancy Narrative (Mt. 1.18-2.23)   163
2. The Baptism Narrative (Mt. 3.13-17)   167
3. The Temptation Narrative and the Jesus-Exodus-Israel
        Parallelism (Mt. 4.1-11)   170

4. The Sermon on the Mount (Mt. 5–7)   175
5. The Last Supper (Mt. 26.17-29)   185
6. Jesus' Moses-Type Farewell Discourse (Mt. 28.16-20
       and Deut. 1–34)   187
7. Matthew's Moses-Jesus Typology in the Light of Son of
       David Themes and Zion Theology   192

Chapter 7
CONFIRMATION OF THE IMPORTANCE OF THE JESUS-MOSES
AND TRANSFIGURATION MOTIFS ELSEWHERE IN THE NEW
TESTAMENT   208
1. The Jesus-Moses Parallelism and Exodus Motifs in the
       Acts Speeches   208
2. The Transfiguration in 2 Peter 1.16-18   211
3. The Jesus-Moses Parallelism and the Letter to the Hebrews   212
4. Moses-Sinai and Transfiguration Motifs in the Fourth Gospel   214
5. Moses-Sinai and Transfiguration Motifs and
       2 Corinthians 3.7-18 and 4.1-6   224

OVERALL CONCLUSIONS   239

Appendix
LUKE'S UNDERSTANDING OF THE TRANSFIGURATION   245

Bibliography   251
Index of References   273
Index of Authors   000

PREFACE

This monograph is a revision of my doctoral dissertation submitted to Westminster College, Oxford in collaboration with Wycliffe Hall, Oxford in 1992. I owe a debt of gratitude to several people who have helped me in various ways during the preparation of this book: above all to my primary supervisor, Dr David Wenham, who read many drafts of this thesis and has given countless hours to discuss the work with me. Dr N.T. Wright, my second supervisor, has contributed significantly through his reading and comments on material presented to him. I am grateful to Wycliffe Hall, Oxford, for the supportive environment provided for me and my family during our time in Oxford; to the University of Oxford for access to its libraries and lectures; and to Tyndale Hall, Cambridge for the use of the resources there.

I would like to thank Ralph and Tisha Dunstan who on several occasions provided me with welcome rest at their home in Devon during my studies.

Finally, I want to thank Clare Wenham and my wife, Vasanthy, for editing the manuscript, and my son, Paul, who has provided inspiration and joy for this work. I dedicate this book to my late parents, who started me off on my theological pilgrimage.

ABBREVIATIONS

AJT	*American Journal of Theology*
ALUOS	*Annual of Leeds University Oriental Studies*
ANRW	*Aufstieg und Niedergang der römischen Welt*
ATR	*Anglican Theological Review*
BETL	Bibliotheca ephemeridum theologicarum lovaniensium
Bib	*Biblica*
BJRL	*Bulletin of the John Rylands University Library of Manchester*
BTB	*Biblical Theology Bulletin*
BZAW	Beihefte zur *ZAW*
CBQ	*Catholic Biblical Quarterly*
CRINT	Compendia rerum iudaicarum ad Novum Testamentum
EBib	Etudes bibliques
EvQ	*Evangelical Quarterly*
ExpTim	*Expository Times*
FzB	Forschung zur Bibel
HeyJ	*Heythrop Journal*
HTR	*Harvard Theological Review*
HUCA	*Hebrew Union College Annual*
IDB	G.A. Buttrick (ed.), *Interpreter's Dictionary of the Bible*
Int	*Interpretation*
ISBE	*The International Standard Bible Encyclopedia*
JBL	*Journal of Biblical Literature*
JETS	*Journal of the Evangelical Theological Society*
JewEnc	*Jewish Encyclopedia*
JJS	*Journal of Jewish Studies*
JQR	*Jewish Quarterly Review*
JR	*Journal of Religion*
JSNT	*Journal for the Study of the New Testament*
JSNTSup	*Journal for the Study of the New Testament*, Supplement Series
JSOT	*Journal for the Study of the Old Testament*
JTS	*Journal of Theological Studies*
NIDNTT	C. Brown (ed.), *The New International Dictionary of New Testament Theology*
NIGTC	The New International Greek Testament Commentary
NovT	*Novum Testamentum*
NTAbh	Neutestamentliche Abhandlungen

NTS	*New Testament Studies*
OTP	*Old Testament Pseudepigrapha*
RB	*Revue biblique*
RechBib	Recherches bibliques
RTP	*Revue de théologie et de philosophie*
SBL	Society of Biblical Literature
SBLMS	SBL Monograph Series
SBT	Studies in Biblical Theology
SJT	*Scottish Journal of Theology*
ST	*Studia theologica*
StudNeot	Studia neotestamentica
TDNT	G. Kittel and G. Friedrich (eds.), *Theological Dictionary of the New Testament*
TynBul	*Tyndale Bulletin*
TZ	*Theologische Zeitschrift*
VT	*Vetus Testamentum*
ZNW	*Zeitschrift für die neutestamentliche Wissenschaft*
ZTK	*Zeitschrift für Theologie und Kirche*

Chapter 1

INTRODUCTION

In the Asian religious context the transfiguration story (Mt. 17.1-8; Mk 9.2-8; Lk. 9.28-36) has been extensively discussed, being compared to stories in the Asian religious tradition, for example, to the concept of 'Avatara' in Hinduism.[1] In the West, however, contemporary scholarship has not given the transfiguration story as significant a place in the discussion on New Testament theology as might be expected. This is not to say that there has been a total absence of discussion,[2] but the difficulties which the text itself poses to the modern exegete—literary, historical and theological—have led scholars to give it relatively little attention.[3]

---

1. D.E. Bassuk, *Incarnation in Hinduism and Christianity* (London: Macmillan, 1987).

2. For a select bibliography see T.F. Best, 'The Transfiguration: A Select Bibliography', *JETS* 24 (1981), pp. 157-61; M. Sabbé, 'La rédaction du récit de la Transfiguration', in E. Massaux (ed.), *La venue du Messie: Messianisme et Eschatologie* (RechBib, 6; Bruges: Brouwer, 1962), pp. 56-100, reprinted and slightly expanded in *Studia Neotestamentica: Collected Essays* (BETL, 98; Leuven: Leuven University Press, 1991), pp. 65-104, esp. pp. 101-104; J.M. Nützel, *Die Verklärungserzählung im Markuesevangelium: Eine redaktionsgeschichtliche Untersuchung* (FzB, 6; Würzburg: Echter, 1973), pp. 317-24. Articles on the transfiguration by M.D. Hooker, A.A. Trites and D. Evans, in D. Hurst and N.T. Wright (eds.), *The Glory of Christ in the New Testament* (Oxford: Clarendon Press, 1987), perhaps suggest interest in this topic; also see R.H. Gundry, *Mark: A Commentary on his Apology for the Cross* (Grand Rapids: Eerdmans, 1993), pp. 457-86.

Recently see D.C. Allison, *The New Moses: A Matthean Typology* (Minneapolis: Fortress Press, 1993), esp. pp. 243-48; D. Wenham and A.D.A. Moses, '"There are Some Standing Here...": Did they Become the "Reputed Pillars" of the Jerusalem Church? Some Reflections on Mark 9.1, Galatians 2.9 and the Transfiguration', *NovT* 36 (1994), pp. 146-63, and more recently, D. Wenham, *Paul: Follower of Jesus or Founder of Christianity?* (Grand Rapids: Eerdmans, 1995), pp. 357-63.

3. Also see D. Evans, 'Academic Scepticism, Spiritual Reality and the Transfiguration', in D. Hurst and N.T. Wright (eds.), *The Glory of Christ in the New Testament* (Oxford: Clarendon Press, 1987), pp. 175-86.

1. *Statement of Purpose*

The literary questions pertaining to the transfiguration pericope include source, form and redaction critical issues. Source critical questions concern, for example, the agreements between Matthew's and Mark's account as against that of Luke, some 'minor agreements' of Matthew and Luke against Mark, and distinctive material in Luke's narrative of the transfiguration which may not be Lukan redaction but may derive from a non-Lukan source.[4] On the form of the transfiguration pericopes scholars have made various suggestions about its genre, nature and origin, with some seeing it as a displaced resurrection story.[5] From a redaction critical point of view, various issues arise. For example, the setting of the transfiguration passages in the synoptics is of particular significance. The differences between the accounts need to be explained;[6] the theological significance of the story for the different evangelists needs to be brought out.

The transfiguration pericope also raises significant theological questions. Various themes are striking within the text itself. For example, the appearances of Moses and Elijah, the cloud motif, the voice from heaven, the transfiguration of Jesus himself and the related themes that arise from it. These themes and ideas need to be seen in the light of the Jewish thinking of the time and the appearance of these motifs elsewhere in the New Testament.

It is, therefore, the purpose of this study to address some of these issues, and, because of the need to limit the scope of the thesis, to focus particularly on Matthew 17.1-9.

2. *Method*

(1) I shall review critically and evaluate scholarly discussion of the interpretation of the transfiguration. The existence of a great divergence of interpretations will suggest that the proper way forward is to study how each evangelist has understood the transfiguration in keeping with his own theological viewpoint.[7] So this section will include a comparison

4.   These issues are addressed in the Appendix: 'Luke's Understanding of the Transfiguration'.

5.   See discussion in Chapter 2.1.

6.   See discussion in Chapters 2, 3, 5 and Appendix.

7.   The importance of the individual 'theologies' of the evangelists has long since

of the relevant synoptic texts in order to ascertain how the different texts relate and to make provisional deductions about the history of the traditions.

(2) I shall evaluate the pervasive influence of the Moses-Sinai transfiguration motifs in Second Temple Judaism. This Jewish framework will allow us to appreciate better, for example, why Matthew emphasised the radiance of Jesus' face, amalgamating Mosaic and Danielic language and motifs. This is a point that will surface throughout my thesis; that is, that Matthew used categories within his socio-cultural and religious world in order to (a) address the Moses ideology of his day, in his dialogue with the Pharisees,[8] and (b) communicate to his readers that the 'coming of God' had taken place in Jesus. The issue of how Matthew by creative use of his sources and redaction produced the present form and order of his transfiguration pericope, and the implications of this for Matthean theology, will engage us in the largest part of this thesis.

(3) I shall examine possible background and parallels to the transfiguration story, particularly looking at literary parallels, especially in Jewish apocalyptic literature, and making form critical comparisons. This will help us to locate Matthew's presentation of the transfiguration in its first-century Jewish, socio-religious and intellectual setting. This section will also show how Matthew responds to this setting, (a) by his distinctive redaction and use of source material, primarily Mark and the tradition behind Mark, in order to (b) produce his distinctive 'vision-form' and so express his own theological interests. Here I shall demonstrate that Matthew has presented his transfiguration pericope within a Danielic 'Son of Man *inclusio*',[9] and this enables him to present the transfiguration in terms of the 'coming of God'. This focus on the 'setting of the transfiguration' in Matthew sets the stage for my exegesis of the passage.

been recognised, and the present day emphasis on 'holistic' appreciation of the evangelist's theology is commendable. On this see R.T. France, *Matthew—Evangelist and Teacher* (Exeter: Paternoster Press, 1989), pp. 41-49.

8.   For Matthew's dialogue with the Pharisees (and the synagogue) see K. Stendahl, *The School of Matthew, and its Use of the Old Testament* (Philadelphia: Fortress Press, 1968), pp. xi-xii; L.E. Keck, 'The Sermon on the Mount', in D.G. Miller and D.Y. Hadidian (eds.), *Jesus and Man's Hope* (2 vols.; Pittsburgh: Pittsburgh Theological Seminary, 1971), II, pp. 311-22; B.T. Viviano, 'Where was the Gospel according to St Matthew Written?', *CBQ* 41 (1979), pp. 533-36.

9.   This is developed in Chapter 4.3 and 4.4. I originally wanted to use the word 'sandwich', but for want of a better word I settled on '*inclusio*'.

(4) I shall do an exegetical study of Mt. 17.1-13 with reference to its immediate context and the Gospel as a whole. Here attention will be given to Matthew's vocabulary, distinct theological motifs, grammar within the passage, and its relation to parallel motifs within Matthew's Gospel. This chapter does not stand on its own, but develops chapter 4 and anticipates chapters 6 and 7; for Matthew's redactional and theological interests in the transfiguration narrative need to be set in the context of the 'holistic' reading of it which will be highlighted in chapter 6.

(5) I shall evaluate how Matthew's transfiguration pericope and its theology function in relation to the overall plot of the Gospel. This will involve a broad sweep through the first Gospel, including Matthew's infancy narrative, baptism, temptation, the sermon on the mount, the last supper and final commissioning.

The implications of my exegesis of Mt. 17.1-13 take us beyond Matthew's Gospel. I shall show, for example, that Matthew's emphasis on Peter at the transfiguration and the elevation Peter received in the early community (partly due to his witness of the transfiguration) may have posed problems for Paul. In 2 Cor. 3–4 he responds to this by viewing his Damascus road experience as comparable to the disciples', particularly Peter's, witness of the transfiguration of Jesus. Thus, (6) in my final chapter I shall discuss 2 Cor. 3–4 and other early Christian writings such as Acts, Hebrews, 2 Peter, and John's Gospel—which will confirm the importance of the Jesus-Moses and transfiguration motifs elsewhere in the New Testament.

3. *Working Assumptions*

In recent years there has been a call for an 'open verdict' on the literary relationships of the synoptics.[10] Scholars have found the two dominant rival positions, the 'Griesbach' and 'Two-Document' theories, to be too neat and perhaps 'simplistic', and it has been argued that these proposed 'solutions' cannot cope with the 'complex web of factual data' thrown

---

10. Cf. E.P. Sanders, *The Tendencies of the Synoptic Tradition* (Cambridge: Cambridge University Press, 1969), pp. 278-79; 'The Overlaps of Mark and Q and the Synoptic Problem', *NTS* 19 (1972/3), pp. 453-65. In general see D.L. Dungan, *The Interrelations of the Gospels* (Leuven: Leuven University Press and Leuven: Peeters, 1990); F. Van Segbroeck *et al.* (eds.), *The Four Gospels: Festschrift Frans Neirynck* (3 vols.; Leuven: Leuven University Press and Leuven: Peeters, 1992).

up by the texts of the Gospel.[11] However, while simple linear solutions to the synoptic problem have been questioned,[12] there is reasonable general agreement that Mark offers us the earliest or most primitive account of the teachings of Jesus.[13] In this thesis I acquiesce to the view that Matthew knew and used Mark; however, I do not advocate a one-stage, purely linear redaction, but allow for Matthew's possible knowledge of other traditions and for the cross-fertilization of traditions both written and oral.[14] Most importantly, Matthew's presentation of the transfiguration needs to be appreciated from a holistic perspective, something that is stressed in chapter 6.

I take the position that Matthew is a Jewish Christian,[15] a literary

11. See France, *Matthew—Evangelist*, pp. 41-42; Sanders, *The Tendencies of the Synoptic Tradition*. For criticism against 'Q' see A. Farrer, 'On Dispensing with Q', in D.E. Nineham (ed.), *Studies in the Gospels* (Oxford: Basil Blackwell, 1955), pp. 55-88; M.D. Goulder, 'On Putting Q to the Test', *NTS* 24 (1978) pp. 218-34.

12. J.A.T. Robinson, *Redating the New Testament* (London: SCM Press, 1985), pp. 94-95.

13. Any work on the synoptic problem would cite the 'Markan priorists' and it is pointless to cite all of them. Recently see D.A. Hagner, *Matthew 1–13* (Dallas: Word, 1993), pp. xlvii-xlviii; W.D. Davies and D.C. Allison, *A Critical and Exegetical Commentary on the Gospel according to Saint Matthew* (Edinburgh: T. & T. Clark, 1988), pp. 73-74, 97-127, who also accept the 'two-source' theory. For a qualified acceptance of Mark as the earliest, see R.T. France, *Divine Government* (London: SPCK, 1990), pp. 3-4; E.P. Sanders and M. Davies, *Studying the Synoptic Gospels* (London: SCM; Philadelphia: Trinity, 1989). For those who accept Markan priority and also Luke's knowledge of Matthew see Farrer, 'On Dispensing with Q', pp. 55-88; Goulder, 'On Putting Q to the Test' (1978), pp. 218-34, 'Mark XVI.1-8 and Parallels', *NTS* 24 (1978), pp. 235-40, *Midrash and Lection in Matthew* (London: SPCK, 1974), pp. 241-442; A.W. Argyle, 'Evidence for the View that St Luke Used St Matthew's Gospel', *JBL* 83 (1964), pp. 390-96; R.H. Gundry, *Matthew: A Commentary on his Literary and Theological Art* (Grand Rapids: Eerdmans, 1982).

14. Cf. Robinson, *Redating the New Testament*, p. 94; Hagner, *Matthew 1–13*, pp. xlvii-xlviii; L. Morris, *The Gospel according to Matthew* (Grand Rapids: Eerdmans; Leicester: IVP, 1992), pp. 15-17.

15. See Hagner, *Matthew 1–13*, pp. lxxvi-lxxvii; Davies and Allison, *Saint Matthew*, I, pp. 7-58; France, *Matthew—Evangelist*, pp. 95-108; J.D.G. Dunn, *Unity and Diversity in the New Testament* (London: SCM Press, 1977), pp. 246-51; Goulder, *Midrash and Lection in Matthew*; E. von Dobschütz, 'Matthew as Rabbi and Catechist', in G. Stanton (ed.), *The Interpretation of Matthew* (Philadelphia: Fortress Press; London: SPCK, 1983), pp. 19-29; G.D. Kilpatrick, *The Origins of the Gospel according to St Matthew* (Oxford: Clarendon Press, 1946), pp. 106-107. For the 'thoroughly Jewish flavour' of the First Gospel see K. Tagawa, 'People and

technician[16] who creatively responds to his socio-cultural and religious setting in his Gospel.[17] He writes to a predominantly Jewish community,

Community in the Gospel of Matthew', *NTS* 16 (1969-70), pp. 149-62; N.T. Wright, *The New Testament and the People of God* (Minneapolis: Fortress Press, 1992), pp. 384-90; Morris, *Matthew*, pp. 2-3; also S.H. Brooks, *Matthew's Community: The Evidence of his Special Material* (JSNTSup, 16; Sheffield: JSOT Press, 1987); Allison, *The New Moses*.

Matthew's Jewishness has not gone uncontested: see K.W. Clark, 'The Gentile Bias in Matthew', *JBL* 66 (1947), p. 165; J.P. Meier, *Law and History in Matthew's Gospel* (Rome: Biblical Institute Press, 1976), pp. 16-20; *The Vision of Matthew* (New York: Paulist Press, 1979), pp. 19-23. For an evaluation of such a view, but concluding that 'the evangelist is unlikely to have been a Gentile', see G. Stanton, 'The Origin and Purpose of Matthew's Gospel: Matthean Scholarship from 1945 to 1980', in H. Temporini and W. Haase (eds.), *Aufstieg und Niedergang der römischen Welt* (Berlin: de Gruyter, 1985), pp. 1916-1921; *A Gospel for a New People: Studies in Matthew* (Edinburgh: T. & T. Clark, 1992); Davies and Allison, *Saint Matthew*, I, pp. 9-10; France, *Matthew—Evangelist*, pp. 102-108; Hagner, *Matthew 1–13*, pp. liii-lxxvii.

Whether Matthew's community was *intra muros* or *extra muros* has been widely debated (on the state of the debate see Stanton, 'The Origin and Purpose of Matthew's Gospel', pp. 1914-1915, who holds the *extra muros* position and that the community was still engaged in defending itself over against Judaism). But France, *Matthew—Evangelist*, pp. 99-100, questions whether the *intra/extra muros* debate needs to be linked with the dating of the Gospel tradition (as it is in Stanton's evaluation). For one could hold an *extra muros* position and still give Matthew an early dating (see C.F.D. Moule, 'St Matthew's Gospel: Some Neglected Features', in F.L. Cross [ed.], *Studia Evangelica II* [Berlin: Akademie-Verlag, 1964], pp. 90-99; reprinted in C.F.D. Moule, *Essays in New Testament Interpretation* [Cambridge: Cambridge University Press, 1982], pp. 67-74, esp. pp. 69, 72).

16. For thematic thinking, linguistic interconnections, affinity for repetition formulas, see Davies and Allison, *Saint Matthew*, I, pp. 58-96; France, *Matthew—Evangelist*, pp. 123-65.

17. That Matthew's community was in conflct with 'formative Judaism' see J.A. Overman, *Matthew's Gospel and Formative Judaism* (Minneapolis: Fortress Press, 1990). But that Matthew's community was a reform movement within Judaism see A.F. Segal, 'Matthew's Jewish Voice', in D.L. Balch (ed.), *Social History of the Matthean Community* (Minneapolis: Fortress Press, 1991), pp. 3-37; A.J. Saldarini, 'The Gospel of Matthew and Jewish-Christian Conflict', in *Social History of the Matthean Community*, pp. 38-61, and more elaborately in his recent book: *Matthew's Christian-Jewish Community* (Chicago and London: University of Chicago Press, 1994). Saldarini tries to argue that Matthew lost the battle for Judaism and his Gospel is a Christian-Jewish attempt to unite Jews and Gentiles (p. 206). Against Segal and Saldarini, and for the view that the church in Matthew is a new people (albeit with

emphasising the motif of fulfilment and portraying Jesus as in continuity with Israel but also as initiating the new Israel. Despite Matthew's emphasis on Jesus' initial message to the 'lost sheep of the house of Israel' (10.6) he shows interest in the Gentiles (4.15; 8.5-13; 15.21-39) and anticipates active mission among them (28.18-20). Whether Matthew's Gospel reflects the church's situation post-Jamnia is an open question,[18] but arguments by Gundry[19] and others for an earlier date need not be dismissed.

intramural problems) with a replaced Torah, differing from the Jews, see R.H. Gundry, 'A Responsive Evaluation of the Social History of the Matthean Community in Roman Syria', in Balch (ed.), *Social History*, pp. 62-67. Given the influence of Hellenism on (Palestinian) Judaism (see I.H. Marshall, 'Palestinian and Hellenistic Christianity: Some Critical Comments', *NTS* 19 [1973], pp. 271-87; M. Hengel, *Judaism and Hellenism* [Philadelphia: Fortress Press 1974]; J. Riches, *Jesus and the Transformation of Judaism* [London: Darton, Longman & Todd, 1980], pp. 62-80; S. Lieberman, *Hellenism in Jewish Palestine* [New York: Jewish Theological Seminary, 1962], pp. 19-20; B.T. Viviano, 'Where Was the Gospel according to Matthew Written?', p. 540) Matthew's exposure to and competence in communicating to a Hellenised Jewish culture cannot be ignored. On this, see Gundry, *Matthew*, p. 622. Hagner, *Matthew 1–13*, p. lxxvii, suggests that the final editing of the Gospel was probably done by a Hellenistic Christian.

18. That Matthew's anti-Pharisaism, anti-Temple emphasis fits the post-Jamnia context see W.D. Davies, *The Setting of the Sermon on the Mount* (Cambridge: Cambridge University Press, 1963), pp. 256-315; esp. p. 315; Davies and Allison, *Saint Matthew*, I, pp. 127-38; Keck, 'The Sermon on the Mount', p. 313. Kilpatrick, *The Origins*, pp. 110-11, links Matthew's συναγωγὴ αὐτῶν with the insertion of the *'Birkat ha-Minim'* to the synagogue liturgy around 85 CE, excluding Christian Jews from the synagogues. But against this see R. Kimelmann, 'Birkat ha-Minim and the Lack of Evidence for an Anti-Christian Jewish Prayer in Late Antiquity', in E.P. Sanders (ed.), *Jewish and Christian Self-definition* (3 vols.; Philadelphia: Fortress Press, 1981), II, pp. 226-44.

19. Gundry, *Matthew*, pp. 600-601, drawing on Paul (Pharisee's persecution of the church: Phil. 3.5-6; Acts 8.3; 9.1-2, 13-14, 21; 22.3-5, 19; 26.9-11; 1 Cor. 15.9; Gal. 1.13; 1 Thess. 2.13-16; 1 Tim. 1.13), has argued, among other things, that the conflict between Pharisaism and Christianity need not be post-Jamnian. Moreover, other groups like the Essenes/Qumran too had an ambiguous attitude towards the Temple and isolated themselves.

Chapter 2

A CRITICAL SURVEY OF SCHOLARSHIP ON THE TRANSFIGURATION

A universally accepted solution has never been reached in understanding the significance of the transfiguration. The purpose of this chapter is critically to evaluate scholarship on the transfiguration, and as a methodological procedure, I shall first do a general survey of some approaches to the transfiguration, not limiting myself to one Gospel, but looking more generally at the issue.

In this general survey, I shall first evaluate those scholars focusing on the post-Easter events and parousia motifs. Secondly, I shall evaluate those views that interpret the transfiguration in the light of events within Jesus' earthly life. Thirdly, I shall evaluate those views which take the Jewish and Hellenistic context seriously. This is important since the purpose of this work is to explore Matthew's treatment of the transfiguration in its Jewish, early Christian, and intellectual context, and it will be shown in the rest of this book that Matthew is sensitive to the climate of his day and responds to it in his portrayal of the transfiguration.

The reader will find some approaches more satisfying than others, and my broadly based analysis will lead us into a preliminary comparison of the transfiguration pericopes of Mk 9.2-13 and Mt. 17.1-13.[1] This initial comparison will open up issues that will be more thoroughly dealt with in the rest of the work.

1. The Transfiguration, the Resurrection, Ascension and Parousia: A Misplaced Resurrection Account

Wellhausen,[2] Bultmann,[3] Carlston,[4] Weeden,[5] Watson[6] and others have

---

1.   The main focus of this thesis is on Matthew; therefore my comments on Luke's treatment of the transfiguration are featured in the Appendix.

2.   J. Wellhausen, *Das Evangelium Marci* (Berlin: G. Reimer, 1909), p. 69.

argued that the transfiguration is a misplaced or reinterpreted pre-Markan resurrection account. Arguments for this view have focused on common terminology, form, redaction, and other considerations. For example, ὤφθη (Mk 9.4 and Mt. 17.3) has been seen as a *terminus technicus* for resurrection appearances,[7] and the use of νεφέλη has been taken as suggestive of a resurrection-ascension appearance (Acts 1.9; Rev. 11.12) and of the parousia (Mk 13.26; 14.62; 1 Thess 4.17). Such arguments are not very weighty. ὤφθη is in fact used in Mk 9.4; Mt. 17.3 of Moses and Elijah, not Jesus; in the Old Testament the 'cloud' motif is also linked to the idea of revelation (Exod. 13.21-22; 14.19-20; Num. 9.15-23; Deut. 5.22; Ezek. 10.3-4) and the transfiguration is very much a 'revelation'. The case against the misplaced resurrection account has been well made by Boobyer, Stein, Alsup, Bauckham, Gundry and

---

3.   R. Bultmann, *The History of the Synoptic Tradition* (Oxford: Basil Blackwell, 1963), pp. 259-60.

4.   C.E. Carlston, 'Transfiguration and Resurrection', *JBL* 80 (1961), pp. 233-40. Also see C.M. Mann, *Mark* (New York: Doubleday, 1986), p. 357; F.W. Beare, *The Gospel according to Matthew* (Oxford: Basil Blackwell, 1981), p. 361; J.B. Bernardin, 'The Transfiguration', *JBL* 52 (1933), pp. 181-89, esp. p. 189.

5.   T.J. Weeden, *Mark-Traditions in Conflict* (Philadelphia: Fortress Press, 1971), pp. 118-26.

6.   F. Watson, 'The social function of Mark's secrecy theme', *JSNT* 24 (1985), pp. 55-56. Others include: W. Schmithals, 'Der Markusschluss, die Verklärungsgeschichte und die Aussendung der Zwölf', *ZTK* 69 (1972), pp. 394-95; B.W. Bacon 'The Transfiguration Story', *AJT* 6 (1902), pp. 236-65, esp. p. 259 n. 29, pp. 262-63; E. Klostermann, *Das Markusevangelium* (Tübingen: Mohr, 1950), p. 86; J.M. Robinson, 'On the Gattung of Mark (and John)', in D.G. Buttrick (ed.), *Jesus and Man's Hope* (Pittsburgh: Pittsburgh Theological Seminary, 1970), pp. 116-18; also 'Jesus: From Easter to Valentinus (or to the Apostle's creed)', *JBL* 101 (1982), pp. 8-10 (who cites the Gospel of Peter and examples from the Gnostic gospels); F.R. McCurley, '"And after Six Days" (Mark 9.2): A Semitic Literary Device', *JBL* 80 (1961), pp. 79-81—who develops on Weeden, *Mark-Traditions*, pp. 121-22; H.D. Betz, 'Jesus as Divine Man', in F.T. Trotter (ed.), *Jesus the Historian* (Philadelphia: Westminster Press, 1968), p. 120. For arguments against giving priority to the Gospel of Peter see R.E. Brown, 'The Gospel of Peter and Canonical Gospel Priority', *NTS* 33 (1987), pp. 321-43; S.E. Schaeffer, 'The Guard at the Tomb (Gos. Pet. 8.28-11.49 and Matt 27.62-66; 28.2-4, 11-16): A Case of Intertextuality?', *SBL* 1991, pp. 499-507.

7.   Weeden, *Mark-Traditions*, pp. 119-20.

others.[8] C.H. Dodd, on form critical grounds has shown the dissimilarities between the two events.[9]

Appeal also has been made to the rather late second century *Apoc. Pet.* 15-17, where the transfiguration is cited in a sequence of events leading up to the ascension,[10] and also to 2 Pet. 1.16-19. But it is clear that *Apoc. Pet.* 15-17 is dependent on the synoptics,[11] and the 2 Peter passage understands the transfiguration as a prefigurement of the parousia, not of the resurrection.[12] So the pre-Markan resurrection hypothesis is inconclusive on several counts.

A Prefigurement of the Resurrection

The argument that the transfiguration prefigures the resurrection has plausibility, and is a view proposed by Thrall, Masson, Mauser, McGuckin and, more recently, Garland.[13] A case could be made that Mark does

8.   G.H. Boobyer, *St Mark and the Transfiguration Story* (Edinburgh: T. & T. Clark, 1942), esp. pp. 1-16, 41-42; R. Stein, 'A Misplaced Resurrection-Account?', *JBL* 95 (1976), pp. 79-96; J.E. Alsup, *The Post-Resurrection Appearance Stories of the Gospel Tradition* (Stuttgart: Calwer; London: SPCK, 1975), pp. 141-44; R.J. Bauckham, *Jude, 2 Peter* (Waco: Word, 1986), pp. 210-11; C. Rowland, *The Open Heaven* (London: SPCK, 1982), p. 368; *Christian Origins* (London: SPCK, 1985), p. 368. Some of the details that the resurrection-appearance advocates are unable to address are: (1) the conversation between Moses, Elijah and Jesus, (2) Peter's proposal to build booths, (3) the cloud, or divine voice that identifies Jesus as God's beloved Son. On this see Morris, *Matthew*, p. 437; Gundry, *Mark*, pp. 471-73.

9.   C.H. Dodd, 'The Appearance of the Risen Christ: An Essay in Form-Criticism of the Gospels', in D.E. Nineham (ed.), *Studies in the Gospels* (Oxford: 1955), pp. 9-35: (1) Unlike in the resurrection accounts, the disciples are with Jesus throughout. (2) Jesus is silent at the transfiguration. (3) There is no heavenly voice at the resurrection. (4) At the transfiguration ὤφθη is used of Moses and Elijah and not of Christ. (5) There is no radiance or light motif in the resurrection appearances.

10.   For text, see M.R. James, *The Apocryphal New Testament* (Oxford: Clarendon Press, 1954), pp. 510-21.

11.   See Boobyer, *St Mark and the Transfiguration Story*, pp. 11-16; Stein, 'A Misplaced Resurrection Account?' (1976), pp. 87-88; Bauckham, *Jude, 2 Peter*, p. 211.

12.   On this see J.H. Neyrey, 'The Apologetic Use of the Transfiguration in 2 Peter 1.16-21', *CBQ* 42 (1980), pp. 504-19; Bauckham, *Jude, 2 Peter*, pp. 211-12.

13.   M.E. Thrall, 'Elijah and Moses in Mark's Account of the Transfiguration', *NTS* 16 (1969-70), pp. 305-17; C. Masson, 'La Transfiguration de Jesus (Marc 9.2-13)', *RTP* 3/14 (1964), pp. 1-14; U.W. Mauser, *Christ in the Wilderness* (London: SCM Press, 1963), pp. 114ff.; Nützel, *Die Verklärungserzählung*, pp. 236-54; J.A. McGuckin, *The Transfiguration of Christ in Scripture and Tradition* (Lewiston,

show considerable interest in the resurrection motif in Mk 9.2-13. For example, in 9.9 Mark speaks about the Son of Man's resurrection (retained by Matthew 17.9, but omitted by Luke). In 9.10-11 the disciples question what 'the rising from the dead' means and this leads into their question about the scribal teaching on the coming of Elijah. It has traditionally been assumed that the teaching concerned was about Elijah as the forerunner of the Messiah (cf. Mk 1.2, 6) but this view has been challenged by M.M. Faierstein, J.A. Fitzmyer and recently J. Taylor.[14] Fitzmyer, noting that the issue in Mk 9.10 (prompted by 9.9) is that of the resurrection, argues that the scribes' teaching alluded to by the disciples (ὅτι λέγουσιν οἱ γραμματεῖς ὅτι Ἠλίαν δεῖ ἐλθεῖν πρῶτον; Mk 9.11) refers to the raising of the dead that Elijah was to initiate (cf. *m. Sota* 9.18; *Sib Or.* 2.185-95). Mark however has linked the idea of Elijah and resurrection with that of Elijah's (i.e. the Baptist's) suffering.

I conclude that the prefigurement theory has weight, though a 'pure' resurrection hypothesis fails to do justice to features in the narrative such as the 'high mountain' (Mk 9.2), the appearance of Moses, Peter's suggestion to build booths and the 'voice' (Mk 9.7).

A Prefigurement of the Ascension
This view, with particular reference to the third Gospel, has been advocated by G.J. Davies,[15] J. Manek,[16] C.H. Talbert[17] and others.[18]

NY: Edwin Mellen Press, 1986), pp. 26-27, D.E. Garland, *Reading Matthew: A Literary and Theological Commentary on the First Gospel* (New York: Crossroad, 1993), p. 181. H.A.A. Kennedy, 'The Purpose of the Transfiguration', *JTS* 4 (1903), pp. 270-73, tries to argue that the transfiguration 'prepared' the three disciples to recognize Jesus at the resurrection, but against this see R. Holmes, 'The Purpose of the Transfiguration', *JTS* 4 (1903), pp. 543-47.

14.   M.M. Faierstein, 'Why do the scribes say that Elijah must come first?', *JBL* 100 (1981), pp. 75-86; J.A. Fitzmyer, 'More about Elijah coming first', *JBL* 104 (1985), pp. 295-96 (partially in response to D.C. Allison, 'Elijah must come first', *JBL* 103 (1984), pp. 256-58 who tries to argue for the traditional forerunner theory); J. Taylor, 'The coming of Elijah, Mt. 17, 10-13 and Mk 9, 1-13: The Development of texts', *RB* 97 (1991), pp. 107-19.

15.   G.J. Davies, 'The Prefiguration of the Ascension in the Third Gospel', *JTS* 6 (1955), pp. 229-33.

16.   J. Manek, 'The New Exodus in the Books of Luke', *NovT* 2 (1958), pp. 8-23, who also includes the parousia.

17.   C.H. Talbert, *Literary Patterns, Theological Themes, and the Genre of Luke–Acts* (Missoula, MT: Scholars Press, 1974), esp. pp. 51-52, who, though not

Davies finds links between passages in Acts and Luke.[19] Some of Davies's links (e.g. Acts 1.18-19; Lk. 9.37-43) are fanciful,[20] but he also finds linguistic and thematic connections, some of which are also used by J. Manek, and recently A.A. Trites.[21] For example: (1) καὶ ἰδοὺ ἄνδρες δύο in Lk. 9.30, 32 (in Luke alone of Moses and Elijah) is compared with the identical καὶ ἰδοὺ ἄνδρες δύο (of heavenly beings) in Acts 1.10. (2) Davies views τῆς ἀναλήμψεως (Lk. 9.51, which follows closely from 9.28-36) as an ascension motif, and suggests that Luke's distinctive τὴν ἔξοδον (9.31) in part refers to the ascension.[22] (3) Luke alone applies δόξα to Jesus (9.32), and Davies links this to the resurrection-ascension (glorification) theme in Acts 3.13 (ἐδόξασεν).

But while these thematic links may exist a 'pure' ascension view seems not to do justice to other features in Luke's narrative: Luke's τὴν ἔξοδον αὐτοῦ ἣν ἤμελλεν πληροῦν ἐν Ἰερουσαλήμ need not be limited merely to the ascension, and other considerations, such as the considerable amount of space Luke gives the figures of Moses and Elijah; his omission of Mk 9.10-13 (with its Elijah-Baptist association); the 'voice' (Lk. 9.35), need to be addressed (see Appendix).

explicitly following Davies, accepts the architectural links in Luke–Acts, and those between the transfiguration and the ascension.

18.   Several years ago G.B. Caird in 'The Transfiguration', *ExpTim* 67 (1955-56), pp. 291-94 argued that a satisfactory explanation of the transfiguration, among other events in Jesus life, also must recognise its connection with the ascension (p. 292). This has been taken up by A.A. Trites, 'Transfiguration in the Theology of Luke', in L.D. Hurst and N.T. Wright (eds.), *The Glory of Christ in the New Testament* (Oxford: Clarendon Press, 1987), pp. 71-81.

19.   Davies finds verbal parallels between Luke and Acts, for example (1) τί ποιήσωμεν; in Lk. 3.12 with the identical question in Acts 2.37, where too the people respond, are called to repentance and are baptised. (2) Jesus' lament over Jerusalem in Lk. 13.34 with Stephen upbraiding Jerusalem in Acts 7.52. (3) Like Jesus, Stephen was cast out of the city in Acts 7.52. (4) Stephen's final words in Acts 7.59-60 resemble those of Jesus in Lk. 23.34.

20.   For example (1) Lk. 9.37-43 with Acts 1.18; but the boy in Lk. 9.37-43 is healed, while Judas in Acts 1.18 dies! (2) Davies parallels 'fire' in Lk. 9.54 with Acts 2.1, 3; but 'fire' in Lk. 9.54 is a negative motif (not made by Jesus) but a positive motif in Acts 2.1, 3.

21.   Trites, 'Transfigurations in Luke', pp. 72-73; also J. Manek, 'The New Exodus', pp. 8-23.

22.   Davies, *JTS* 6 (1955) pp. 229-33. According to A.E. Burn, 'The Transfiguration', *ExpTim* 14 (1902-1903), pp. 442-47, esp. p. 444, Moses and Elijah are figures of 'ascension'.

A Prolepsis of the Parousia

G.H. Boobyer[23] while rejecting the resurrection hypothesis, has argued that the transfiguration prefigures the parousia, a view also supported by W.L. Lane, T.J. Weeden and others.[24] Boobyer (1) takes 8.38 as a reference to the parousia, and (2) links 9.1 with 8.38 and 9.2-8 and hence (3) concludes that Mark views the transfiguration as an anticipation of the parousia.[25] In support of his position he cites the Apocalypse of Peter, the Pistis Sophia, and also 2 Pet. 1.16-18. The Apocalypse of Peter however is late and unreliable, but, as we have noted, the 2 Peter passage does support Boobyer's view.[26]

Boobyer has, however, overworked his case, and it is doubtful if Mark himself (Boobyer's main focus) wanted to emphasise the motifs that Boobyer suggests. His treatment of Mk 9.1 is simplistic, and does not address the complex issues pertaining to its interpretation. He attempts to present Moses and Elijah as 'parousia' figures. But although this may fit Luke with his focus on δόξα (associated with Moses, Elijah and Jesus Lk. 9.31, 32) and with his description of Moses and Elijah as ἄνδρες δύο (being redactionally linked with the two angels (ἄνδρες δύο) of Lk. 24.4; Acts 1.10) it does not obviously fit Mark. Mark by redaction and arrangement presents Elijah as a suffering figure, who by his identification with the Baptist in Mk 9. 1-13 (Mt. 17.10-13) prefigures Jesus' sufferings. Boobyer fails to recognise this function of Elijah in Mk 9.1-8. He attempts to make every detail in Mk 9.2-8 congruous with the parousia story, in a way that is unacceptable.

Thus we have seen that the misplaced resurrection account theory is unpersuasive. The prefigurement of the resurrection theory with

23. Boobyer, *St Mark and the Transfiguration Story* (Edinburgh: T. & T. Clark, 1942); 'St Mark and the Transfiguration', *JTS* 41 (1940), pp. 119-40.

24. Cf. Weeden, *Mark-Traditions*, pp. 124-25; C.E.B. Cranfield, *The Gospel According to St Mark* (Cambridge: Cambridge University Press, 1963, pp. 287-88; also 'Thoughts on New Testament Eschatology', *SJT* 35 (1982), pp. 503-12. Cranfield takes the transfiguration as a pointer and foretaste of the resurrection, which in turn is a foretaste of the parousia. So also W. Lane, *The Gospel of Mark* (Grand Rapids: Eerdmans, 1974), pp. 313-14; A. Moore, *The Parousia in the New Testament* (Leiden: E.J. Brill, 1966), p. 127; K. Barth, *Church Dogmatics* (eds. G.W. Bromiley and T.F. Torrance; Edinburgh: T. & T. Clark, 1955–77), Vol. III.2, pp. 478-79. Also see Gundry, *Mark*, p. 486.

25. Boobyer, *St Mark and the Transfiguration Story*, pp. 58-64.

26. J.H. Neyrey, 'The Apologetic Use of the Transfiguration in 2 Peter 1.16-21', *CBQ* 42 (1980), pp. 504-19; Bauckham, *Jude, 2 Peter*, p. 211.

reference to Mark has weight, but a 'pure' resurrection-prefigurement hypothesis (as also the prefiguration of the ascension or parousia theories) fails to do justice to the other features of the transfiguration narrative, and particularly, as I shall further show, to the figures of Moses and Elijah. Boobyer's 'parousia' theory is supported by the independent witness to and application of the transfiguration story in 2 Pet. 1.16-18, but in this passage the writer dispenses with details that are irrelevant to his purposes, Moses and Elijah, the echo of αὐτοῦ ἀκούσεσθε (Deut. 18.15 LXX) and others. And so the 2 Peter passage cannot be used to decide what the synoptic evangelists themselves have done with their transfiguration pericopes.

2. *The Transfiguration and the Theme of Suffering*

If the views discussed so far associate the transfiguration with post-resurrection events, the next group of views links the transfiguration with certain events within the earthly life of Jesus.

The Confirmation Hypothesis

The transfiguration has been linked to the motif of suffering and also to Peter's confession. Several considerations point to this:

(1) The most natural way to view Mark's καὶ μετὰ ἡμέρας ἓξ (also Mt. 17.1; Luke has ὡσεὶ ἡμέραι ὀκτὼ) is in relation to the immediately preceding pericopes; that is, the first prediction of the cross in 8.31-32, and parallels, and then to the whole teaching section that follows, 8.31-9.1 and parallels.[27] Given this temporal connection it is natural to conclude that Mark links the transfiguration with the passion and suffering motifs in the preceding pericopes; see 8.31-33, 34-38.[28] The ἀκούετε αὐτοῦ in 9.7 may be taken as referring in particular to Jesus's teaching in 8.31-38.[29]

27.   Luke makes this clearer by the insertion Ἐγένετο δὲ μετὰ τοὺς λόγους τούτους. On this see A.A. Trites, 'The Transfiguration of Jesus: The Gospel in Microcosom', *EvQ* 51 (1979), pp. 70-72.

28.   See E. Schweizer, *The Good News According to Mark* (London: SPCK, 1971), pp. 181-82; M.D. Hooker, *The Son of Man* (London: SPCK, 1967), pp. 122-23, and 'What Doest Thou here Elijah?', in L.D. Hurst and N.T. Wright (eds.), *The Glory of Christ in the New Testament* (Oxford: Clarendon Press, 1987), pp. 61-62; E.L. Schnellbächer, 'ΚΑΙ ΜΕΤΑ ΉΜΕΡΑΣ ᾽ΕΞ (Markus 9.2)', *ZNW* 71 (1980), pp. 252-57; Morris, *Matthew,* p. 437; A.M. Ramsey, *The Glory of God and the Transfiguration of Christ* (London: Longmans, Green & Co., 1949), pp. 144-46.

29.   According to E. Schweizer, *The Good News According to Mark,* p. 183,

(2) As for Peter's confession of Christ, Taylor, Nineham, Hunter, Burkill, Best, Beasley-Murray and Davies[30] have argued that the transfiguration can be seen as divine confirmation of the Petrine Christology, as well as of what Jesus had said about suffering—this being a key theme in Mark's central section. The argument is: (a) in the preceding section (Mk 8.29; Mt. 16.16; Lk. 9.18) Peter had formally declared that Jesus is the Messiah. (b) In turn the disciples had received teaching about the way this Son of Man-Messiah was to accomplish his work (via death), and hence (c) now at the transfiguration the truth of their (Peter's) declaration (Mk 8.29 par.) is confirmed by the appearance of the transfigured Jesus.

The merit of this view is that it majors on the function of the event in Mark's central section (8.27-9.13), a point that perhaps could also be extended to Luke,[31] and particularly Matthew, who alone has Peter confessing Jesus' sonship (Mt. 16.16 compare 17.5).[32] But while there is value in this 'confirmation hypothesis' it is not entirely satisfactory, for it does not explain other details of the transfiguration narrative: notably the appearance of Moses and Elijah. Moreover, perhaps an important point to note here, and one that will be developed later, is that the voice at the transfiguration has more parallels with the voice at the baptism (Mk 1.11; Mt. 3.17; Lk. 3.22) than with Peter's confession in Mk 8.29 (Mt. 16.16; Lk. 9.20).

Mark interprets Peter's suggestion in 9.5 as equal to his mistake in 8.32 and dismisses the importance of 8.38 and 9.1 by holding that Mark places 9.2-8 after 8.27-9.1 'because he wanted another opportunity to designate 8.31 as the centre of his gospel'. That 9.1 is fulfilled in 9.7—which refers to Jesus' teaching on the way of suffering in 8.31-32 see M.A. Tolbert, *Sowing the Gospel: Mark's world in Literary-Historical Perspective* (Minneapolis: Fortress Press, 1989), pp. 206-207.

30.　V. Taylor, *The Gospel According to St Mark* (London: Macmillan; New York: St Martins, 1966), pp. 388-89; Nineham, *Saint Mark*, p. 233; A.M. Hunter, *The Gospel According to Saint Mark* (New York: 1960), pp. 93-94; T.A. Burkill, *Mysterious Revelation, An Examination of the Philosophy of Mark* (Ithaca: Cornell, 1963), pp. 145-64, especially pp. 156-57; E. Best, *Following Jesus: Discipleship in the Gospel of Mark* (JSNTSup, 4; Sheffield: JSOT Press, 1981), pp. 55-58. On Matthew see G. Beasley-Murray, *Matthew* (London: Scripture Union, 1984), pp. 73-74; M. Davies, *Matthew* (Sheffield: JSOT Press, 1993), pp. 123-24.

31.　D.A.S. Ravens, 'Luke 9.7-62 and the Prophetic Role of Jesus', *NTS* 36 (1990), pp. 119-29.

32.　Matthew has five non-Markan passages in which Peter is named: Mt. 14.28-31; 15.15; 16.17-19; 17.24-27; 18.21.

The Transfiguration and Gethsemane

A closely related view connects the transfiguration with the Gethsemane scene. This has been well argued by A. Kenny—a view also supported by E. Schweizer and C.R. Kazmierski.[33] Kenny for example has shown that there are several coincidences between the circumstances of the two events. Not all of Kenny's parallels are persuasive,[34] but he usefully observes that: (1) both events took place on a mountain, and (2) both were witnessed by Peter, James and John. But (3) the weightier argument is based on the verbal and thematic similarities between Mk 9.2 and 14.33. Thus (a) he notes the occurrence of παραλαμβάνει,[35] τὸν Πέτρον καὶ τὸν Ἰάκωβον καὶ τὸν Ἰωάννην, εἰς ὄρος ὑψηλὸν (εἰς τὸ ὄρος in 14.26). (b) A parallel also has been seen between Jesus' cry ἀββὰ ὁ πατήρ in 14.36 and the divine words οὗτός ἐστιν ὁ υἱός μου ὁ ἀγαπητός (9.7). (c) οὐ γὰρ ᾔδει τί ἀποκριθῇ in 9.6 is comparable to καὶ οὐκ ᾔδεισαν τί ἀποκριθῶσιν αὐτῷ in 14.40. Kenny goes on to show that these links are not obvious in Matthew. He allows that Luke's τὴν ἔξοδον αὐτοῦ, ἣν ἤμελλεν πληροῦν ἐν Ἰερουσαλήμ (9.31) and other parallels may indicate such a link, but here the arguments are strained;[36] it is mainly a Markan motif.

Kenny's linguistic arguments with regard to Mark are quite plausible. Moreover, (1) if as K. Brower[37] has argued, Mk 9.1 anticipates the motifs of the passion and the cross, and (2) if καὶ μετὰ ἡμέρας ἓξ (among other things) is to be seen in relation to the passion prediction of

33.   A. Kenny, 'The Transfiguration and the Agony in the Garden', *CBQ* 19 (1957), pp. 444-52; E. Schweizer, 'Mark's Contribution to the Quest of the Historical Jesus', *NTS* 10 (1964), p. 428; C.R. Kazmierski, *Jesus, the Son of God: A Study of the Markan Tradition and its Redaction by the Evangelist* (FzB, 33; Würzburg: Echter, 1973), p. 107.

34.   E.g. Kenny, 'The Transfiguration', p. 444 refers to the textually disputed Lk. 22.43-44 as evidence for Jesus' physical change at Gethsemane, (though some ancient variants support it: see K. Aland, [ed.], *Synopsis Quattuor Evangeliorum* [Stuttgart: Deutsche Bibelgesellschaft, 1984], p. 456, note on Lk. 22.43.44 [= *SQE*]).

35.   Kenny observes that παραλαμβάνω occurs six times in Mark, once in the sense of 'receiving a tradition', five times in the same sense as here (4.36; 5.40; 9.1; 10.32; 14.33). Each time it occurs in a context where Peter is an eyewitness, suggesting that the transfiguration and Gethsemane pericopes belong to a Petrine tradition, which is quite plausible.

36.   Kenny, 'The Transfiguration', pp. 445-52.

37.   K. Brower, 'Mark 9.1 Seeing the Kingdom in Power', *JSNT* 6 (1980), pp. 17-26.

Mk 8.31-32, then these 'passion' motifs strengthen Kenny's arguments for linking the transfiguration in Mark to the motifs of suffering, death, Gethsemane and the events to follow. It is probably this suffering motif that makes Mark stress the Elijah motif in the transfiguration: he places Elijah before Moses to lead into the following passage which explicitly connects Elijah, the Baptist and the suffering Son of Man.

The Transfiguration, Gethsemane and the Temptation Narratives

H. Baltensweiler[38] claims that the period of the feast of tabernacles was the general 'external' setting for the transfiguration pericopes. He goes on to argue that from a Markan perspective the circumstances leading to the transfiguration suggest a crisis experience of Jesus, similar to the temptation he had faced before (Mk 1.12-13 and par.), and that he would face from Peter (Mk 8.31-33 and par.), and especially at Gethsemane. The temptation was to reject the cross and take up a Zealot type messiahship. So, as at Gethsemane, he took with him his inner circle of three disciples to support him during the temptation.

Baltensweiler goes on to argue that this temptation is heightened by the 'external setting', that is, the period of the feast of the tabernacles, a time when eschatological hopes and the expectation of a political Messiah reached a high point. So he argues that Jesus went up the mountain to spend the seventh and greatest day of the feast in solitude, to be strengthened for his chosen mission of suffering and death.[39]

Baltensweiler has made an interesting case. The importance of the feast of the tabernacles for Jews in the first century is attested by Josephus: it was a 'most holy and most eminent feast' (*Ant.* 7.4.1) and 'very much observed among us' (*Ant.* 15.3.3). The feast evoked memories of the great Davidic and Solomonic era when it was celebrated for fourteen days upon the dedication of the Temple (*Ant.* 8.4.5). The political and popular theological significance of this festival is seen in *Ant.* 13.13.3: when Alexander attempted to offer a sacrifice upon the altar, the Jews, questioning his pedigree, pelted him with citrons and brought a great slaughter on themselves.

---

38. H. Baltensweiler, *Die Verklärung Jesu* (Zürich: Zwingli Verlag, 1959), pp. 37-38.

39. Baltensweiler, *Die Verklärung Jesu*, pp. 55-62. In Jn 7.1-2, it was precisely on the last day of the feast of tabernacles that Jesus uttered his famous words (vv. 37-38). On this see G.R. Beasley-Murray, *John* (Waco: Word, 1987), pp. 114-15; J.W. Bowker, 'The Origin and Purpose of St John's Gospel', *NTS* 10 (1964-65), pp. 398-408.

The idea of a link between the transfiguration and the feast of the tabernacles is not novel, and has been suggested by several scholars: among others Badcock, Lohmeyer, Swete, Turner, Riesenfeld, Ramsey, Farrer, Stendahl, Daniélou, Bonnard, Hahn.[40] According to Bonnard, the 'six days' are the days separating the day of atonement, from the feast of the tabernacles;[41] in his view the first passion prediction (Mk 8.31-33; Mt. 16.21-23; Lk. 9.22) occurred on the day of atonement and the transfiguration with its booth motif on the first day of the week. According to Baltensweiler the 'six days' refers to the feast itself with Jesus going up the mountain on the sixth day in order to spend the seventh day with the 'inner circle' of disciples.[42] The whole period of the feast, particularly the last day, evoked much nationalistic excitement associated with the expectation of a political messiah.

But the theory has not gone without criticism. (1) People have questioned whether Jesus could have traveled from Caesarea Philippi to this mountain during the feast. (2) Luke's ὡσεὶ ἡμέραι ὀκτώ, in contrast to Mark's precise καὶ μετὰ [μεθ'] ἡμέρας ἕξ, (followed by Matthew) causes problems for this theory. But it must be noted that, while it is true that the Jews would be more likely to remain in one place during the feast, the most preferred place being Jerusalem (Zech. 14.16; Jn 7),[43] an exception was made for those already on a journey;[44] and Jesus was journeying in Caesarea Philippi according to Mk 8.27 (Mt. 16.13). As for

40.   F.J. Badcock, 'The Transfiguration', *JTS* 22 (1921), p. 326; E. Lohmeyer, 'Die Verklärung Jesu nach dem Markus-Evangelium', *ZNW* 21 (1922), pp. 185-215; A.M. Ramsey, *The Glory of God and the Transfiguration* (London: Longmans, Green & Co., 1949); A.M. Farrer, *A Study in Mark* (London: Dacre, 1951), p. 214; C.H. Turner, *The Gospel According to St Mark* (London: SPCK, 1928), p. 42; H.B. Swete, *The Gospel According to St Mark* (London: Macmillan, 1927), p. 190; K. Stendahl, 'Matthew', in M. Black and H.H. Rowley (eds.), *Peake's Commentary on the Bible* (Edinburgh: Thomas Nelson, 1962), p. 788; P. Bonnard, *L'Evangile selon saint Matthieu* (Neuchatel: Delachaux et Niestlé, 1963), p. 254; J. Daniélou, 'Le symbolisme eschatologique de la Fête des Tabernacles', *Irenikon*, 31 (1958), pp. 19-40; F. Hahn, *The Titles of Jesus in Christology* (London: Lutterworth, 1969), p. 342 n. 15.

41.   Bonnard, *L'Evangile selon saint Matthieu*, p. 254.

42.   Baltensweiler, *Die Verklärung Jesu*, pp. 37-52.

43.   R. de Vaux, *Ancient Israel: Its Life and Institutions* (London: Darton, Longman & Todd, 1961), pp. 495-96.

44.   According to Lev. 23.43 they were to live in booths in memory of the *sukkoth* in which they lived when they were brought out of Egypt. So it also had an exodus significance.

Luke's ὡσεὶ ἡμέραι ὀκτώ, this is a fair point. But it could be that Mark and Matthew allude to this festival while Luke does not, or, as Daniélou[45] has argued, Luke's approximate time-note fits the 'feast of the tabernacles' theory, since the feast lasted six to eight days. However, on the eighth day the booths were pulled down and not erected, which perhaps makes Peter's suggestion (in Mk 9.5; Mt. 17.4; Lk. 9.33) less appropriate.[46]

So we have seen that the 'confirmation hypothesis' is probably right in linking the 'voice' motif at the transfiguration (Mk 9.7; Mt. 17.5; Lk. 9.35) with the sayings about suffering and Peter's confession (Mk 8.29; Mt. 16.16; Lk. 9.20), though the link is more forceful in Matthew—'you are...the Son of the living God', Mt. 16.16—than in Mark or Luke. But also to be taken into account is the link between the voice at the baptism (Mk 1.11; Mt. 3.17; Lk. 3.22) and the transfiguration, a link made more explicit by Matthew with his use of the third person of the baptism-voice (Mt. 3.17). We have also seen that Kenny made a good case that

---

45. J. Daniélou, 'Le symbolisme eschatologique', pp. 19-40. For the 'eight' day duration of the feast see 2 *Macc.* 10.6-8; R. de Vaux, *Ancient Israel,* pp. 497-98.

46. It must be noted that Luke's ὡσεὶ ἡμέραι ὀκτώ has been taken variously: (1) By inclusive reckoning (e.g. as in Jn 20.26) it could be taken as 'on the seventh day', an indirect way of indicating the lapse of approximately one week (so W. Liefeld, 'Luke', in F.E. Gaebelein [ed.], *The Expositor's Bible Commentary* [Grand Rapids: Zondervan, 1984], p. 926, also J.M. Creed, *The Gospel According to St Luke* [New York: Harper & Row, 1960], p. 134). (2) Luke is using a Hellenistic form of reckoning *contra* the Jewish seven day week (so W. Grundmann, *Das Evangelium nach Lukas* [Berlin: Evangelische Verlagsanstalt, 1974], p. 192; E.E. Ellis, *The Gospel of Luke* [New York: Nelson, 1966], pp. 142, 275-76). (3) Luke's ὡσεὶ indicates that he is giving an approximation to Mark's figure (so E. Weiss, *Die Evangelien des Markus und Lukas* [Göttingen: Vandenhoeck & Ruprecht, 1885], p. 382). (4) It refers to the eighth day of the festival of booths (so Daniélou, 'Le symbolisme eschatologique', p. 17). Or (5) that it was influenced by his scheme of eight days, e.g. the resurrection on the eighth day, the meal at Emmaus the eighth meal. (6) According to I.H. Marshall, *Commentary on Luke* (NIGTC, Grand Rapids: Eerdmans, 1978), p. 381, continuing oral traditions lie behind Luke's reworking of Mark's narrative. (7) Trites, 'The Transfiguration of Jesus', pp. 70-72 attempts to solve it by recourse to audience criticism (pp. 70-71), and by reckoning that the Petrine confession at Caesarea Philippi took place two days before the declaration of the principles of discipleship. It is with the latter that Matthew and Mark link their transfiguration pericopes, and hence have 'after six days'. Luke links it both with the Petrine confession and Jesus' teaching on discipleship, and hence has 'about eight days'.

Mark has linked the transfiguration with Gethsemane. Baltensweiler's 'temptation' hypothesis and its links with the festival of booths is an interesting hypothesis, but speculative.[47] All three views, while making interesting points, fail to do justice to other features of the narrative including the figures of Moses and Elijah.

3. *The Transfiguration Viewed within Jewish and Hellenistic Categories*

It is important to take into consideration the Jewish and Hellenistic context in which the evangelists wrote, and in this case particularly Matthew, for I shall later show that Matthew has blended Old Testament and Jewish apocalyptic categories in his presentation of the transfiguration. Here I shall therefore briefly evaluate the influence of the Jewish and Hellenistic background.

The Transfiguration and Enthronement

A view that has been put forward by several scholars is that the transfiguration was symbolic of Jesus' enthronement.[48] Riesenfeld, rejecting Boobyer's 'parousia' hypothesis, has linked the transfiguration with the feast of booths and the enthronement festival, that is, the Messiah's enthronement.[49] Here he is building on Mowinckel's original theory of an annual feast of the enthronement of Yahweh in Israel.[50] In

47.   W.L. Groves, 'The Significance of the Transfiguration of Our Lord', *Theology*, 11 (August, 1925), pp. 80-92, tries to argue that Jesus was offered translation into heaven (for death was not the natural end of a good man, and Moses and Elijah were representatives of such good men), but chose the path of suffering and death instead. But this eccentric view does not recognize the significance of the face-radiance motif, cloud or voice, and in view of 9.32-33, it makes Moses and Elijah those who dissuade Jesus from the cross! Against Groves, see A.D.F. Mckenzie, *Theology*, 11 (November, 1925), pp. 279-81.

48.   For recent acceptance of this (in relation to Ps. 2.7) see T.L. Donaldson, *Jesus on the Mountain* (Sheffield: JSOT Press, 1985), pp. 146-49 (for Matthew). For my arguments against Donaldson see chapter 5.

49.   H. Riesenfeld, *Jésus transfiguré: L'arrière-plan du récit évangélique de la transfiguration de Notre-Seigneur* (Copenhagen: Ejnar Munksgaard, 1947), pp. 292-99 for criticisms on Boobyer's theory; pp. 276-79 for view on the festival of booths.

50.   In addition to S. Mowinckel's writings he draws from A.R. Johnson, 'The Role of the King in Jerusalem Cultus', *The Labyrinth* (1935), pp. 71-111, who expands on this in his later *Sacral Kingship in Ancient Israel* (Cardiff; University of Wales Press, 1955). Riesenfeld also argues that originally the tent was the place of

various ways this enthronement theme is also referred to by M. Sabbé, M. Horstmann and J. Daniélou.[51] However, this supposed connection between the 'feast of tabernacles' and the motif of 'enthronement', indeed the 'enthronement festival' itself,[52] has been challenged by Roland de Vaux.[53] There is a case for saying that in later times the feast took on eschatological characteristics that it did not originally have;[54] the chief support for this is Zech. 14.16-19.[55] However, the feast continued mainly to be associated with the sojourn in the wilderness.[56]

So the significance that Riesenfeld gives to this feast is quite hypothetical.[57] Moreover, Riesenfeld himself admits that the appearance of

divine nuptials (p. 152), and that the enthronement was also a wedding celebration (p. 160). During the feast, Yahweh dwells in the tent (p. 176) and from this developed the idea that the Messiah too would live in a booth (p. 257). He connects Heb. 1.3-14, Rev. 1.12-17; 5.1-12; 7.9-12 with the idea of 'enthronisation' of the Messiah, the shining garments of Jesus with kingly robes, Peter's words 'it is good for us to be here' with the sabbath rest of the messianic age. These connections at best are highly speculative, and he gives no consideration to the place of the history of the traditions and their dating.

51. Daniélou, 'Le symbolisme eschatologique', pp. 19-40; M. Sabbé, 'La rédaction du récit de la Transfiguration', pp. 65-100; M. Horstmann, *Studien zur markinischen Christologie: Mk 8,27-9,13 als Zugang zum Christusbild des zweiten Evangeliums* (NTAbh, 6; Münster: Aschendorff, 1969), pp. 80-103.

52. This has been developed in the Scandinavian school of thought. The works of S. Mowinckel gave the original impetus, and has influenced others like H. Ringgren, *The Messiah in the Old Testament* (London: SCM Press, 1961).

53. De Vaux, *Ancient Israel*, pp. 495-502. For refutation of the 'enthronement festival' hypothesis see pp. 504-506, also see 502-504. Also see J.A. Ziesler, 'The Transfiguration Story and the Markan Soteriology', *ET* 81 (1970), pp. 263-8 and Kazmierski, *Jesus, the Son of God*, pp. 108-10.

54. Cf. Daniélou, 'Le symbolisme eschatologique', pp. 19-40; Baltensweiler, *Die Verklärung Jesu*, pp. 60-61.

55. According to de Vaux, the two items; 'adoration before the king, Yahweh Sabaoth' and 'to celebrate the feast of tents', cf. Zech. 14.17-18, are merely accidental. Its primary feature was not, as some have tried to show, the celebration of creation, and of Yahweh's victory over chaos, see p. 506.

56. Cf. Ziesler, 'The Transfiguration Story', pp. 263-68, esp. p. 264.; also see T.F. Glasson, *Moses in the Fourth Gospel* (London: SCM Press, 1963), pp. 48-50, 66; J.C. Rylaarsdam, 'Booths, Feast of', *IDB*, I, p. 457; I. Abrahams, *Studies in Pharisaism and the Gospels* (Second series; Cambridge: Cambridge University Press, 1924), II, pp. 51-54.

57. Donaldson rejects the feast significance but accepts the Ps. 2.7 enthronisation motif to fit his Zion theology. Donaldson, following S. Pedersen, 'Die

Moses and Elijah does not fit into his theory,[58] and he stretches his case when arguing that exodus motifs—which he sees in the transfiguration pericope (e.g. 'cloud', 'tent')—are projections of things experienced in the feast of tabernacles, a highly speculative idea. Moreover, Riesenfeld (and all those who argue for an enthronement idea in the transfiguration) assumes that 2 Sam. 7.14 and Ps. 2.7 (set within an enthronement context) lie behind the voice: οὗτός ἐστιν ὁ υἱός μου ὁ ἀγαπητός.[59] But this is debatable, since in addition to Ps. 2.7, the influence of passages such as Exod. 4.22;[60] Gen. 22.2;[61] Isa. 42.1[62] (singly or in combination[63]) has been advanced. So far as the Son of God motif in Matthew goes I disagree with an explicit application of Ps. 2.7 in the transfiguration context, something that I shall discuss later. Finally, perhaps the single most telling criticism is that Riesenfeld makes the transfiguration story so allusive that it is doubtful if any of Mark's readers would have got the point or would have been enough in touch with Jewish thought forms and feasts to have understood it thus.

Proklamation Jesu als des eschatologischen Offenbarungsträgers (Mt.xvii.1-13)', *NovT* 17 (1975), pp. 260-61, argues that Peter's suggestion about 'three tents' is 'most awkward' since 'if Peter was suggesting booths for the booths of a messianic feast, one would have expected six booths, i.e. for the disciples as well'. But this argument is weak since the tents that were built during this period of festivity were large enough at times to accommodate three to four people or more. On this see Daniélou, 'Le symbolisme eschatologique', pp. 19-40 and Baltensweiler, *Die Verklärung Jesu*, pp. 60-61.

58.   For example, Riesenfeld finds it difficult to accommodate the 'voice' motif (with its Deut. 18 prophet-like-Moses significance) into his scheme (see *Jésus transfiguré*, pp. 250-52). He meets the same difficulty with Moses and Elijah who he admits 'cannot be classified with the themes' he has already given the transfiguration (cf. pp. 254-56).

59.   Riesenfeld, *Jésus transfiguré*, pp. 69-70, and 252.

60.   P.G. Bretscher, 'Exodus 4.22-23 and the Voice from Heaven', *JBL* 87 (1968), pp. 301-11.

61.   G. Vermes, *Scripture and Tradition* (Leiden: Brill, 1961), pp. 222-23, for its importance in the New Testament see pp. 218-27; C.H. Turner, 'Ο ΥΙΟΣ ΜΟΥ Ο ΑΓΑΠΗΤΟΣ', *JTS* 27 (1926), pp. 113-29, also see chapter 6.

62.   J. Jeremias, *TDNT* 5, pp. 701-702; O. Cullmann, *Baptism in the New Testament* (London: SCM Press, 1950), p.17; R.H. Fuller, *The Foundations of New Testament Christology* (London: Collins, 1969), p. 170.

63.   That Ps. 2.7 and Isa. 42.1 were already combined in the early church see T.W. Manson, *The Sayings of Jesus* (London: SCM Press, 1947), pp. 110-13; D. Hill, *The Gospel of Matthew*, p. 98. For arguments against the influence of Ps. 2.7 see Kazmierski, *Jesus, the Son of God*, pp. 108-10.

The Transfiguration and Apocalyptic Categories
An old, but recently revived, view is that the transfiguration needs (1) to be interpreted in Hellenistic categories, or (2) to be seen as an amalgamation of Hellenistic and Jewish apocalyptic categories. In part, this discussion impinges on literary parallels and the vision-form considerations in relation to the transfiguration pericope, which will feature later, so here I shall make only some preliminary comments.

View (1) was initially suggested by E. Lohmeyer,[64] but in his later work he viewed the transfiguration within Jewish, and Jewish-apocalyptic categories.[65] W. Gerber, U.B. Müller, J. Nützel and others[66] have seen the influence of both Jewish and Hellenistic characteristics. Müller and Betz view the transfiguration in terms of θεῖος ἀνήρ categories.[67] Müller, in particular, gives prominence to the idea of Moses' deification, and he views Moses and Elijah as figures who had been translated, as θεῖοι ἄνδρες.[68]

It is commendable that Müller has given the figures of Moses and Elijah some weight. But his application of θεῖος ἀνήρ categories to the transfiguration is not persuasive, for the whole idea of θεῖος ἀνήρ Christology has been severely called to question.[69]

So Riesenfeld, Lohmeyer, Gerber, Müller, Nützel, Sabbé and others

64. E. Lohmeyer, 'Die Verklärung Jesu nach dem Markus-Evangelium', *ZNW* (1922), pp. 203-204.

65. E. Lohmeyer, *Das Evangelium des Markus* (Göttingen: Vandenhoeck & Ruprecht, 1967), pp. 175-76. He finds eschatological symbolism for example in (1) Moses and Elijah symbolising the end times, and (2) reference to σκηνάς, which is associated with the feast of the tabernacles, the tabernacling of God with his people and their eschatological association.

66. W. Gerber, 'Die Metamorphose Jesu. Mk 9, 2f par.', *TZ* 23 (1967), pp. 385-95; U.B. Müller, 'Die christologische Absicht des Markusevangeliums und die Verklärungsgechichte', *ZNW* 64 (1973), pp. 159-93; Nützel, *Die Verklärungserzählung*, pp. 179-80.

67. Müller, 'Die christologische Absicht', pp. 182-85; H.D. Betz, 'Jesus as Divine Man', in F.T. Trotter (ed.), *Jesus and the Historian* (Philadelphia: Westminister Press, 1967), pp. 114-30.

68. Müller, 'Die christologische Absicht', pp.182-85.

69. Cf. M. Hengel, *The Son of God* (ET 1967; Philadelphia: Fortress Press, 1976), pp. 31-32; W.L. Lane, '*Theios Aner* Christology and the Gospel of Mark', in R.N. Longenecker and M.C. Tenney (eds.), *New Dimensions in New Testament Study* (Grand Rapids: 1974), pp. 144-61; C.R. Holladay, *Theios Aner in Hellenistic Judaism: A Critique of the Use of This Category in New Testament Christology* (Missoula, MT: Scholars Press, 1977).

are right in highlighting the Jewish and also Hellenistic setting of the idea
of the transfiguration. But neither Riesenfeld's enthronement idea nor
Müller's θεῖος ἀνήρ categories is entirely persuasive. Müller has at least
highlighted the importance of Moses and Elijah, which most views
evaluated so far have neglected. As I shall show below, the manner in
which the evangelists have portrayed these two figures (for Luke's
treatment see Appendix) gives us a vital clue into their understanding of
the transfiguration, and a survey of scholars who have taken them
seriously is my next task.

4. *The Transfiguration and the Function of Moses and Elijah*

My survey of scholarship thus far shows that by and large scanty
attention has been given to the figures of Moses and Elijah. This hardly
does justice to the fact that these two figures occupy a high proportion
of space in the various transfiguration pericopes (Mk 9.2-8 and 9-13; Mt.
17.1-9 and 9-13; Lk. 9.28-36). In Lk. 9.28-36 Moses and Elijah occupy
four out of nine verses, which amounts to nearly 50% (without considering v. 35 where there is an allusion to their absence). In Mk 9.2-8,
Moses and Elijah are referred to in two out of seven verses (discounting
v.8), and Elijah figures in three out of five verses in Mk 9.9-13 and
parallels; Mt. 17.9-13 (omitted by Luke). The evangelists then give
Moses and Elijah considerable prominence, and so must any explanation
of the transfiguration. A brief survey of views concerning their function
is necessary for the total development of this thesis.

Symbols of Suffering
Recently M.D. Hooker, focusing on Mark's Elijah emphasis at the transfiguration, presents Elijah as a suffering figure, who prefigures Jesus'
suffering. Hooker also associates Moses with the idea of suffering. She
argues that (1) the clue to the presence of Elijah and Moses is found in
Jesus' specific teaching that his disciples will have to face suffering. Here
Elijah and Moses are examples of those who have already suffered. (2)
Hooker connects καθὼς γέγραπται ἐπ᾽ αὐτόν in 9.13 with γέγραπται
ἐπὶ τὸν υἱὸν τοῦ ἀνθρώπου of 9.12 and οὐδὲ τὴν γραφὴν ταύτην
ἀνέγνωτε of 12.10 and concludes that, just as it is written that Elijah
must suffer, it is also written that Jesus must suffer. (3) Elijah and
Moses are prototypes of those who must suffer for Christ's sake, a
message that Jesus had plainly taught his disciples in 8.34-38. (4) In the

transfiguration three disciples see a vision of Jesus' glory, which he will have when he returns as the triumphant Son of Man. Those seen with him are prototypes of those who have suffered. Therefore at the triumphal returning of the Son of Man (Mk 8.38), only those who have suffered for his sake will be able to share his glory.[70]

Hooker does well in relating Mk 9.2-8 to the suffering motifs of the Son of Man in 8.31-33, of discipleship in 8.34-37, and also in relating it with 9.9-13; 12.10 and 8.38. Mark 9.10-13 lends weight to the view that Elijah (alias the Baptist) prefigures Jesus' suffering. Recently M. Davies has viewed Mt. 17.1-13 in a similar manner. She points out that Matthew's transfiguration pericope is almost bracketed by references to the Baptist (16.14; 17.12-13)—and Matthew devotes space to describing John's execution (14.3-12). Hence like the prophets before—Moses and Elijah who were rejected by their own people but vindicated by God— both John and Jesus, followed by their disciples will suffer persecution.[71]

However, it is doubtful if Mark (and Matthew) intends Moses to be seen as a prototype of suffering. Elsewhere in Mark (and Matthew) Moses is not a suffering figure, but the great leader/teacher whom Jesus supercedes. So while Hooker's and Davies's Elijah-suffering association may be accepted, the Moses-suffering association does not have much support. It also needs to be pointed out that, although Mark (and Matthew) associates Elijah with the motif of suffering through the Baptist (Mk 9.13, more explicitly in Mt. 17.12-13), in this context this seems to be an association made by the evangelist(s) rather than a well known way of viewing Elijah at the time. The Elijah expectation, following scribal teaching, was one that associated Elijah with the idea of the resurrection; Mark, however, has linked this with the idea of suffering qua the Baptist. This, as I shall show later, is adopted by Matthew but omitted by Luke. So while Hooker has made a valid point, to argue solely that Mark portrays Elijah and Moses as 'figures of suffering' prefiguring Jesus' suffering is not adequate.

---

70.   Hooker, 'What Doest Thou here Elijah?', pp. 69-70; *The Gospel According to St Mark* (London: A. & C. Black), pp. 216-17; *The Son of Man in Mark*, pp. 127-28. Also see M. Pamment, 'Moses and Elijah in the Story of the Transfiguration', *ExpTim* 92 (1981), pp. 338-39; A. Feuillet, 'Les perspectives propres à chaque évangéliste dans les récits de la transfiguration', *Bib* 39 (1958), pp. 281-301, esp. pp. 284-85.

71.   M. Davies, *Matthew*, pp.123-24.

A Contrast to Jesus' True Status

M.E. Thrall[72] has argued that Moses and Elijah are introduced in order
to assert that Jesus by virtue of his resurrection has attained a far greater
status than theirs, or any other Old Testament saint.

It is true that Jesus identified as God's Son (Mk 9.7) enjoys a higher
status than Moses and Elijah, and this theme is not exclusive to Mark.
But Thrall has missed other important aspects, including: (a) the Markan
association of Jesus with Elijah as a suffering figure and (b) Mark's
linking of Jesus' resurrection with the scribal association of Elijah with
resurrection. So, there is more to the story than a pure contrast of status
between Jesus and these two Old Testament figures.

Figures Representing the Parousia

G.H. Boobyer[73] argues that the transfiguration prefigures the parousia
and so Moses and Elijah are figures representing the parousia. His
arguments are: (1) The belief concerning the eschatological coming of
Elijah and of other prophets is seen in the New Testament. Of Elijah: Mk
6.15 (Lk. 9.8); 8.28 (Mt. 16.14; Lk. 9.19); 9.11-13 (Mt. 17.10-13); 15.35-
36 (Mt. 27.47). Of others: Mt. 8.11; Mk 12.25-27; 13.27, and echoes in 1
Cor. 10.1-4; Heb. 11; 12.2; 1 Pet. 1.11, among others.[74] This is in
keeping with Jewish eschatology, according to which many prominent
figures, Enoch, Elijah, Moses, Ezra, Baruch, Jeremiah, perhaps even Job
(LXX, Job 42.17), are associated with the expectation of the new age.[75]
Moses and Elijah represent such a group. (2) Mk 9.11-13; Mt. 17.10-13,
assign to Elijah a future function in the establishment of the messianic
kingdom, in the second advent. The work of Elijah in the person of John
the Baptist in 'restoring all things' (ἀποκαθιστάνει πάντα Mk 9.12;
ἀποκαταστήσει πάντα Mt. 17.11), though frustrated by his enemies,
will not be thwarted, and will be resumed at Christ's second coming. (3)
Boobyer also understands Moses and Elijah as representatives of the law
and the prophets. For he points out that, according to Mk 13.21-22,
false prophets and false christs will arise in the last days; and it is through
Moses and Elijah, representatives of the law and the prophets, that these

---

72.   M.E. Thrall, 'Elijah and Moses in Mark's Account of the Transfiguration',
NTS 16 (1969-70), pp. 305-17.
73.   Boobyer, *St Mark and the Transfiguration Story*, pp. 70-71.
74.   Boobyer, *St Mark and the Transfiguration Story*, p. 72.
75.   Boobyer, *St Mark and the Transfiguration Story*, p. 70.

false prophets will be confounded, at the parousia, when Moses and Elijah descend with Christ.[76]

Boobyer raises an interesting issue as to whether the 'coming of Elijah' is fully exhausted in the coming and ministry of John the Baptist. Luke for example omits Mk 9.9-13 (Mt. 17.9-13) and in view of the parallels he brings out between Elijah/Elisha and Jesus it could be argued that he sometimes sees Jesus himself as the new Elijah, in which capacity he also has a future eschatological role (Acts 3.19-21; 1.6, and on Luke, see Appendix). Boobyer's view that Moses and Elijah will confound false prophets and christs at the parousia, however, is speculative; the consistent picture in the New Testament is that it is Christ who brings judgment upon the false prophets and christs (Mt. 24.30; 25.41; 2 Thess. 1.7-8; 2.8). Furthermore, Boobyer is oblivious to aspects of Mark's handling of his tradition which I have noticed, for example the Elijah-Baptist-Jesus-suffering/death parallelism that Hooker has pointed out, and also the Elijah-resurrection theme in Mk 9.10-13. 2 Pet. 1.16-17 supports Boobyer's general thesis connecting the transfiguration and the parousia, but he seems to have pressed every detail of the transfiguration story to fit the parousia theme (e.g. Moses and Elijah as parousia men) and so overstated his case.

Deathless Witnesses

B.D. Chilton[77] has argued that in Mk 9.1 (and Mt. 16.28; Lk. 9.27) Jesus 'swears by immortal witnesses the efficacy of the kingdom in power'. He argues as follows: (1) By a judicious use of redaction criticism, he attempts to arrive at the pre-Markan tradition. He concludes that the phraseology of Mk 9.1, ἀμὴν λέγω ὑμῖν, οὐ μὴ γεύσωνται θανάτου, echoes themes found in apocalyptic and rabbinic material, and that the phrase is an authentic saying of Jesus.[78] (2) He compares οἵτινες οὐ μὴ γεύσωνται θανάτου with similar phraseology in *R. Gen.* 21.5; *4 Ezra* 6.25, 26 and concludes that the phrase is a technical reference to

76. Boobyer, *St Mark and the Transfiguration Story*, p. 76.
77. B.D. Chilton, *God in Strength* (Freistadt: F. Plöchl, 1977), pp. 251-74; 'An Evangelical and Critical Approach to the Sayings of Jesus', *Themelios*, 3 (1977-78), pp. 78-85; 'The Transfiguration: Dominical Assurance and Apostolic Vision', *NTS* 27 (1980), pp. 115-24.
78. Like A. Ambrozic, *The Hidden Kingdom: A Redaction-Critical Study of the References to the Kingdom of God in Mark's Gospel* (Washington: Catholic Biblical Association of America, 1972), pp. 208-209, so also Chilton, *God in Strength*, p. 268.

'immortals.'[79] In *R. Gen.* 21.5 Elijah was granted the privilege of not tasting death. In *4 Ezra* 6.25, 26, those who have not tasted death are to appear with the Messiah.[80] (3) He takes Luke's use of συνεστῶτας (9.32), in comparison with ἑστηκότων of Mk 9.1, as confirming his position that 'the ones standing' refers not simply to bystanders, but to the deferential attitude of a heavenly court.[81] (4) So Jesus refers to 'immortals' in Mk 9.1 and parallels, and the function of Moses and Elijah is to represent these immortals. Mark places 9.1 before 9.2-10 because in the transfiguration just such an immortal group is gathered.

Interestingly, some years ago B.W. Bacon,[82] argued on similar lines when he held that it is one of the characteristics of the forerunners that they 'had not tasted death' and Mk 9.1 is fulfilled literally in 9.4, in the presence of Moses and Elijah.[83] If Chilton and Bacon are correct, some major problems in the interpretation of Mk 9:1 and parallels are solved. However, Chilton's position poses some difficulties: (1) Chilton eliminates ὧδε as a Markan redaction and thus designates τῶν ἑστηκότων οἵτινες as 'immortals'. But the natural meaning is that Jesus is referring to those in his immediate audience. (2) It is true that, in 2 Kings 2.11 Elijah was translated into heaven, and so was 'deathless', but according to Deut. 34.5 Moses died. Certain Jewish traditions suggest that Moses escaped death, but the evidence is ambiguous. Chilton's theory of 'deathless' witnesses is at least uncertain.[84]

Typological and Eschatological Figures
W.L. Liefeld has argued that the role of Moses is primarily typological, while that of Elijah is primarily eschatological.[85] In the light of the possible echo of Deut. 18.18 themes (e.g. αὐτοῦ ἀκούσεσθε 18.15

79.   Chilton, *God in Strength*, pp. 268-69.
80.   Chilton, *God in Strength*, pp. 268-69.
81.   Chilton, *God in Strength*, p. 272.
82.   B.W. Bacon, 'The Transfiguration Story', *AJT* 6 (1902), pp. 251-52.
83.   Bacon, 'The Transfiguration Story', p. 251.
84.   In 'The Transfiguration', pp. 115-24 Chilton compares Peter, James and John with Aaron, Nadab and Abihu who were with Moses on Mount Sinai, but according to Lev. 10.1-8, Nadab and Abihu were consumed by divine fire! For critique of Chilton's view see Gundry, *Mark*, p. 476-477; Carson, *Matthew*, pp. 380-82; Wenham and Moses, *NovT* 36, 2 (1994), p. 149 n. 5; p. 152 n. 10.
85.   W.L. Liefeld, 'Theological Motifs in the Transfiguration Narrative', in R.N. Longenecker and M.C. Tenney (eds.), *New Dimensions in New Testament Study* (Grand Rapids: Zondervan, 1974), pp. 171-74.

LXX) in Mk 9.7; Mt. 17.5 (ἀκούετε αὐτοῦ, and αὐτοῦ ἀκούετε in Lk. 9.35 and in manuscripts C L W V *f*[13] of Mt. 17.5) he argues that the presence of Moses signifies that the 'type' (Deut. 18.18) is fulfilled in Jesus, but that Elijah has eschatological significance.

However, Liefeld himself wonders if such a distinction can be made.[86] Certain examples from Second Temple Judaism (admittedly few) suggest that Moses himself was given an eschatological role, for example the first century CE *Liv. Proph.* 2.14-15; and the sixth–tenth century Midrash *R. Deut.* 3.17. Moreover, the idea that Sinai and Sinai-type experiences will accompany the 'Day of the Lord' perhaps fueled such expectations (*Liv. Proph.* 2.14-15; Mic. 1.3; Ps. 96.13).[87] While certain of these materials expressing such expectations are late, they could well preserve earlier traditions. For example, the saying in Midrash *R. Deut.* 3.17 is attributed to Johanan ben Zakkai, who lived in the first century CE.[88]

The Law and the Prophets

Boobyer, Nineham, Mauser, Trilling, Meier, Morris and several others[89] hold that Moses and Elijah function as representatives of the 'law and the prophets'. The familiar argument here is that with the coming of Jesus, the law and the prophets are fulfilled, the old covenant is superseded by the new.

This view has been criticised by those who argue that (1) it gives too much individual importance to both figures.[90] (2) Elijah is not a 'canonical' prophet. (3) Moreover, there is an overlap of function in both

---

86. Liefeld, 'Theological Motifs', p. 178.

87. On this see T.F. Glasson, 'Theophany and Parousia', *NTS* 34 (1988), pp. 259-70, who agues that passages like Mic. 1.3, Ps. 96.13 suggest that the divine coming of the future reflects the theophany at Sinai.

88. On this see Glasson, *Moses in the Fourth Gospel*, p. 12; I. Abrahams, *Studies in Pharisaism and the Gospels* (2 vols.; Cambridge: Cambridge University Press, 1924), II, p. 54 n. 5.

89. Cf. Nineham, *Saint Mark*, p. 235; Mauser, *Christ in the Wilderness*, p.113; W. Trilling, *The Gospel According to St Matthew* (New York: Herder & Herder, 1969), p. 110; J.P. Meier, *Matthew* (Wilmington: Michael Glazier, 1980), p. 190; Morris, *Matthew*, p. 439; F.V. Filson, *A Commentary on the Gospel according to St Matthew* (London: A. & C. Black, 1960), p. 192; Burn, 'The Transfiguration', *ExpTim* 14, (1902-1903), p. 444; J.C. Fenton, *Saint Matthew* (Harmondsworth: Penguin Books, 1976), pp. 275-77.

90. Cf. Liefeld, 'Theological Motifs in the Transfiguration Narrative', p. 171; Gundry, *Mark*, p. 478.

these figures: for Moses was not only a lawgiver, but also a prophet (Deut. 34.10; *Quaest. in Exod.* 2.46; *Mos.* 2.187-291; *Ant.* 2.327; 4.165, 320; Qumran *1QS* 1.3; 8.15; *CD* 5.21b-6.1a). And Elijah was not only a prophet but, according to Mal. 4.4-6, one aspect of his future ministry was to turn people's hearts back to the 'covenant' (see also Sir. 48.1-12). In later Jewish literature, Elijah was to resolve halakhic difficulties (*m. b. Mes.* 1.8; 2.8; 3.4; *b. b. Mes.* 114a; *b. Sabb.* 108a; *b. Menah.* 63a; *b. Pesah.* 13a) and to further the study of the Torah both written and oral.[91] So any compartmentalisation of Moses and Elijah as 'law' and 'prophet' presents difficulties. But since both Elijah and Moses motifs are seen in Mal. 4.4-6 this view has value, albeit limited, in illuminating their function at the transfiguration.

From the above discussion, it is clear that the figures of Moses and Elijah raise a host of issues, and, excepting Hooker's observations on the Jesus-Elijah-suffering function of the Elijah motif in Mark, none of the views has satisfactorily explained their presence at the transfiguration. Some crucial issues which are of significance for any discussion on the transfiguration, are: (1) Why do they appear at all? (2) What was their significance in first century Judaism? (3) How do the evangelists portray their presence and, for this thesis in particular, how does Matthew understand them especially in the light of current ideas about Moses (see Chapter 2). The argument of this thesis is that to do justice to the figures of Moses and Elijah, as well as to other details of the narrative, is of vital importance in unlocking the significance of the transfiguration.

5. *The Transfiguration and Moses-Sinai Symbolism*

Several scholars, recent and not so recent, Klostermann, Mauser, Johnson, Davies and Allison and others,[92] have suggested that a number

91. Also see L. Ginzberg, *The Legends of the Jews* (6 vols.; Philadelphia: Jewish Publication Society of America, 1938), VI, p. 333 n. 8; A. Wiener, *The Prophet Elijah in the Development of Judaism, A Depth-Psychological Study* (London: Routledge & Kegan Paul, 1978). In addition to these views, A.T. Fryer, 'The Purpose of the Transfiguration', *JTS* 5 (January 1904), pp. 214-17 suggests that Moses as the consecrator of the first high priest represents the 'typical high priest' and Elijah was the 'typical prophet', but against this view see W.C. Braithwaite, 'The Teaching of the Transfiguration', *ExpTim* 17 (1905-6), p. 375.

92. On Mark, cf. Klostermann, *Das Markusevangelium,* pp.98; Mauser, *Christ in the Wilderness*, pp. 111-19; S.E. Johnson, *The Gospel according to St Mark* (London: Adam & Black, 1960), pp. 156-58. On Matthew, see Gundry, *Matthew,*

of features within the narrative point to a background in the Moses-Sinai and exodus tradition.

Moses-Sinai Parallels

The following Moses-Sinai motifs have been noted (here I will focus on Mark and Matthew alone; my comments on Luke are featured in the Appendix): (1) The time reference: The unusually precise time reference[93] καὶ μετὰ ἡμέρας ἓξ in Mk 9.2 and Mt. 17.1 (καὶ μεθ᾽ ἡμέρας ἓξ) is said to recall Exod. 24.16-17, where for six days the cloud covered Mount Sinai, and on the seventh day Yahweh called Moses out of the midst of the cloud.[94] (2) The mountain: In both stories (Exod. 24.16 and Mk 9.2-8 and par.) the setting is a mountain. In Mark and Matthew it is ὄρος ὑψηλὸν (and Luke merely τὸ ὄρος); in Exodus 24 it is Mount Sinai. (3) The cloud: In both stories a cloud overshadows the mountain: Mark uses ἐπισκιάζουσα, but the LXX of Exod. 40.34-35, uses both ἐκάλυψεν and ἐπεσκίαζεν. (4) The voice: In both stories, the divine voice speaks out of the cloud: look at Exod. 24.16 with Mk 9.7 and parallels. (5) Moses: Moses features in both stories: and if going beyond Exodus 24 to its larger context, in 34.29 the face of Moses shines due to his meeting with God, which may be compared with Matthew's καὶ ἔλαμψεν τὸ πρόσωπον αὐτοῦ ὡς ὁ ἥλιος (Mt. 17.2) and Luke's τὸ εἶδος τοῦ προσώπου αὐτοῦ ἕτερον (Lk. 9.29).[95] Further, (6) Chosen companions: Both accounts have the idea of chosen companions: in Exodus 24 Moses separates himself first from the people, taking with him the seventy elders and Aaron, Nadab and Abihu (Exod. 24.1, 9) and later, further up the mountain, takes only Joshua (Exod. 24.13). This parallels (not in every detail)[96] Mk 9.2-3, and parallels, where Jesus takes

---

pp. 99-101; P. Dabeck, '"Siehe, es erschienen Moses und Elias" (Mt. 17.3)', *Bib* 23 (1942), pp. 175-89, esp. pp. 175-80; Feuillet, 'Les perspectives propers a chaque evangeliste dans les recits de la transfiguration', p. 293; Davies and Allison, *Saint Matthew*, II, pp. 685-86.

93.   The only other parallel of a precise reference to time in Mark is 14.1.

94.   Klostermann, *Das Markusevangelium*, p. 98; B.W. Bacon, 'After Six Days', *HTR* 8 (1915), pp. 94-95; Nineham, *Saint Mark*, p. 234; Lane, *The Gospel of Mark*, pp. 317-18; McCurley, '"And after Six Days"', pp. 67-81.

95.   On Luke see G.B. Caird, 'The Transfiguration', *ExpTim* 67 (1956), pp. 291-94.

96.   Bultmann, *The History of the Synoptic Tradition*, p. 260, objects here that there is no strict parallel, but this would be only if one limits oneself to Exod. 24.15-18. But as McCurley, '"And after Six Days"', p. 76 n. 23 has rightly pointed out

with him the three disciples. (7) Theophany: Moses and Elijah too received theophanies on mountains (Moses in Exod. 3.1-2, 24-34 and Elijah in 1 Kgs 19).[97] (8) Other parallels, albeit of lesser significance, have been suggested: Mauser, for example, has compared the fear motif in Mk 9.6 (used variously in Mt. 17.6-7 and Lk. 9.34) with Exod. 34.30, and suggests that the 'cloud' in Mk 9.7 recalls the cloud in the wilderness traditions.[98]

Some Differences

Despite these comparisons, the parallelism is not certain or total. For example (1) καὶ μετὰ ἡμέρας ἕξ (Mk 9.2, Mt. 17.1) has been taken variously, and without reference to Exodus 24, for example (a) as a simple chronological link between the transfiguration pericope and Jesus' preceding teaching.[99] (b) According to Thrall, μετὰ ἡμέρας ἕξ implies 'on the seventh' day, and so for Mark the significance, as for the resurrection, is that the transfiguration occurred on the sabbath day.[100] (c) For Riesenfeld and Bonnard, the six days represents the interval between the day of atonement and the feast of the tabernacles, and so Jesus went up the mountain on the first day of the feast. H. Baltensweiler argues that the 'six days' are the period of the feast of tabernacles, with

that the use of the Old Testament by New Testament writers is not always so precise and limited.

97.   Like Moses, Elijah too is closely associated with a Sinai/Horeb context, see Josephus *Ant.* 8.13.7; Ginzberg, *Jewish Legends*, 4, p. 200.

98.   Cf. Mauser, *Christ in the Wilderness*, p. 119-20. Moses and Elijah are men of the wilderness par excellence, and this fits in with Mauser's overall theme that Jesus' work was inaugurated in the wilderness (at his baptism), and whose way, driven by the spirit, was to be a way through the desert (p. 116); hence there is striking similarity between the transfiguration story and the wilderness tradition, particularly Exod. 24 (pp. 114-19).

99.   See Braithwaite, 'The Teaching of the Transfiguration', *ExpTim* 17 (1905-1906), pp. 372-75, esp. 372-73; Schnellbächer, 'ΚΑΙ ΜΕΤΑ ʽΗΜΕΡΑΣ ΕΞ (Markus 9.2) ', pp. 252-57; Mauser, *Christ in the Wilderness*, pp. 111-12; Johnson, *The Gospel According to St Mark*, p. 156; H. Anderson, *The Gospel of Mark* (London: Oliphants, 1976), pp. 223-24; Hooker, 'What Doest Thou here, Elijah?' pp. 60-61.

100.   Thrall, 'Elijah and Moses in Mark's Account of the Transfiguration', *NTS* 16 (1969-70), p. 311. Also according to Burn, 'The Transfiguration', pp. 442-47, esp. p. 443, Jesus ascended on a 'sabbath's eve', and according to Anderson, *The Gospel of Mark*, p. 223, the 'six days' represents a 'sabbath's rest'.

Jesus going up on the final and great day, the seventh day.[101] (d) According to another view, 'six days' parallels the days that a priest waited in the temple to cleanse himself. (2) Further, the 'voice' in Exodus 24–31; 33–34 is addressed to Moses, while at the transfiguration it is directed at the disciples (not Jesus). (3) Peter's proposal to build τρεῖς σκηνάς (Mk 9.5; Mt. 17.4; Lk. 9.33) has no parallel in Exodus 19–34; it is Yahweh who gives Moses plans for the tabernacle (Exod. 25.10-31.11). (4) In Exod. 24.16 the cloud covered the mountain for six days, and on the seventh Yahweh called Moses; at the transfiguration the cloud alights only at a specific moment and after they had ascended the mountain.[102]

So given that these 'differences' exist,[103] there is not necessarily a one-to-one parallelism in the typological use of the Old Testament by New Testament writers.[104] To compare Mk 9.2-9 and parallels with Exod. 24.15-18, and the wider corpus in 19–24, 32–34: There are certain common motifs, (1) mountain, (2) cloud, (3) the radiance of the face, (4) the voice, which do suggest a Sinai typology.

Mark and the Moses-Sinai Motif

Although I take this view to be true and important, it is debatable whether Mark has exploited the Sinai background. The purpose of this thesis is to explore Matthew's portrayal of the transfiguration in its Jewish and early Christian context. But since, as a working hypothesis, I accept that Matthew redacted Mark, a brief analysis of Mark's portrayal of the transfiguration is essential for my thesis. For any attempt to determine Matthew's redaction of Mark also needs to take into account Mark's treatment of the transfiguration and the possibility that Matthew

101. Riesenfeld, *Jesus transfiguré*, pp. 276-77; Baltensweiler, *Die Verklärung Jesu*, pp. 46-51.

102. Further see McCurley, '"And after Six Days"', p. 77.

103. These differences perhaps make the following scholars see very little Moses-Sinai typology in Mt. 17.1-9 and parallels; see R.C.H. Lenski, *The Interpretation of St Matthew's Gospel* (Minneapolis: Augsburg 1964), p. 652; A. Plummer, *An Exegetical Commentary on the Gospel according to St Matthew* (London: Robert & Scott, 1909), p.238; W.C. Allen, *A Critical and Exegetical Commentary on the Gospel according to St Matthew* (Edinburgh: T. & T. Clark, 1912), pp. 183-85; P. Gaechter, *Das Matthäus-Evangelium: Ein Kommentar* (Innsbruck: Tyrolia-Verlag, 1963).

104. On use of typology see R.T. France, *Jesus and the Old Testament* (London: Tyndale, 1971), pp. 38-43, 76-78; *Matthew: Evangelist*, pp. 186-89; J. Goldingay, *Approaches to Old Testament Interpretation* (Leicester: Apollos, 1990), pp. 97-115.

not merely used Mark as a source but also in some sense understood what Mark was doing with his material, Mark's emphases and so on. It is this understanding, in addition to Matthew's own theological emphases, that contributed towards Matthew's end product in 17.1-13. With this Matthew-Mark relationship in view, Mark's possible demotion of the Moses motif at the transfiguration may be highlighted by the following arguments:

(1) Mark when first referring to the appearance of Moses and Elijah has Ἠλίας σὺν Μωυσεῖ rather than the traditional, more natural, and chronologically proper Μωυσῆς καὶ Ἠλίας of Mt. 17.3/Lk. 9.30. Since Mark reverts to the more natural order in Peter's suggestion in Mk 9.5 καὶ Μωυσεῖ μίαν καὶ Ἠλίᾳ μίαν, it is arguable that this order was found in the tradition behind Mk 9.2-8, and that Mark chose to change it in 9.4. It is arguable that he does this to suit his Elijah emphasis, (a) the Elijah-resurrection link made by the disciples (based on scribal expectations Mk 9.10-11) and also (b) the Elijah-Baptist-suffering association prefiguring Jesus' suffering.

(2) Unlike Matthew and Luke, Mark is silent on the radiance of Jesus' face. Had he intended to emphasise the parallel between Mk 9.3 and Moses in Exod. 34.30 he might have been expected to refer to Jesus' shining face. Whether the pre-Markan tradition had such a reference, retained by Matthew (and Luke) but omitted by Mark, is unclear,[105] but such an omission would fit in with Mark's demotion of Moses below Elijah in 9.5. Not that Mark can avoid the Moses motif evident in his tradition; note the echo of Deut. 18.15 in the ἀκούετε αὐτοῦ of Mk 9.7.

(3) Lane, Swartley, Mauser and others have shown, that Mark is interested in the 'exodus' motif, and Mark does portray Jesus as having greater authority than Moses.[106] Hints of a new and greater Moses theme may also be detected in Mark. For example, in 12.29-31. Jesus combines Deut. 6.5 and Lev. 19.18, in a way that has parallels in rabbinic

105. B.H. Streeter, *The Four Gospels: A Study of Origins* (London: Macmillan, 1926), p. 316 raises the possibility that at one time πρόσωπον may have been found in the Markan text. But his suggestion needs to be set in the context of his main argument, softening the minor agreement between Mt. 17.2 and Lk. 9.29. Moreover, the absence of πρόσωπον in Mark (hence muting a Sinai echo) argues well for the priority that he gives Elijah in placing him before Moses in 9.4.

106. Lane, *The Gospel of Mark*, pp. 39-62; W.M. Swartley, 'The Structural Function of the Term "Way" (Hodos) in Mark's Gospel', in H. Charles (ed.), *The New Way of Jesus* (Kansas: Faith & Life, 1980), pp. 73-85; Mauser, *Christ in the Wilderness*.

literature,[107] and here Jesus may possibly be seen as going beyond Moses, in that the levitical identification of 'neighbour' as the 'the sons of your own people' is probably not presupposed by the Markan Jesus.[108] In 10.3-9, Jesus' teaching (on divorce) is superior to Moses' concession. In certain passages Mark also portrays Jesus as law abiding, for in 1.44 (Mt. 8.4; Lk. 5.14) he underscores Jesus' compliance with the Mosaic regulations[109] and in 7.10 (Mt. 15.4)[110] Jesus approvingly cites Moses and the fifth commandment almost verbatim (Exod. 20.12 LXX (Deut. 5.16) also Exod. 21.16 LXX (Lev. 20.9). In 10.19 (cf. Mt. 19.18; Lk. 18.20) Jesus is positive about the Old Testament, teaching that the man who obeys the law will live.[111] And in 12.26 (Mt. 22.31; Lk. 20.37) reference is made to the 'Book of Moses' and in particular to Exod. 3.6, and is used in defence of the resurrection.

But even though the transfiguration pericope provides him with ample opportunities to exploit the Moses theme, he does not. Despite its significance in Second Temple Judaism, he seems in his transfiguration pericope (Mk 9.2-10 and 11-13) to give Elijah a greater role than Moses. This failure to highlight the Moses-Sinai theme is not exclusive to Mark; the probably independent witness to the transfiguration in 2 Pet. 1.16-18 does not bring out the Moses-Sinai (nor the Elijah) theme;[112] there is not even the 'hear him' (of Deut. 18.15) when the heavenly voice is described.

---

107. See Lane, *The Gospel of Mark*, p.432 n. 48 and 49.

108. Lane, *The Gospel of Mark*, p. 433.

109. According to R.A. Guelich, *The Sermon on the Mount* (Waco: Word, 1982), pp. 75-77, this may also reflect Jesus' attitude to the Law, and here in Mk 1.44 it was perhaps offered as 'evidence against' those who accused Jesus of having disregarded the Law. Like Mt. 17.24-27, 5.23-24 this verse may have played a role in the early church's struggle within Judaism.

110. In Mark alone the emphasis is on 'Moses', Μωυσῆς γὰρ εἶπεν (Mk 7.10) in contrast to Matthew ὁ γὰρ Θεὸς εἶπεν (Mt. 15.4).

111. Cf. Deut. 30.15-16; Ezek. 33.15. With the exception of the prohibition of fraud, which appears to be an application of the eight and ninth commandment, the requirements cited are drawn from the decalogue (Exod. 20.12-16; Deut. 5.16-20).

112. On this see Gundry, *Mark*, pp. 475-76. Given Mark's (most likely) gentile audience, Augustín Del Agua's thesis that Mk 9.2-8 is a derashich hermeneutic (more than a midrash) patterned after Exod. 24 and 34 ('The Narrative of the Transfiguration as a Derashic Scenification of a Faith Confession [Mark 9.2-8 PAR)', *NTS* 39 [1993], pp. 340-54) is highly speculative.

Matthew: Some Preliminary Remarks

In contrast with Mark, Matthew emphasises the Moses-Sinai-Jesus parallelism. I shall engage in a substantial source and redaction critical study of Matthew's account of the transfiguration shortly. Here I shall make some preliminary comments about distinctive features of Matthew: (1) In 17.2 Matthew adds καὶ ἔλαμψεν τὸ πρόσωπον αὐτοῦ ὡς ὁ ἥλιος which is reminiscent of Exod. 34.29-30, 35, of Moses' shining face. (2) Matthew changes Mark's order to the more natural Μωυσῆς καὶ Ἠλίας thereby reversing Mark's Elijah emphasis to a Moses emphasis. (3) Matthew drops Mark's reference to the fuller (Mk 9.3) and adds ὡς τὸ φῶς, thus giving the transfiguration a more 'heavenly' and apocalyptic setting. (4) He omits Mark's οὐ γὰρ ᾔδει τί ἀποκριθῇ, and perhaps presents Peter as having meant what he said in 17.4; certainly Peter receives special emphasis in Matthew's account. His suggestion of τρεῖς σκηνάς may be connected with the building metaphor in Mt. 16.16-20. (5) In 17.5 Matthew adds φωτεινὴ to Mark's simple νεφέλη, and this, with the idea of overshadowing ἐπεσκίασεν αὐτούς, strengthens the allusion to Exod. 24.15-16; 40.34-38. (6) Matthew's description of the transfiguration as τὸ ὅραμα has apocalyptic connotations, reminiscent of passages like Dan. 7.13.

Given Matthew's redaction on Mark and also the common material in Matthew and Mark, including Mosaic motifs which Mark could not avoid (e.g. ἀκούετε αὐτοῦ Mk 9.7; cf. Deut. 18.15) but did not exploit, I will show that Matthew exploits these motifs and has blended together Moses-Sinai and apocalyptic themes (e.g. from Daniel 7). I will show that Matthew accommodates Mark's Elijah motif, but it has a different function than in Mark. These and other observations will be developed in this thesis.

Conclusions

It is evident that there is a great divergence in interpretation of the transfiguration. The misplaced resurrection account theory is unacceptable. The prefigurement theories in relation to the resurrection, and post-resurrection themes such as the ascension and the parousia have certain weight, but nevertheless are inadequate. A similar point may be made about links made with Peter's confession (the confirmation hypothesis) and Gethsemane (more relevant to Mark). No one of these theories gives a comprehensive view of the evangelists' understanding of the transfiguration, but all leave important details unexplained. Theories giving due consideration to the Jewish and Hellenistic context of the idea of transfiguration and transformation point in the right direction; but we have seen that neither Riesenfeld's enthronement view nor Müller's θεῖος ἀνήρ categories are persuasive.

We have also seen that in the transfiguration pericopes, Moses and Elijah figure prominently, occupy considerable space, and hence need to be given adequate attention.

My broadly based analysis also led us into a preliminary comparison of the transfiguration pericopes of Mk 9.2-13 and Mt. 17.1-13. Here I have argued that the Moses-Sinai-Jesus parallelism is the most convincing framework within which the tradition as a whole, perhaps including the pre-Markan tradition, is set. Mark plays down the Moses-Sinai parallelism, in order to emphasise (a) the Elijah-resurrection and hence Jesus-resurrection theme, and (b) the Elijah-Baptist-Jesus-suffering motif. In this, Mk 9.9-13 exerts a hermeneutical control on his transfiguration pericope. At a preliminary level I have shown that Matthew, by his redaction on Mark, emphasises the Moses-Sinai parallelism. The amalgamation of this with apocalyptic motifs, particularly Daniel 7, will be explored later.

The Task Ahead
My conclusions, even at this preliminary stage of this study, indicate that the Moses-Sinai typology plays an important role in Matthew's portrayal of the transfiguration. In order to understand the wider theological implications of this, and also to set Mt. 17.1-13 within the wider framework of Matthew's theology and in its first century milieu, a reconstruction of Matthew's context is necessary. In order to do this we need to explore the influence of Moses-Sinai and transfiguration motifs in Second Temple Jewish literature.

Chapter 3

A SURVEY OF MOSES-SINAI AND TRANSFIGURATION THEMES
IN SECOND TEMPLE JUDAISM

It is indisputable that Moses was a towering figure in the Old Testament, and this has been well documented in the writings of G.W. Coats, E. Auerbach, J. Bright and others.[1] Moses plays a prominent role in the Hexateuch and his figure rises at key points both in the Old Testament (e.g. Hos. 12.14; Neh. 1.8; Ezra 7.6) and the New Testament. The story of Moses was also the 'story' of God, for according to Exod. 14.31 Israel 'believed in the Lord and in his servant Moses'. It is due to this unique relationship between Yahweh and Moses that the Torah was both Yahwistic and Mosaic and, as J. Bright remarks, it is with Moses that 'Israel's distinctive faith begins'.[2]

Since Moses' important role in the Old Testament has been well documented, it is pointless to engage in a study of Moses motifs in the Old Testament as such, but I shall focus on a period of history which is crucial for this thesis, that of Second Temple Judaism. The scope of this chapter is wide, for methodological reasons I shall focus on pre-Christian and first-century material. My purpose is to set the synoptic account of

1.   G.W. Coats, *Moses: Heroic Man, Man of God* (Sheffield: JSOT Press, 1988) (and note works cited there); E. Auerbach, *Moses* (Detroit: Wayne, 1975); J. Bright, *A History of Israel* (London: SCM Press, 1980), pp. 125-28; H. Seebas, 'Moses', in C. Brown, (ed.), *NIDNT*, II, pp. 635-42.

2.   Bright, *A History of Israel*, p.128. Recently Allison, *The New Moses*, pp. 11-95 has argued that Moses is so important that 'Moses-types' are seen in important figures in the 'Jewish scriptures', these include: Joshua, Gideon, Samuel, David, Elijah, Josiah, Ezekiel, Jeremiah, Ezra, Baruch, 'The Suffering Servant', Hillel, 'The prophet like Moses' of Deut. 18.15-19, and 'The Messiah.' He also finds Moses-typology applicable to Jesus, Peter (here Allison is unable to cite New Testament passages, apart from Mt. 16.17 in relation to 1 Cor. 10.1-4), Paul (cf. 2 Cor. 3.1-4.6) and other Christian figures (see pp. 96-134). He stoutly defends the role of 'typology' and its cumulative force in the scriptures.

the transfiguration, particularly Matthew's, against its religious and intellectual background.

1. *Moses-Sinai and Moses-Transfiguration Language and Themes in Philo*

Philonic studies have been fruitfully applied to New Testament exegesis in recent years by, among others, Dodd, Borgen, Meeks and Thurston.[3] Philo's emphasis on Moses has been commented on by Goodenough,[4] Wolfson,[5] Meeks,[6] Tiede[7] and Holladay.[8] Those scholars have studied

---

3.   C.H. Dodd, *The Interpretation of the Fourth Gospel*, Cambridge: Cambridge University Press, 1953, pp. 54-73; P. Borgen, 'God's Agent in the Fourth Gospel', in J. Neusner (ed.), *Religions in Antiquity* (Leiden: Brill, 1968), pp. 137-48, reprinted in *Logos was the True Light and Other Essays in the Gospel of John* (Trondheim: 1983), pp. 121-32; *Philo, John and Paul* (Atlanta: Scholars Press, 1987), pp. 233-54; W.A. Meeks, *The Prophet King* (Leiden: Brill, 1967), pp. 100-31; 'The Divine Agent and his counterfeit in Philo and the Fourth Gospel', in E.S. Fiorenza (ed.), *Aspects of Religious Propaganda in Judaism and Early Christianity* (Notre Dame: University of Notre Dame Press, 1976), pp. 43-67; D. Aune, *Prophecy in Early Christianity and the Ancient Mediterranean World* (Grand Rapids: Eerdmans, 1983), pp. 147-53; E.R. Goodenough, *Jewish Symbols in the Greco-Roman Period*, I (New York: Pantheon, 1953), pp. 3-58; R.W. Thurston, 'Philo and the Epistle to the Hebrews', *EvQ*, 58 (1986) pp. 133-43; R. Williamson, *Philo and the Epistle to the Hebrews* (Leiden: Brill, 1970).

4.   E.R. Goodenough, *By Light, Light—The Mystic Gospel of Hellenistic Judaism* (New Haven: Yale, 1935); *An Introduction to Philo Judaeus* (Oxford: 1962), pp. 33-35, 145-52; 'Philo's Exposition of the Law and his de vita Mosis', *HTR* 27 (1933), pp. 109-26. As to the influence of Goodenough's writings see Meeks, *The Prophet King*, pp.101-102; R.S. Eccles, *Erwin Ramsdell Goodenough: A Personal Pilgrimage* (Chico: Scholars Press, 1985); E.S. Freriches and J. Neusener, *Goodenough on The History of religion and on Judaism* (Atlanta: Scholars Press, 1986); D.M. Hay, 'Review', in D.T. Runia (ed.), *The Studia Philonica Annual: Studies in Hellenistic Judaism*, I (Atlanta: Scholars Press, 1989), pp. 128-34, where he highlights the phenomenal rise in Philonic studies in the last fifty years, see pp. 74-81.

5.   H.A. Wolfson, *Philo: Foundations of Religious Philosophy in Judaism, Christianity, and Islam* (Cambridge, MA: Harvard, 1948).

6.   Meeks, *The Prophet King*, pp. 100-31.

7.   D.L. Tiede, *The Charismatic Figure as Miracle Worker* (Missoula, MT: University of Montana, 1972), pp.123-27, 138-77, 241-92.

8.   C.R. Holladay, *'Theios aner' in Hellenistic-Judaism* (Missoula, MT: Scholars Press, 1977), pp. 103-98; Hengel, *The Son of God*, pp. 31-32; Lane, *'Theios*

Philo's portrayal of Moses from various angles and for various purposes.[9] Our purpose, however, is to note Philonic teaching on Moses on Sinai and Moses-transfigured and then to compare our findings with, especially, Matthew's presentation of the transfiguration.[10]

Transformation Motifs in Philo

In *Mos.* 1.158-59 Philo interprets Moses' ascent on Sinai in terms of mystical transformation. At Sinai Moses enjoyed deep κοινωνία with God, he was 'named God and King of the whole nation' (ὠνομάσθη γὰρ ὅλου τοῦ ἔθνους Θεὸς καὶ βασιλεύς),[11] and 'entered into the darkness where God was' (Exod. 21; cf. *Mut. Nom.* 7). Through his mystical ascent on Sinai, and in related events, Moses is initiated into the office as king (*Mos.* 1.158-59), high priest (*Mos.* 2.67-71, 74, 75-76) and hierophant (*Gig.* 53-54). These 'Sinai transformation' themes are also clear in *Mos.* 2.70 (Exod. 24.18; 34.28-29):

> 'he ascended an inaccessible (ὑψηλότατον) and pathless mountain, the highest and most sacred in the region...he descended with a countenance far more beautiful than when he ascended,...nor even could their eyes continue to stand the dazzling brightness that flashed from him like the rays of the sun'.[12]

Aner Christology and the Gospel of Mark', pp. 144-61; B.L. Blackburn, '"Miracle working ΘΕΙΟΙ ΑΝΔΡΕΣ" in Hellenism (and Hellenistic Judaism)', in D. Wenham and C. Blomberg (eds.), *Gospel Perspectives* (6 vols.; Sheffield: JSOT Press, 1986), VI, pp. 185-218, is a corrective against hasty application of *theios-aner* categories to the figure of Jesus.

9.   Also see Williamson, *Philo and the Epistle to the Hebrews*, pp. 449-80, for a concise summary of Philo's view of Moses. Against Williamson's dismissal of any Philo-influence on 'Hebrews' see Thurston, 'Philo and the Epistle to the Hebrews', pp. 133-43 also his 'Midrash and "Magnet" Words in the New Testament', *EvQ* 51 (Jan. 1979), pp. 22-39.

10.   Philo describes his 'sources' as 'the sacred books' which Moses left behind him, and material 'from some of the elders of the nation' (*Mos.* 1.4). See Meeks, *The Prophet King*, p. 101. Moses also features in Graeco-Roman Hellenistic literature (see J.G. Gager, *Moses in Greco-Roman Paganism* [Nashville: Abingdon, 1972]), and it is possible that Philo, aware of such works, contextualised his faith and Moses within the language and categories familiar to the gentile inquirer (see Goodenough, *By Light, Light*, ch. 10).

11.   G.P. Goold (ed.), *Philo* (Loeb Classical Library; 10 vols.; London: Heineman/Cambridge: Harvard, 1925), VI, pp. 357-59.

12.   *Philo*, VI, pp. 482-85.

The εἰς γὰρ ὄρος ὑψηλότατον...here makes an interesting comparison with Mark's (and Matthew's) emphasis on εἰς ὄρος ὑψηλὸν (Mk 9.2/Mt. 17.1), and also Philo's description of Moses' transformed face κατὰ τὴν προσβολὴν ἡλιοειδοῦς φέγγους ἀπαστράπτοντος is not unlike Matthew's καὶ ἔλαμψεν τὸ πρόσωπον αὐτοῦ ὡς ὁ ἥλιος (Luke uses ἐξαστράπτων but of Jesus' clothes) though Matthew is probably incorporating Danielic language (cf. Mt. 13.34 and Dan. 12.3).[13]

In book 2 of Philo's *Quaest. in Exod.*,[14] Moses-Sinai and related events (Exod. 20.25-26) feature prominently. *Quaest. in Exod.* 2.37, speaks of 'God's descent' at Sinai and Moses the 'theologian' (θεολόγου) was privileged, was 'most suitable' and 'worthy' to 'see' God.[15] In *Quaest. in Exod.* 2.45 the coming of the 'glory of God' on Mount Sinai is associated with 'an appearance of the coming of God' (compare καὶ κατέβη ἡ δόξα τοῦ Θεοῦ ἐπι τὸ ὄρος τὸ Σινά of Exod. 24.16 LXX). In *Quaest. in Exod.* 2.46-47. Moses is called up on the seventh day (Exod. 24.16) and is 'changed' from an earthly man. Due to his experience at Sinai, Moses is presented as the 'intelligent man and prophet' (*Quaest. in Exod.* 2.51-2/Exod. 25.7-8). Philo also stresses the sacredness and inaccessibility of Mount Sinai, for 'the mountain...is most suitable to receive the manifestation' (τὴν ἐπιφάνειαν),[16] an emphasis also found in Josephus (*Ant.* 2.264-65).

Philo's use of μετεμορφώθη in reference to Moses makes for a productive comparison with its use in Mk 9.2, and, given Matthew's Moses emphasis, particularly with Mt. 17.2. In *Mos.* 1.57, as Moses spoke to the unjust shepherds (cf. Exod. 2.15b-22) 'he grew inspired and was transfigured into a prophet' (μεταμορφούμενος εἰς προφήτην).[17] This transformation here is in relation to Moses' mind.[18] In *Quaest. in Exod.* 2.29 'he is changed into the divine so that such men become kin

---

13. Similar language is also found in 1 *En.* 14.20; 39.7; 71.11; 2 *En.* 22.8-9; *T. Abr.* 12.4-5. Also note Dan. 12.3 in Mt. 13.34, further see ch. 5.

14. That the Armenian version has preserved all six books of the original treatise see R. Marcus, *Philo*, Supplement I, in Loeb Series, p. xi.

15. For the association of this idea with Israel see *Conf. Ling.* 146; *Leg. All.* 1.43.

16. On Philo's Sinai-Horeb association through word-play see Marcus, *Philo*, Supplement I, p. 90.

17. And in *Leg. Gai.* 95 μετεμορφοῦτο denotes the transformation of one of the gods, but in *Spec. Leg.* 4.147 μεταμορφώσει is perhaps used in the plain sense.

18. Similar idea is found in Rom. 12.2 μεταμορφοῦσθε...τοῦ νοός; also cf. *Mos.* 2.280.

to God and truly divine'. In *Mos.* 2.288-89, Moses' departure and 'exaltation' (not death) is described in transformation language: 'the Father transformed his whole being into mind, pure as sunlight' (μεθαρμοζόμενος εἰς νοῦν ἡλιοειδέστατον).[19]

Having noticed this prominent Moses-transformation motif in Philo, there are certain Sinai-related themes in Philo which have relevance to this discussion of the transfiguration of Jesus. One such example is the Moses-Israel-Sinai link in Philo which may be compared with a similar Jesus-disciples and new Israel/new Sinai association in Mt. 17.2-8.

Typological Understanding of the 'Six Days' in Exod. 24.16
In *Quaest. in Exod.* 2.46-47, and by means of typological reasoning, Philo compares the 'six days' in Exod. 24.16 with the 'six days' in the creation story (Gen. 1.3-31). He then parallels the creation motif with the 'birth of the nation of Israel' and its 'election' at Sinai. This typological interpretation of the 'six days' both at Sinai and creation makes an interesting comparison with ἡμέρας ἓξ, νεφέλη, of Mk 9.2,7; Mt. 17.1, 5; Lk. 9.34.

Like Moses, Israel Sees' God at Sinai and is υἱοὶ θεοῦ
Quaest. in Exod. 2.51-52 describes Moses as 'seeing God' at Sinai. In relation to this, Peder Borgen[20] has drawn attention to the fact that, like Moses at Sinai, in *Conf. Ling.* 146 and *Leg. All.* 1.43 the idea of one 'who sees God' is applied to Israel. It is this 'seeing' and experiencing Sinai that qualifies Israel to be called 'those who live in the knowledge of the One' and υἱοὶ Θεοῦ (*Conf. Ling.* 146).

The description of Israel as 'Son of God', 'first born', 'the Word', inevitably reminds one of similar titles used of Jesus. The Israel-Son of God identification, for example, compares well with the Jesus-Israel-Son of God parallelism in Mt. 2.15 (Hos. 2.15). Moreover the Jesus-Son of God association features at the transfiguration (Mt. 17.5; Mk 9.7; Lk. 9.35) and is an important Matthean motif (cf. 3.17; 4.3, 6; 14.33; 16.16; 26.64; 27.54). Philo's Israel-Son of God association is not unique to him, being in the Old Testament (e.g. Hos. 2.15; Deut. 14.1; 32.6). In the evangelists' application of it to Jesus, however, as I shall show with

---

19.　Moses' continuing intercessory ministry is seen in the *Assumption of Moses* 11.7. See J.H. Charlesworth, *The Old Testament Pseudepigrapha* (2 vols.; London: Darton, Longman & Todd, 1983), I, p. 934 (hereafter known as *OTP*).

20.　See Borgen, 'God's Agent', pp. 145-46.

particular reference to Matthew, the Jesus-Israel-Son of God association (Mt. 2.15; 3.17; 4.3, 6; 17.5) is only part of a larger understanding of Jesus' unique, filial relationship to the Father (Mt. 7.21; 10.32-33; 12.50; 15.13). Thus Sinai theophany is crucial for both Moses and also for Israel, as those who 'see God'.[21] Moses was the true representative of Israel.[22]

Likewise, the obvious biblical theme of Moses and the Sinai law too is elaborated by Philo. In *Sacr.* 50; *Migr. Abr.* 23; *Spec. Leg.* 2.104, he is the 'great law giver' (ὁ νομοθετης); and in *Mos.* 1.162, Moses is the very incarnation of the law (νόμος ἔμψυχος τε καὶ λογικός), and as king he is a 'living law' (*Mos.* 2.4).

Summary

(1) It is evident that the Sinai event was the launching pad for Philo's eulogisation of Moses. His emphasis on Moses' mystical ascent on Sinai and the transfiguration language parallel the mystical experiences of the adept in Jewish apocalyptic and mystical literature (e.g. *4 Ezra* 7.97; *2 Bar.* 50.10; *1 Enoch* 14.20; 38.4; 50.1).[23]

(2) Philo associates Sinai with the 'appearance of the coming of God' (*Quaest. in Exod.* 2.44), a prominent emphasis in Josephus (παρουσίαν του Θεοῦ *Ant.* 3.80) and also, as we shall see, in Matthew's presentation of the transfiguration.[24] Like Israel (*Conf. Ling.* 146; *Leg. All.* 1.43)

---

21. See Borgen, 'God's Agent', pp. 145-46, views the idea of Israel (and Moses) 'seeing' God at Sinai in the light of Jn 6.46 and 1.18: i.e. with the idea of Jesus having 'seen God' and its Sinai 'echoes' in the fourth gospel.

22. On this see Wolfson, *Philo*, II, pp. 333-34.

23. He supercedes all the patriarchs: See *Poster. C.* 173; *Dec.* 18; *Migr. Abr.* 14; *Leg. All.* 3.173; *Virt.* 75; *Gig.* 53; *Conf. Ling.* 95-97; compare Mt. 12.41, 42; Heb 3.1-6). Moses is the *mystagogue*, and receives direct revelation (*Deus.* 109-10). Moses is God's friend and shares God's treasures, and even God's title, cf., *Mos.* 1.156-57; *Sacr.* 130; *Ebr.* 94; *Migr.* 44-45; *Rev. Div. Her.* 21; *Somn.* 1.193-94. In *Quaest. in Exod.* 2.54; *Sacr.* 9; *Poster. C.* 28; *Gig.* 47-48, he is 'the divine and holy Moses', is 'many named' (πολυώνυμος, cf. *Mut. Nom.*, 25-26; *Ebr.* 92),—a term frequently applied to deities by classical writers. Moses was the ideal philosopher, (*Rev. Div. Her.* 301), a sage, (*Ebr.* 92; *Leg. All.* 2.87, 93; 3.45, 131, 140, 144, 147), the 'great theologian' (*Quaest in Gen.* 2.33, 59, 64, 81, 3.5, 21; 4.137; *Quaest. in Exod.* 2.37, 87-88, 108, 117).

24. He is ideal model and king. According to Philo, the four characteristics of a perfect ruler, kingship, the faculty of legislation, priesthood and prophecy, are found in Moses, see *Praem. Poen.* 56. For Moses is (1) θεὸς καὶ βασιλεύς (*Mos.* 1.158), the ideal-king representative of Israel (also *Mos.* 1.1, 8f., 18-31; 32; 48). His being a

Moses 'sees God' (*Quaest. in Exod.* 2.46). This makes him the supreme representative of Israel. This makes an interesting parallel with Mt. 17.1-8, where, given the echo of Exod. 34.40, (a) Jesus may be said to 'see' God, and (b) the disciples (representatives of new Israel) 'see' the transfigured Jesus, hear the voice from heaven, 'see' the cloud; in short, like Israel in Philo, they witness a theophany and 'see God'. This representative role in some sense also compares with Matthew's Jesus-Moses and Jesus-kingship motifs (cf. Mt. 2.12; 13.41; 16.28; 19.28; 21.4-5; 25.31, 34; 28.18).

(3) Philo's emphasis on the 'high mountain' (εἰς γὰρ ὄρος ὑψηλότατον) compares well with Mark's and especially Matthew's emphasis (considering his Moses and Sinai emphasis). And Philo's theological interpretation of the 'six days' in *Quaest. in Exod.* 2.46, and of Moses being called up on the seventh in terms of Gen. 1.1-2. and the new birth concept, at least suggest to us that this temporal reference in Exod. 24.16 lent itself to such typological interpretation. Since typology was important for Matthew, it is conceivable that he adopted such an approach in describing various features of the transfiguration, for example in interpreting the significance of καὶ μεθ' ἡμέρας ἓξ, σκηνάς.

(4) Philo's understanding of Israel as 'Son of God' in an Exodus-Sinai context (*Conf. Ling.* 146) compares well with Matthew's understanding of Israel as 'Son of God' in Mt. 2.15 (Hos. 11.1).

(5) Philo uses μετεμορφώθη and its derivatives of Moses (*Mos.* 1.57; 2.288). Since the verb μεταμορφόω is not found in the LXX, its appearance in Mk 9.2; Mt. 17.2; 2 Cor. 3.18 (also Rom. 12.2, compare *Mos.* 1.57 where Moses' 'mind' experiences transformation), while not suggesting dependence, may not be unconnected with Philo's usage.[25] Philo

'shepherd' qualifies him to be the ideal king (*Mos.* 1.60; 148-162; 249, 328) and ruler (*Mos.* 1.71), ἡγεμων (1.152; 155f). See Meeks, *The Prophet-King*, pp.107-117. (2) Moses was high priest (*Mos.* 1.158-59; *Mos.* 2.5, 66-186, *Praem. Poen.* 56); this compares well with Jesus' intermediary motifs in the New Testament, especially in Heb.7-10. (3) In *Quaest. in Exod.* 2. 46 Moses is πρωτοπροφητης, and is featured as 'supreme prophet' in *Mos.* 2.187-291; *Mut. Nom.* 103, 125; *Somn.* 2.189; *Quaestum in Gen.* 1.86; *Fug.* 147; *Leg. All.* 3.43; *Migr. Abr.* 151, *Congr.* 170.

25.   For parallels between Matthew and Philo see E. Schweizer, 'Christianity of the circumcised and Judaism of the uncircumcised: the background of Matthew and Colossians', in R.G. Hammerton-Kelly and R. Scroggs (eds.), *Jews, Greeks and Christians: Religious Cultures in Late Antiquity: Essays in Honour of W.D. Davies* (Leiden: Brill, 1976), pp. 45-56. He has among other things compared some of the ascetic elements in Matthew, (1) abstinence from marriage, (perhaps alluding to

also uses the language and motifs of transformation, in the Sinai context (*Mos.* 1.158-59; 2.70; *Quaest. in Exod.* 2.45) and elsewhere (*Mos.* 2.280—μεταβαλὼν εἰς εἶδος; *Mos.* 2.288-89—μεθαρμοζόμενος).

Even though there may be no direct connection between Philo and Matthew, it is arguable that in some sense, both reflect a common heritage, atmosphere and common ideas. At least Philo's presentation of the Moses, Moses-Sinai and Moses-transformation themes, with its interesting parallels with Matthew's presentation of the transfiguration, is an independent witness to the importance of the Moses motif in first-century Judaism.

2. *Moses-Sinai and Transfiguration Motifs in Josephus*

The significance of Josephus to New Testament studies needs no defence,[26] and my purpose, as in the previous section of this chapter, is

passages like Mt. 19.11-12 on 'eunuchs for the sake of the kingdom'), and (2) abstaining from property (Mt. 6.19) with asceticism in Qumran, and especially with the *Therapeutae* passages in Philo. But since 'asceticism' was quite a common theme in the Old Testament (Num. 6.3; Judg. 13.4-5; Jer. 35.6; Amos 2.12) and among ascetic groups of that time, this comparison may not be too strong, except that it suggests common motifs, trends and perhaps traditions (compare *Omn. Prob. Lib.* 75-91).

Other Philo–Matthew comparisons perhaps are more forceful, e.g. (1) 'hungering and thirsting after excellence' (*Fug.* 139) with 'hungering and thirsting for righteousness' (Mt. 5.6); (2) 'true wealth is stored in heaven' (*Praem. Poen.* 104) with 'lay up for yourself treasure in heaven' (Mt. 6.20); (3) 'what a man would hate to suffer he must not do himself to others' (*Hypo.* 7.6), with 'So whatever you wish that men would do to you, do so to them' (Mt. 7.12).

26. L.H. Feldman, 'Editors' Preface', in L.H. Feldman and G. Hata (eds.), *Josephus, Judaism, and Christianity* (Leiden: Brill, 1987), pp. 13-16—in the same 'Editors Preface' also see G. Hata, pp. 16-17; L.H. Feldman, *Josephus and Modern Scholarship (1937–1980)* (Berlin: de Gruyter, 1984), pp. 152-53; L.H. Feldman and G. Hata (eds.), *Josephus, the Bible, and History* (Detroit: Wayne, 1989). Josephus must be used critically, for his apologetic intent colours his approach, and at times his political expediency makes him inconsistent. Consider for example his once negative and later positive view of the Pharisees (cf. M. Smith, 'Palestinian Judaism in the First Century', in M. Davis (ed.), *Israel: Its Role in Civilization* (New York: 1956), pp. 67-81; and J. Neusner, 'Josephus' Pharisees: A Complete Repertoire', in *Josephus, Judaism, and Christianity*, pp. 274-92). On the importance of Josephus for 'Jesus' studies, cf. G.H. Twelftree, 'Jesus in Jewish Traditions', in D. Wenham (ed.), *Gospel Perspectives: The Jesus Tradition Outside the Gospels*, (6 vols.; Sheffield: JSOT Press, 1985), V, pp. 289-341, esp. pp. 290-310.

to determine Josephus' use of Moses[27] and Sinai traditions in order (1) to reconstruct the function of Moses-Sinai traditions in first century Judaism, and (2) to apply this to my study of Matthew's use of the Moses-Sinai motif in his understanding of the transfiguration.

The Sacredness of Sinai

Josephus describes Sinai as 'the highest of the mountains in this region' (ὑψηλότατον *Ant*. 2.264-65; compare Mk 9.2; Mt. 17.1; *Mos*. 2.70), the abode of the 'Deity' (θεὸν) and as 'unapproachable' (*Ant*. 3.76). It was a place where Moses 'witnessed an amazing prodigy' (θαυμάσιον), and had 'other visions' (φαντάσματα). This stress may be (1) polemic against the Samaritans' view of Gerizim[28] and also (2) proof of his presentation of the Jews as a people of 'the mountain', Mount Sinai (*Ant*. 3.77; also 2.291; 2.323, 349, 283-284, 291; 3.1-62).

Moses' Transformation at Sinai

Josephus does not go so far as Philo in elaborating the biblical Sinai-narrative (*Ant*. 3.75-76). But still at Sinai, Moses is 'nourished by the food of angels' (*Ant*. 3.99). In *Ant*. 3.82-83 Moses' transfiguration is briefly described: 'Moses appeared, radiant and high-hearted (ἐπιφανεται Μωυσῆς γαῦρός τε καὶ μέγα φρονῶν)'.[29] Josephus did not major on the Moses-transfiguration motif, but on the 'coming of God' at Sinai.[30]

27.   In general the Moses motif has been commented on by: J. Jeremias, Μωυσῆς, *TDNT*, IV, pp. 862-63; Meeks, *The Prophet King*, pp. 131-46; Tiede, *Charismatic Figure*, pp. 197-240; Holladay, *'Theios Aner'*, pp. 67-79; G. Hata, 'The Story of Moses Interpreted within the Context of Anti-Semitism', in *Josephus, Judaism, and Christianity*, pp. 180-97; O. Betz, 'Miracles in the Writings of Flavius Josephus', in *Josephus, Judaism, and Christianity*, pp. 212-35.

28.   As F. Dexinger, 'Limits of Tolerance in Judaism: The Samaritan Example', in E.P. Sanders, A.I. Baumgarten and A. Mendelson (eds.), *Jewish and Christian Self-Definition* (3 vols.; London: SCM Press, 1981), II, pp. 88-114, esp. 96-108, and R.J. Coggins, 'The Samaritans in Josephus', in *Josephus, Judaism, and Christianity*, pp. 257-73 have shown, Josephus is biased against the Samaritans (*Ant*. 9.288-291; 10.184; 11.84-88, 346-47; 12.257-64), and their temple at Mount Gerizim (*Ant*. 9.302-303; 12.10; 13.74-75).

29.   Josephus presents Moses as a military figure (cf. *Ant*. 4.117, 159, 176-77). He was 'leader of Israel' (*Ant*. 3.11, 12), 'commander' (*Ant*. 2.238-39; 268; 4.176-77, 329; 5.117), 'leader' (*Ant*. 20.230; 3.66; *Apion* 1.250). In *Ant*. 2.238-39, he is general of the Egyptian army; see Feldman, *Josephus and Modern Scholarship*, pp. 151-52.

30.   See L. Smolar and M. Aberbach, 'The Golden Calf Episode in Post Biblical Literature', *HUCA* 39 (1968), pp. 91-116. As to his polemic against anti-semitism see

The Coming of God and Sinai
The Sinai theophany is described graphically by Josephus: according to him the Sinai event was not dependent on natural causes. The cloud enveloped the spot where they (Israel) had pitched their tents (σκηνάς). He then goes on to describe the cataclysmic happenings at Sinai, a motif which, as I shall show, is found in certain New Testament eschatological passages.[31]

Josephus interprets these happenings as revealing (ἐδήλουν), or making clear 'the advent of God' (τὴν παρουσίαν τοῦ θεοῦ cf. *Ant.* 3.80), a theme noted already in Philo (*Quaest. in Exod.* 2.45 cf. Exod. 24.14). Josephus also uses the word παρουσία in *Ant.* 3.203 in the context of God taking his 'abode' κατεσκήνωσε(ν) and of his 'entry' (παρουσίαν) at the consecration of Solomon's Temple. This use naturally evokes interest, since in its New Testament usage in relation to Christ, παρουσία nearly always signifies his messianic advent in glory to judge the world at the end of this age.

Sinai, Moses and the Law of Moses in Josephus's History of Israel
It was due to the Sinai experience, more than any other reason, that the Hebrews were to listen to him 'not merely as an ordinary person addressing them in a human tongue, but that he was God's interpreter', οὗτος ὑμιν τούτους Χαρίζεται τοὺς λόγους δι' ἑρμηνέως ἐμοῦ (*Ant.* 3.87).[32] According to *Ant.* 3.93 hearing Moses the lawgiver (ὀνομοθέτης), was hearing God (cf. Deut. 18.15-18).[33] In *Ant.* 3.26-27, Josephus incorporates haggadic elements, implying that the manna was

D.J. Silver, 'Moses and the Hungry Birds', *JQR,* 64 (1973-74), pp. 123-53.

31.   Mt. 24.3, 27, 37, 39; 1 Cor. 15.23; 1 Thess. 3.13; see also, 2.19; 4.15; 5.23; 2 Thess. 2.1, 8; 2 Pet. 1.16, 3.4; 1 Jn 2.28.

32.   On the link between the God of the patriarchs and Moses see J.L. Bailey, 'Josephus' Portrayal of the Matriarchs', in L.H. Feldman and G. Hata (eds.), *Josephus, the Bible, and History*, pp. 170-71 (also cf. *Ant.* 4.328-29).

33.   The 'laws of Moses' (*Ant.* 3.93, 287, 320, 6.93, 12.36-37, 110, *Apion* 2.170) were the product of God's speech (*Ant.* 3.89), they were 'learnt from God' and 'transmitted in writing' (*Ant.* 3.286), and faithfully kept (*Ant.* 5.1, 39-40; *Ant.* 5.91, 96; *Ant.* 5.117; *Ant.* 5.126-127; *Ant.* 6.86, 88; 6.133). For Josephus, Moses is the 'sage' who legislates for others (*Ant.* 1.19), had a superior philosophy (*Ant.* 1.18-26), and so was greater than ancient legislators (*Ant.* 1.18-19, 2.145, 151-54, 168-71). The fact that Josephus intended to write further on Moses' Laws (*Ant.* 3.94, also cf. *Ant.* 1.25; 4.198; 20.268)—a project apparently not completed—suggests Josephus' polemical use of the figure of Moses.

first received by Moses, who then introduced it to the Hebrews.[34] This for example, makes an interesting comparison with the 'feeding miracles' in the Gospels, for example, where Jesus, the new Moses, feeds the crowd (Jn 6.31).[35]

Summary

Our findings are that the figure of Moses plays the most important role in Josephus' reconstruction of Israelite history,[36] and in this Sinai plays a crucial role. As for Philo, for Josephus the Jews were a people of 'the Mountain', an emphasis which was used apologetically. He interprets Sinai in terms of the παρουσίαν του Θεοῦ, which has ramifications for Jewish eschatological thinking. Josephus briefly speaks of Moses' transfiguration, without elaborating on it like Philo or Ps-Philo. Josephus counters anti-Semitic and anti-Moses propaganda by Hellenistic authors,[37] and in *Ant*. 3.180 he calls him Θεῖον ἄνδρα (cf. Philo's *Virt*. 177).[38]

34.   See G. Vermes, *Post-biblical Studies* (Leiden: Brill, 1975), p. 143; B.J. Malina, *The Palestinian Manna Tradition: The Manna Tradition in the Palestinian Targums and Its Relationship to the New Testament Writings* (Leiden: Brill, 1968), pp. 54-55.

35.   Josephus also cites messianic pretenders who promise Moses-Exodus type signs and wonders, which suggests that this type of Moses-messiah concept was at least popular among some. See J. Jeremias, *TDNT*, IV, p. 862; Tiede, *Charismatic Figure*, pp. 197-240; O. Betz, 'Miracles in the Writings of Flavius Josephus', in *Josephus, Judaism, and Christianity*, p. 222-23; M. Smith, in *Josephus, Judaism, and Christianity*, pp. 236-37. Theudas in *Ant*. 20.97 is generally taken with Acts 5.36, but see A.C. Headlam, 'Theudas', in J. Hastings (ed.), *Dictionary of the Bible*, IV (1902), p. 750.

36.   In contrast to Philo, he does not present Moses as king. Meeks, *The Prophet King*, pp. 134-35 argues that this was because Josephus was pro-theocracy (*Apion* 2.164-167), and anti-monarchy (*Ant*. 4.223). In *Ant*. 4.223-24, Moses makes provision for a king (Deut. 17.14-15) but the general force of Meek's argument is in order.

37.   Josephus' whole work *Against Apion* was to counter anti-semitic (and also anti-Moses) sentiments.

38.   Moses is not presented as a high priest, because that office belongs to Aaron (*Ant*. 3.188-92; 20.200), even though Moses executes some priestly functions (*Ant*. 3.63), makes a feast (*Ant*. 4.79). According to Meeks Moses spurned the title 'high priest' because of his 'humility' (*Ant*. 3.212; 4.28)—a feature of *Theios Aner*. According to L. Ginzberg, *Legend of the Jews*, (Philadelphia: Jewish Publication Society of America, 1938), III, pp. 256-57, VI. p. 90 n. 490, 'meekness' too was characteristic of 'extraordinary' heroes, so also J.R. Porter, *Moses and the Monarchy* (Oxford: Basil Blackwell, 1963).

The upshot of this study is as follows: (1) Josephus' use of the Moses, Sinai, and law themes helps us appreciate what we may call the 'Moses propaganda' of the time, and the Jewish social and intellectual climate, in which Matthew was writing. (2) Josephus' description of the Sinai event as τὴν παρουσίαν τοῦ Θεοῦ (*Ant.* 3.80), as we shall see, is a parallel to Matthew's presentation of the transfiguration.

3. *Moses-Sinai and Transformation Motifs in Qumran Literature*

The relevance of the Qumran scrolls to biblical studies, and the relationship between this textual deposit of Palestinian Judaism and the New Testament have been and continue to be the subject of voluminous writings.[39] Given our particular focus, we may note that the relevance of the Dead Sea Scrolls (DSS) to Matthaean studies has been shown by K. Stendahl, M. Black, W. Brownlee, W.D. Davies, J.M. Allegro, J.A. Fitzmyer, G. Vermes and others.[40] In this section, my primary purpose is to study the Moses-Sinai-transfiguration and other related motifs in the scrolls. This study then will be part of the comprehensive study of such motifs in order to set Matthew's understanding of the transfiguration and its Moses-Sinai significance in its socio-religious and intellectual context.

The Teacher of Righteousness and Moses' 'Transfiguration'

J.A. Fitzmyer followed by R. Martin and recently L.L. Belleville[41] have shown that several passages in the scrolls allude to the Moses-glory

---

39.   Cf. G. Vermes, *The Dead Sea Scrolls: Qumran in Perspective* (London: SCM Press, 1982), pp. 224-25; J.A. Fitzmyer, *The Dead Sea Scrolls Major Publications and Tools for Study* (Missoula, MT: Scholars Press, 1977), pp. 119-38.

40.   K. Stendahl, *The School of St Matthew* (Philadelphia: Fortress Press, 1968), pp. 183-217; K. Stendahl (ed.), *The Scrolls and the New Testament* (London: SPCK, 1957); M. Black, *The Scrolls and Christian Origins* (New York: Charles Scribner's Sons); W.D. Davies, '"Knowledge" in the Dead Sea Scrolls and Matthew 11.25-30', *HTR* 46 (1953), pp. 113-39; J.A. Fitzmyer, 'The Use of Explicit Old Testament Quotations in Qumran Literature and in the New Testament', *NTS* 7, 1960-61, pp. 297-333 reprinted in J.A. Fitzmyer, *Essays on the Semitic Background of the New Testament* (London: Chapman, 1971), pp. 3-58, also 'The Son of David tradition and Mt. 22.41-46', *Concilium* 10/2 (1966) pp. 40-46, reprinted in *Essays on the Semitic Background,* pp. 113-26; J.M. Allegro, *The Dead Sea Scrolls* (Harmondsworth: Penguin, 1956), pp. 135-47; W. Brownlee, 'Messianic Motifs of Qumran and the New Testament', *NTS* 3 (1956-57), pp. 12-30 and 195-210.

41.   See J.A. Fitzmyer, 'Glory Reflected on the Face of Christ (2 Cor. 3.7–4.6)

theme of Exodus 34. In 1QH 4.5-6, there is an interesting link between the Teacher of Righteousness, the idea of the covenant and of Moses being transfigured.

> I thank Thee, O Lord, for Thou hast illumined my face by thy Covenant,...I seek Thee and sure as the dawn Thou appearest as [perfect Light] to me...[42]

Here the motifs of 'face', 'light', 'covenant', are reminiscent of Exod. 34.28-35. The phrase 'by thy covenant' is significant, for the community considered itself living the בברית אל in a new sense (1QS 5.8; CD 5.1), and the expression 'new covenant' of Jer. 31.31 is used in CD 6.19; 1QpHab 2.3 (implied). These considerations suggest that 'thy covenant' in 1QS 4.5 is a renewed understanding of the old Mosaic covenant, which is clearly set out in 1QS 5.7-9. It is this renewed understanding of the Mosaic covenant, in Exodus 34 fashion, that illumines the Teacher. In 1QH 16.9 the Teacher speaks of his glory thus:

> Behold, Thou art pleased to favour [Thy servant], and hast graced me with Thy spirit of mercy and [with the radiance] of Thy glory.[43]

This perhaps is also echoed in 1QH 7.23-25:

> And I shall shine in a seven-fold light in [the Council appointed by] Thee for Thy glory...for Thou hast enlightened me through Thy truth.[44]

The Community and the Transfiguration Motif
In 1QH 4.27-29, for example, this 'illumination' motif is applied to the community, but only 'through the Teacher of Righteousness'.

> Through me Thou hast illumined the face of the Congregation and shown Thine infinite power. For Thou hast given me knowledge through Thy marvelous mysteries, and hast shown Thyself mighty within me...for the sake of Thy glory.[45]

Here too, a Moses-type illumination seems to be in focus. For, just as Moses radiated God's glory (Exod. 34.29-35), so here the Teacher of

and a Palestinian Jewish Motif', *TS* 42 (1981), pp. 639-44; R.P. Martin, *2 Corinthians* (Waco: Word, 1986), pp. 80-81; L.L. Belleville, *Reflections of Glory: Paul's Polemical Use of the Moses-Doxa tradition in 2 Corinthians 3.1-18* (Sheffield: JSOT Press, 1991), pp. 46-47.

42. Translation from G. Vermes, *The Dead Sea Scrolls in English* (Harmondsworth: Penguin, 1988), p. 174.

43. Vermes, *The Dead Sea Scrolls in English*, p. 204.

44. Vermes, *The Dead Sea Scrolls in English*, p. 186.

45. Vermes, *The Dead Sea Scrolls in English*, p. 176.

Righteousness passes on God's reflected glory to 'the face of the Congregation'.

These examples suggest that the idea of facial illumination was current at Qumran. The background to 1QH 4.5-6; 27-29 may be Moses' experience on Sinai (Exod. 34), this being applied in particular to the Teacher of Righteousness, and, by extension, to his followers. This contributes to the world view which the evangelists confronted, and, given Matthew's Moses-Sinai emphasis, the radiance of the Teacher of Righteousness may be a significant parallel to Mt. 17.1-8 (Mk 9.2-8; Lk. 9.28-36).

Sinai Remembered and Re-enacted Through Covenant Renewal
At Qumran, the covenant renewal ceremony was held at Pentecost.[46] It was a time when the desert brotherhood and those following the sect in the city congregated in the desert (1QS 2.22-23), for a covenant renewal ceremony based on Moses' instruction (Deut. 31.9-13, cf. 2 Chron. 15.10-13). New members were formally admitted during this ceremony (1QSa 1.4-5), which underlies its significance (1QS 2.19-25a).[47] By their study of the Mosaic law the covenanters 'prepared the way of the Lord' in the desert (1QS 8.15; 9.19 cf. Isa. 40.3), and since they believed that they were living on the threshold of the eschaton (4Q Flor 1.2, 12, 15, 19) it was the proper keeping of the 'law of Moses' that would determine judgment or redemption.[48]

So at the covenant renewal ceremony, allegiance was given to the Torah, also called 'the well' (CD 6.2-3).[49] In CD 15.5-11, for example, returning to the law of Moses is in fact equivalent to joining the 'new

46. A.C.R. Leaney, *The Rule of Qumran and its Meaning* (London: SCM Press, 1966), pp. 95-96; G. Vermes, *The Dead Sea Scrolls: Qumran in Perspective* (London: SCM Press, 2nd edn, 1982), p. 108; M.A. Knibb, *The Qumran Community* (Cambridge: Cambridge University Press, 1987), p. 89. For similar calendrical reckoning in the Jubilees see O.S. Wintermute, *Jubilees*, in *OTP*, II, 1985, pp. 67-68. On Qumran calendrical issues, differing from their opponents, see J. Obermann, 'Calendrical Elements in the Dead Sea Scrolls', *JBL*, LXXV, 1956, pp. 285-97.

47. In 1QS 8.12-15 the caption 'the Way' referred, above all, to the strict observance of the Mosaic law and its interpretation in the community.

48. D. Dimant, 'Qumran Sectarian Literature', in M.E. Stone (ed.), *Jewish Writings of the Second Temple Period* (CRINT Section 2; Van Gorcum: Fortress Press, 1984), pp. 483-550.

49. In 1QH 5.29-32 the Teacher's 'radiance turned to decay' since the law was sealed up within him (due to opposition cf. 1 QH 5.11-12). See Belleville, *Reflections of Glory*, p. 46; Vermes, *The Dead Sea Scrolls in English*, p. 178.

covenant' (also 1QS 5.8-9; 6.19; 1QSa 1.2-3), though it is likely that allegiance was also given to the teachings, expositions of the law, 'mysteries' (1QH 4.5-6, 24-28) and 'hidden things' (CD 1.11; 1QpHab 7.4) revealed to the Teacher of Righteousness (CD 6.2-11) and communicated to the community (CD 3.10-14).[50] In 1QH 5.11, the revelation that God imparts to the Teacher itself is called law or Torah. So the 'new covenant', expressly called הברית החדשה in CD 6.19; (1QpHab 2.[3]; cf. Jer. 31.31 ברית הדשה; LXX 38.31 διαθήκην καινὴν)[51] is in continuity with the old Mosaic covenant and law,[52] as are the 'new' and formerly 'hidden' things.

The Teacher of Righteousness and the Prophet-like-Moses (Deut. 18.15-19)

It is generally argued that the Qumran Teacher of Righteousness functioned as a prophet-like-Moses, and the 'second exodus' eschatological community at Qumran were to listen to his word (1QpHab 2.7-8).[53]

50. See E.P. Sanders, *Paul and Palestinian Judaism* (London: SCM Press, 1982), pp. 240-42.

51. The covenant idea is also emphasised in CD 8.21; 119.33; 20.12.

52. See Fitzmyer, 'Glory Reflected on the Face of Christ', p. 642.

53. Any eschatological reckoning of the Teacher of Righteousness needs to be seen in relation to several factors:

(1) The Teacher has been identified with both the coming of Elijah and the prophet-like-Moses, or new Moses concept. (a) On Elijah-association see M. Burrows, 'The Messiah of Aaron and Israel (DSD IX,11)', *ATR* 34 (1952), pp. 202-206, esp. p. 105. That this Elijah–Messiah precursor idea grew up in Christian circles (e.g. Mt. 11.13; 17.12) see J.A.T. Robinson, 'Elijah, John and Jesus: An Essay in Detection', *NTS* 4 (1957-58), pp. 263-81; *Twelve New Testament Studies* (London: SCM Press, 1962), pp. 28-52; A.J.B. Higgins, 'Jewish Messianic Belief in Justin Martyr's Dialogue with Trypho', *NTS* 9 (1967), pp. 298-305. (b) On Moses-identification see B.Z. Wacholder, *The Dawn of Qumran: The Sectarian Torah and the Teacher of Righteousness* (Cincinnati: Hebrew Union, 1983), p. 137; G. Vermes, *The Dead Sea Scrolls: Qumran in Perspective*, pp. 185-86; Meeks, *The Prophet King*, pp. 172-73; N. Weider, 'The "Law-Interpreter" of the Sect of the Dead Sea Scrolls: The Second Moses', *JJS* 4 (1953), pp. 158-75. Even before the scrolls were found, J. Jeremias argued for this on the basis of examples from Josephus, the New Testament and the Damascus Document alone, cf. J. Jeremias, 'Μωυσῆς', *TDNT*, p.861.

The concentration of Deuteronomic passages in 4Q Testimonia (Deut. 5.28-29; 18.18-19, see J.M. Allegro, 'Further Messianic References in Qumran Literature', *JBL* 75 (1956), esp. pp. 186-87), if applied to the Teacher, makes a strong case for a prophet-like-Moses identification. Moreover the idea of a 'second-exodus–eschatological community' (CD 4.4,11; 8.12-15; 1QS 8.13-14), coupled with the

But those who disobey his 'word' are unfaithful and are condemned (1QpHab 2.8).

This makes an interesting comparison with Matthew's emphasis on Jesus' teaching and words, and on obedience (or disobedience) determining one's reward or condemnation (Mt. 7.21-27; 11.28-30; 28.20), and also on the ἀκούετε αὐτοῦ of 17.5 with its echo of Deut. 18.15 (αὐτοῦ ἀκούσεσθε).

Summary

The Moses-transfiguration, Sinai and associated themes are quite prominent in Qumran literature (1QH 4.5-6; 5.29-32; 7.23-25; 16.9). The covenant renewal ceremony held at Pentecost with its wilderness, Sinai-law and new covenant themes illustrate the influence of Moses themes in the community. The new covenant (CD 6.19; 1QpHab 2.3 cf. Jer. 31.31) entailed a renewed understanding of the old covenant (1QS 5.7-9), therefore a fresh interpretation of the Sinai covenant with particular reference to the sect's place in history.

For our purposes, since the Sinai motif plays a dominant part in Matthew's understanding of the transfiguration, this association in

study of the Law, calls for a Moses-like leader figure (CD 6.2-10; 3.16; 1QS 9.11), who 'led men in the way of God's heart' (CD 1.11; 1QpHab 2.2; 7.4; 1QH 5.11).

(2) The attribution of eschatological motifs to the Teacher also has raised the issue whether at some point the Teacher of Righteousness himself is to be considered as a messianic figure. See F.M. Strickert, 'Damascus Document VII, 10-20 and Qumran Messianic Expectation', *RQ* 47, XII (December, 1986), p. 345; B.Z. Wacholder, 'The «Sealed» Torah versus the «Revealed» Torah: An Exegesis of Damascus Covenant V, 1-6 and Jeremiah 32, 10-14', *RQ*, No. 47, XII, (December, 1986), pp. 351-68; Dimant, 'Qumran Sectarian Literature', p. 540 n. 270. He was also a priest (1QpHab 2.7-8) confirmed by 4QpPss[a] = 4Q177; see also, Fitzmyer, 'Qumran, Ebionites and their literature', ESBNT, p. 461 n. 55; Vermes, *The Dead Sea Scrolls*, p. 185; Meeks, *The Prophet King*, p. 171. But this issue needs to be viewed in relation to the development of messianic thought in Qumran, see J.A. Fitzmyer, 'Aramaic "Elect of God" text from Qumran', in his *Essays on the Semitic Background*, pp. 130-35; Strickert, 'Qumran Messianic Expectation', pp. 327-49. That 'single' and 'multiple' Messiah' concepts existed side by side, see G.J. Brooke, 'The Amos–Numbers Midrash (CD 7.13b-8.1a) and Messianic Expectation', *ZNW* 92 (1980), pp. 397-403. For multiple messianism see R.E. Brown, 'J. Starcky's Theory of Qumran Messianic Development', *CBQ* 28 (1966), pp. 51-57; Dimant, 'Qumran Sectarian Literature', p. 540 n. 267. And this in contrast to L. Silberman, 'The Two Messiahs of the Manual of Discipline', *VT* 5 (1955), pp. 77-82; M. Smith, 'What is Implied by the Variety of Messianic Figures?', *JBL* 78 (1959), pp. 66-72—who virtually dismisses messianic expectation in Qumran.

Qumran of Moses, Sinai and new covenant ideas both indicates the pervasive influence of the Moses-Sinai motif in pre-Christian and first century Palestinian Judaism, and also provides a Palestinian background for the images, vocabulary, Moses and Sinai themes used in Matthew.

All this illustrates the significance of the Moses ideology of the time, and suggests part of the socio-religious and intellectual background which Matthew had to address. For, (1) if this Moses-eschatological motif figured so prominently at Qumran, and (2) if this was also closely associated with the Teacher of Righteousness, the Torah, the 'new covenant', then it is possible that Matthew, in presenting Jesus as the new and greater Moses, was perhaps conscious of such categories and was responding to it.[54]

4. *Moses-Sinai and Moses-Transfiguration Themes in Samaritan Literature*

In recent years there has been an upsurge in Samaritan studies led by such as J. Macdonald, C.H.H. Scobie, R.J. Coggins, S. Lowy and A.D. Crown.[55] The value of Samaritan literature and its relevance to New

54. On Matthew–Qumran 'parallels' see: Stendahl, *The School of Matthew*, who sees parallels with the Qumran Habakkuk commentary; Rowland, *Christian Origins*, p. 153. Atonement motifs have been applied to the Teacher (1QpHab 8.1)— a motif also associated with (1) the community 1QS 5.6; 9.4-5 (2) the priest (1QM 2.5), and (3) the 'council of the community' (1Qs 8.4-10; 1Qsa 1.3), see Sanders, *Paul and Palestinian Judaism*, pp. 299-300, 321-323; W. Brownlee, 'Messianic Motifs of Qumran and the New Testament', *NTS* 3 (1956-57), pp. 25-26. This theme may be compared with (1) the Jesus–atonement theme (Mt. 26.28), and also (2) with 4Q 504 where 'Moses atoned for Israel'. That Moses was a suffering figure, see C. Chavasse, 'Jesus: Christ and Moses', *Theology*, Vol. 54, No. 373 (July 1951), pp. 244-50, continued in Vol. 54, No. 374, (Aug. 1951), pp. 289-96; *The Servant and the Prophet*, 1972. In Talmud Sotah, Isaiah 53 is applied to Moses, see I. Epstein, *Babylonian Talmud* (London: Soncino, 1961), p. 73.

55. C.H.H. Scobie, 'The Origin and Development of Samaritan Christianity', *NTS* 19 (1972/3), pp. 390-414; R.J. Coggins, *Samaritans and Jews* (Oxford: Basil Blackwell, 1975); 'The Samaritans and Acts', *NTS* 28 (1982), pp. 423-34; 'The Samaritans in Josephus', pp. 257-73; S. Lowy, *The Principles of Samaritan Exegesis* (Leiden: Brill, 1977); A.D. Crown, (ed.), *The Samaritans* (Tübingen: Mohr, 1989). The works of older scholars like A.E. Cowley, M. Gaster, J.A. Montgomery, and of more recent ones like J. MacDonald, F. Dexinger and others will be cited below. J. Bowman's 'The Importance of Samaritan Researches' (Leeds University Oriental Society: 1960), pp. 43-54 gives an excellent summary of the salient features of Samaritanism and also a good lead into the topic.

Testament studies (suggested a century ago by E.H. Plumptre,[56] then H. Odeberg, and more recently by J. Bowman, A. Spiro, C.H.H. Scobie, O. Cullmann and others[57]), is beginning to be appreciated.[58] The purpose of this section, however, is to look particularly at the Moses, Sinai, transfiguration themes in Samaritanism, for the figure of Moses dominates Samaritan theology. In this study of Samaritanism preference will be given to first-century and previous 'external' sources, Josephus, relevant New Testament passages, and certain Samaritan documents containing early haggadic traditions.[59]

An Evaluation of the Samaritan Prophet-like-Moses Motifs in Josephus, John 4 and Acts 7
Several recent scholars, including R.J. Coggins, M. Mor, B.H. Sydney, A.D. Crown and F. Dexinger[60] have shown that, despite the paucity of

56.   E.H. Plumptre, 'The Samaritan Elements in the Gospels and Acts', *The Expositor*, 10 (1887), pp. 22-40; A.E. Cowley, 'The Samaritan Doctrine of the Messiah', *The Expositor*, I, Fifth Series, (1895), pp. 171-72.

57.   J. Bowman, 'The Samaritan Studies', *BJRL* 40 (1958), pp. 298-327; *The Samaritan Problem: Studies in the Relationships of Samaritanism, Judaism, and Early Christianity* (Pittsburgh: Pickwick Press, 1975); A. Spiro, 'Stephen's Samaritan Background', in J. Munk, *The Acts of the Apostles* (New York: Doubleday, 1967), pp. 285-300; C.H.H. Scobie, 'Samaritan Christianity', pp. 390-414; O. Cullmann, *The Johannine Circle* (London: SCM Press, 1975); H. Odeberg, *The Fourth Gospel interpreted in its Relation to Contemporaneous Religious Currents in Palestine and the Hellenistic-Oriental World*, cited in K. Haacker, *DNTT*, III, pp. 464-66.

58.   In addition to Scobie and Cullmann, see E.D. Freed, 'Did John Write his Gospel Partly to Win Samaritan Converts?', *NovT* 12 (1970), pp. 241-56; R. Pummer, 'Samaritan Pentateuch and the New Testament', *NTS* 22 (1976), pp. 441-43; G.W. Buchanan, 'The Samaritan Origin of the Gospel of John', in J. Neusner (ed.), *Religions in Antiquity* (Leiden: Brill, 1968), pp. 149-75; Belleville, *Reflections of Glory*, pp. 48-52.

59.   For defence of this position see Lowy, *The Principles of Samaritan Exegesis*; Meeks, *The Prophet King*, pp. 239-240; Belleville, *Reflections of Glory*, pp. 48-52. Some of the primary sources are: J. MacDonald, *Memar Marqah* (The Teaching of Marqah; 2 vols.; BZAW 83; Berlin: Alfred Topelmann, 1963); M. Gaster, *The Asatir* (The Samaritan book of the 'Secrets of Moses' together with the Pitron or Samaritan Commentary and the Samaritan Story of the Death of Moses; London: The Royal Asiatic Society, 1927); J. MacDonald, *The Samaritan Chronicle No II* (Berlin: de Gruyter, 1969); A.E. Cowley, *The Samaritan Liturgy* (2 vols.; Oxford: Clarendon Press, 1909).

60.   Coggins, 'The Samaritans in Josephus', pp. 257-73 argues that in spite of his biases, Josephus attests that Samaritanism was essentially one variant within

material and knowledge of the Samaritans just before and after the beginning of the Christian era, Josephus' accounts about the Samaritans (however biased) are valuable. In *Ant.* 18.85-86, Josephus speaks of an unnamed man who gathered a mass of armed followers at Mount Gerizim, and promised to unearth the Temple vessels which Moses had hidden.[61] His intent, apparently, was to bring back the '*Rahuta*', the period of divine favour, which originally had been initiated by Moses but had ended with the evil priest Eli.[62]

This *Rahuta* was linked to the coming *Taheb*,[63] and in *Memar Marqah* 3 it is associated with Moses' second coming. So it is possible that the unnamed 'prophet' in *Antiquities of the Jews* 18.85 was conceived to be such a second Moses or prophet-like-Moses figure.[64]

Judaism (p. 271). Also see Coggins' earlier work, *The Samaritans and Jews*, pp. 93-99; M. Mor, 'The Persian, Hellenistic and Hasmonaean Period', in *The Samaritans*, pp. 4-14; B.H. Sydney, 'From John Hyrcanus to Baba Rabbah', in *The Samaritans*, pp. 30-40. A.D. Crown, 'The Samaritan Diaspora', in *The Samaritans*, pp. 197-98, observes that Josephus is the only non-Samaritan to speak of Samaritan participation in Alexander's army (*Ant.* 11.345-47). Also see Dexinger, 'Limits of Tolerance in Judaism', p. 106f. On the polemical use of 2 Kings 17 and idea of 'Cuthaean' see A. Tal, 'Samaritan Literature', *The Samaritans*, p. 446 n. 94. A concise treatment is found in E. Schürer (ed.), *The History of the Jewish People in the Ages of Jesus Christ*, II (new edition ed. G. Vermes and F. Millar; Edinburgh: T. & T. Clark, 1973-1987), pp. 16-20.

    61.   *Ant.* 18.85, in Feldman, 9, trans. p. 61. On this see E.M. Smallwood, 'The Date of the Dismissal of Pontius Pilate from Judaea', *JJS* 5 (1954), pp 12-13.

    62.   On *Rahuta* and the return of the sacred 'tent' at Mount Gerizim see F. Dexinger, 'Samaritan Eschatology', in *The Samaritans*, pp. 276-79; M. Gaster, *Samaritan Oral Law and Ancient Traditions* (Search, 1932), pp. 223-24; A.D. Crown, 'Some Traces of Heterodox Theology in Samaritan Book of Joshua', *BJRL* 50 (1967), pp. 178-98.

    63.   On *Taheb-Rahuta* links and *Taheb* expectations see Dexinger, 'Samaritan Eschatology', pp. 272-76; Gaster, *The Samaritan Oral Law and Ancient Traditions*, pp. 223-29; J. MacDonald, *The Theology of the Samaritans* (London: SCM Press, 1964), pp. 362-65.

    64.   For *Taheb*-prophet-like-Moses links see Lowy, *The Principles of Samaritan Bible Exegesis*, p. 245, according to whom he will restore true worship by restoring vessels of the sanctuary. Also Dexinger, 'Samaritan Eschatology', pp. 273-74. In the fourth century *Memar Marqah* these Moses-*Taheb* connections were made more explicit, for example, the poem about the *Taheb* in *Memar Marqah* 1.9, p. 33 is similar to the poem about Moses in *Memar Marqah* 2.8, p. 63, implying that the *Taheb* was a Moses *redivivus*.

The Prophet-like-Moses-Taheb, *John 4 and Acts 7*

Interestingly, the next external source for the study of the Samaritan Moses motif is certain New Testament passages, especially John 4 and Acts 7. Samaritanists and New Testament scholars have been intrigued by the parallels in language and theological motifs in John's gospel, Hebrews, Luke–Acts, and other New Testament material and those found in Samaritan documents.[65]

(1) *Jn 4.25*: Parallels between John's gospel and Samaritan theology have been highlighted by H. Odeberg[66] and in the works of J. Bowman,[67] whose thesis has been developed by more recent scholars such as G.W. Buchanan,[68] and E.D. Freed.[69] For example, O. Cullmann[70] (i) links his 'Johannine circle' with the Hellenists in Acts, noting their theological standpoint and concern for mission in Samaria, and (ii) sees other common points between Stephen's speech, with its echo of heterodox Judaism, and the fourth Gospel.

In Jn 4.22, it is plain that salvation is of the Jews (4:22) and the Jewish term Χριστός is used. But, as G.R. Beasley-Murray,[71] following Bowman, Buchanan and others, has shown, the Samaritan woman's claim οἶδα ὅτι Μεσσίας ἔρχεται,...ὅταν ἔλθῃ ἐκεῖνος, ἀναγγελεῖ ἡμῖν ἅπαντα (4.25) is an echo of the Samaritans' messianic expectation defined not by the prophetic books but by the Pentateuch, notably Deut.

---

65. Scobie, 'Samaritan Christianity', pp. 390-414; Coggins, 'Samaritans and Acts', pp. 423-34; Freed, 'Did John Write his Gospel Partly to Win Samaritan Converts?', pp. 241-56; Plumptre, 'Samaritan Elements', pp. 22-40; Spiro, 'Stephen's Samaritan Background', pp. 285-300; Pummer, 'The Samaritan Pentateuch', pp. 441-43.

66. H. Odeberg, *The Fourth Gospel*, in K. Haacker, *DNTT*, III, pp. 464-66.

67. Bowman, 'The Samaritan Studies', pp. 298-27.

68. G.W. Buchanan, 'The Samaritan Origin of the Gospel of John', pp. 149-75; G.R. Beasley-Murray, *John* (Waco: Word, 1987), p. 62.

69. Freed, 'Did John Write his Gospel Partly to Win Samaritan Converts?', pp. 241-56, supports Bowman's thesis in 'The Samaritan Studies', pp. 298-327, and like Meeks, *The Prophet King*, p. 290, argues that in Samaritan literature it was Moses who received the 'sacred name'—which is to be compared with ἐγώ εἰμι used of Jesus (pp. 251-251).

70. Cullmann, *The Johannine Circle*, pp. 52-53.

71. Beasley-Murray, *John*, p. 62, who also takes him to be another Moses. But Cowley, 'The Samaritan Doctrine of the Messiah', pp. 171-75, differentiates Moses from the *Taheb*. But that the *Taheb* will function like the prophet-like-Moses of Deut. 18.18 (seen in the Samaritan Pentateuch as in 4QTestimonia) has been established by Dexinger, Bowman and others.

18.15-18, of the *Taheb*. It is he who will restore true worship (see on *Ant*. 18.85-86 above) and to this end ἀναγγελεῖ ἡμῖν ἅπαντα. It is likely that the evangelist has translated the *Taheb* into the Jewish messianic term Χριστός, by which also he stresses ὅτι ἡ σωτηρία ἐκ τῶν Ἰουδαίων ἐστίν (4.22).[72]

Additional support for this *Taheb*–Jesus parallelism may also be inferred from Jn 4.9 where the woman 'perceives' Jesus to be a prophet, because, for the Samaritans, there was, and could be, no prophet after Moses, with one exception, their Messiah or *Taheb*, the prophet-like-Moses promised in Deut. 18.18.[73] The whole dialogue suggests that the woman, and eventually the Samaritans (4.28-30), view Jesus as the *Taheb*. But the evangelist has skillfully cast it within Jewish-Χριστός categories.

(2) *Acts 7.37*: Two factors govern the discussion on Acts 7: (i) the pro-Samaritan stance taken by Luke–Acts and (ii) the supposed Samaritan elements in Stephen's speech in Acts 7. Taking the former, over a century ago E.H. Plumptre argued that there are distinctly favourable Samaritan elements in Luke (Lk. 10.33-37, 17.11-18, despite Lk. 9.52-53) John 4 and Acts (ch. 7; 8.4-25). Similar motifs have been recognised in more recent years by Bowman and others.

Taking the second factor, E.H. Plumptre, and recently A. Spiro and C.H. Scobie, have been attracted by the idea that Stephen's speech (Acts 7) has significant parallels in the Samaritan Pentateuch and Samaritan theology and emphasis.[74] Some of the supposed parallels, however, have been challenged by K. Haacker, and R.J. Coggins.[75] For example, the version of Deut. 18.15 cited in Acts 7.37 has been taken as reflecting a pro-Samaritan text-type. But this is an inadequate argument, for E. Tov and R. Pummer[76] have rightly observed that the Samaritan

72. That the fourth Gospel's non-Davidic type *Taheb* categories would have attracted the Samaritans, see Buchanan, 'Samaritan Origin of the Gospel of John', pp. 149-75. But it must be noted that the writer does not deny Davidic sonship of the Messiah in Jn 7.41-42 (citing Mic. 5.2 also in Mt. 2.5-6), but he does not press the point. Also see Beasley-Murray, *John*, pp. 118-19.

73. For Bowman, it is quite possible that the Samaritans understood the *Taheb* to be a Moses returning to earth again, and he takes 'the prophet' in Jn 1.21; 6.14; 7.40 in the light of Deut. 18.18, the Samaritan messianic proof text.

74. Plumptre, ' Samaritan Elements', pp. 22-40; Spiro, 'Stephen's Samaritan Background', pp. 285-300; Scobie, 'Samaritan Christianity', pp. 390-414.

75. K. Haacker, *DNTT*, III, pp. 464-66; Coggins, 'Samaritans and Acts', pp. 423-34.

76. E. Tov, 'Proto-Samaritan Texts and the Samaritan Pentateuch', in *The*

Pentateuch is only one of the several witnesses to the state of the text (of the Old Testament) in Palestine.[77] However, other Samaritan-type motifs in Acts 7 cannot be disregarded. For example, in contrast to the Old Testament but in line with Samaritan literature, Stephen cites Shechem (Acts 7.16) as the place where the patriarchs were buried. Here according to (the otherwise cautious) Coggins it is 'certainly plausible to see a Samaritan background underlying the speech'.[78]

It is in this setting that the prophet-like-Moses theme in Acts 7 needs to be viewed. In Acts 7.37, for example, Deut. 18.15 has been inserted in the middle of a series of references from Exodus. This is reminiscent of the Samaritan Pentateuch, where after Exod. 20.17 there is the insertion of Deut. 5.26-27; 18.18-22 and 5.27. This, as we have already seen, is similar to the arrangement and emphasis in *4Q Testimonia*. All this only goes to highlight the 'prophet-like-Moses' theme of Deut. 18.15-18, and the prominence it enjoyed in first century CE. This prophet-like-Moses theme attested in these external sources, *Ant.* 18.85-86, Jn 4, Acts 7, is found also in some Samaritan literature.

Moses-Sinai and Transfiguration Motifs in Samaritan Literature
The Samaritan documents cannot be dated with certainty earlier than the third or fourth century CE; and so, like rabbinical literature, they need to be used with caution. Having said this, however, Bowman, recently Lowy and others have shown that they contain haggadic traditions stemming from an early period.[79] With the possible exception of Philo, no other writer eulogises the figure of Moses, as do authors of the Samaritan religious literature. In *Memar Marqah* 1.1, p.4, Moses is

Samaritans, pp. 397-407; Pummer, 'The Samaritan Pentateuch', pp. 441-43.

77.   According to Cullmann, *The Johannine Circle*, p. 50, Stephen's speech should also be compared with 'those tendencies in non-conformist Judaism'. That Stephen belonged to an 'heterodox' Jewish group, see R. Scroggs, 'The Earliest Hellenistic Christianity', in *Religions in Antiquity* (1968), pp. 176-77.

78.   Coggins, 'Samaritans and Acts', pp. 423-34.

79.   Macdonald, *The Theology of the Samaritans*, pp. 420-21, and in contrast to his earlier 'The Samaritan Doctrine of Moses', *SJT* 13.2 (1960), pp. 149-62, and 'Comprehensive and Thematic Reading of the Law by Samaritans', *JJS* 10 (1959) pp. 67-74, suggests that Johannine literature influenced the development of Samaritan doctrine, but he is uncertain and adds the reverse is not 'entirely impossible'! (p. 421). But for a forceful defence of Samaritan conservatism in hermeneutics, and hence in theology and transmission of early tradition see Cowley, 'The Samaritan Liturgy', pp. 121-40; Lowy, *The Principles of Samaritan Exegesis*, passim; Meeks, *The Prophet King*, esp. pp. 239-40, 257.

described as the 'great prophet', 'illuminer of the whole family of mankind'. He is 'the last of the world's Righteous', God's 'viceregent', and 'prophet' (an often repeated title). In *Memar Marqah* 1.1, p.12 Moses and Aaron are 'two great lights' who will illumine the congregation of Israel. Horeb is crucial to Samaritan theology, in *Memar Marqah* 1.1, pp. 3-4, God taught Moses 'secrets in the bush' and it was at Horeb that he was 'vested with prophethood and the divine Name'.

(1) *Moses and transfiguration*: At Mount Sinai Moses transcends the barrier and penetrates the veil between the two worlds:

> The cloud enveloped him and the angels magnified him. The great glory honoured him...He stood at the very foundations of the Creation... (*Memar Marqah* 4.3, p. 143).

In *Memar Marqah* 6.3 (pp. 224-25) the writer links Moses' reception of the Torah with his transformation. When Moses received 'the autograph of God'

> 'his body was mingled with the angels, his speech was like the speech of his Lord...and thus he was magnified above all the human race...with his feet he trod the great fire...'

It is because Moses received the Torah from God's hand, that God's 'image dwelt on him' (*Memar Marqah* 6.3, pp. 223-24).

(2) *Moses' transfiguration and Adam*: The link made between Moses and Adam in certain texts is striking. For example, in the *Asatir* 9.22, the 'rod of Adam' and Adam's radiant clothes were given to Moses on the day he was commissioned.[80] Moses was the 'light' of Israel (compare the emphasis on the 'garment' in Merkavah literature, and the Palestinian Targum[81]) and in *Memar Marqah* 6.8 Moses' light 'shines more brightly than the light of the sun'. Moses is 'light' as recipient of the Torah, which itself was 'Divine light' (*Memar Marqah* 1.2, p. 65). In *Memar Marqah* 1.2, Moses is the 'illuminer of the whole house of Adam', and in *Memar Marqah* 6.9 (p. 240) there is no prophet like Moses in the whole human race'. Due to his elevation at Sinai, 'he who

80.   I.H. Gaster, 'Samaritans', *IDB*, IV, p. 190, postulates a 13th century dating for the *Asatir*. While this may be, there is weight in M. Gaster's arguments that the brevity of the *Asatir* points to its antiquity. It is remarkably concise and does not show signs of elaborate additions which is normally seen in a later work. But as to how early, it cannot be said with certainty.

81.   M. Gaster, *The Asatir*, p. 280; Bowman, 'The Samaritan Studies', pp. 303-304.

believes in Moses also believes in God' (*Memar Marqah* 4.8, p. 167; 4.8, p. 162), an idea also found in the so called Samaritan creed.[82]

(3) *Transfiguration motifs and Moses' departure*: In *Memar Marqah* 4.12, p.186 Moses' departure is presented as being 'gathered with the angels', and 'crowned with light, all the hosts of the heavenly angels gathered to meet him' (*Memar Marqah* 5.3, p. 202 also 5.2, p. 198). His departure is very much like an assumption or ascension story influenced by Sinai motifs and Sinai type cataclysmic happenings and language: 'All the powers descended on to Mount Nebo...the Glory drew near to him and embraced him' (*Memar Marqah* 5.3, p. 203). According to *Memar Marqah* 5.4, p. 207 'The shining light which abode on his face is with him in his tomb'. These examples show that the Moses-transfiguration theme plays an important role in Samaritan theology.

(4) *The law emphasis*: Given, their adherence only to the Pentateuch, the Torah emphasis is understandable. The Torah originated from God and was written down by Moses at God's command (*Memar Marqah* 5.4, p.209).[83] It was infallible,[84] it was symbolic of life[85] and light,[86] and Moses was its everlasting guardian. At Sinai Moses had a vision of Israel's past and of what was yet to come, including the coming day of judgment.[87] It is also worth noting that in scores of passages from fourth–eighteenth century Samaritan literature the theophany on Mount Sinai is directly transferred to Mount Gerizim.[88]

82.   The primitive beliefs of the Samaritan creed are belief in God, Moses, the Law and in the Holy Mount. For fuller discussion; see MacDonald, *The Theology of the Samaritans*, pp. 49-55.

83.   See Lowy, *The Principles of Samaritan Exegesis*, p. 97.

84.   That the Torah was created before the world, see Lowy, *The Principles of Samaritan Exegesis*, p. 99; Moore, *Judaism*, 1, p. 526. For examples from Philo see Wolfson, *Philo*, I, p. 183.

85.   J. MacDonald, 'The Theological Hymns of Amram Darah', *Annual of Leeds University Oriental Studies*, II (1961), pp. 70-72.

86.   That the Law was 'light' (also 'well' and 'shepherd') is seen in *2 Bar.* 59.2; 77.13-15; also in the DSS where everything is determined by the contrast between light and darkness: see Leaney, *The Rule of Qumran and its Meaning*, pp. 41, 80; Lowy, *The Principles of Samaritan Exegesis*, pp. 77-78. Lowy argues that the Samaritans took the identification of the 'primal light' with the Torah much more literally (*Memar Marqah* 2.12; 4.2, 3, 7).

87.   Lowy, *The Principles of Samaritan Exegesis*, p. 77-78; *Memar Marqah* 4.3.

88.   MacDonald, *The Theology of the Samaritans*, p. 77, and pp. 142-22 for a useful section on Moses. On the importance of the Temple at Gerizim in Samaritan history, but viewed in relation to Israelite history, and scriptures see: H.H. Rowley,

Summary: (1) This study has shown that Moses-Sinai themes were fundamental for Samaritan theology. Transfiguration motifs are initially applied to the Horeb commissioning, but the climax was at Sinai. Also at his departure, Moses was 'crowned with light'.

(2) We have also seen that prophet-like-Moses-*Taheb* ideas (of Deut. 18.18) feature also in relation to the unnamed 'prophet' in *Ant.* 18.85-86, to the messianic expectation of the woman of Samaria in John 4, and also to Stephen's speech in Acts 7.37 which has Samaritan elements. So just as Matthew presents Jesus as the fulfilment of Jewish expectations, so the authors of Luke–Acts and of the gospel of John present Jesus as the fulfilment of the *Taheb* expectations of the Samaritans.

(3) Even though until recently the Samaritan documents have been neglected as a source for shedding light on the New Testament, they help emphasise the Mosaic orientation of the Jewish world, which the New Testament and Matthew in particular had to address.

5. *Moses-Sinai and Transfiguration Motifs in the Apocrypha and Pseudepigrapha*

As in previous sections, the purpose here is to study Moses-Sinai and transformation motifs. I shall first survey these motifs in the Apocrypha, the Pseudepigrapha and rabbinic literature.[89]

The Transfiguration Theme

Sir. 44.23–45.5 eulogises Moses, and in 44.23 Moses is 'a man, who found favour in the sight of all living', he is *'beloved of God and men'* (45.1), Yahweh made him *'glorious as God'* (45.2-3; cf. Exod. 4.16; 7.1-11; Deut. 4.34; 24.12). Ben Sira does not explicitly describe Moses' transfiguration, but adds phrases like Yahweh 'showed him His glory' (Exod. 33.18, 34.6) or Yahweh made him 'glorious as God' (45.2-3). In 45.5-6, Moses is allowed to draw nigh into the dark cloud (Exod. 20.21,

---

'Sanballat and the Samaritan Temple', *BJRL*, Vol. 38, No.1 (1955), pp. 166-98. On Jewish polemic against this see J. Heinemann, 'Anti-Samaritan Polemics in the Aggadah', in *Proceedings of the Sixth World Congress of Jewish Studies* (August, 1973; 3 vols.; Jerusalem: Hacohen, 1977), III, pp. 57-69.

89.   J.H. Charlesworth, *Jesus within Judaism* (London: SPCK, 1988), pp. 30-53, argues for the importance of pseudepigraphical material—there has been an 'astronomical leap' from the seventeen in R.H. Charles's 1913 publication to sixty-five documents, opening up a whole territory of exploration.

24.18), suggesting a mystical ascent (also Sir. 24.23-24; cf. Exod. 19.7;
32.15; Deut. 6.1; Ezek. 20.11).

A more appropriate transformation motif is seen in the first century
pseudepigraphical writing of Pseudo-Philo's *Bib. Ant.* 12.1-2, which is
based on Exod. 34.29-35:

> he had been bathed with invisible light, he went down to the place where
> the light of the sun and the moon are; and the light of his face surpassed
> the splendour of the sun and the moon.

This depicts Moses as ascending into the heavenly realm and being
transformed. In *Bib. Ant.* 19.2-29 this 'transformation' is linked to
Moses' death: 'his appearance became glorious; and he died in glory'.
God gave him a 'public burial.'[90]

The Significance of the Sinai Theophany
The importance of Mount Sinai as a theophany and a 'coming of God'
is emphasised in several pseudepigraphical materials. For example (1) the
second-century BCE *Book of Jubilees*[91] is a work that is supposed to be
based on the revelation communicated to Moses during his forty days
spent on Mount Sinai (echoes Exod. 24.18, 28; 31.18, 32.15, Deut. 9.11,
etc.). (2) This Sinai theophany is also forcefully presented in the first-
century *Bib. Ant.* 11.5, the late-first-century *4 Ezra* 3.18-19 and the
second-century CE *2 Bar.* 59.4-12, where, the writer uses apocalyptic
language to describe the Sinai theophany, the cataclysmic happenings
associated with it, and the giving of the law. Undoubtedly the Sinai-law
giving and the Sinai event elevated Moses.[92] (3) The second-century CE
2 Bar. 59.4-12, using apocalyptic language, describes the historical
coming of Moses and comments on the cataclysmic happenings at Sinai
(v. 3). Like Philo and Josephus, the second-century BCE *Jub.* 2–4 stresses
the sacredness of Sinai, for it is the 'Mountain of the Lord', where

---

90.   Also see Josephus *Ant.* 4.8.48; *Ass. Mos.* 1.15.
91.   See O.S. Wintermute, 'Jubilees', *OTP*, II, p. 35.
92.   Also cf. *Bib. Ant.* 15.5-6; 23.10; 32.7-8. On 'Moses' and 'Moses-law'
emphases see *Jub.* 1.1-2; 11.5; *Bib. Ant.* 11.15; 15.5-6; 23.10; and 32.7-8; first-
century CE *4 Ezra* 3.18-19; second-century CE *2 Bar.* 59.4-12; *Sib. Or.* 3.256. It is
the Sinai law-giving that elevated Moses (*Bib. Ant.* 11.14; 13.1-10; 12.2-10; 32.7-8; *3
En.* 48D.; *Jub.* 1.2-4; 23.32; *b. Sanh* 38b; prior to first-century CE *Eupolemus* 26.1;
second-century BCE *Aristobulus* 2.3, 6; the second–third-century CE *T. Jac.* 7.3). At
Sinai Moses becomes Israel's instructor (*Bib. Ant.* 13.1-10) and lawgiver (12.2-10).

Moses receives 'revelation': 'both what (was) in the beginning and what will occur (in the future)...' (1.4-5).

A strong case can also be made for the view that Sinai motifs have influenced the content and description of apocalyptic and eschatological literature.[93] I will explore the coming together of sinaitic and apocalyptic ideas subsequently.

Mount Sinai at the Eschatological Age and The Eschatological Moses
It must be stated that evidence for the second coming of Moses himself is slender in Jewish literature. However, the following texts are pertinent to my discussion.

(1) The first-century *Lives of the Prophets* assumes the doctrine of the resurrection (cf. 2.15; 3.12) and states that at the resurrection the Ark of the Law will be the first to be resurrected and 'will come out of the rock and be placed on Mount Sinai' (*Liv. Proph.* 2.15); no one is going to bring out the ark 'except Aaron', and it is Moses, 'God's Chosen one', who is allowed to 'open the tablets'.[94] All this is to happen at the restoration of the cult implements at the eschatological age, and this implies that Moses himself (also Aaron) will be given an eschatological function in association with a new and future Sinai. It is possible that Moses himself or a Moses-like figure was considered as a returning messiah. For example, *Liv. Proph.* 2.8[95] may suggest that the coming messiah would be a Moses-like figure[96] who will overthrow the pagan culture of Egypt.

(2) In the sixth- to ninth-century CE *Midrash Rabba Deuteronomy* 3.17, for example, Moses and Elijah are to 'come together'. The lateness of this text calls for caution, nevertheless since it is attributed to the first-century Johanan ben Zakkai it may be of some relevance.

(3) Finally, the first-century CE *Testament or Assumption of Moses* does not speak explicitly of the 'coming of Moses' as such, but Moses motifs are associated with the final deliverance. In this work, (1) Moses

93.   This would include Ezekiel, Daniel (see ch. 4).

94.   According to *Liv. Proph.* 2.11, the Law which Jeremiah rescued before the destruction of the Temple will be the first to be resurrected, and will be placed on Mount Sinai.

95.   The second part of this verse is very likely a Christian gloss but for rabbinic tradition concerning Moses' miraculous birth see D. Daube, *The New Testament and Rabbinic Judaism* (London: 1956), pp. 6-7.

96.   On this see D.R.A. Hare, 'The Lives of the Prophets', *OTP*, II, p. 387 n. 8.

via God's revelation is given insight into the past and the future (3.11-12; 12.4-5). (2) God's eschatological intervention is at hand (10.1-12), and his covenant promises are certain (1.8-9; 3.9; 4.2-6; 12.7-13). (3) Just as Israel's previous deliverance and guidance in the wilderness were not due to Moses' strength (12.7) nor the people's piety (12.8), so also the final deliverance would solely be due to God's action predetermined by his covenant oath (12.3).

So the evidence for the 'coming of Moses' himself is slender and needs to be put in perspective. But the idea of 'Sinai at the eschatological age' (*Liv. Proph.* 2.14-15) and Moses' role as 'God's chosen one' to open the tablets in the ark of the Law (2.14) at least suggest a future role for him. It is also possible that there was an expectation in certain circles that the Messiah would incorporate within himself Mosaic features. For as D.R.A. Hare has pointed out it could be argued that the author of the *Lives of the Prophets* adhered to 'that segment of Jewish eschatology which expected not a Davidic but a Mosaic deliverer'.[97] All this evidence shows the importance of the Moses idea in the first-century, and it is my thesis that Matthew writes in this context.

6. *A Survey of Moses-Sinai and other Moses Motifs in Rabbinic* halakah *and* haggada

S. Sandmel, M. Smith, R. Bloch, G. Buchanan and others[98] have highlighted the difficulties posed in the study of rabbinic literature. There are difficulties in dating the traditions and, since Judaism underwent major changes in post 70 CE, rabbinic material needs to be used with caution.[99] Nevertheless, as Renee Bloch[100] has shown, later material (both halakhic and haggadic traditions) could reflect earlier traditions. The purpose in my study of rabbinic literature is not to infer literary dependence, but to establish a broader Jewish framework for my study of Mt. 17.1-13.

97. Hare, *OTP*, II, p. 383.
98. S. Sandmel, 'Parallelomania', *JBL* 81 (1962) pp. 1-13; M. Smith, 'A Comparison of Early Christian and Early Rabbinic Tradition', *JBL* 82 (1963) pp. 169-76; Renee Bloch, 'Methodological Note for the Study of Rabbinic Literature', in W.S. Green (ed.), *Approach to Ancient Judaism: Theory and Practice* (Missoula, MT: Scholars Press, 1978), pp. 51-75; G. Buchanan, 'The Use of Rabbinic Literature in New Testament Research', *BTB* 7 (1977), pp. 110-22.
99. Sanders, *Paul and Palestinian Judaism*, pp. 25-26.
100. Renee Bloch, 'Methodological Note for the Study of Rabbinic Literature'.

The Significance of Mount Sinai

The Sinai theophany is the overriding motif in haggadic tradition. For example, the Sinai event was considered as the sixth revelation (literally sixth descent) of God in the world,[101] and its summit towered into the heavens, and touched the feet of the divine throne.[102] The Sinai event is so important that in another *Haggada*, the slaves and the bond women who were present at the revelation of the Torah on Sinai were said to have seen more of the glory of God than the prophets Isaiah and Ezekiel.[103] Sinai was an antidote to sin (*b. Yebam.* 103a; *b. Sabb.* 145b-46a).

Sinai elevated Moses, for often a rabbinic tradition is considered a '*halakah* of Moses at Sinai' (*b. Sabb.* 61b; *b. Erub.* 4a, 97a; *b. Hag.* 3b; *b. Megillah* 19b; *b. Ber.* 4b) and is thought to have been 'orally communicated by God to Moses at Sinai' (*m. Pe'a* 2.6; *b. Ta'an.* 3a; *b. Ned.* 37b). This indicates clearly that Moses and the Sinai theophany had become a fundamental reference point.

The Moses-Transfiguration Motif

As in Philo *Mos.* 1.57; 2.292; *Bib. Ant.* 12.1 (cf. Exod. 34), Moses' transfiguration and heavenly ascent are important. Moses ate no food like the angels,[104] but, like the angels, was sustained by the radiance of the *shekinah*.[105] At Moses' death, Yahweh reminded him of his earlier 'transfiguration' experience, addresses him as 'Son' (also cf. Ezek. Trag. 96-100) and affirms that his transfiguration will also continue into the future world.[106]

The Radiance

Several traditions suggest that the radiance of Moses' face, as in Exodus 34, is due to the 'coming of God' at Sinai, and Moses' encounter with this theophany. According to certain traditions, Moses inherited the

---

101.   B.R. 38.9; see Ginzberg, *Legend*, 3, pp. 93-94, also vol 6 n. 206 for sources. In this section I am using Ginzberg's findings and the sources he has cited.

102.   Cf. Ginzberg, *Legend*, 3, pp. 93-94; 6 n. 206; also cf. Philo, *De Decalogo* 11. The second century Tanna stresses the transcendence of God, and hence denies Moses' ascent into heaven (Ginzberg, *Legend*, 4 n. 206).

103.   Cf. Ginzberg, *Legend*, 6 n. 207.

104.   Ginzberg, *Legend*, 3, pp. 142-43.

105.   That the righteous will feast on the brightness of the divine presence see *b. Ber.* 17a.

106.   Ginzberg, *Legend*, 3, pp. 430-31.

radiance emitting from the exposed tablet given at Sinai.[107] In another tradition (based on Exod. 33.18-19) Moses, though hidden in a cave at Sinai,[108] caught the reflection of the passing light.[109]

Moses' radiance was also associated with the 'primordial light' concept. Certain traditions held that the primordial light,[110] which God had hidden shortly after its creation, shone upon Moses.[111] Other traditions, in language reminiscent of *Merkavah* literature and of the transfiguration of Enoch in *3 En.* 15.1-2,[112] associate Moses' transfiguration with the theophany at Horeb (Exod. 3).[113] This suggests that the Moses-Sinai-law-radiance link was an important motif. It is this 'radiance' factor that Matthew links with Jesus.

Moses–Adam and the Radiance Factor

In Sir. 49.16 *'above every living thing was the beauteous glory of Adam'*. The thought here is that Adam, created by God and without human parentage, enjoyed a glory not shared by any other human being, an idea that played an important part in the development of the messianic doctrine, of the second Adam.

In rabbinic literature, however, this glory of Adam is applied to Moses (also hinted at in Philo, hence an early motif). In discussing with Adam as to who is superior, Moses argues that he is superior, because Adam lost God's glory (so also in the Samaritan *Memar Marqah* 2.2-3) but he 'retained the radiance of his flesh forever'.[114] There is an interesting link implied here between the primal man and (a) Moses and (b) the expected Messiah. Moses himself seems to be presented as a new Adam,

107. Ginzberg, *Legend*, 3, p. 119; 6 n. 260.

108. Moses and Elijah used the same cave, which protected them from the divine light (Ginzberg, *Legend*, 3, p.137; 4 n. 294 and 295).

109. Cf. Ginzberg, *Legend*, 3, p. 137; 6 n. 295; Moses' radiance was like the sun and outshone Joshua's (Ginzberg, *Legend*, 3, p. 441). In another tradition his radiance was a reward for his intercession for Israel (Ginzberg, *Legend*, 3, pp. 140-41); His radiance was from the *shekinah* at Sinai (Ginzberg, *Legend*, 6, p. 50 n. 260).

110. Ginzberg, *Legend*, 1, pp. 8-9.

111. On the appearance of celestial lights at the birth of heroes see Ginzberg, *Legend*, 1, p. 145. On Moses-light associations see Ginzberg, *Legend*, 2, pp. 265, 267; 3, pp. 469-70, 479; 6 n. 260.

112. In this passage Enoch is transformed into fire (cf. *OTP*, I, pp. 267-68).

113. For the idea that Moses changed into fire see Ginzberg, *Legend*, 2, pp. 305-306.

114. See Ginzberg, *Legend*, 3, pp. 479-80.

for at Sinai he regained Adam's lost glory and radiance, and so perhaps is a prototype of the future Messiah's 'radiance'.

Moses' Radiance and the Rays Expected to Emit from the Messiah's Countenance
Taking the previous point further, it is to be noted that certain traditions held that the rays which will emanate from the countenance of the Messiah will spread a stronger lustre than those of Moses and Joshua. The implication that the Messiah will be greater than Moses is seen in the idea that the Messiah is greater than the (three) patriarchs, more exalted than Moses, and is superior to the angels.[115] Since the Messiah himself was associated with light (*T. Levi*. 8.11-12; *T. Jud*. 24), it is instructive to view the above discussion in the light of the messiah-radiance theme in Mt. 17.2: καὶ ἔλαμψεν τὸ πρόσωπον αὐτοῦ ὡς ὁ ἥλιος, for Matthew may have been keen to insist on Jesus as the new and greater Moses and also as the expected radiant Messiah.

Thus Rabbinic literature heightens and further elaborates the Moses-Sinai, Moses-transfiguration themes already discussed, and, despite the difficulties involved in the use of these post-Christian post-70 CE materials, they do confirm our findings about the importance of Moses in first-century Judaism.

7. *A Survey of Moses-Sinai Motifs in the Fragments of Lost Judeo-Hellenistic Works*

Since some of the fragments of lost Judeo-Hellenistic works are pre-Christian, they contain useful material for my evaluation of Moses-Sinai motifs. In the case of Ezekiel the Tragedian (see below), its combination of both Sinai and Daniel 7 motifs will feature in my discussion on Mt. 17.1-13 in chapter 5.

Moses-Sinai and 'Coming of God' Motifs in Aristobulus (Second Century BCE)
In fragment 2.12b-17 of this second-century BCE Jewish philosopher, Aristobulus, Sinai was the place where God 'descended'.

---

115.   Ginzberg, *Legend*, 4 n. 836 where he cites *Tehillim* 21, 179. According to *Tanḥ. B*. 1.139 the Messiah will be more exalted than Moses and will be superior to the angels.

It is said in the book of the Law that there was a descent of God upon the
mountain, at the time when he was giving the Law, in order that all might
see the action of God. For this descent was manifest;...the mountain was
burning with fire, so says the Law, on account of God's coming down...[116]

Here Aristobulus interprets the Sinai event in terms of the 'coming of
God', a motif also seen in Josephus' *Ant.* 3.80 (παρουσίαν τοῦ θεοῦ).
He stresses the cataclysmic happenings at Sinai (cf. 2.13-16) and
portrays a great theophany (also cf. *Bib. Ant.* 11.5; *4 Ezra* 3.18-19). This
divine descent, or 'coming of God', motif will feature prominently in my
consideration of Matthew's understanding of the transfiguration.

*Moses-Sinai and Daniel 7 Motifs in Ezekiel the Tragedian (Second
Century BCE)*
In this second-century BCE work, the writer Ezekiel the Tragedian
synthesises the Exodus narrative (especially Exod. 1–15) with the literary
form of Greek tragic drama. The whole drama centres around the figure
of Moses, and in it the writer incorporates elements such as: (1) Moses'
birth (Ezek. Trag. 1-31). (2) His early childhood (vv. 32-38). (3)
His flight into the wilderness and marriage to 'Sepphorah' (vv. 39-67).
(4) His call to lead Israel out of Egypt, being dramatised in two ways:
(a) The first scene is presented in the form of a dream or vision seen by
Moses: *'On Sinai's peak I saw what seemed a throne'* [v. 68], this
being interpreted by his father-in-law vv.68-89. And (b) secondly, the
scene (vv. 90-192) initiated by the burning bush episode describes how
God commands Moses to lead his people out of Egypt (Exod. 3), and
culminates at Elim (Exod. 15.27).[117]

(1) *The importance of Sinai*: In the 'plot' of his 'drama' the writer
places the Sinai theophany before the burning bush theophany, which
suggests that he wishes to stress its importance. The text of this Sinai
'dream' of Moses is most illuminating:

v. 68   'On Sinai's peak I saw what seemed a throne
v. 69   so great in size it touched the clouds of heaven.
v. 70   Upon it sat a man of noble mien,
v. 71   becrowned, and with a sceptre in one hand
v. 72   while with the other he did beckon me.
v. 73   I made approach and stood before the throne.
v. 74   He handed over the sceptre and he bade

116.   See A. Yarbro Collins, 'Aristobulus', *OTP*, II, pp. 838-39.
117.   See R.G. Robertson, 'Ezekiel the Tragedian', *OTP*, II, pp. 804-806.

v. 75   me mount the throne, and gave to me the crown;
v. 76   then he withdrew from the throne.
v. 77   I gazed upon the whole earth round about;
v. 78   things under it, and high above the skies.
v. 79   Then at my feet a multitude of stars
v. 80   fell down, and I their number reckoned up.
v. 81   They passed by me like armed ranks of men.
v. 82   Then I in terror wakened from the dream' (Ezek. Trag. 68-82).[118]

This dream is then interpreted by Moses' father-in-law positively as meaning that Moses shall cause a mighty throne to rise (v. 85), and shall rule and govern men (86), and Moses shall be *shown* things past present and future (87-89). So, as in *Jub*. 1.4-5, Moses is gifted with foreknowledge and associated with it is the motif of prophecy.

(2) *Sinai, Ezekiel and Danielic themes*: The vision of the man of noble mien (φῶς γενναῖος),[119] a vision of God in human form seated on the throne, is reminiscent of (a) the reign of God in human form in Ezek. 1.24 (this has been combined by the writer with the Sinai event in Exod. 24, 'On Sinai's peak I saw what seemed a throne' [Ezek. Trag. 68]); and (b) the description, especially in vv. 74-76, where God 'handed over the sceptre and made me mount the throne, and gave to me the crown; then he himself withdrew from off the throne'. This echoes Daniel 7, where (i) the *Ancient of Days* is seated on the throne (7:9-10) and (ii) 'one like a son of man comes to the Ancient of Days, and was presented before him, And to him was given dominion and glory and the kingdom...' (7.13-14). (c) Ezekiel the Tragedian (v.79) speaks of 'a multitude of stars' falling down at Moses' feet, which is reminiscent of Joseph's dream in Genesis 37. Moreover, Moses' statement 'and I their number reckoned up' could be compared to Ps. 147 where God counts all the heavenly bodies.

Perhaps there is a combination of motifs in the passages of the Tragedian, the most prominent being (a) the description of God in the 'likeness as were of human form' (Ezek. 1.26), and (b) the account in Daniel 7 of the 'Ancient of Days' giving dominion and eternal kingship

118. Robertson, *OTP*, II, pp. 811-12.
119. Here φῶς is a poetic form for ἀνήρ, see Liddell and Scott, p.1968 and Robertson, *OTP*, II, p. 812 n. b2. Further see P. van der Horst, 'Moses' Throne Vision in Ezekiel the Dramatist', *JJS* 34 (1983), pp. 21-29; C.R. Holladay, 'The Portrait of Moses in Ezekiel the Tragedian', *SBL Seminar Papers* 1976 (Missoula, MT: Scholars Press, 1976), pp. 447-52; A.F. Segal, 'Paul and Ecstasy', in K.H. Richards (ed.), *SBL Seminar Papers* 1986 (Chico: Scholars Press, 1986), pp. 564-65.

to 'one like a son of man'—one of human appearance.

(3) *Daniel 7 themes applied to Moses*: If this Ezekielian and Danielic influence is accepted in Ezek. Trag. 70-76, then several conclusions may be drawn. (a) The enigmatic vision of Daniel 7 has been applied to Moses; so at least to the writer of this drama, he functions as 'one like the son of man' of Dan. 7.13. For he receives the sceptre, the throne, the crown, and also incorporates within himself the characteristics and functions of this 'man'. All this is at the withdrawal of the *man of noble mien* from 'the throne', which is a unique scene not paralleled in Daniel 7 (or in the enthronement of Enoch in *3 Enoch*). (b) The other important factor is that all this is set in the context of Moses' Sinai experience (Ezek. Trag. 68). So the Sinai theophany is associated with an anthropomorphic representation of God as 'man', in terms of the 'throne vision' of Ezekiel 1; and Moses' Sinai ascent is linked with Daniel 7.

So it may be argued that in this fascinating piece of literature the 'man', God (reminiscent of Ezek. 1.26), gives kingship and dominion to the 'man' Moses. This interpretation of the 'man' Moses is substantiated by Ezek. Trag. 96, where God addresses Moses as 'best of men', 'son' v. 100, 'mortal man' v. 101. Since in v. 76 God himself 'withdraws', Moses himself functions as the 'man' of v. 70 (with its Ezek. 1.26 significance) and like the 'son of man' of Daniel 7.

Implications for Matthew 17

This combination of both Ezek. 1.26 and Daniel 7, and their application to Moses, is particularly interesting because of the application within the Gospels of Son of Man and Moses motifs to Jesus. It is of special relevance to Matthew 17 with (1) its strong emphasis on Moses (on Sinai) and on the 'coming of God' and (2) in view of the framework of the 'Son of Man' sayings in which the transfiguration is set (see chs. 4 and 5).[120]

---

120. The pervasive influence of the Book of Daniel on works such as Qumran, Josephus (who however, does not comment on Daniel 7), the Apocalypses, has been pointed out by J.E. Goldingay, *Daniel* (Dallas: Word, 1989), pp. xxv-xl, and it is against this backdrop that one needs to view the influence of Daniel on Ezekiel the Tragedian, Matthew's Gospel and the New Testament in general.

Conclusions

My study of Moses motifs in Jewish literature has indicated that the experience of Moses on Sinai is central in Jewish theology of Moses. It is this event that elevates Moses as *Beloved of God* (Sir. 45.1), *God's chosen one* (*Liv. Proph.* 2.14-15), *God's son* and as the 'one like the son of man' of Daniel 7 (Ezek. Trag. 96-100). It was primarily at Sinai that Moses experienced a 'heavenly ascent' (Sir. 45.5, *Bib. Ant.* 12.1; *Orphica* 30-41).

The idea of transfiguration and transformation too has been applied to Moses (*Bib. Ant.* 12.1; Ezek. Trag. 68-82; also cf. *Mos.* 1.57, 158-59; *Mos.* 2.70, 280, 288-89; *Quaest. in Exod.* 2.46-47; *Ant.* 3.82-83; *Memar Marqah*, 4.3, 6; 5.3) and in certain rabbinic literature Moses regained Adam's lost glory and radiance. In *Bib. Ant.* 19.2-29 Moses is also transformed at his death and in *T. Levi.* 8.11-12, *T. Judah* 24 the Messiah himself is associated with light.

At Sinai Moses fellowshipped with angels, became the *prophet-pre-eminent* (Sir. 46.1), was endowed with *foreknowledge* and became Mediator of Israel (*T. Mos.* 1.14). Some traditions also hint at Moses' *'pre-existence'* (*T. Mos.* 1.14). In Ezekiel the Tragedian and some other literature, at Sinai Moses was elevated as king and leader of Israel and achieves near-divine status.

The Sinai theophany also elevated Mount Sinai above all other mountains (Aristobulus 2.13-16, *2 Apoc. Bar.* 4.1-7). It is worth comparing this with the Samaritan glorification of Gerizim. According to some early traditions, Mount Sinai will have a crucial role in the eschatological age and according to *Liv. Proph.* 2.14-15, Mount Sinai will feature at the resurrection. In Samaritan literature a similar role is attributed to Moses, but on Mt. Gerizim (*Ant.* 18.85-86). Sinai also attests *the descent or coming of God* (Aristobulus 2.12b-17; *Ant.* 3.80).

It is very obvious that in Jewish biblical and non-biblical literature, the Torah is intrinsically related to Mount Sinai and to Moses. In the Mishnah and the Babylonian Talmud, the oral Torah too is attributed to Moses at Sinai, also certain Halakah (cf. *m. Pe'a* 2.6; *m. Abot.* 1.1; *m. Ed.* 8.7; *b. Ned.* 37b). No other event in Moses' life was given such prominence and elaboration as the Sinai event. Mount Sinai and all that it signified was determinative for Jewish theology and thinking about Moses.

Chapter 4

MATTHEW 17.1-13 IN THE LIGHT OF LITERARY PARALLELS
AND DANIEL 7-SINAI CONSIDERATIONS

In the previous chapter we have seen that transfiguration language and
motifs are important in Second Temple Jewish literature. I shall demonstrate in due course how Matthew with his emphasis on the radiance of
Jesus' face and on 'light' has heightened the Moses-Sinai-radiance
Exodus 34 motif in the transfiguration narrative. But Matthew's presentation also reflects interest in certain apocalyptic motifs, and the purpose
of this chapter is to compare Mt. 17.1-13 with the language and imagery
of the transfiguration stories in Hellenistic and Jewish apocalyptic literature and to determine how and with what purpose he has combined
these motifs with the Moses-Sinai theme.

In this chapter I will be suggesting a formal and theological framework
within which Matthew's transfiguration narrative should be understood.
I suggest that by unique use of the 'Son of Man' *inclusio*, Matthew has
blended Moses-Sinai and Danielic themes in order to demonstrate that
the 'coming of God' had taken place in Jesus. I will establish in what
follows: (1) Matthew's use of Danielic categories and (2) his amalgamation of these with Moses-Sinai categories. An important argument in my
thesis is that for Matthew *it is precisely because Jesus is the Danielic
Son of Man, who is also Son of God, that he is the new and greater
Moses, whose transfiguration is a new and greater Sinai event.*

1. The Transfiguration in the Light of Parallels in Graeco-Hellenistic Literature

Transformation language and motifs are found in ancient Hellenistic
literature. For example the idea that gods and spirits can transform themselves before others and examples of such transformations are found in

the first-century Latin poet Ovid's *Metamorphoses*.[1] Ovid was not alone: as J. Behm has observed, this type of mythical thinking produced a whole literary genre, the chief motif of which was that the gods, in drawing near to men, change themselves into earthly perceptible beings.[2] Similar motifs are also found in Asian religions. In the *Bhagavad Gita* 11.12 for example, Krishna is transfigured before (the human) Arjuna, and the face of Krishna is described as 'one as bright and terrible as the radiance of a thousand suns'.[3]

E. Lohmeyer[4] believed that such concepts of transformation in Hellenistic literature formed the backdrop for the synoptic account of the transfiguration. In his commentary on Mark's Gospel, however, he rightly abandoned this theory in favour of a Jewish and Jewish-apocalyptic setting, for the strongly Jewish context of the transfiguration (including the figures of Moses and Elijah) tells against the Hellenistic setting.[5] Furthermore it has been rightly pointed out that, in contrast to certain of these examples from Hellenistic literature, the synoptic accounts do not convey the idea of 'deification'.[6]

1.   See *Metamorphoses*, 1, pp. 233-39; 10.235-42; 11.291-95. In 11. 410-748 Ovid describes the transformation of Ceyx and his wife Alcyone; in 14.757-58 of Anaxarete 14.757-58, of Daphne 1.551-552. Further see 2.508-31; 4.264-70; 6.374-76, 378; 732-45; 8.254-59; 14.576-80 in *Ovid in Six Volumes*, IV; *Metamorphoses* (English trans. F.J. Miller; Harvard: Harvard University Press and London: W. Heineman), p. xxxiv; J.B. Solodow, *The World of Ovid's Metamorphoses* (London: Chapel Hill, 1988), pp. 192, 194; 'Ovid', in W.H. Harris and J.S. Levey, (eds.), *Columbian Encyclopedia* (New York: The Columbia University Press, 1975), p. 2034; 'Ovid' in *Encyclopedia Britannica* (16 vols.; 1976), pp. 797-800.

2.   See J. Behm, 'μεταμορφω', *TDNT*, IV, p. 756, and note 7; W.L. Liefeld, 'μεταμορφω', *DNTT*, III, p. 861.

3.   *The Bhagavad Gita* (New York: Penguin, 1962).

4.   'Die Verklärung Jesus', *ZNW* 21 (1922) pp. 230-31, e.g. *Hom. Dem.* 233-34, where Demeter changes her appearance and light emits from her skin. In *Corp. Herm.* I:1-2, Poimandres is transfigured into a heavenly being etc.; also see Behm, 'μεταμορφω', *TDNT*, IV, p. 757.

5.   E. Lohmeyer, *Das Evangelium des Markus*, pp. 174-75.

6.   See Behm, 'μεταμορφω', p. 756. Even though 2 Pet. 1.4 uses Θείας κοινωνοὶ φυσεως of the believer, it is significant that in the independent attestation to the transfiguration in 2 Pet. 1.16-18—which at least enables one to see how one early tradition interpreted it—the emphasis is not on deification or any other related motif but that God has appointed Jesus as the eschatological king and judge. See Bauckham, *Jude, 2 Peter*, p. 205.

2. *The Transfiguration in the Light of Parallels in Apocalyptic Literature*

In his commentary, Lohmeyer compares the transfiguration with passages such as *4 Ezra* 7.97, *2 Bar.* 50.10; Dan. 12.3.[7] This view has been developed in various ways in relation to the Enoch corpus, *T. Abr.* 12 and others, by W. Gerber, U.B. Müller, S. Pedersen, M. Sabbé, C. Rowland and others.[8] Gerber (pp. 391-92) also suggests parallels in Jewish mystical literature, the *Hekhalot Rabbati* 3.4 and *Midrash Ketappuach.*

Transfiguration Motifs in 1 Enoch Material
It is interesting to compare the transfiguration language and motif in the Enoch corpus in particular with Matthew's portrayal of the transfiguration. Compare, for example, Matthew's distinctive 'sun-garment' analogy (17.2) with *1 En.* 14.20 where the 'gown' of the 'Great Glory' was 'shining more brightly than the sun, it was whiter than any snow'. This has a parallel in Mt. 13.43, which, as we shall see later, is linked by the evangelist with 17.2. Or compare Matthew's (and Luke's) emphasis on the brightness and transformation of Jesus' face with *1 En.* 38.4, where

---

7.   Lohmeyer, *Das Evangelium des Markus*, p. 174; Nineham, *Saint Mark*, p.234; Cranfield, *The Gospel according to St Mark*, p. 290, cites Daniel 12.3; *2 Baruch* 51.3, 5, 10, 12, *1 En.* 38.4; 54.2; *4 Ezra* 7.97; E. Schweizer, *The Good News according to Matthew* (London: SPCK, 1976), pp. 348-49; H. Anderson, *The Gospel of Mark* (London: Oliphants, 1976), p. 224; Johnson, *A Commentary on the Gospel according to Mark*, p. 157. Visions are also cited in Gen. 35.13, also see Joseph's experience in Gen. 32.24; Judg. 6.21, 20.

8.   H.P. Müller, 'Die Verklärung Jesu', *ZNW* 51 (1960) pp. 56-64, esp. pp. 61-62; Gerber, *TZ* 23 (1967) pp. 385-95, esp. p. 387-88; U.B. Müller, 'Die christologische Absicht des Marksevangeliums und die Verklärungsgesichte', *ZNW* 64 (1973) pp. 159-93, esp. p.180-81; S. Pedersen, 'Die Proklamation Jesu als des eschatologischen Offenbarungsträgers (Mt. xvii.1-13)', *NovT* 17 (1975) pp. 241-64, esp. pp. 258-59. A number of scholars however have paralleled parts of it with Rev. 1.14; 4.4; 11.19; 12.1, 3; Dan. 10.6; 12.3 etc. cf. Müller, 'Die christologische Absicht' pp. 62-63; J. Schmid, *Das Evangelium nach Matthäus* (Regensburg: Pustet, 1965), p. 263; A. Schlatter, *Der Evangelist Matthäus* (Stuttgart: Caliver, 1959), pp. 526-30 (who also gives rabbinic parallels); D.W. Michaelis, *Das Evangelium nach Matthäus* (2 vols.; Zürich: Zwingli Verlag, 1948-49), II, p. 378; B. Weiss, *Das Matthäus-Evangelium* (Gottingen: Vandenhoeck & Ruprecht, 1898), p. 304; Rowland, *The Open Heaven*, pp. 367-68.

men are not able to behold the faces of the holy ones, for 'the light of the Lord of the Spirits has shined upon the face of the holy, the righteous, and the elect'.

The 'light' motif, commonplace in apocalyptic literature, is also present in *1 En.* 39.7, where 'all the righteous and the elect...shall be as intense as the light of fire', and in 62.15-16, 'The righteous and elect ones shall rise from the earth and shall cease being of downcast face... They shall wear the garments of glory...' *1 En.* 71.1 speaks of the 'sons of the holy angels' whose 'garments were white...and the light of their faces was like snow' (perhaps compare this with Dan. 10.5-6).[9]

Examples from Other Apocalyptic Literature
Similar ideas are found in other apocalyptic literature; for example, in the late first century *2 En.* 22.8-9, Enoch, who is anointed with oil, appeared 'greater than the greatest light...like the rays of the glittering sun.'[10] In the first to second century CE *T. Abr.* A. 12.4-5, Abel is transformed and appears on a throne as 'a wondrous man, bright as the sun, like unto a son of God...'[11] In the late first century CE *4 Ezra* 7.97 the 'faces' of the departed are to 'shine like the sun' and are to be made like 'the light of the stars'.[12]

Examples from Jewish Mystical Literature
In the *Hekhalot Rabbati* 3.4 the *Merkavah* mystic 'beholds' Yahweh's garment, the throne of his glory, and experiences a transformation, his 'eyes sending forth torches of fire'.[13] In the rather late (5th to 6th

---

9.　On this see I. Gruenwald, *Apocalyptic and Merkavah Mysticism* (Lieden: Brill, 1980), p. 44; P.D. Hanson, *Old Testament Apocalyptic* (Nashville: Abingdon, 1988), pp. 25-26.

10.　Trans. F.I. Andersen, *OTP*, I, pp. 138, 139.

11.　Trans. E.P. Sanders, *OTP*, I, p. 889; Rowland, *The Open Heaven*, p. 367.

12.　Trans. B.M. Metzger, *OTP*, I, p. 540.

13.　From a translation by G.G. Scholem, *Jewish Gnosticism, Merkaba Mysticism, and Talmudic Tradition* (New York: Jewish Theological Seminary of America, 1960), pp. 59-60. Also cf. Gerber, *TZ* 23 (1967) p. 392. Gruenwald, *Apocalyptic and Merkavah Mysticism*, pp. 32-71, 127-28, has shown that the mystical and 'ascent' motifs developed in later *Merkavah* literature are already present in *1 En.* 17.9/Ezek. 1.22, 2 Kgs 2.11; *1 En.* 39.3; 52.1; 70.2; 71, in shorter passages like *1 En.* 18.8-9; 25.3, and also in the Similitudes of Enoch: Chs 36–71; 39.3; 32.3; 40.23, 8; 67.3; *2 En.* 3.1 etc. Antecedents to mystical vision are also seen in biblical material: 1 Kgs 22.19; Isa. 6.1-2, Ezek. 1.3, 22-23, 8.1-2, 10; Dan. 7.9-10. And in a

century CE) *3 En.* 15, Enoch describes his transformation thus: 'my flesh turned to flame, my sinews to blazing fire,...my eyeballs to fiery torches,...and the substance of my body to blazing fire...' (also cf. ch. 7, 19.2, 22.4, 26.4). In *3 En.* 48C the transformed Metatron appears like 'lightning, and the light of the sun'.[14]

So it is evident that transfiguration language and motifs are at home in apocalyptic literature. The crucial issue, though, is how far the gospel accounts of the transfiguration are dependent on such Jewish apocalyptic. C. Rowland argues plausibly for dependence, noting that (1) *1 En.* 14.20-21, mentions two aspects of divinity, Enoch's clothing and his face; which are precisely the two elements mentioned in Mt. 17.2 and Lk. 9.29 (contra Mark); (2) that no less than five words are used in both the transfiguration and in *1 Enoch*, sun, face, white, snow and clothing.[15] It is of interest to observe that Matthew's transfiguration narrative is more apocalyptically oriented than Mark's more mundane account (compare Mt. 17.2 with Mk 9.3).[16] This, together with his description of the event as a ὅραμα and his setting of the narrative within a framework of Son of Man sayings (see below), gives the Matthean version of the story a distinct apocalyptic–Danielic flavour.

3. *The 'Vision-Form', Matthew's Use of* τὸ ὅραμα *and Danielic Motifs*

A common feature in Jewish apocalypses is the vision-form, the revelation being based on the seer's visionary experiences. Of the evangelists Matthew (alone) categorises the transfiguration as τὸ ὅραμα.[17] This

---

broader sense one may also include Moses-Sinai motifs of Exod. 19-34; Deut. 5.19-24, and some cite the prologue of Job (Rowland, *The Open Heaven*, p. 29). Closely associated with these themes is the '*Kabbalah*', i.e. the esoteric teachings of Jewish mysticism (cf. G.G. Scholem, '*Kabbalah*', *Encyclopaedia Judaica*, X, pp. 495-97) some of which pre-date Christianity. Josephus for example speaks of Essenes possessing magical literature (cf. Scholem, *Jewish Gnosticism*, p. 497), and Qumran possessed such material, which also spoke of a 'divine chariot'.

14. Trans. P. Alexander, in *OTP*, II, p. 312.

15. Cf. Scholem, *Jewish Gnosticism*, p.56.

16. ἐξαστράπτων in Lk. 9.29 has also been paralleled with ἀστραπη in *1 En.* 14.11, 17, LXX of Ezek. 1.4 (ἐξαστράπτον) and Dan. 10.6 ἀστραπῆς.

17. ὅραμα occurs in Acts to denote visions (9.12; 10.3, 17, 19; 11.5; 16.9). In Acts 12.9 however, ἐδόκει δὲ ὅραμα βλέπειν is used in distinguishing a 'vision' from a real experience.

usage functions as a window into his unique understanding of the transfiguration, since he blends Moses-Sinai particularly with Danielic motifs.
This blending in his transfiguration story also contributes to his understanding of the passage in terms of the 'coming of God'. Due to its
importance for understanding Mt. 17.1-9, his use of τὸ ὅραμα merits
further comment.

The Concept of 'Vision' in Daniel and Matthew 17
Daniel as a whole and chapter 7 in particular are full of visions. The
chapter opens with a description of Daniel having a dream and 'visions';
there are further references to visions in vv. 12, 13 and 15. Verse 13 is
the particularly important verse referring to the coming of the one like a
son of man,[18] and interestingly the LXX there uses ὅραμα (the word
used by Matthew of the transfiguration) rather than the more usual
ὁράσις, thus ἐθεώρουν ἐν ὁράματι τῆς νυκτός. Since (1) Matthew
shows considerable interest in Daniel 7 and Danielic motifs,[19] and since

---

18. The voluminous discussion on the title 'the Son of Man' has generally been
focused on the 'origin' and 'meaning' of the term. See M. Casey, 'Method in our
madness, and madness in their methods. Some approaches to the Son of Man
problem in recent scholarship', *JSNT* 42 (1991), pp. 17-43, who critisises the views
of O. Betz, S. Kim and especially C.C. Caragounis, (who are heavy on the influence
of Dan. 7). Following G. Vermes, M. Casey and B. Lindars, *Jesus Son of Man*
(London: SPCK, 1983), have taken *bar nash* and *bar nasha* as a form of self reference in Aramaic. Casey and Lindars in particular have campaigned for the exclusive
'generic' use of the term (also see B. Lindars, 'Response to Richard Bauckham: The
idiomatic use of bar enasha', *JSNT* 23 [1985], pp. 35-41; Casey, 'Method in our
Madness', pp.17-23). But against this exclusive-generic significance see R. Bauckham,
'The Son of Man: "A man in my position" or "someone"'? *JSNT* 23 (1985),
pp. 23-33. It is known that Ps. 8; 80; Ezek. 2.1; *1 En.* 37-71 too have been featured;
on Ps. 80 see W. Wifall, 'Son of Man—A Pre Davidic Social class?' *CBQ* 37
(1975), pp. 331-40; D. Hill, '"Son of Man" in Psalm 80 v. 17', *NovT* 15 (1973),
pp. 261-69. But little attention has been paid for example for 'any distinctive features
of its use in the gospels individually except John' (France, *Matthew—Evangelist*,
p. 288). That Matthew was interested particularly in the Danielic Son of Man, see
M. Pamment, 'The Son of Man in the First Gospel', *NTS* 29 (1983), pp. 116-29;
France, *Matthew—Evangelist*, pp. 290-91.

19. France, *Matthew—Evangelist*, pp. 288-92; *Jesus and the Old Testament*,
passim; D. Hill, 'The Figure of Jesus in Matthew's Story: A Response to Professor
Kingsbury's Literary-Critical Probe', *JSNT* 21 (1984), pp. 49-51; D.A. Carson,
'Excursus: "The Son of Man" as a Christological Title', in *Matthew*, pp. 209-13;
D.E. Orton, *The Understanding Scribe: Matthew and the Apocalyptic Ideal*
(Sheffield: JSOT 1989), pp. 145-46.

(2) he brackets his transfiguration pericope with four Son of Man verses (16.27; 16.28—17.1-8—17.9; 17.12), we may reasonably infer that Matthew has been influenced by Daniel 7.

It must be borne in mind that the LXX of Exod. 3.3 speaks of Moses' 'vision' at Horeb/Sinai as τὸ ὅραμα τὸ μέγα τοῦτο; (cf. Acts 7.31). Therefore, as an 'idea' it belongs both to Sinai and Daniel 7, something which as I shall argue could have been exploited by Matthew.

The 'Vision' and 'Vision-Interpretation-Form' in Daniel 7.13-18 and Matthew's Portrayal of the Transfiguration

Dan. 7.13-28 is a passage that includes (1) a 'vision' (7.13-14), (2) the seer's reaction to the vision (7.15 also 28), (3) request for its explanation (7.16, also v. 19), and finally (4) interpretation of the vision (7.16-27, which also takes into consideration the vision in 7.2-12). Matthew's portrayal of the transfiguration is somewhat similar. For (1) the disciples see the 'vision' (τὸ ὅραμα) of the transfiguration (Mt. 17.2-5). (2) They react to what they saw and heard (17.6-8). (3) They query Elijah's coming (Mt. 17.9-13), presumably prompted by his appearance at the transfiguration, and (4) receive an explanation from Jesus, with Matthew alone stressing that they 'understood'. Mt. 17.9-13, of course, parallels Mk 9.9-13, but Matthew alone describes the transfiguration as τὸ ὅραμα (compare Dan. 7.13 LXX), and, given his use of apocalyptic language in 17.2 (to be compared with 13.34 and Dan. 12.3 etc.), the comparison with Dan. 7.13-18 is arresting.

The Son of Man inclusio Displayed by Matthew 16.27/16.28 and 17.9/ 17.12

As already mentioned, it is notable that Matthew's transfiguration pericope (17.1-8) is preceded and followed by two Son of Man sayings (16.27; 16.28 and 17.9; 17.12). I shall argue that these Son of Man sayings when taken together form a Danielic Son of Man *inclusio*, which has direct bearing on Matthew's theology of the transfiguration.

Recent studies based on available Jewish evidence show that 'Son of Man' was not a recognised title for an apocalyptic figure, and so, except in some places where the allusion is unmistakable (e.g. Mk 14.62), references in the gospels to 'the Son of Man' cannot be assumed to be alluding to Daniel 7.[20] However, with regards to Matthew's use of the

20. See Bauckham, 'The Son of Man', pp. 23-33, esp. pp. 27-28; Casey, 'Method in our Madness', pp. 17-43, esp. pp. 27-28.

title, I side with those who consider that the *primary* background must be found in Dan. 7.13-14, and Matthew's use of the term reflects the conviction that those verses provided a pattern which it was Jesus' mission to fulfil.[21] For the *majority* of Matthew's distinctive uses are set in the context of the future vindication and glory of the Son of Man[22] and many of the relevant passages echo Daniel 7 themes: clouds, heaven, coming, glory, kingdom, judgment and the like.[23]

It is with this in view that the 'Son of Man' *inclusio* provided by 16.27; 16.28; 17.9; 17.12 needs to be considered. The relevant passages are set out as follows:

(1) The 'Son of Man' double bracket I part 1:

Mt. 16.27	Mk 8.38	Lk. 9.26
	ὃς γὰρ ἐὰν ἐπαισχυνθῇ με καὶ τοὺς ἐμοὺς λόγους ἐν τῇ γενεᾷ ταύτῃ τῇ μοιχαλίδι	ὃς γὰρ ἂν ἐπαισχυνθῇ με καὶ τοὺς ἐμοὺς λόγους,
μέλλει γὰρ ὁ υἱὸς τοῦ ἀνθρώπου ἔρχεσθαι ἐν τῇ δόξῃ τοῦ πατρὸς αὐτοῦ μετὰ τῶν ἀγγέλων αὐτοῦ, καὶ τότε ἀποδώσει ἑκάστῳ κατὰ τὴν πρᾶξιν αὐτοῦ.	καὶ ἁμαρτωλῷ, καὶ ὁ υἱὸς τοῦ ἀνθρώπου ἐπαισχυνθήσεται αὐτόν, ὅταν ἔλθῃ ἐν τῇ δόξῃ τοῦ πατρὸς αὐτοῦ μετὰ τῶν ἀγγέλων τῶν ἁγίων.	τοῦτον ὁ υἱὸς τοῦ ἀνθρώπου ἐπαισχυνθήσεται, ὅταν ἔλθῃ ἐν τῇ δόξῃ αὐτοῦ καὶ τοῦ πατρὸς καὶ τῶν ἁγίων ἀγγέλων.

The relation between Mk 8.38 and the 'Q' passages (Lk. 12.8-9/ Mt. 10.32-33) has been widely discussed.[24] Whatever their relation,[25] in Mt. 16.27; Mk 8.38; Lk. 9.26 the Son of Man tradition is shared by all three evangelists, and so also are the themes of 'glory', 'angels' and 'judgment'. Since Mk 8.38 (and par.) leads into 9.1 (and par.) with its reference to 'kingship': τὴν βασιλείαν τοῦ Θεοῦ Mk 9.1, Lk. 9.26 (in Mt. 16.28 it is τὸν υἱὸν τοῦ ἀνθρώπου ἐρχόμενον ἐν τῇ βασιλείᾳ αὐτοῦ) the influence of Dan. 7.13-14 on both Mk 8.38 (and par.) and

21. See France, *Matthew—Evangelist*, esp. pp. 290-91.

22. The exceptions are: 13.37; 16.13; 26.2; see France, *Matthew—Evangelist*, p. 291.

23. See Mt. 16.27; 28; 19.28; 24.30; 25.31-32; 26.64.

24. For recent discussion, see G.R. Beasley-Murray, *Jesus and the Kingdom of God* (Grand Rapids: Eerdmans; Exeter: Paternoster, 1987), pp. 219-29, 291-96.

25. See Marshall, *Luke*, pp. 541-16 for the view that 'Son of Man' must have stood in Luke's source behind 12.8-9 (in view of v. 10) attested by Mk 8.38, but that Matthew and Luke may have had different versions of Q at this point.

Mk 9.1 (and par.) is recognised by scholars.[26]

In Matthew's version of the saying (16.27), the theme of judgment is emphatic: ἀποδώσει...κατὰ τὴν πρᾶξιν αὐτοῦ. The divine prerogative of judgment is here exercised by the 'Son of Man.' The background to this may well be in Daniel 7, where the 'one like the son of man' comes to share in the authority of the 'Ancient of Days.'[27]

(2) The 'Son of Man' double bracket I part 2:

Mt. 16.28	Mk 9.1	Lk. 9.27
	Καὶ ἔλεγεν αὐτοῖς·	
ἀμὴν λέγω ὑμιν ὅτι	ἀμὴν λέγω ὑμῖν ὅτι	λέγω δὲ ὑμῖν ἀληθῶς,
εἰσίν τινες τῶν ὧδε	εἰσίν τινες ὧδε τῶν	εἰσίν τινες τῶν αὐτοῦ
ἑστώτων οἵτινες οὐ μὴ	ἑστηκότων οἵτινες οὐ	ἑστηκότων οἳ οὐ μὴ
γεύσωνται θανάτου ἕως	μὴ γεύσωνται θανάτου	γεύσωνται θανάτου ἕως
ἂν ἴδωσιν τὸν υἱὸν τοῦ	ἕως ἂν ἴδωσιν τὴν	ἂν ἴδωσιν τὴν
ἀνθρώπου ἐρχόμενον	βασιλείαν τοῦ Θεοῦ	βασιλείαν τοῦ Θεοῦ.
ἐν τῇ βασιλείᾳ αὐτοῦ.	ἐληλυθυῖαν ἐν δυνάμει.	

These parallels are important for the development of my thesis. So we need to make some preliminary points before coming to conclusions on Matthew's redaction of Mk 9.1 and its implications.

(a) *Various interpretations of Mk 9.1*: The enigmatic Mk 9.1 (and its parallels) has been taken variously. It has been argued that (1) it refers to Jesus' death. K. Brower[28] links Jesus' death with the 'idea' of the 'day of the Lord'. For in Mk 15.37-39, Jesus's death was associated with (i) the 'torn temple curtain', (ii) the centurion's confession, (2) Mk 9.1 has been seen as referring to the resurrection,[29] (3) the ascension, in

26. See Beasley-Murray, *Jesus and the Kingdom of God*, pp. 291-96 where he argues that both Q (Lk. 12.8-9/Mt. 10.32-33) and Mk 8.38 reflect the judgment scene of Dan. 7.9-10, 13-14; also see France, *Divine Government* (London: SPCK, 1990), pp. 80-81.

27. See Mt. 13.41-43. The interpretation (13.41-43 to parable in 13.24-30) perhaps tells us more of Matthew (redaction) than Jesus, see Gundry, *Matthew*, pp. 261-62; but the 'point' in both is the same, Hill, *The Gospel of Matthew*, p. 235; France, *Matthew*, p. 224.

28. See Brower, 'Mark 9.1: Seeing the Kingdom in Power', *JSNT* 6 (1980), pp. 17-26.

29. See France, *Divine Government*, p. 69, who also lists other views. For a similar list of views see Cranfield, *St Mark*, pp. 285-89; Brower, 'Mark 9.1 Seeing the Kingdom in Power', pp. 17-26; Carson, *Matthew*, pp. 380-82, and Beasley-Murray, *Jesus and the Kingdom of God*, pp. 187-93. Rom. 1.4 links δυνάμει (compare Mk 9.1) with the resurrection, but in 2 Pet. 1.16 δύναμιν is referred to in

which Jesus took his seat at God's 'right hand' or according to Mk 14.62 at 'the right hand of power',[30] (4) the coming of the Spirit on the church (Acts 2)[31] and the church's expansion,[32] (5) the fall of Jerusalem in 70 CE,[33] (6) the parousia,[34] or (7) a series of events, including everything so far mentioned above.[35]

(b) *The primary focus of Mk 9.1 and parallels*: It is true that all these

the context of parousia, followed by the transfiguration in vv. 17-18.

30. Cf. France, *Divine Government*, p. 69. On 'ascension' and 'parousia' themes in Mk 14.62 see W.W. Wessel, 'Mark', in F.E. Gaebelein (ed.), *The Expositor's Bible Commentary* (12 vols.; Grand Rapids: Zondervan, 1984), VIII, p. 769.

31. See H.B. Swete, *The Gospel According to Mark* (London: Macmillan, 1913), p. 186.

32. Such a view perhaps also could accommodate Dodd's understanding of ἐληλυθυῖαν (Mk 9.1) in terms of realised eschatology, see C.H. Dodd, *Parables of the Kingdom* (New York: Charles Scribner's Sons, 1961) (revised ed.), p. 53. In relation to Mt. 16.28 see Carson, *Matthew*, p.382, cited also in France, *Divine Government*, p. 69.

33. See France, *Divine Government*, p. 119 n. 6.

34. See Anderson, *The Gospel of Mark*, pp. 221-22; N. Perrin, *The Kingdom of God in the Teaching of Jesus* (London: SCM; Philadelphia: Westminster Press, 1963), pp. 137-38; Ambrozic, *The Hidden Kingdom*, pp. 209-10; Nineham, *Saint Mark*, pp. 231-32, who also argues that Matthew (16.28 with 16.27) understood it as such. Also see Hill, *The Gospel of Matthew*, p. 266. That Luke by his plain τὴν βασιλείαν τοῦ Θεοῦ avoids the problem of the parousia expectation see Ambrozic, *The Hidden Kingdom*, pp. 214-15, and H. Conzelmann, *The Theology of St Luke* (New York: Harper & Row, 1960), p. 104.

35. See France, *Divine Government*, p. 69. For such a view on the parallel passage in Mt. 16.27 see Carson, *Matthew*, p. 382; France, *Matthew*, p. 261. Beasley-Murray, *Jesus and the Kingdom of God*, p. 193 concludes that Mk 13.30 is prior to Mk 9.1 and provides its inspiration. This is an interesting observation. But while I accept the position that the primary focus of Mk 9.1 (and par.) is the transfiguration pericope, setting Mk 9.1 in its 'wider' context, I suggest that a case could be made that, just as it is possible to view that the relationship between Mk 13.30-31 and Mk 13.24-27 is that between the event of 70 CE (that ushers the nearness of the parousia, i.e. a 'prophetic perspective of the parousia') and the parousia (on this see A.L. Moore, *The Parousia in the New Testament* [Leiden: Brill, 1966], pp. 131-36; D. Wenham, '"This Generation Will Not Pass..." A Study of Jesus' Future Expectation in Mark 13', in H.H. Rowdon [ed.], *Christ the Lord* [Leicester: IVP, 1982], pp. 127-50; and T.J. Geddert, *Watchwords: Mark 13 in Markan Eschatology* [Sheffield: JSOT Press, 1989], pp. 223-55) suggest that the relation between Mk 8.38 and 9.1 perhaps could be seen in similar fashion: Mk 8.38 and 13.24-27 refer to the parousia and Mk 9.1 includes the events of 70 CE (like its parallel tradition in 13.30) but also a whole series of events.

events (except the parousia) were *visible* to some who heard Jesus and could be the point of the saying. But more plausible than any is the view that Mk 9.1 should be connected with the immediately following event of the transfiguration. In favour of this: (1) It is observed that Mark's temporal prediction τινες ὧδε τῶν ἑστηκότων οἵτινες οὐ μὴ γεύσωνται θανάτου ἕως ἂν ἴδωσιν...(Mk 9.1) is immediately followed by an unusually precise temporal link καὶ μετὰ ἡμέρας ἕξ. R.T. France makes the point that 'there seems no reason to assume that this happened by accident, and that Mark was unaware of the effect produced', suggesting that Mark intended 9.1 in some sense to be linked to 9.2-8.[36] (2) It is also entirely possible to see Mk 9.1 as a transitional saying, picking up the themes of the preceding verses which included the call to suffer and lose their lives and then of the Son of Man coming in judgment. Mk 9.1, however, promises that some of the disciples will see the glorious kingdom before tasting death, and leads into the transfiguration narrative. (3) C.K. Barrett, followed by H. Anderson and others,[37] objects that it is odd to say that 'some will not taste death until...' of something that then happens a few days later, but: (a) on a purely narrative level it is not necessary to assume that Jesus knew that his prediction was going to be fulfilled in a few days; (b) it is not certain that the evangelists would have found it odd to have Jesus' prediction that something would happen relatively soon fulfilled 'after six days'. It is possible that whoever first brought together the saying of Mk 9.1 and the transfiguration included the specific note of time 'after six days' in order to make it clear that the transfiguration was the coming of the kingdom which Jesus said would happen before too long.[38] (4) In any case the reference to some 'not tasting death' is not primarily a chronological observation in its present context, but is picking up the preceding comments about disciples being called to suffer. France, for example,

36. France, *Divine Government*, p. 71. For this view also see Cranfield, *St Mark*, pp. 287-89; Pesch, *Das Markusevangelium*, 2, p.67; Davies and Allison, *Saint Matthew*, 2, p. 677; Gundry, *Mark*, pp. 457-58; Boobyer, *St Mark and the Transfiguration*, pp. 58-64 links Mk 9.1 with the transfiguration and the parousia.

37. C.K. Barrett, *Jesus and the Gospel Tradition* (London: SPCK, 1967), p. 85; Anderson, *The Gospel of Mark*, p. 221; G.R. Beasley-Murray, *Jesus and the Future* (London: Macmillan, 1954), p. 185.

38. Wenham and Moses, '"There Are Some Standing here...": Did they Become the "Reputed Pillars" of the Jerusalem Church? Some Reflections on Mark 9.1, Galatians 2.9 and the Transfiguration', *NovT* 36, 2 (1994) pp. 148-51.

argues that the idea of tasting death[39] (rather than 'dying') made emphatic by οὐ μή is the idea of *martyrdom*, picking up the theme of the previous verses which speak of Jesus' death (8.31) and of choosing to follow him, and to take up the cross (8.34-7); it is not just a statement that they will survive for a week.[40]

(c) τῶν ἑστηκότων *(Mk 9.1 and par.) and Peter, James and John as the 'standing ones'*: This interpretation may be supported by three observations: first, there is evidence that the transfiguration helped to elevate Peter (James and John); the participation in this event gave him (and the other two) a special position in the early church. Secondly, Peter, John and James (the Lord's brother) were known as 'pillars' in the early Jerusalem church (Gal. 2.9).[41] How and why they got this title has never been explained. Thirdly, I wish to make the point that one of the main Hebrew/Aramaic words for pillar is עמוד, a word which etymologically means 'standing one' and which is regularly translated in the LXX by στῦλος.[42] Given these three observations, it is possible to go on to argue that the saying of Jesus in Mk 9.1 τινες ὧδε τῶν ἑστηκότων οἵτινες οὐ μὴ γεύσωνται θανάτου ἕως ἂν ἴδωσιν τὴν βασιλείαν τοῦ Θεοῦ ἐληλυθυῖαν ἐν δυνάμει was linked to the transfiguration narrative from an early date, and that this explains how Peter, James and John came to be called the pillars of the church (στῦλοι cf. Gal. 2.9). They were the privileged three who witnessed the transfiguration; they were thus 'the standing ones'—or, by a play on words, 'the pillars'— who did not taste death before witnessing the revelation of the kingdom represented by the transfiguration. If this view is accepted, it would

39. The language of tasting death is unusual, though it has a parallel in Jn 8.52; Heb. 2.9 (both passages possibly deriving the usage from the synoptic verse; cf. *4 Ezra* 6.26). It is slightly reminiscent of Jesus' use of the 'cup' imagery to refer to his death (cf. Mk 10.39; 14.36), and the association of ideas may confirm that in Mk 9.1 and parallels, the thought is of martyrdom and the cross rather than just of natural death. On this see Wenham and Moses, '"There Are Some Standing here…"', p. 150 n. 7.

40. France, *Divine Government*, pp. 71-72, also see Cranfield, *St Mark*, p. 287, and 'Thoughts on New Testament Eschatology', *SJT* 35 (1982) pp. 503-504.

41. F.F. Bruce, *The Epistle of Paul to the Galatians* (Exeter: Paternoster Press, 1982), p. 123 suggests that Peter, John and James constituted the original Jerusalem στῦλοι (Gal. 2.9) and after the latter's execution, James the Lord's brother took his place. On this see Wenham and Moses, '"There Are Some Standing here…"', pp. 153-55.

42. Wenham and Moses, '"There Are Some Standing here…"', pp. 155-62.

(1) confirm the view that Mk 9.1 has primary reference to the transfiguration, and (2) also suggest that Mk 9.1 was not a so called 'floating-*logion*' which Mark placed before the story of the transfiguration, but was already associated with the transfiguration in earlier tradition.

(d) *Mt. 16.28 and Mk 9.1*: Matthew (like Luke) while redacting Mk 9.1, retains the theme of the 'standing ones' (τῶν ὧδε ἑστώτων compare ὧδε τῶν ἑστηκότων); like Mark he probably relates the saying to the event of the transfiguration that follows (thus his retention of Mark's temporal καὶ μεθ' [μετὰ] ἡμέρας ἓξ etc.). But what is important for my argument is that Matthew *alone* speaks of the coming of 'the Son of Man' instead of 'the kingdom coming'. Since ὁ υἱὸς τοῦ ἀνθρώπου has occurred in the previous verse, Matthew's use of the expression here also is probably deliberate and significant. The way that Matthew specifically links the ideas of 'Son of Man and 'kingdom' (ἐρχόμενον ἐν τῇ βασιλείᾳ αὐτοῦ)—contrasts with Mark's τὴν βασιλείαν τοῦ Θεοῦ ἐληλυθυῖαν ἐν δυνάμει (9.1)—is explicable in terms of Dan. 7.13-14.[43] It is also interesting that Matthew has omitted Mark's καὶ ἔλεγεν αὐτοῖς, thereby linking more closely than Mark the saying of 16.28 with the preceding saying about the Son of Man coming in judgment.

Even if Mt. 16.28 is not referring to the transfiguration it is still the case that Matthew has made the framework of the narrative more strongly Danielic than Mark. If it is rightly taken as a reference to the transfiguration, then the transfiguration is explicitly referred to in Matthew as a coming of the Son of Man, that is, in Danielic, apocalyptic terms.

(3) The 'Son of Man' bracket part II: If the transfiguration in Matthew

---

43. France rightly emphasises that the 'kingdom' language here refers to the 'abstract idea of God being king, his sovereignty'; it points to God and is not describing something called 'kingdom'. See R.T. France, 'The Church and the Kingdom of God: Some Hermeneutical Issues', in D.A. Carson (ed.), *Biblical Interpretation and the Church* (Exeter: Paternoster Press, 1984), pp. 30-44; *Divine Government*. For a similar view also see J. Riches, *Jesus and the Transformation of Judaism* (London: Darton, Longman & Todd, 1980), pp. 87-111, who while stressing the themes of love, forgiveness etc., does not adequately address the theme of judgment associated with the kingship idea in the NT (e.g. Mt. 16.27-28; 19.28; 25.31-32). Mt. 16.27-28, however, (as in 13.38-43; 19.28; 25.31-32) speaks of the Son of Man's kingdom, like the 'one like a son of man' in Dan. 7.13-14, Jesus is the representative and mediator of the kingdom of God (see Beasley-Murray, *Jesus and the Kingdom of God*, pp. 221-22).

is preceded by two Danielic Son of Man sayings, it is also followed by two others, 17.9 referring to the resurrection of the Son of Man and 17.12, referring to the 'suffering' Son of Man. The transfiguration is thus enclosed by a Son of Man bracket. Since vv. 9-12 are discussed fully in the next chapter, there is no need to set them out here, but the following points may be made:

The idea of resurrection is not seen in Daniel 7, but there is some evidence of *Matthew* applying Daniel 7 to Jesus' resurrection elsewhere, (a) in Jesus' saying anticipating resurrection (26.64) and (b) in his post-resurrection appearance and exaltation (28.19-20). The latter will be dealt with in Chapter 6. In 26.64 where Jesus' inquisitors are told that 'from now on' they will see the Son of Man coming..., the force of ἀπ' ἄρτι has often been missed. ἀπ' ἄρτι here, as in 23.39; 26.29, signifies a new period *beginning from now*; and it is arguable that this must in context include the immediately forthcoming events, including Jesus' death-resurrection (note also Matthew's distinctive 'saints-resurrection' motif in 27.52-53). Thus it is arguable that *theologically* Matthew has linked the resurrection with Daniel 7.

Another general but contributory argument is that the concept of 'resurrection' is found in Dan. 12.2-3. This Danielic description of resurrection is drawn on in the M passage Mt. 13.41-43, where it is applied to the final vindication of the 'righteous'. This Matthean passage will feature in the next chapter, where I show that it is possible that Matthew has theologically and redactionally linked 13.43 with 17.2 through the identical use of the phrase ὡς ὁ ἥλιος.

So in view of the strong Daniel 7 motifs in 16.28 and 27, and perhaps also in view of Matthew's distinctive description of τὸ ὅραμα (17.9), it is certainly possible that Matthew veiledly alludes to a Danielic Son of Man in 17.9.

(4) The saying that completes the Son of Man double bracket is 17.12, where like Mark (9.12), with certain redactional changes; Matthew portrays Jesus as the 'suffering Son of Man'. The 'Son of Man' here has been taken as referring (a) to Elijah;[44] (b) to the lowly/earthly son of man, similar to בן־אדם in Ezek. 2.1; Dan. 8.17.[45] But M.D. Hooker,[46] has

---

44. See J. Taylor, 'The coming of Elijah, Mt. 17, 10-13 and Mk 9, 11-13. The Development of texts', *RB* (1991), pp. 107-19.

45. On Ezek. 2.1/Mk 9.12 comparison see W.H. Brownlee, *Ezekiel 1–19* (Waco: Word, 1986), p. xli.

46. Hooker, *The Son of Man*, pp. 30-32; also see N.T. Wright, 'Jesus, Israel and

well argued that if כבר־אנש in Dan. 7.13 in a very definite sense represents the קדישי עליונין (v. 18) who suffer (v.21), then here too such an association is possible. Certainly the idea of Jesus' suffering (16.21; 17.22-23), his representative status and his solidarity with the disciples' suffering are well attested (Mt. 5.11/Lk. 6.22; Mt. 16.25 and par). So, again, given (a) Matthew's interest in the Danielic Son of Man,[47] (b) the possible Danielic motifs in the previous verse (17.9), and (c) the rather forceful presence of Daniel 7 motifs in the first Son of Man bracket (16.27; 16.28), the cumulative effect of my arguments suggests that Mt. 17.12 too contributes toward this Danielic framework within which Matthew has portrayed his account of the transfiguration.

So Mt. 17.1-8 is sandwiched between two 'Son of Man' double brackets (16.27/16.28 and 17.9/19.12), which in *Matthew* suggest a Daniel 7 significance. At first sight, *Matthew's* Son of Man double bracket I (16.27; 16.28; for the Son of Man reference is absent in Mk 9.1 and Lk. 9.27) seems more strongly Danielic than his 'Son of Man' double bracket II (17.9; 17.12; found in Mark but heightened in Matthew). But in the context of my cumulative argument all four sayings are probably to be seen against a background of Daniel 7. In this argument, *16.28 with its distinct Matthean redaction and insertion bringing out the Danielic Son of Man/kingdom theme* is of particular importance; significantly it is the immediate context of the transfiguration.

A Comparison of Daniel 7.13-18 and Matthew 17.1-13
The Son of Man *inclusio* in Mt. 16.27; 16.28—17.1-8—17.9; 17.12 taken by itself may be represented by the following outline:

> 16.27 The Son of Man coming for deliverance and judgment
> > 16.28 The Son of Man coming in his kingdom
> > > 17.1-8 The transfiguration (The glory of the Son of Man)
> > 17.9 The Son of Man and the resurrection
> 17.12 The suffering Son of Man

the Cross', in K.H. Richards (ed.), *SBL 1985 Seminar Papers* (Atlanta: Scholars Press, 1985), pp. 75-95, esp. pp. 84-85; C.F.D. Moule, 'Neglected Features in the Problem of 'the Son of Man'', in *Essays in New Testament Interpretation* (Cambridge: Cambridge University Press, 1982), pp. 76-77.

47. On this see France, *Matthew—Evangelist*, pp. 288-92, 312-17; M. Pamment, 'The Son of Man in the First Gospel', *NTS* 29 (1983) pp. 116-29; Orton, *The Understanding Scribe*, pp. 140-51, 171-72.

In addition to this, the form, structure and themes of Mt. 17.1-13 when compared with the structure of Dan. 7.13-18 (also vv.19-28) may be represented by the following tabulation.

Dan. 7.13-18 (19-28)   Mt. 17.1-13

Structure and arrangement of tradition:

(1) *The vision*:

The vision (ἐν ὁράματι 7.13) of the ὡς υἱὸς ἀνθρώπου	The vision (τὸ ὅραμα 17.9) of ὁ υἱὸς τοῦ ἀνθρώπου (Mt. 16.27, 28) who is also Son of God (17.5) at the transfiguration

Corresponding motifs:

(a) ὡς υἱὸς ἀνθρώπου	(a) ὁ υἱός μου (Jesus)
(b) τῶν νεφελῶν (7.13)	(b) νεφέλη φωτεινὴ (17.5)
(c) use of ἰδού frequently linked with theophany/angelophany (Gen. 18.2; Ezek. 1.4 etc.)	(c) καὶ ἰδού...Μωυσῆς καὶ Ἡλίας (v.3); ἰδοὺ νεφέλη (v. 5a); καὶ ἰδοὺ φωνὴ (v. 5b)
(d) 'Ancient of Days'	(d) Voice: implies God, the Father (cf. use of μου, v. 5)
(e) audience: heavenly implied (7.13, cf. v. 10)	(e) heavenly: Moses and Elijah, earthly: three disciples.
(f) giving of dominion, power,	(f) Jesus' authority confirmed by heavenly voice: ἀκούετε αὐτοῦ 'Sonship' motif, etc., also anticipates 28.18.

(2) *The discussion of the meaning of the vision in response to a question by the seer*:

(a) Daniel asks for help in interpreting 'vision' (7.16-17)	(a) Disciples ask help in interpreting the Elijah issue prompted by his appearance in the 'vision' (17.3) and the scribal teaching about Elijah associated with the idea of the resurrection
(b) Daniel 'kept the matter in his heart' (7.28)	(b) Silence motif, but 'until' the resurrection (17.9)

This tabulation shows the broad similarity in 'vision-form' and perhaps also in a certain amount of 'content' between Mt. 17.1-9, 10-13 and Dan. 7.13-14, 15-28. It is not a rigid one to one parallelism, but in view of Matthew's creative use of Old Testament parallels (cf. 1.13-23) and of his interest in Daniel 7 motifs (13.41; 16.27; 16.28; 19.28; 24.30; 25.31;

26.64; 28.18), it may be that Matthew has been influenced by the 'vision-form' of Daniel 7 as well as by its content. No other place gave him so much scope for utilising the 'vision-form' and 'content' of Daniel 7, as the transfiguration, where he presents Jesus the Son of Man (esp. 16.27; 16.28) who is also the Son of God (17.5) in whom the 'coming of God' has taken place (also cf. 1.23; 3.3-4), and also will take place (16.27; 28; 24.30; 25.31; 26.64).

In any case, the general sweep of Danielic themes is apparent in Mt. 17.1-9: note also the 17.2/13.43/Dan. 12.2-3 parallelism. Before I draw further conclusions from this comparison and in particular from the amalgamation of Sinai and Danielic motifs, my case is further strengthened by noting other thematic parallels with 'vision' passages in the book of Daniel.

Other Thematic Parallels

(1) In the Dan. 7.9 'throne vision' the 'raiment' of the 'Ancient of Days' was λευκὸν ὡσεὶ χιών. This analogy may be compared with Matthew's τὰ δὲ ἱμάτια αὐτοῦ ἐγένετο λευκὰ ὡς τὸ φῶς (17.2) contrasting with Mark's mundane comparison καὶ τὰ ἱμάτια αὐτοῦ ἐγένετο στίλβοντα λευκὰ λίαν, οἷα γναφεὺς ἐπὶ τῆς γῆς οὐ δύναται οὕτως λευκᾶναι (9.3). (2) Matthew alone has the disciples falling on their faces ἔπεσαν ἐπὶ πρόσωπον αὐτῶν 17.6. This may be compared with Dan. 8.17 (also cf. Ezek. 1.28; Rev. 1.17) where Daniel on seeing a 'vision' (τὴν ὅρασιν) of the 'appearance of a man' (ὡς ὅρασις ἀνδρός) and on 'hearing the voice of a man' (ἤκουσα compare the 'voice' in Mt. 17.5) 'fell upon his face' (καὶ πίπτω ἐπὶ πρόσωπόν μου also v.18).[48] (3) Matthew alone records Jesus 'touching' and encouraging them καὶ προσῆλθεν ὁ Ἰησοῦς καὶ ἁψάμενος αὐτῶν εἶπεν· ἐγέρθητε καὶ μὴ φοβεῖσθε. This compares well with Dan. 8.17-18, where (a) Gabriel speaks to Daniel εἶπε πρὸς μὲ, σύνες

48. Certain other 'call-visions' display similar motifs: see Isa. 6.7; Acts 9.4; 22.7; 26.4. In view of my arguments (Son of Man *inclusio* etc.) it is in another 'apocalypse', (Apocalypse of John) that we see a comparable 'vision-form': for John (1) has a revelation (Ἀποκάλυψις 1.1) and a Christophany (vv. 12-16); (2) hears a voice, 1.12, (3) falls down as though dead 1.17; (4) is 'touched' by Christ (1.17); and (5) receives encouragement. For comparison between Mt. 17.2-8 and Dan. 10.5-21 see M. Sabbé, 'La rédaction du récit de la Transfiguration', pp. 66-67. Nützel, *Die Verklärungserzählung*, pp. 282-86 questions whether Sabbé's Matthean apocalyptic structure is the most original form. Mine is an independent study of these Danielic motifs.

υἱὲ ἀνθρώπου, (b) and in v.18 there is the motif of 'touch' and 'encouragement' καὶ ἥψατό μου, καὶ ἔστησέ με ἐπὶ πόδας (4) A comparison of lesser value perhaps is that both Mt. 17.9 and Dan. 8.19 share a silence motif until events come to pass. In Mt. 17.9 it is conditioned by the resurrection and in Dan. 8.19 what Daniel is shown was to come to pass in the 'eschaton' ἐπ' ἐσχάτων τῆς ὀργῆς and the 'vision' (ἡ ὅρασις) was for a yet-to-be-appointed time.

A similar sequence is also found in Dan. 10.6-21, for (1) Daniel sees a vision of a 'man clothed in linen' whose 'face was the appearance of lightning' καὶ τὸ πρόσωπον αὐτοῦ ὡς ἡ ὅρασις ἀστραπῆς (v. 6, to be compared with καὶ ἔλαμψεν τὸ πρόσωπον αὐτοῦ ὡς ὁ ἥλιος of Mt. 17.2, also εἶδος τοῦ προσώπου αὐτοῦ ἕτερον of Lk. 9.29, note ἐξαστράπτων of raiment v. 29b). (2) He hears a voice, ἤκουσα τὴν φωνὴν (Dan. 10.9, to be compared with φωνὴ...ἀκούσαντες of Mt. 17.5, 6). (3) He falls with his face to the earth καὶ τὸ πρόσωπόν μου ἐπὶ τὴν γῆν (Dan. 10.9, compare ἔπεσαν ἐπὶ πρόσωπον αὐτῶν Mt. 17.6). (4) In 10.10 Daniel is 'touched' ἁπτομένη which may be compared with ἁψάμενος (Mt. 17.7). (5) Here significantly, the command μὴ φοβοῦ Δανιήλ 10.12, (also v. 19) may be compared with Jesus' command μὴ φοβεῖσθε of Mt. 17.7. (6) The idea of lifting up one's eyes and beholding καὶ ἦρα τοὺς ὀφθαλμούς μου of Dan. 10.5 too may be compared with ἐπάραντες δὲ τοὺς ὀφθαλμοὺς of Mt. 17.8. (7) Finally, just as Jesus 'approaches', 'touches' and 'said' (εἶπεν) in Mt. 17.7, so in Dan. 10.10-11, the hand of the 'man' 'touches', 'raises' and 'says' (καὶ εἶπε v.11).

Some of these ideas may be commonplace in Jewish apocalyptic visions. But given Matthew's interest in the Danielic motifs—especially as I have shown in reference to the transfiguration pericope—the cumulative thrust of these Danielic parallels is strong.

So my tabulation has shown similarity in 'vision-form' between Mt. 17.1-9, 10-13 and Dan. 7.13-14, 15-28. There is also a certain amount of thematic overlap with other Danielic visions. The use of ὅραμα in Dan. 7.13 and Mt. 17.9 too is interesting. There seems to be a good deal of overlap in form, themes, and also terminology which encourages comparison between Daniel 7 and Matthew 17.

This conclusion should not, however, lead us to minimise the importance of the Sinai background of the transfiguration. A conspicuous absence in Dan. 7.13 is any reference to the radiance of the 'one like a son of man' or to his face. This motif does appear in Enochic material, but particularly in Exodus 34. The appearance of Moses and Elijah who among other things are associated with Horeb/Sinai (Exod. 19–20; 1 Kings 19) perhaps heightens the Exodus 34 significance. Moreover, we have already noted that τὸ ὅραμα in Exod. 3.3 (LXX) denotes Moses' 'vision' at the Horeb/Sinai (burning bush) event: εἶπε δὲ Μωυσῆς, παρελθὼν ὄψομαι τὸ ὅραμα τὸ μέγα τοῦτο. Significantly, this is identical to Stephen's description of the Horeb/Sinai event: ὁ δὲ Μωυσῆς ἰδὼν ἐθαύμαζεν τὸ ὅραμα (Acts 7.31).

It would be hazardous to build much on the one word ὅραμα, but given the setting of the transfiguration, and Matthew's emphasis on Jesus' radiant face, it seems quite likely that Matthew has amalgamated both Daniel 7 categories and Moses-Sinai motifs. For this blending of Mosaic and Danielic motifs, Matthew has a precedent in Ezekiel the Tragedian, pp. 68-82.

So my argument here is that Sinai and Daniel 7 constitute the basic framework within which Matthew has presented his account of the transfiguration. Some further comments on the Sinai motif in relation to Daniel 7 are in order.

4. *The Sinai-Daniel 7 Conceptual Setting: The Relationship between Matthew's Presentation of the 'Coming of the Son of Man' (16.27-28), the 'Coming of God' at Sinai, Daniel 7 and Matthew 17.1-13*

The 'Coming of God' and Sinai

There is no event in the history of the Jewish people that so clearly demonstrated the 'coming of God' as the theophany at Mount Sinai (Exod. 19-20), which Josephus called παρουσίαν τοῦ Ωεοῦ (*Ant.* 3.80). In the previous chapter we have seen that this concept of God coming at Sinai is in various ways also stressed by Philo *Quaest. in Exod.* 2.44; *Memar Marqah* 1.1-2, 4.3, Sir. 44.23-45.5; Ps.-Philo 11.5; 15.5-6, *Jub.* 1.1-2, 2 *Bar.* 59.4-12 and in rabbinic literature.

Israel experienced the 'coming of God' in judgment/deliverance (Exod. 7.14-12.42), in Yahweh's personal protection (13.17-22), in deliverance through the sea (14.1-15.21) and other ways. But it was at Sinai (Exod. 19.1-25, as previously to Moses at Horeb in Exod. 3) that God 'descended' (καταβήσεται v.11) before all the people. For God had 'descended' (καταβεβηκέναι) upon Sinai in fire (ἐπ᾽ αὐτὸ τὸν Θεὸν ἐν πυρί v. 18, also see v. 20 κατέβη δὲ Κύριος ἐπὶ τὸ ὄρος τὸ Σινὰ). Hence for Israel, the 'coming of God' par excellence, was at Sinai.

The Programmatic Influence of the Sinai 'Coming of God' Motif
In view of this, R.E. Clements, R.J. Clifford and recently G.R. Beasley-Murray have shown that the 'coming of God' concept in Jewish literature is inextricably linked to the Sinai theophany in Exodus 19–20, (see Judg. 5.4-5; Ps. 68.7-8, 17-18; Isa. 64; Hab. 3.1-15; Ezek. 40–48).[49] So much so that Sinai motifs are taken up by writers like Ezekiel and the Psalmist into the formulation of Zion traditions.[50] The same is true of Daniel for, as D.C.T. Sheriffs has shown, Daniel 9 is a good example of a combination of Exodus-Sinai and Jerusalem Temple (Zion) traditions.[51] Moreover, the fact that the Sinai tradition was faithfully remembered and re-enacted in Israel's covenant renewal celebrations (e.g. at Qumran) and in pilgrimages to Sinai (Deut. 1.2; 1 Kgs 19.7-18)[52] shows that, even though Israel had come to Canaan, then to Jerusalem and Zion, the idea of God's presence was both cultic in its expression and was rooted in a historical tradition of the founding of the covenant at Sinai. As R.E. Clements, *God and Temple*, has well stated:

> Yahweh's revelation in the past became the pattern and promise of his revelation in the present, so that his presence with Israel was an inseparable feature of the covenant faith. Yahweh was the God of Mount Sinai, but he was also the Holy One in the midst of Israel (p. 22).

It is this 'coming of God' par excellence *from* Mount Sinai that is clearly echoed in passages such as Judg. 5.4-5; Ps. 68.7-8; 17-18; Isa. 64; Hab. 3.1-15.[53] In such passages it is the 'coming of God' at Sinai which acts

49. Beasley-Murray, *Jesus and the Kingdom of God*, pp. 3-10; R.E. Clements, *God and Temple* (Oxford: Basil Blackwell, 1965), pp. 17-18; *Old Testament Theology* (London: Marshall, Morgan & Scott, 1978), pp. 82-83; R.J. Clifford, *The Cosmic Mountain in Canaan and the Old Testament* (Cambridge, MA: Harvard University Press, 1972), pp. 107-108; T.B. Dozeman, *God on the Mountain* (Atlanta: Scholars Press, 1989).

50. See D. Levenson, *Theology of the Program of Restoration of Ezekiel 40–48*, (Missoula: Scholars Press, 1976), pp. 7-44; J.M. Roberts, 'Zion in the Theology of Davidic-Solomonic Empire' in T. Ishida, Yamakawa-Shuppansha (ed.), *Studies in the Period of David and Solomon and other Essays* (Tokyo, 1982), pp. 93-108.

51. See D.C.T. Sheriffs, '"A tale of two cities"—Nationalism in Zion and Babylon', *TynBul* 39 (1988), pp. 19-57, esp. p.42.

52. These pilgrimages seem to have dropped off when Israel came to Canaan, Clements, *God and Temple*, p.21. But Elijah returns to Sinai (1 Kings 19.7-18) suggesting Sinai's continuing importance even though 'Zion' was established at Jerusalem since David's time.

53. 'Exodus-deliverance/sea traditions' are echoed in Ps. 77.16; Isa. 51.9-10.

as a model for the expression of the 'coming of God'; and Sinai-related themes recur: revelation, covenant-Israel (and hence kingdom cf. Exod. 15.18; Deut. 33.1-5), deliverance/vindication (of Moses Exod. 19.9; 34.29-35), and judgment (Exod. 19.5, 21).[54]

Sinai and Daniel 7

It is significant that similar motifs, especially of judgment and vindication, are clearly seen in the vision-theophanies in Daniel. This is highly relevant to my thesis, since Matthew, as I have shown, has presented the transfiguration within a Moses-Sinai and Danielic framework.

(a) *The coming of God motif*: Just as Sinai is portrayed as 'God's coming' (ירד MT, καταβαίνω Exod. 19.11, 18, 20 LXX) so in Dan. 7.21-22, the oppression of the tyrant continued 'until the Ancient of Days came' (ἦλθεν LXX) and in these verses, God 'comes' that he may give 'judgment' and 'the kingdom' to the saints.[55]

Beasley-Murray, following J. Jeremias and others, has stressed that even though biblical traditions (e.g. 'Rahab the dragon' in Isa. 51.9-10) reflect such a borrowing of language (also see G.B. Caird, *Language and Imagery of the Bible* [London: Duckworth, 2nd edn, 1988]) they are more indebted to the Exodus-Sinai traditions than Babylonian theophanies.

54. Another motif that arises from the Sinai tradition is the 'vindication of Moses': For example (1) in 19.9 Yahweh was coming (ἰδού ἐγὼ παραγίνομαι LXX) specifically to or for the sake of Moses (πρὸς σέ), that the people 'may believe in Moses for ever'. So in 19.9 the 'coming of God' was to legitimise Moses' position among Israel; so also at the transfiguration 'coming of God' motif legitimises Jesus' role among his (chosen) disciples, the nucleus of the new Israel, the church (Mt. 16.16-19); who are to listen to him ἀκούετε αὐτοῦ (Mt. 17.5)—which compares well with καὶ σοὶ πιστεύσωσιν εἰς τὸν αἰῶνα of Exod. 19.9.

55. There has been a debate among scholars whether the 'coming of the one like a son of man' to the Ancient of Days was an 'ascent' or 'descent' and hence as to its relevance to the 'coming of the Son of Man' passages in the gospels: Mk 8.38 (and par.), 13.26 (and par.); 14.62 (Mt. 26.64); Mt. 16.28. See T.F. Glasson, *The Second Advent* (London: Epworth, 1945), pp. 52-56; 'Theophany and Parousia', *NTS* 34 (1988) p. 261; J.A.T. Robinson, *Jesus and His Coming* (London: SCM Press, 1957), p. 56; for recent discussion see France, *Divine Government*, pp. 76-81; also his earlier work *Jesus and the Old Testament*, pp. 227-39. Interestingly, Goldingay, *Daniel*, pp. 167 has argued that Dan. 7.2-12 seems to imply symbolically that the Ancient of Days is enthroned 'on earth' and this gives the 'one like a son of man' a 'descent' motif. On the other hand, Beasley-Murray, *Jesus and the Kingdom of God*, pp. 28-29 points out that what was depicted in Daniel 7 would mean less if it had no relevance for those on earth. Whatever the case may be, it is not in dispute that the one like a son of man came to (or was brought to) the Ancient of Days, and this 'coming

(b) *The kingdom motif.* Another significant motif shared by both the book of Daniel and Sinai, and one that is important to Matthew's theology (with particular reference to 17.1-8), is the concept of the kingdom of God. It is very clear that God's kingship/the kingdom of God is a dominant theme in Daniel (2.44; 4.17, 25-26, 34-35, 37; 5.21-23; 7.9-10, 14, 22, 27), and the fact that this is set against the 'earthly' kings and kingdoms, makes it all the more prominent. This kingship of God and the idea that Israel, the covenant-nation, was the 'earthly' constituent of God's reign and so God's kingdom (earthly) is also precisely what is demonstrated at Sinai. For example, in the 'sea tradition' of the 'song of Moses' in Exodus 15, Moses and Israel celebrate Yahweh's deliverance through the (Red) sea. In vv. 17-18, the redactor, who has probably taken up Sinai traditions into Zion traditions, affirms this Yahweh-kingdom concept by the phrase: 'The Lord will reign for ever and ever'. In addition, the 'Blessing of Moses' in Deut. 33.1-2, while stating that 'The Lord came from Sinai...', in v.5 speaks of his kingship over Israel: 'Thus the Lord became king in Jeshurun'; i.e., Israel (32.15; 33.26).

Commenting on these passages, P.C. Craigie, *The Book of Deuteronomy*,[56] has rightly pointed out that the kingship of God in early Israel rests on three basic premises: (1) the liberation of his people in the Exodus (e.g. Exod. 15.18); (2) the giving of the law at Sinai (Deut. 33.4); (3) the victory (which in Deut. 33 is still in the future) by which God would grant to his people the promised land (p. 394). Craigie continues:

> That unique event, emerging from the Exodus and the forming of the covenant at Sinai, was the formation of the kingdom of God in the nascent, theocratic state of Israel, in which the Lord was king (Exod. 15.18; Deut. 33.5) (p. 406).

It is in the founding of this earthly 'kingdom of God' that Moses played so important a part. Hence the 'kingdom' motif in Daniel 7 is a parallel to that of Sinai; as seen by Ezekiel the Tragedian, who has combined Sinai, Daniel 7, and Ezekiel motifs and applied them to Moses: 'On Sinai's peak I saw what seemed a throne...' (Ezek. Trag. 68).

---

to' theme parallels a similar idea found at the transfiguration where Jesus (the Son of Man, Mt. 16.27, 28; 17.9, 12) went up the mountain to meet with God (his Father implied by the 'son' theme in 17.5).

56. P.C. Craigie, *The Book of Deuteronomy* (Grand Rapids: Eerdmans, 1976).

The 'Coming of God' at Sinai and the 'Coming of the Son of Man'
Passages in Matthew
In order to relate what I have been saying to Matthew's transfiguration narrative, I need now to demonstrate that the 'coming of the Son of Man' concept in Matthew too is influenced by the 'coming of God' concept and language of the Sinai event. For I am convinced this has direct bearing on Matthew's presentation of the transfiguration, especially in view of (1) Matthew's Son of Man *inclusio* (especially note 16.28 ἐρχόμενον ἐν τῇ βασιλείᾳ αὐτοῦ), (2) the kingdom-glory concept and (3) the Moses-Sinai, Danielic motifs in Mt. 17.1-9. Certain of these motifs are reflected also in other passages in Matthew and contribute to Matthew's theology of the transfiguration.

In the passages to be considered Daniel 7 is perhaps more obvious than Exodus-Sinai themes, but the following arguments are worth noting. In Mt. 24.30-31 for example, several features of the passage echo both Daniel 7 and Sinai motifs: (1) the coming (ἐρχόμενον) on the clouds (v. 30, compare Dan. 7.13) is to be compared with Exod. 19.16; and especially 34.5 where καὶ κατέβη Κύριος ἐν νεφέλῃ is to be set in the context of God's 'coming' *for* Israel on earth. (2) The theme of 'glory' (Mt. 24.30; cf. 16.27; 25.31) parallels Exod. 33.19-23 and Dan. 7.14. (3) Perhaps less plausibly, the 'loud trumpet' (σάλπιγγος μεγάλης), which is normally associated with the gathering of the exiles in Isa. 27.13; 11.12; 49.22, may be linked to Exod. 19.16, 19, (φωνὴ τῆς σάλπιγγος ἤχει μέγα LXX) where Israel is 'gathered' at Sinai (19.10, 14).[57]

---

57. I suggest that a similar line of argument is also applicable to 2 Thess. 2.1-12; Rev. 4-5. That Danielic themes seen in the Olivet discourse are also seen in 2 Thess. 2.1-12 (which explains 1 Thess. 4.13-18) has been argued by D. Ford, *The Abomination of Desolation in Biblical Eschatology* (Lanham, MD: University Press of America, 1979), pp. 193-40; and D. Wenham, *The Rediscovery of Jesus' Eschatological Discourse* (Sheffield: JSOT Press, 1984). But the theme of the Lord 'descending' from heaven (καταβήσεται 1 Thess. 4.16, compare Exod. 19.18 LXX); and the 'trumpets' (σάλπιγγι Θεοῦ 1 Thess. 4.16, compare Exod. 19.16, 19 also use of φωναὶ Exod. 19.19 with 1 Thess. 4.16) may be said to evoke Sinai-type themes. For Danielic motifs in Revelation 4–5 see Brownlee, *Ezekiel 1–19*, pp. xli-xlii; G.K. Beale, 'The Use of Daniel in the Synoptic Eschatological Discourse and in the Book of Daniel', in D. Wenham (ed.), *Gospel Perspectives* (6 vols.; Sheffield, JSOT Press, 1984), V, pp. 129-53; L. Hartman, *Prophecy Interpreted: The Formation of Some Jewish Apocalyptic Texts and of the Eschatological Discourse Mark 13 Par.* (Lund: Gleerup, 1966), p. 174. This blending of Daniel 7 and Sinai

It is true that in these examples, the Daniel 7 themes are stronger than Exodus-Sinai themes. But there is evidence in the Old Testament and in certain Jewish literature that the 'coming of God' at the end time was associated with Sinai. T.F. Glasson, referring to the 'coming of God' themes in Mic. 1.3 'the Lord comes forth out of his place, and will come down (καταβήσεται LXX)'; Ps. 96.13 'He comes to judge the earth', and other passages, points out that

> These divine comings of the future reflect the theophany at Sinai, and the conviction grew that as the Lord had come down at the beginning of Israel's history, so he would come down at the end.[58]

Moreover, we have seen that according to *Liv. Proph.* 2.14-15, Sinai will feature at the resurrection. And so in view of these arguments, the link between both Daniel 7 and Sinai themes in the 'coming of God' (through the coming of the Son of Man) in Mt. 24.30-31 is plausible.

Sinai-Daniel 7 and Matthew 17.1-9

So I suggest that it is with a similar Sinai-Daniel 7 background that we need to evaluate the 'coming of God' theme in Matthew's presentation of the transfiguration. In the table which follows shortly I shall more comprehensively set out the parallels between Sinai, Daniel 7, and Mt. 17.1-8 (also Ezek. Trag. 66-82), but here I shall make some general points:

(1) As Moses along with his chosen companions went up Sinai to meet with God, so at the transfiguration Jesus goes up the mountain. (2) In addition, just as a 'one like a son of man' went up to the Ancient of Days (Dan. 7.13), Matthew views Jesus' ascent as a proleptic enthronement. (3) Moses' ascent at Mount Sinai resulted in his receiving the law for Israel at the foot of the mountain, and the coming of the 'one like a son of man' to the Ancient of Days to receive dominion and glory, was as representative of the 'saints' and hence ultimately for the execution of this authority on earth. Similarly Jesus' transfiguration was to have significance for 'his community', and especially the nucleus of the new Israel constituted by his chosen companions, Peter, James and John, who

themes is perhaps supported by the fact that in Jewish tradition Sinai motifs were to reappear at the end of days (see *2 Bar.* 59.3).

58. See Glasson, 'Theophany and Parousia', pp. 259-70; G.R. Beasley-Murray, 'Resurrection and Parousia of the Son of Man', *TynBul* 42.2 (1991), pp. 298-309; R.J. Bauckham, *Jude and the Relatives of Jesus in the Early Church* (Edinburgh: T. & T. Clark, 1992), pp. 288-89.

probably became the pillars of his community, the church. Furthermore, (4) I wish to suggest that just as when Moses came down from the mountain he confronted Israel's apostasy (Exod. 32), and just as the enthronement of the one like a son of man (Dan. 7.13-14) needs to be set in the context of the authority of the 'beasts', so on Jesus' descent from the 'high mountain' he confronts unbelief (Mt. 17.17; Mk 9.19; Lk. 9.41, the condemnation of which echoes of Deut. 32.5, 20), and he confronts τὸ δαιμόνιον (Mt. 17.18; τῷ πνεύματι τῷ ἀκαθάρτῳ Mk 9.25; Lk. 9.42) which makes for a parallel with the 'beasts' in Daniel 7.[59]

The following table will help to show this parallelism more clearly:

Sinai—Daniel 7—Matthew 17.1-8

Sinai	*Daniel 7*	*Mt. 17.1-8*
εἰς τὸ ὅρος τοῦ	The 'one like a son of man'	εἰς ὅρος ὑψηλόν (17.1).
Θεοῦ (Exod. 19.3, 14, 11, 12, 14). Moses going up (ἀνέβη) the 'mount of God'; in 24.9 (ἀνέβη) with his three chosen companions	coming to the 'Ancient of Days' ὡς υἱὸς ἀνθρώπου ἐρχόμενος Dan. 7.13 LXX	Jesus with his three chosen companions (ἀναφέρει Mt. 17.1)
The 'coming of God' (διὰ τὸ καταβεβηκέναι ἐπ' αὐτὸ τὸν Θεὸν ἐν πυρί 19.18-19)	Dan. 7.9-10, 13 The Ancient of Days enthroned, 'thrones were set' (Dan. 7.9-12)	μετεμορφώθη by divine encounter demonstrated by the presence and 'coming of God' in the 'bright cloud' and the 'voice out of the cloud' (17.5)
Μωυσῆς μόνος πρὸς τὸν Θεὸν (Exod. 24.2) in 34.29-30 Moses was transfigured' δεδόξασται LXX	Dan. 7.13 focus on 'one like a son of man' ὡς υἱὸς ἀνθρώπου כבר אנש	Jesus alone μετεμορφώθη, hence main focus, see also Ἰησοῦν μόνον (17.8)

59. C.C. Caragounis, *The Son of Man: Vision and Interpretation* (Tübingen: Mohr, 1986), p. 243, argues that as in Daniel 7, the Son of Man and the Kingdom of God are linked in Jesus' teaching, and as in Daniel 7 (with respect to the one like a son of man) Jesus challenges the kingdom of the beasts, seen in his fight against the powers of darkness.

Moses' office legitimised (19.9) covenant made, law given. God's earthly kingdom among nations, tongues instituted through Moses (Exod. 15.18/Deut. 33.5)	'one like a son of man' given dominion, glory, kingdom, all peoples to serve him.	Son of God's (17.5b) mission, ministry confirmed by God's voice ἀκούετε αὐτοῦ (cf. 7.24-27; 11.28-30; 28.18-20).
Audience: The heavenly hosts (Deut. 33.2)/Moses and Joshua/Israel at the base of Mount Sinai	The heavenly hosts 7.10, court v.11. The 'saints'—Israel represented by 'one like a son of man' vv. 18, 22, 27	The heavenly visitors are Moses and Elijah. Peter, James and John are representatives of 'new Israel' (16.17-20) with the rest of 'the twelve' at the base of the mountain
Response: Exod. 34.8 καὶ σπεύσας Μωυσῆς, κύψας ἐπὶ τὴν γῆν προσεκύνησε	In 7.28 Daniel's thoughts greatly alarmed, καὶ ἡ μορφή μου ἠλλοιώθη. In 8.18, he falls to the ground, is touched, is raised, in 10.12 μὴ φοβοῦ Δανιὴλ	Mt. 17.6 disciples ἔπεσαν ἐπὶ πρόσ-ωπον, ἐφοβήθησαν σφόδρα, Jesus προσῆλθεν, ἁψάμενος, says μὴ φοβεῖσθε
Descent: from the mountain κατέβη Exod. 19.14, κατέβαινε 34.29 for ministry for and within Israel	The symbolism 'the one like a son of man' brought to God on the throne signifies him representing the saints, hence its ultimate relevance on earth (7.22, in association with 'coming' ἦλθεν ὁ παλαιὸς ἡμερῶν)	καὶ καταβαινόντων αὐτῶν ἐκ τοῦ ὄρους (Mt. 17.9). Immediately followed by ministry, where 17.17 echoes Deut. 32.5, 20. Even within his disciples, the unbelief of γενεὰ (cf. 12.38-45) is seen. Jesus' confrontation with τὸ δαιμόνιον in 17.14-21 makes for an interesting parallel with the beast in Daniel 7
Moses meets unbelief (through the golden calf incident Exod. 32) at the base of Sinai		

Apart from these parallels, other thematic parallels (some further emphasising those tabulated above) may be cited:

1. *The 'Coming of God'*

Exodus 19–35: 'God-cloud-rider' (19.16-17; 24.15-18)	Dan. 7.9-10, 13-14 (7.13)	Mt. 17.5, and transfiguration in v. 2 due to God's act. (note νεφέλη φωτεινὴ v. 5) and God's voice attesting his visitation and 'coming'

2. *The Kingdom of God*

Exod. 19.5-6 'all the earth is mine, you shall be to me βασίλειον ἱεράτευμα καὶ ἔθνος ἅγιον'	ἐδόθη...ἡ βασιλεία. to 'one like a son of man' (7.14)	In part, 17.1-8 to be viewed in context of 16.28 τὸν υἱὸν τοῦ ἀνθρώπου ἐρχόμενον ἐν τῇ βασιλείᾳ αὐτοῦ. Also Son of Man framework[60]

3. *The Glory of God*

כבוד MT, δόξα LXX Exod. 24.16-18; 33.18, 22; (40.34)	קר׳, ἡ τιμὴ (Dan. 7.14)	μετεμορφώθη... ἔλαμψεν...ὡς ὁ ἥλιος...ἱμάτια... λευκὰ ὡς τὸ φῶς (v. 5)

4. *'Coming of God' for Judgment and Vindication*

Exod. 19.5 'if you keep my covenant...'	Judgment on kingdoms, 7.26	ἀκούετε αὐτου Mt. 17.5 echoes Deut. 18.15-16, which includes judgment on those who do not

---

60. Matthew's kingdom-Son of Man association needs to be set against certain twentieth-century scholarship that denies this: P. Vielhauer, who is rightly challenged by H.E. Tödt, *The Son of Man in the Synoptic Tradition* (London: SCM Press, 1965), pp. 329-47. Also see Caragounis, *The Son of Man*; I.H. Marshall, 'The Hope of a New Age: the Kingdom of God in the New Testament', *Themelios* 11.1 (1985) pp. 5-15; esp. 10-11; Beasley-Murray, *Jesus and the Kingdom of God*, pp. 71-312. The Son of Man-Kingdom (Dan. 7.13-14), and God-Kingdom (Dan. 2.44; 4.3, 17, 25-26, 32, 34; 5.12) are very much Danielic themes, see D. Wenham, 'The Kingdom of God and Daniel' *ExpTim* 98 (1986-87) pp. 132-34; Sheriffs, '"A Tale of Two Cities"', pp. 41-43.

heed: 'I myself will
require it of him.' A
similar motif is
implied in Mt. 8.24-
27; 28.20

5. *Suffering and Vindication of God's Agent and Israel*

Exod. 19.9 (above)	'The 'saints' who enjoy	Mt. 17.9-13, death-
Divine descent	solidarity with 'one like a son	resurrection of Son
that Moses may be	of man' are persecuted (7.21)	of Man. Suffering
vindicated and	but are vindicated. 'One like a	linked to Elijah-John-
'believed for ever',	son of man' represents Israel	Jesus equation. Jesus
Moses representative		embodies 'new Israel'
of Israel		and is the suffering
		Son of Man. The
		disciples share
		suffering (16.24-28)

Conclusions

In the light of this I suggest that Matthew, who is known for his hermeneutical method of combining Old Testament texts and applying them to Jesus, has portrayed the transfiguration within a Moses-Sinai and Danielic framework. We have seen that (1) Matthew by his use of tradition and redaction aligns the transfiguration with the biblical 'vision-form' (Exod. 3.1-4.17, 19–34; Isa. 6.1-13; 1 Kings 22.19), and in particular with the vision-form of biblical and non-biblical apocalyptic literature (Ezekiel 1–2, 43.1-2, Dan 7; 8.18; 10.5-6; *1 En.* 14.20; *T. Abr.* 12, *2 Bar.* 51.10). (2) Matthew's 'Son of Man' *inclusio* resembles a literary technique used by the writer of Daniel 7. (3) Without pressing for rigid form critical comparisons, we have seen that the vision-form and to an extent the content of Mt. 17.1-8, 9-13 resembles the vision-form and content of Dan. 7.13-18. (4) Matthew has amalgamated Daniel 7 and new-Sinai motifs to portray the transfiguration as a sign and prolepsis of the 'coming of God' motif.

I emphasise that I am not suggesting a rigid one-to-one parallelism; Matthew works more freely in his creative use of Old Testament typology (cf. 1.13-23). So I am suggesting that in view of Matthew's interest in Danielic and Moses categories, and at times also in the amalgamation of these motifs (cf. 28.16-20), the proposed Daniel 7, Moses-Sinai framework for Mt. 17.1-9 is quite feasible. Moreover, Matthew's application of these motifs to Jesus' transfiguration is in keeping with his portrayal of the 'coming of the Son of Man' elsewhere in his Gospel. Since, as I shall further show, Matthew portrays the Son of Man as Son of God, and in 1.23 has proclaimed Jesus as Ἐμμανουήλ ὅ ἐστιν μεθερμηνευόμενον μεθ᾽ ἡμῶν ὁ Θεός, to whom in 28.18 (with its Daniel 7 echo) is given πᾶσα ἐξουσία ἐν οὐρανῷ καὶ ἐπὶ γῆς, the 'coming of the Son of Man' is also the coming of God. I am convinced that Matthew views the transfiguration as a prolepsis of the 'coming of the Son of Man' and the 'coming of God', and hence uses the Moses-Sinai-Danielic framework to convey this.

Having argued for a Moses-Sinai, Daniel 7 framework for Matthew's presentation of the transfiguration, I move on to study Matthew's redaction of his tradition. This will substantiate my arguments and also will provide the cue for relating Mt. 17.1-9 to the network of concepts, beliefs, language and theology in the rest of his Gospel.

Chapter 5

AN EXEGESIS OF MATTHEW 17.1-13 IN THE LIGHT OF SOURCE AND REDACTION CRITICAL ISSUES

Comparisons with literary parallels and vision-form considerations in my previous section confirmed that Matthew's presentation of the transfiguration is reminiscent of (1) apocalyptic 'visions' especially those found in the book of Daniel, and (2) the Moses-Sinai theophany. In this section I shall substantiate my earlier findings by detailed exegetical study, taking into account source and redaction critical considerations. (It may be worth saying in advance that the full effect and weight of arguments in this chapter will only be appreciated in the light of chs. 6 and 7 that follow. Chapters 4 to 7 hang together as a cumulative argument).

1. *Matthew 17.1 and Mark 9.2a*

Mt. 17.1 Καὶ μεθ' ἡμέρας ἓξ παραλαμβάνει ὁ 'Ιησοῦς τὸν Πέτρον καὶ 'Ιάκωβον καὶ 'Ιωάννην τὸν ἀδελφὸν αὐτοῦ καὶ ἀναφέρει αὐτοὺς εἰς ὄρος ὑψηλὸν κατ' ἰδίαν.

Mk 9.2a Καὶ μετὰ ἡμέρας ἓξ παραλαμβάνει ὁ 'Ιησοῦς τὸν Πέτρον καὶ τὸν 'Ιάκωβον καὶ τὸν 'Ιωάννην καὶ ἀναφέρει αὐτοὺς εἰς ὄρος ὑψηλὸν κατ' ἰδίαν μόνους.

What does a comparison of Matthew and Mark suggest here?

Καὶ μεθ' ἡμέρας ἓξ: Matthew retains Mark's Καὶ μεθ' ἡμέρας ἓξ (9.2) with μεθ' an insignificant stylistic change. This rare time reference in all three Gospels stresses the continuity of the transfiguration narrative with the preceding pericopes (note Luke's distinctive μετὰ τοὺς λόγους τούτους). A good case can be made for viewing Mt. 16.13-17.13 as a structural unit. U. Luz[1] describes it as a 'christological text', with several

---

1.   U. Luz, 'What Does it Mean, to Understand the Traditions about Jesus and

interconnected themes: note, (1) 'sonship' in 16.16 (Matthew alone) and 17.5, (2) the 'Peter' theme in 16.16-19; 22-23; 17.4-5, (3) the motif of suffering in 16.21, 21-26, 17.12-13 and perhaps in 17.5, if there is an echo there of the Genesis 22 story of the binding of Isaac, (4) the 'Son of Man' 16.13 (Matthew alone), 16.27, 28; 17.9, 12 (the *inclusio*), (5) the resurrection in 16.21 and 17.9. These and other themes form a 'network of ideas' which bind 16.13-17.13 together as a unit.[2]

In view of this large context we can see that, just as Mk 9.1 anticipates 9.2-8, the transfiguration pericope being the *primary* focus of Mk 9.1, so Mt. 16.28 is probably to be related to 17.1-8. This linkage is supported by (1) Matthew's Son of Man *inclusio* (16.27; 28—17.1-8—17.9; 12) bracketing the transfiguration pericope, and (2) the way Matthew (alone) speaks of 'seeing' the 'Son of Man coming in his kingdom' (16.28). It is arguable that the transfiguration was a sign of the kingdom, comparable to Jesus' exorcisms and miracles (e.g. 12.28), but witnessed only by Jesus' three chosen companions.

There is more to be said, however, since in Matthew καὶ μεθ' ἡμέρας ἓξ has probably acquired a deeper meaning. In ch. 2, I suggested that (1) Mark's καὶ μετὰ ἡμέρας ἓξ perhaps reflected his source, in which the time reference had a parallel in Moses' mountain experience in Exod. 24.15-18. Mark, however, was not particularly interested in his source's Moses-Sinai motif, but stressed the Elijah motif (of suffering and the resurrection), hence the order Ἠλίας σὺν Μωυσεῖ. (2) Matthew, however, is very interested in Moses and Sinai motifs; he reinstates the original Moses-Elijah order and further emphasises the Moses typology. It is likely, then, that he sees Mosaic significance in the καὶ μεθ' ἡμέρας ἓξ.

Peter and the Nucleus of New Israel
παραλαμβάνει ὁ Ἰησοῦς τὸν Πέτρον καὶ Ἰάκωβον καὶ Ἰωάννην τὸν ἀδελφὸν αὐτοῦ: The omission of Mark's τὸν before James and John, but retained before Peter (τὸν Πέτρον) may be due to

---

his History, in the Light of the Gospel according to Matthew?', a talk delivered at Oxford on 24 October 1991.

2.   On the importance of giving attention to the network of ideas within a pericope, the intention of the writers, critical use of language, see J. Riches and A. Millar, 'Conceptual Change in the Synoptic Tradition', in A.E. Harvey (ed.), *Alternative Approaches to New Testament Study*, pp. 42-48.

grammatical economy,[3] but in view of Matthew's Peter-emphasis in v. 4, and elsewhere in his gospel,[4] τὸν Πέτρον places the emphasis on Peter, implying: 'the Peter' who has just been mentioned (prominently in 16.16-19, and also 22-23).[5] By this Matthew emphasises Peter's leadership role in the inner circle;[6] he also links the transfiguration (via the Peter motif) back to Peter's confession in 16.13-20, and to Jesus' teaching on his own necessary death and on discipleship, which is initially rejected by Peter (16.22-23). It also anticipates Peter's role in 17.4-5.

Matthew attaches τὸν ἀδελφὸν to Ἰωάννην characteristically (cf. 4.21; 10.2). By introducing John to his community specifically as the brother of the martyred James (Acts 12.2), he may be deliberately distinguishing him from John Mark (who came from Jerusalem) and at the same time distinguishing James from the 'other' James-Joseph in Mt. 27.56 (Mk 15.40), and perhaps from James of Jerusalem (Acts 15.13; Gal. 2.9). The latter theory is most likely if James was the leader of the Jerusalem church at the time.

3.   That τὸν does service for all three names see Davies and Allison, *St Matthew*, II, p. 694.

4.   On this see M.J. Wilkins, *The Concept of Disciple in Matthew's Gospel* (Leiden: Brill, 1988), pp. 173-216; Kilpatrick, *The Origins*, pp. 37-44, 95-96, 138; E. Schweizer, 'Matthew's Church', in G.N. Stanton (ed.), *The Interpretation of Matthew* (Philadelphia: Fortress Press; London: SPCK, 1983), pp. 135-37; G. Bornkamm, 'The Authority to "Bind" and "Loose" in the Church', in G.N. Stanton (ed.), *Interpretation*, pp.93-95; U. Luz, 'The Disciples in the Gospel according to Matthew', in G.N. Stanton (ed.), *Interpretation*, pp.98-99; 102, 108. Peter is not always portrayed in positive light, see 14.31; 19.27, but according to Luz this at times 'redactional blackening of Peter's character' serves Matthew's presentation of Peter as a 'type' of the disciples (see pp. 102, 122, n. 36). On this also see Luz's, article: 'Das Primatwort Matthäus 16.17-19 aus Wirkungsgeschichtlicher Sicht', *NTS* 37 (1991), pp. 415-33, esp. pp. 422-26.

5.   For such use of the article to distinguish a well known person from others see F. Blass, *Grammar of New Testament Greek* (London: Macmillan, 1898), pp.162-63. In Mt. 17.1, some manuscripts (א D Θ *pc* add τὸν before Ἰάκωβον, and some manuscripts in Mark) omit τὸν before Ἰωάννην (cf. K. Aland, *Synopsis Quattuor Evangeliorum* [Stuttgart: Deutsche Bibelgesellschaft, 1976], p. 236 [*SQE*]). But the weightier manuscripts (Mt. 17.1) have τὸν only before Peter, which is conspicuous.

6.   The inner core to the twelve makes a striking parallel to a similar phenomenon among the Qumran Essenes: see, C.S. Mann, 'The Organization and Institutions of the Jerusalem Church in Acts', in J. Munk, *The Acts of the Apostles* (New York: Doubleday, 1967), Appendix IV; Albright and Mann, *Matthew* (New York: Doubleday, 1971), p. 203.

καὶ ἀναφέρει αὐτοὺς εἰς ὄρος ὑψηλὸν κατ' ἰδίαν
Matthew omits Mark's μόνους after κατ' ἰδίαν as redundant, the
more so since he retains it (cf. Mk 9.8) in v. 8 οὐδένα εἶδον εἰ μὴ
αὐτὸν Ἰησοῦν μόνον. He retains Mark's εἰς ὄρος ὑψηλὸν κατ'
ἰδίαν and probably intends an allusion to Sinai (as becomes clear in the
subsequent description of Jesus' radiant face). Moreover, in view of his
Son of Man '*inclusio*', we may see a parallel with Daniel 7 where the
'one like a son of man' comes and 'is brought' to the Ancient of Days
(ἐρχόμενος...προσηνέχθη αὐτῷ LXX v. 13, see tabulation in ch. 4).
As I have shown, this combination of the Moses-Sinai, Daniel 7 themes
has a precedent in the second-century BCE Ezekiel the Tragedian 68–82,
and it is not impossible that Matthew was influenced by this. In any case
the parallel is interesting.[7]

εἰς ὄρος ὑψηλὸν *in the Light of Matthew's Use of Geographical
Motifs*
εἰς ὄρος occurs frequently in Matthew (4.8; 5.1, 14; 8.1; 14.23; 15.29;
our 17.2, 9; 17.20; 18.12; 21.1, 21; 24.3, 16; 26.30; 28.16) meaning
generally 'into the hills'. Only in 17.2 and 4.8 does Matthew speak of
εἰς ὄρος ὑψηλὸν and on both occasions there is a probable allusion to
Moses' mountain. The mountain in 17.2 seems to tower over every
other mountain.[8] Given Matthew's interest in (theological) geography it
is interesting to consider what he had in mind in the ὄρος ὑψηλὸν.[9]

7.   That Matthew was a Galilean Jew, the tax collector from Galilee (Mt. 9.9;
10.3 with Mk 2.14; Lk. 5.27), see France, *Matthew–Evangelist*, pp. 66-69; Gundry,
Matthew, pp. 620-21. On his literary capabilities, see Moule, 'St Matthew's Gospel:
Some Neglected Features', in F.L. Cross (ed.), *Studia Evangelica* II (Berlin:
Akademie-Verlag, 1964) pp. 67-74; E. von Dobschütz, 'Matthew as Rabbi and
Catechist' in G.N. Stanton, *Interpretation*, pp. 19-29; Kilpatrick, *The Origins*,
pp. 137-39. On the influence of Hellenism on Palestine and elsewhere—making it all
the more possible for the writer of the first gospel to be acquainted with Hellenistic
writings—see works of I.H. Marshall, M. Hengel, J. Riches, S. Lieberman,
B.T. Viviano cited in ch. 1, p. 18 n. 17.
8.   Donaldson, *Jesus on the Mountain,* has woven a whole thesis around
Matthew's mountain passages, stressing the importance of Mount Zion. For my
critique of Donaldson's views see ch. 6.6.
9.   ὄρος ὑψηλόν compares well with Ezek. 40.2 where Ezekiel is set on a
'high mountain' καὶ ἔθηκέ με ἐπ' ὄρος ὑψηλὸν σφόδρα (LXX), where he sees
δόξα Θεοῦ Ἰσραήλ (43.1-5). Other parallels may also be seen in Ezekiel's throne
vision (chs. 1–2). E.g. (1) compare the idea of 'vision' ὄρασις (Ezek. 1.4, 5 etc.)
with τὸ ὅραμα (Mt. 17.9); (2) νεφέλη associated with φέγγος κύκλῳ (Ezek. 1.4)

Mount Tabor in Galilee and Mount Hermon have been suggested as possible locations of Jesus' transfiguration. Mount Tabor, however, is a weak candidate being not very high (588 m) and having a settlement on top (Josephus *War* 2.573; 4.54-55, contrast κατ' ἰδίαν). Mount Hermon (2,814 m), immediately north of Caesarea,[10] is a stronger candidate. As R.J. Clifford, J.T. Milik, J. Allegro and G.W.E. Nickelsburg and S. Freyne[11] have shown, Mount Hermon, which already in the Old Testament featured as a place of religious significance (Ps. 29.6; 42.6; 89.12; 133.3), had acquired religious and theological significance in the exilic and post exilic period.

R.J. Clifford has convincingly shown that during the intertestamental period Israel experienced a change in its mountain ideology. It was no longer Mount Zion, but 'only Mount Hermon seems to be the bearer in intertestamental times of ancient tradition of the Holy mountains'.[12] In

with νεφέλη φωτεινή (Mt. 17.5). But it does not prove anything if one finds a parallel to one thing in Ezekiel 1 and another in Ezekiel 40. On the other hand, as we have seen in chs. 4.3 and 4.4, given Matthew's interest in Daniel 7, the influence of the form and content of Daniel 7 on Matthew's presentation of the transfiguration with its Son of Man *inclusio* technique, combined with Moses-Sinai themes, is strong and provides for a more fruitful comparison. On the role of mountains in Jewish eschatology also see Zech. 14.4; Rev. 21.10, and on the link between mountains and thrones see Pss. 2.6; 48.2; Jer. 8.19; *Jub.* 1.27-9; *1 En.* 18.18. ὑψηλός is used of mountains in LXX Gen. 7.19, 20; Isa. 14.13; 28.4 (also see Davies and Allison, *St Matthew*, II, p. 695).

10.   For Mount Hermon/Hermon range theory see P.A. Micklem, *St Matthew* (London: Methuen, 1917), p. 172; A.W. Argyle, *The Gospel According to Matthew* (Cambridge: Cambridge University Press, 1963), p.132; G.B. Caird, *Saint Luke* (Harmondsworth: Penguin, 1963), p. 131; Trites, 'The Transfiguration of Jesus', pp. 72-73. W.A. Liefeld, 'Mark', in *The Expositor's Bible Commentary*, vol. 8 (Grand Rapids: Zondervan, 1984), p.167, n. 27 plausibly suggests Mount Miron (3,926 feet). Certain manuscripts have ὡς χιών in Mk 9.3 which may favour a Hermon hypothesis since the top of Hermon is said to be perpetually covered in snow (cf. A D Φ 22.33.118 *pl* lat sy[s.p] bo[pt] in *SQE*, p. 237), but these are not particularly weighty.

11.   R.J. Clifford, *The Cosmic Mountain in Canaan and the Old Testament* (Cambridge: Harvard University Press, 1972), pp. 187-88; J.T. Milik, 'Le Testament de Lévi en Araméen', *RB* 62 (1955), p. 405, n.2; J. Allegro, *The Dead Sea Scrolls* (Harmondsworth: Penguin, 1956), pp. 142-43; S. Freyne, *Galilee, Jesus and the Gospel* (Dublin: Gill & Macmillan, 1988), pp. 188-89. For recent archaeological findings at this cite attesting religious significance etc., see G.W.E. Nickelsburg, 'Enoch, Levi and Peter: Recipients of Revelation in Upper Galilee', *JBL* 100/4 (1981), pp. 575-600

12.   Clifford, *The Cosmic Mountain*, p. 189.

the Enochic corpus, and in the *Testament of Levi*, with their anti-Jerusalem-priest stance, Mount Hermon features as the polar opposite to Mount Zion in Jerusalem.[13] These arguments cause problems for T.L. Donaldson's hypothesis about the importance of Zion for Matthew. Moreover, Enoch in *1 En.* 13.7-10, and Levi in *T. Levi* 2.3-5, have visions at the 'waters of Dan', at the base of Mount Hermon, the source of the Jordan.

In view of these observations, various scholars have argued for the importance of Mount Hermon and its geographical surroundings particularly in relation to Matthew's account of Peter's confession, and his commission in the 'district of Caesarea Philippi' (Mt. 16.13-14).[14] J.T. Milik,[15] makes an interesting suggestion that the region near Mount Hermon was known for its deep ravines called 'the gates of Hell', and that Jesus' reference to πύλαι ᾅδου in Mt. 16.18 was perhaps evoked by such a setting. Milik's observation makes a 'geographical link' between the place where Peter's confession took place and the general (Hermon range) location of the transfiguration.[16] But besides this, other

13.   Similarly the Qumran covenanters seem to have emanated from among disaffected Jerusalem priests. Interestingly, W.F. Albright and C.S. Mann, *Matthew* (New York: Doubleday, 1971), pp. clxxvii-clxxviii, clxxxiii-clxxxiv, have suggested that Matthew the Levite (Mk 2.14; Lk. 5.27 with Mt. 9.9; 10.3) took to tax-collecting to seek a livelihood and so forfeited the respect of his fellow-Levites with their orthodox Pharisaic background. If some such background is given to Matthew, his emphasis on Galilee, and here Hermon/range as opposite to Jerusalem is possible. But it will remain a hypothesis.

14.   See Milik, 'Le Testament de Lévi', p. 405 n. 2; Allegro, *The Dead Sea Scrolls,* pp. 142-43; K. Stendahl, 'Matthew', in M. Black and H.H. Rowley (eds.), *Peake's Commentary on the Bible* (London: Nelson, 1962), p.787 draws attention to similarity in 'motifs' between *T. Levi.* 2–7 and Mt. 16.17-20. Also see Nickelsburg, 'Enoch, Levi and Peter', pp. 575-600.

15.   Milik, 'Le Testament de Lévi', p. 405. Milik commenting on the fragment of the Aramaic fragment on *T. Levi.* 2.3-5 argues that Mount Hermon had importance for Jewish apocalyptists. Its height contrasted with the deep ravines below communicated heaven and hell. The vision of Levi took place here. He suggests that the missing word for 'mountain' in this fragment could very well be *Kepha*—and *Kepha,* is used in another Qumran Aramaic fragment from the 89th chapter of Enoch to describe the 'rock' on which Moses received revelation for Israel. Historically this was of course Sinai, but Mount Hermon near the Jordan became a literary figure in Jewish apocalyptic thought.

16.   This is followed by Allegro, *The Dead Sea Scrolls,* p. 142; also see Clifford, *The Cosmic Mountain,* pp. 187-88. Josephus in *War* 4.3 casually mentions the

redactional and thematic links between Mt. 16.13-20 (the Peter motif) and 17.4 will be developed below. Here, I simply comment that whatever view one may have about the transfiguration 'event' itself, the idea of 'theological-geographical typology' is perfectly suitable for Matthew (cf. 2.13-23).

2. *Matthew 17.2 and Mark 9.2b-3*

Mt. 17.2   καὶ μετεμορφώθη ἔμπροσθεν αὐτῶν, καὶ ἔλαμψεν τὸ πρόσωπον αὐτοῦ ὡς ὁ ἥλιος, τὰ δὲ ἱμάτια αὐτοῦ ἐγένετο λευκὰ ὡς τὸ φῶς.

Mk 9.2-3   καὶ μετεμορφώθη ἔμπροσθεν αὐτῶν, καὶ τὰ ἱμάτια αὐτοῦ ἐγένετο στίλβοντα λευκὰ λίαν, οἷα γναφεὺς ἐπὶ τῆς γῆς οὐ δύναται οὕτως λευκᾶναι.

The Transfiguration and the Disciples
Matthew agrees with Mark's καὶ μετεμορφώθη ἔμπροσθεν αὐτῶν,[17] suggesting that the transfiguration occurred for the disciples' sake. Since

'temple of the golden calf' as he describes the region where the Jordan rises (I owe this observation to Freyne, *Galilee, Jesus and the Gospels*, p. 184) and probably associated any worship there as similar to the old Israelite idolatry. In view of this it is interesting to note that in Mt. 17.14-20 just as when Moses descended the mountain he was confronted by Israel's apostasy (Exodus 32), so also Jesus confronts unbelief (17.17, 20), and moreover 17.17 echoes Deut. 32.5, 20.

17.   Luke drops Mark's μετεμορφώθη and has τὸ εἶδος τοῦ προσώπου αὐτοῦ ἕτερον and this as has been suggested, was to avoid viewing the transfiguration in a Hellenistic sense (so I.H. Marshall, *The Gospel of Luke* [Grand Rapids: Eerdmans, 2nd edn, 1986], p. 383). But Luke's use of τὸ εἶδος is significant, for in the LXX it is synonymous with ὁμοίωμα, and also has links with μορφή. Like Matthew, Luke emphasises Jesus' face with its Exodus 34 links. Luke uses the masculine ὁ ἱματισμός (contra Mark's τὰ ἱμάτια [Mk 9.3] and Matthew in τὰ δὲ ἱμάτια [Mt. 17.2]) and has λευκὸς ἐξαστράπτων for Mark's ἐγένετο στίλβοντα λευκὰ λίαν, and omits Mark's 'earthly' example: οἷα γναφεὺς ἐπὶ τῆς γῆς οὐ δύναται οὕτως λευκᾶναι. As in Mt. 17.2 (λευκά) Luke uses λευκός (cf. 24.4), which in Acts 1.10; Mk 16.5; Rev. 2.17; 3.4-5; 6.2; 20.11, is the colour of heavenly or angelic garments (cf. J.A. Fitzmyer, *The Gospel according to Luke*, vol. 1 [New York: Doubleday, 1981–85], p.799; W. Michaels, λευκός, *TDNT* IV, pp. 241-50. Luke's use of ἐξαστράπτων (also in 10.18; 11.36; 17.24, and in Acts 9.3; 22.6) is stronger than Mark's στίλβοντα, and shares the same apocalyptic motifs seen in LXX of Dan. 10.6 where it is used to describe an angel-like figure. Hence, it is arguable that like Matthew, Luke is presenting the transfiguration within apocalyptic categories. Further see Appendix.

these disciples,[18] certainly Peter and John, became 'pillars' (στῦλοι) in the early church (cf. Gal. 2.9), it is conceivable that their witness to this special and exclusive revelation (Mt. 17.1, 9) contributed to their elevation. If there was one event that set the three apart from the rest of the twelve it was the revelation at the transfiguration.[19]

μετεμορφώθη

This verb is rare before New Testament times,[20] but is used by Philo (*Mos.* 1.57, 2.288), also by Paul in 2 Cor. 3.18, Rom. 12.2. Its root μορφή is not found elsewhere in Matthew, but once in the extended version of Mk 16.12 (ἐν ἑτέρᾳ μορφῇ, of a resurrection appearance) and in Phil. 2.6-7 (ὃς ἐν μορφῇ Θεοῦ...μορφὴν δούλου). Its derivatives, however, are seen especially in Pauline writings.[21] It is pertinent to my arguments that μορφή, εἰκών[22] and δόξα[23] are closely connected concepts. The LXX describes Moses' transfiguration as δεδόξασται (Exod. 34.29), καὶ ἦν δεδοξασμένη ἡ ὄψις τοῦ χρώματος τοῦ προσώπου αὐτοῦ (v. 30) and δεδόξασται (v. 35). Even though, unlike Luke, Matthew's use of μετεμορφώθη is probably to be seen as some sort of parallel to Moses' 'glorification' (δεδόξασται) in Exod. 34.29, 30, 35.

18. F.F. Bruce, *The Epistle of Paul to the Galatians* (Exeter: Paternoster Press, 1982), p. 123 suggests that the Jerusalem στῦλοι were originally Peter, James and John (the sons of Zebedee) and when James was martyred his place was taken by his namesake James, Jesus' brother. Also see Wenham and Moses, '"There Are Some Standing here"', pp. 153-55; Wenham, *Paul: Follower of Jesus or Founder of Christianity?*, p.360-63.

19. On this see Wenham and Moses, '"There are Some Standing Here"'.

20. Seen in Ps. 33.1 Sym.

21. E.g. Gal. 4.19 (μέχρις οὗ μορφωθῇ Χριστὸς ἐν ὑμῖν); Rom. 2.20 (ἔχοντα τὴν μόρφωσιν τῆς γνώσεως καὶ τῆς ἀληθείας ἐν τῷ νόμῳ; 2 Tim. 3.5 (ἔχοντες μόρφωσιν εὐσεβείας).

22. R.P. Martin. *Carmen Christi* (Cambridge: Cambridge University Press, 1967), p. 107; O. Cullmann, *The Christology of the New Testament* (ET, London: SCM Press, 2nd edn, 1963), pp. 176-77.

23. Martin, *Carmen Christi*, p. 109; L.H. Brockington, 'The Septuagintal Background to the New Testament use of δόξα', in D.E. Nineham (ed.), *Studies in the Gospels* (Oxford: Basil Blackwell, 1955), p. 2, notes that Gen. 1.27 is cited in 1 Cor. 11.7, where δόξα is virtually a synonym of εἰκών, and also δόξα translates תמנה, 'form' in Num. 12.8, Ps. 17 (16), 15. Martin notes that תמונה is translated as μορφή in LXX Job 4.16. Also see S. Kim, *The Origin of Paul's Gospel* (Grand Rapids: Eerdmans, 1982), pp. 195-205.

The Radiance Factor and Matthew's Moses-Sinai Motif

A most important addition to Mark is the statement καὶ ἔλαμψεν τὸ πρόσωπον αὐτοῦ ὡς ὁ ἥλιος, being reminiscent of Exod. 34.29 but pointing beyond it. That Moses was covered in the invisible light of the *shekinah* is well attested in several Jewish writings (cf. Ps.-Philo 12.1; the Samaritan *Memar Marqah* 4.8; 6.9; *Asatir* 9.22 etc.). In other Jewish traditions, the light that shone on Moses at Sinai and remained with him is said to be the primordial light withdrawn from primal man Adam shortly after creation.[24] So Moses is portrayed in terms of a new Adam. According to certain other traditions the Messiah himself was supposed to emit radiance, a motif explicable in terms of the Moses-Sinai-Adam-primal light connection. Given such a background there is a case for saying that the radiance at the transfiguration (1) helps confirm Jesus as Messiah; (2) also sets the agenda for the later ἀκούετε αὐτοῦ (17.5) with its application of Deut. 18.15-19 to Jesus' teaching and words at Mt. 7.21-27; 28.20. For just as the radiance legitimised Moses and his words to Israel, so here Jesus' radiance legitimises Jesus as the new and greater Moses and his words, stressed by the heavenly voice (17.5).

The radiance is particularly stressed by Matthew with his 'sun' (ὁ ἥλιος) and 'light' (τὸ φῶς) language; in contrast to Mark's 'earthly' analogy of the fuller's whiteness. 'Light' and 'radiance' language is common place in apocalyptic literature, and, in view of Matthew's Son of Man *inclusio* and my arguments in ch. 4 (see tabulation there), the radiance language in 17.2 may be particularly reminiscent of Danielic language and motifs. It is in view of these associations that Matthew's use of μετεμορφώθη (with its μορφή, εἰκών, δόξα, εἶδος, ὁμοίωμα associations) needs to be viewed. The cumulative force of the following arguments will elucidate this:

1. Matthew adds καὶ ἔλαμψεν[25] τὸ πρόσωπον αὐτοῦ ὡς ὁ ἥλιος; this resembles apocalyptic, especially Danielic, language and imagery (Dan. 12.3 use of λάμψουσιν, also τῶν δικαίων...ὡς οἱ ἀστέρες εἰς τοὺς αἰῶνας). Already in Mt. 13.43, Matthew says that the righteous (οἱ δίκαιοι; i.e. οἱ

---

24. See Ginzberg, *The Legends of the Jews*, vol. 1, pp. 8-9; G.C. Nicholson, *Death as Departure: The Johannine Descent–Ascent Schema*, SBLDS 63 (Atlanta: Scholars Press, 1983), pp. 91-98; E. Haenchen, *John I: A Commentary on the Gospel of John Chapters 1–6* (Philadelphia: Fortress Press, 1930), p. 204; Brown, *The Gospel according to John*, I, p. 145.

25. According to R.H. Gundry, *The Use of the Old Testament in St Matthew's*

υἱοὶ τῆς βασιλείας (v. 38) will ἐκλάμψουσιν ὡς ὁ ἥλιος ἐν τῇ βασιλείᾳ τοῦ πατρὸς αὐτῶν.

2. Facial radiance is not associated with the 'one like the son of man' in Dan 7.13-14. The idea is found elsewhere in Jewish apocalyptic, applied to individuals, (*1 En.* 38.4; 62.15; 71.1; 1QH 4.5-6; 5.29-32; Rev. 1.16), but in view of Matthew's interest in Moses, 17.2 is clearly Mosaic, echoing Exod. 34.29-30. The prophet-like-Moses motif in 17.5—ἀκούετε αὐτοῦ (Deut 18.15-19)—adds weight to this Moses interpretation.

3. Matthew retains Mark's 'garment' and the idea of Jesus' clothes being transfigured, but, as we have noted, sets it within an apocalyptic setting,[26] with language reminiscent of passages like *1 En.* 14.20; *2 En.* 1.5; *3 En.* 15.1-2; *2 Bar.* 51.3, 5, 10; Rev. 1.16; 10.1; and particularly (as we shall see) of Dan. 12.3.

Facial Radiance and Matthew's Danielic Language and Motifs, Especially Matthew 17.2 and 13.43 (M)

I need not repeat my earlier discussion on the structural and thematic parallelism between Daniel 7, Sinai and Mt. 17.1-8. But that discussion needs to be kept in mind, for it contributes to my consideration of Matthew's use of ὡς ὁ ἥλιος in 17.2 and the identical occurrence in 13.43. The texts to be compared are as follows:

Gospel (Leiden: Brill, 1975), p. 83, Matthew's use of ἔλαμψεν in the active voice (17.2) is much nearer the Hebrew קרן (Exod. 34.29) than δεδόξασται in the LXX. Matthew's ὡς ὁ ἥλιος makes an interesting parallel with the identical phrase in Rev. 1.16, and R.H. Mounce, *The Book of Revelation* (Grand Rapids: Eerdmans, 1977), p.80 makes mention of the transfiguration in this context.

26.   For Matthew's use of apocalyptic see G.N. Stanton, 'The Gospel of Matthew and Judaism', *BJRL* 66 (1984), pp. 264-84, especially, pp. 278-83. Stanton argues that Matthew uses apocalyptic motifs polemically, and that this is prompted by his 'social circumstances' (i.e. the trauma of the parting of the ways from Judaism, p. 281). But this could also be said of Matthew even if an *intra-muros* (contra Stanton) position is adopted. Given Matthew's polemic against the Pharisees (e.g. ch. 23), the use of apocalyptic motifs at the transfiguration is explainable; in Mt. 17.1-8 Matthew intends presenting Jesus the (Danielic) 'Son of Man' as the 'true' king. It is as 'Danielic Son of Man' that Jesus is the new and greater Moses. On Church/Israel polarity in Matthew also see S. Brown, 'The Two-fold Representation of the Mission in Matthew's Gospel', *ST* 31 (1977), pp. 21-32; 'The Mission to Israel in Matthew's Central Section (Mt. 9.35–11.1)', *ZNW* 69 (1978), pp. 73-90.

Mt. 17.2	Mt. 13.43
καὶ ἔλαμψεν τὸ πρόσωπον αὐτοῦ	τότε οἱ δίκαιοι ἐκλάμψουσιν
ὡς ὁ ἥλιος, τὰ δὲ ἱμάτια αὐτοῦ	ὡς ὁ ἥλιος ἐν τῇ βασιλείᾳ
ἐγένετο λευκὰ ὡς τὸ φῶς.	τοῦ πατρὸς αὐτῶν.

The obvious similarity between the two texts is the identical use of ὡς ὁ ἥλιος. In addition, both passages speak of 'shining', ἔλαμψεν (17.2) and ἐκλάμψουσιν (13.43). Since 'sun' language is common in the Scriptures (e.g. LXX of Judg. 5.31; Isa. 30.26; Mal. 4.2 and Rev. 1.16; 10.1; 12.1) and in apocalyptic literature (*1 En.* 14.20; *Odes* 11.13; *2 En.* 11; *T. Adam* 1.11 etc.) the identical use of ὡς ὁ ἥλιος in Mt. 17.26 and 13.43 could be insignificant. But (1) Matthew is fond of repetition of formulae: he uses similar phrases sometimes in close proximity (e.g. 2.22-23 with 4.14; 3.1/3.13), sometimes not in close proximity (3.17/17.5; 3.7/23.33; 4.10/16.23) By this literary technique, he often seems to link passages and ideas and so hold his material together. In view of this, it is possible that Matthew makes a deliberate redactional and thematic link between 13.43 and 17.2.

2. I have argued that Matthew's transfiguration narrative is Danielic. It is interesting therefore that an echo of Dan. 12.3 in Mt. 13.43 is recognised by several scholars,[27] though neither the LXX nor Theodotion have the expression ὡς ὁ ἥλιος in Dan. 12.3.

3. Mt. 13.36-43 is usually seen as heavily redactional,[28] so it is all the more possible that Matthew has theologically and redactionally linked 13.43 with 17.2 through the common phrase ὡς ὁ ἥλιος. The following arguments will strengthen such a view.

4. There are also several common theological motifs shared by the

---

27. See W.C. Allen, *A Critical and Exegetical Commentary on the Gospel According to St Matthew* (Edinburgh: T. & T. Clark, 1912), p. 153; A. Plummer, *An Exegetical Commentary on the Gospel According to St Matthew* (London: Robert & Scott, 1915), p.196; A.H. McNeile, *The Gospel According to Matthew* (London: Macmillan, 1915), p. 202; D. Hill, *The Gospel of Matthew* (Grand Rapids: Eerdmans, 1972), p. 237; Gundry, *The Use of the Old Testament*, p. 138; *Matthew*, p. 274; France, *Matthew*, p. 227; Carson, *Matthew*, p. 327.

28. According to Gundry, *Matthew*, pp. 261-62, the parable (13.24-30) and its interpretation (13.36-43), both M passages, are edited by Matthew 'to the point of composition' and comprise a conflation of Mk 4.26-29 and 4.1-23, also Allen, *St Matthew*, pp. 149-50. But Hill, *The Gospel of Matthew*, p.235; France, *Matthew*, pp. 224-25, point out that the interpretation (13.36-43) corresponds with the point of the parable (13.24-30).

transfiguration pericope and its immediate surroundings and Mt. 13.24-30 and 36-43. (a) There is the 'Son of Man-kingdom' association (13.38, 41; 16.28). In 13.41 it is the Son of Man's kingdom in which the 'gathering' takes place; this may be compared with 'the Son of Man (Matthew alone) coming in his kingdom' (16.28). (b) There is the motif of judgment (13.30, 40-42; compare with 16.27;16.28) and vindication (13.43; 16.27; also Jesus' resurrection alluded to in 17.9). In 13.37 the Son of Man is the 'sower' and (with his 'angels') the chief harvester, who brings judgment and vindication (v. 41); in 16.27 the Son of Man will come with his 'angels' to repay every one. As I have already suggested, Matthew, by redacting Mk 9.1 and arranging 16.27 by the side of 16.28, has produced a powerful 'coming of the Son of Man' motif in association with other motifs such as 'glory', 'kingdom', which are quite Danielic (and also Sinaitic); so are the themes that feature in Mt. 13.36-43. (c) The theme of 'resurrection' may also link 17.2 with 13.43. If the enigmatic 16.28 is seen not only to refer to the transfiguration event, but also to later manifestations of the kingdom including the resurrection, then the transfiguration in Matthew may function as a foretaste of the resurrection; this perhaps receives support from the instruction in 17.9 to the disciples to remain silent about their witness to the transfiguration 'until' (ἕως) the Son of Man is raised from the dead.

Finally, (d) if there is both a theological and redactional link between 17.2 and 13.34, with Matthew applying the same ideas and phraseology (e.g. ὡς ὁ ἥλιος) to 'the righteous' (ch. 13) and Jesus (ch. 17), the probable conclusion must be that he is indicating Jesus' solidarity with the righteous, with Jesus functioning as a sort of 'firstfruits' of the righteous' resurrection (like Paul in 1 Cor. 15.23). This is confirmed by the evidence of Mt. 13.36-43, and especially v. 43 where the righteous are said to shine 'in the kingdom of their father'. For Matthew, Jesus is the Son of God par excellence and the kingdom is his preeminently (v. 41 'his kingdom'), but his followers are identified with him in the kingdom and in sonship. Jesus' solidarity with his followers is brought out frequently in Matthew, not least in Mt. 25.31-46, where we find a very similar conjunction of ideas to what we find in 13.36-46: the Son of Man is 'king' (v. 34), Son of God (v. 34, 'my father'); he identifies with the 'righteous' and the kingdom is given to them. There is the same circle of ideas in the transfiguration narrative: the Son of Man is also 'my Son' and he is the one who shines like the sun and will bring others to share this kingdom glory.

So I suggest that Matthew has redactionally and theologically linked Mt. 17.1-9 with 13.36-43. Matthew sees Jesus as Son of Man, Son of God, 'the Son' of the kingdom and 'the righteous one', who is in solidarity with 'the sons of the kingdom' (13.38). In view of this, and in view of Matthew's redactional and thematic linking of 13.43 and 17.2, I conclude that the radiance of Jesus in 17.2 (ὡς ὁ ἥλιος) is a probable prolepsis of the reward of the 'righteous' at their resurrection, those who are to ἐκλάμψουσιν ὡς ὁ ἥλιος ἐν τῇ βασιλείᾳ τοῦ πατρὸς αὐτῶν (Mt. 13.43/Dan. 12.3). Moreover, by his emphasis on the face-radiance and 'light' motifs Matthew has blended Moses-Sinai (Exod. 34.29-35) and Danielic (12.3) motifs. This compares well with the general Son of Man *inclusio* and Moses-Sinai framework he has given the transfiguration.

Possible Links with the "Light" Motif in the Sermon on the Mount and the Moses-Radiance Motif
Since the 'Jesus as light' motif is important for Matthew (3.16; also 2.9), and since Matthew stresses Jesus' solidarity with his disciples (the good seed/the sons of the kingdom/the righteous cf. 13.37-38; 43), it is fruitful to compare the 'Jesus as light' motif in 17.2 with the 'disciples as light' theme in the 'Sermon on the Mount', especially 5.14-16 (a fuller discussion on the links between Mt. 17.1-9 and the sermon on the mount in Matthew 5–7 will feature in ch. 6). In 5.14 the disciples are described as τὸ φῶς, and they are to λαμψάτω τὸ φῶς ὑμῶν ἔμπροσθεν τῶν ἀνθρώπων that others may see their good works and 'give glory to your Father who is in heaven' (v. 16). Note also other 'light' terminology, for example, λύχνον, λάμπει v. 15. Both 5.14-16 and 13.46 share the common "disciples–light" motif. This could be insignificant, since one is in the context of mission–witness (5.14-16)[29] and the other in the context of judgment–vindication–resurrection, but given Matthew's fondness for repetition formulas, phrases and motifs, there may be a subtle relation between the two passages.

---

29.   Viewing 5.14-16 in relation to 5.13, (with v. 16 as 'summarizing key of the pericope', see U. Luz, *Matthew 1–7*, p.252), the emphasis here is that the disciples (the renewed Israel) are light of the world by letting their works shine. But in 4.16 Matthew's readers have already been reminded of Isa. 59.1-9 with special reference to the *Galilee of the Gentiles*. My point is, since the transfiguration did take place in 'Gentile territory', it is possible that Matthew makes a subtle relation between 5.14-16 and 17.1-8.

Moreover, so far as the transfiguration goes, there are certain verbal similarities between 5.14-16 and Mt. 17.2. For example, compare: (a) ὄρος (17.1) with ὄρους (5.14). Since mountains play a prominent role in the First Gospel, this comparison is perhaps significant. (b) ἔλαμψεν (17.2) with λαμψάτω (5.16), (c) τὸ φῶς (17.2) with τὸ φῶς (5.14, 16). (d) The use of μετεμορφώθη in 17.2 in conjunction with 17.2b itself is associated with a light motif. This may be compared with the recurring light motif in 5.14-16. (e) Jesus was transfigured ἔμπροσθεν αὐτῶν which perhaps may be compared with ἔμπροσθεν τῶν αὐτῶν in 5.16.

It may be that these suggested links are over-subtle, but the comparisons at least point to a possible thematic relationship between Matthew 17 and 5.14. It is worth recalling that the scene in both cases is Jesus on a mountain; so the contexts are parallel in this respect. In addition to this, but of secondary importance, I wish to suggest that Matthew shows significant interest in Jesus and by extension his disciples as light to the Gentiles. In Matthew's infancy narrative, for example, the advent of Jesus is heralded by heavenly light (2.2), and it is the Gentile Magi who inquire after it. In 4.16 Jesus, in the 'Galilee of the Gentiles',[30] fulfils Isa. 9.1-2 and becomes to those who sat in darkness the 'great light' (φῶς...μέγα). Although he offered his message of restoration (via repentance) first to Israel (10.16-17; 15.24), Matthew sees the messianic kingdom as eventually embracing the Gentiles (28.19); they will receive the 'kingdom of God' taken away from the Jews (21.43). It is this light that disciples share with him in 5.14-16 (and by extension in 13.46) and hence become themselves 'lights'. And so my arguments suggest that it is quite possible that Matthew has theologically and redactionally linked 17.2 with 13.43 and 5.14-16, thereby giving the transfiguration pericope a pivotal role in his structure and theology.

3. *Matthew 17.3 and Mark 9.4*

Mt. 17.3	Mk 9.4
καὶ ἰδοὺ ὤφθη αὐτοῖς Μωυσῆς καὶ Ἠλίας συλλαλοῦντες μετ' αὐτοῦ.	καὶ ὤφθη αὐτοῖς Ἠλίας σὺν Μωυσεῖ, καὶ ἦσαν συλλαλοῦντες τῷ Ἰησοῦ.

Here, the use of ἰδού is particularly characteristic of Matthew (cf. 1.20; 2.1, 13, 19; 9.10, 18, 32; 12.46; 17.5; 26.47; 28.11), and points to

---

30. On the importance of Galilee, see Freyne, *Galilee, Jesus and the Gospels*, pp. 89-91; Nickelsburg, 'Enoch, Levi and Peter', pp. 575-600.

something unexpected. ἰδού and its semitic equivalents are often associated with angelic appearances or theophanies (Gen. 18.2; 28.13; Ezek. 1.4; Dan. 7.13; Lk. 24.4; Acts 1.10; Jude 14; Rev. 19.11).[31] It may be that by adding the word here Matthew heightens the idea that Moses and Elijah are 'heavenly' beings, thus adding to the theophanic setting of Mt. 17.1-8.

Μωυσῆς καὶ Ἠλίας: Matthew has changed Mark's Ἠλίας σὺν Μωυσεῖ to the more natural order Μωυσῆς καὶ Ἠλίας.[32] As I have argued, it is probable that this was the order found in the pre-Markan tradition which Mark chose to change in order to stress his Elijah motif.[33] Matthew reinstates the original order. This is in keeping with his Moses emphasis elsewhere. Matthew omits Mark's καὶ ἦσαν before συλλαλοῦντες[34] as redundant, and has μετ' αὐτοῦ for Mark's τῷ Ἰησοῦ for stylistic reasons.

Both Moses and Elijah were towering figures, and, while Matthew does not ignore the Elijah motif (cf. 11.14; 17.10-13),[35] by changing Mark's order he lays emphasis on the Moses motif, and presents Jesus as the greater Moses. This Moses-Christology was perhaps in response to the Moses propaganda of the time.

Apart from these observations, Matthew seems to give Moses and Elijah separate functions: (1) With his 'high mountain', 'face/radiance', and citing Moses before Elijah, he emphasises the Moses-Jesus typology and heightens the Sinai parallelism. (2) We shall shortly see that like Mark (but more plainly) he gives Elijah a 'present' significance (realised in the Baptist, whose suffering prefigures Christ's). But Matthew's portrayal

31. See Davies and Allison, *St Matthew*, II, p. 206, also ch. 4 (tabulation).

32. Too much must not be made of the use of Matthew's καί and Mark's σύν, for σύν alone does not suggest Elijah or Mosaic priority, but that Matthew (and Luke) have changed Mark's order to its natural and chronological sequence does suggest their interest in the Moses motif.

33. In Mk 9.1-13, the change of order perhaps was to liken it with the Elijah issue occurring in 9.9-13.

34. Davies and Allison, *St Matthew*, II, p. 697 point out that συλλαλέω is used of Moses in LXX 34.35, at the end of the account of his transfiguration, and 34.29 associates Moses' transfiguration with the act of talking with God.

35. In Mt. 11.10, the Baptist is associated with the 'messenger' of Mal. 3.1. There is some debate if this messenger may be identified with Elijah or not (for the state of the debate see P.A. Verhoef, *The Books of Haggai and Malachi* (Grand Rapids: Eerdmans, 1987), pp. 285-86), if not, then John is more than Elijah and a messenger.

needs also to be set in the perspective of themes associated with the 'coming together' of Moses and Elijah which may have been current.

1. For example, we have no problem about Moses as a figure of transfiguration (cf. Exod. 34; Sir. 45.2; Ps.-Philo 19.16 linked to Exod. 3 and 19–34). As for Elijah, he is translated (2 Kgs 2.11-12); but, since according to Jewish mystical and Merkabah traditions one cannot enter the heavenlies without being transformed, transformation motifs were also applied to Elijah: Sir. 48.1-12; *Liv. Proph.* 21.2; *Quest. in Gen.* 1.86, based on 2 Kgs 2.11-12. According to *Liv. Proph.* 21.1-15 at his birth, Sobacha Elijah's father saw men of white greeting Elijah, wrapping him in fire and giving him flames of fire to eat, and it was said of Elijah 'his dwelling will be light'. In view of these traditions, it is apparent that the motif of transformation may be applied to both Moses and Elijah. Moreover, since according to some Jewish literature Moses was translated, that motif too could be common to both figures.

2. At Sinai both witnessed the 'coming of God' in a spectacular manner. For according to *Ant.* 7.13, 7 (also *b. Meg.*19b), both had their theophanies at Horeb/Sinai, and Elijah in the identical cave of Moses. This too fits Matthew's portrayal of the transfiguration in terms of Sinai and Daniel 7.

3. Moses and the law are obviously associated, but Elijah too was seen as one who fought to revive Mosaism (Sir. 48.2; *1 Macc.* 2.58; *b.t.b. Mes.* 114a).

4. In *Midrash Rabbah Deut.* 3.17 Moses and Elijah are to 'come together'. It is true that this work is dated late (sixth to ninth century CE), but the saying itself is attributed to Johanan ben Zakkai, who lived in the first-century CE, and it is arguable that it reflects early tradition. Admittedly such traditions need to be used with caution and perhaps are inconclusive, but they may be of some relevance.[36]

5. Furthermore, in the often cited Mal. 3.22-24 (4.4-6), the writer brings his work to a climax by focusing on both Moses the

---

36. On this see T.F. Glasson, *Moses in the Fourth Gospel* (London: SCM Press, 1963), p. 12. Some see Moses and Elijah paired in Jn 1.21 (Moses indirectly), Rev. 11.3 (possibly). According to *Pesiq. Rab.* 4.2 'Moses and Elijah are equal to each other in everything' (see Davies and Allison, *St Matthew*, II, p. 698).

lawgiver and Elijah the prophet who is to come before the
'great and terrible day of the Lord'. In order to survive the
coming judgment the people must (1) remember the law of
Moses, which God commanded him at Horeb/Sinai—the
Sinaitic covenant 'for all Israel', and (2) respond to Elijah's
ministry of 'restoration' (cf. Mt. 17.10-13)—both social (v. 24)
and religious—and to his renewal of the covenant which they
had broken (Mal. 3.7). One important point though is that
Elijah's mission was to be taken seriously, since the final verse
of Malachi posed the possibility that he might not succeed, the
consequence being judgment: 'I will come and strike the land
with the ban', the 'coming of God for judgment'. This warning
parallels Deut. 18.18-19 where disregard for the words of the
prophet-like-Moses is said to merit a similar judgment.

So, in view of this passage and points (1) to (5), I suggest that it is
conceivable that both Moses (law) and Elijah (prophet of a restored
covenant) were associated with the ideas of (a) 'restoration', (b) resurrection, a closely associated motif, with particular reference to Elijah (see
below), and (c) 'the coming of God' (Mount Sinai, Exod. 19–34; 1 Kgs
19.8-18; *Ant.* 7.13, 7; *b. Meg.* 19b). As in Mal. 3.22-24 (4.4-6) the
'coming of God' is (d) for 'deliverance and judgment' (Exod. 32; 1 Kgs
18.36-40), depending on their heeding (or not heeding) the teaching: 'or
else I will come and strike...' (Mal. 4.6 in response to Elijah's words/
ministry); 'if you obey my voice...' (Exod. 19.5). This is also applicable
to the words/teaching of the prophet like Moses: 'whoever will not give
heed to my words which he shall speak in my name' (Deut. 18.19),
compare ἀκούετε αὐτοῦ in 17.5.

4. *Matthew 17.4 and Mark 9.5*

Mt. 17.4 ἀποκριθεὶς δὲ ὁ Πέτρος εἶπεν τῷ Ἰησοῦ· κύριε, καλόν
ἐστιν ἡμᾶς ὧδε εἶναι· εἰ θέλεις, ποιήσω ὧδε τρεῖς σκηνάς,
σοὶ μίαν καὶ Μωυσεῖ μίαν καὶ Ἠλίᾳ μίαν.

Mk 9.5 καὶ ἀποκριθεὶς ὁ Πέτρος λέγει τῷ Ἰησοῦ· ῥαββί, καλόν
ἐστιν ἡμᾶς ὧδε εἶναι, καὶ ποιήσωμεν τρεῖς σκηνάς, σοὶ
μίαν καὶ Μωυσεῖ μίαν καὶ Ἠλίᾳ μίαν.

In this comparison, (1) Matthew omits Mark's καί but adds δέ before ὁ
Πέτρος. Matthew may want to make a distinction between the

conversation in 17.3 and Peter's suggestion in 17.4, but the change could be purely stylistic. (2) Matthew's ἀποκριθεὶς...εἶπεν for Mark's λέγει is in keeping with Matthew's style elsewhere (e.g. ἀποκριθεὶς εἶπεν 17.11; also cf. 22.1; 28.5). (3) Matthew has κύριε for Mark's ῥαββί, (Lk. ἐπιστάτα 9.33). It is significant that Matthew uses ῥαββί only twice, and on both occasions he puts it on the lips of Judas (26.25, 49). Κύριε in the gospels is sometimes used merely as a polite form of address, a usage which is also seen in Mt. 13.27, 21.30, 25.20, but in Matthew it is also used to denote a deeper and more religious meaning, recognising Jesus' authority and his exalted status (e.g. 7.21, 8.2, 6, 15.22, 20.30-31).[37] Thus in 17.4, viewed from its post resurrection setting, Matthew's redaction stresses Jesus' Lordship. Moreover, Matthew's addition εἰ θέλεις confirms this, for according to Matthew, Peter will do nothing unless Jesus wills it.[38]

Matthew 17.4, 16.16-19 and Matthew's Peter Emphasis
This redaction also highlights Matthew's focus on Peter in the transfiguration (as elsewhere).[39] The significance of Peter's statement: εἰ θέλεις, ποιήσω ὧδε τρεῖς σκηνάς has been debated, and Davies and Allison conclude that 'no one has yet put forward a convincing theological or literary explanation for Peter's remarks about booths'.[40] I

37. According to B.T. Viviano, 'Matthew', in *The New Jerome Bible Commentary* (Englewood Cliffs, NJ: Prentice Hall, 1990), p. 601, Matthew correctly translates Mark's ῥαββί, which in Mark does not refer to a Jewish teacher but represents an older Aramaic usage, literally meaning 'my great one' (used of God, angels and earthly sovereigns). That Matthew's κύριε signifies a deeper meaning see: France, *Matthew*, p. 148; E. Schweizer, *The Good News according to Matthew* (London: SPCK, 1976), pp. 210-11; Davies and Allison, *St Matthew*, II, p. 699.

38. Davies and Allison, *St Matthew*, II, p. 699 have pointed out that as in 16.24; 19.17, 21 εἰ θέλεις is redactional. But Matthew may have simply added εἰ, for it is possible that the text of Mk 9.5 (θέλεις D W Θ f¹³ 543 565 b ff² i) is correct. On this see C.E.B. Cranfield, *The Gospel according to St Mark* (Cambridge: Cambridge University Press, 1963), p. 291; V. Taylor, *The Gospel According to St Mark* (London: Macmillan; New York: St Martin's, 1966), p. 390.

39. See 4.18 (par. Mk 4.16), 14.28-33; 16.16-19; 22-23.

40. Davies and Allison, *St Matthew*, II, p. 692. They toy with the idea of the 'tent of meeting' (pp. 699-700), but then go along with Cyril of Jerusalem that Peter thought that the kingdom of God had come—a view supported by some biblical texts according to which God was to tabernacle among the saints at the end (Ezek. 37.27; 43.7, 9; Zech. 2.10-11; 8.3, 8; 14.6-9; Rev. 21.3). But this is not entirely a novel idea (see A.M. Ramsey, *The Glory of God and the Transfiguration of Christ* (London:

suggest that *Matthew's* distinctive: 'I will make' ποιήσω ὧδε (for Mark's καὶ ποιήσωμεν) not only reiterates Matthew's interest in Peter and his leadership role, but also and significantly is probably to be linked back to the Peter-building motif already seen in 16.13-20 (which too is Matthean). In support of this the following arguments need to be considered:

1. I suggest that just as Israel was enthusiastic about 'building' the tabernacle (of the tent of meeting) *immediately* after Israel and Moses had 'seen' the Sinai theophany (Exodus 35–40), so here in Mt. 17.4 Peter (in Mark and Luke it is 'let us build') intends building three tents.

2. According to 16.16-19, Jesus is to 'build' (οἰκοδομήσω μου τὴν ἐκκλησίαν Mt. 16.18) on Peter, the 'rock', as the foundation of Jesus' new community.[41] It is tempting to link this (οἰκοδομήσω) 'I will build' (Jesus) in 16.18 with the similar (ποιήσω) 'I will make' (Peter) in 17.4, and Matthew's redaction could imply such a link.

3. If there is a link, Peter's 'if you are willing, I will make' could be seen as Peter offering to play his part with Jesus in the building of the ἐκκλησία-βασιλεία (cf. 16.18-19). Preoccupied with Jesus' promise to him and now finding himself in a Christophanic setting heightened by the two 'eschatological' figures Moses and Elijah, and being conscious of Jesus' initial message of restoration to Israel (10.5-6) and of his place as leader of 'the twelve', the first to be chosen (4.18-19), the Matthean Peter may have taken it that the messianic age of rest had dawned (κύριε, καλόν ἐστιν ἡμᾶς ὧδε εἶναι, also cf. Acts 1.6), and that he was now to do his part in the ἐκκλησία building project predicted in 16.18.

Peter's intention to build tents could reflect popular belief about the fulfilment of passages such as Ezek. 17.22-24, where Yahweh promises

Longmans, Green & Co., 1949), pp.110-11). They also allude to the idea that saints in heaven have dwellings (*1 En.* 39.4-8; 41.2; 71.16; Jn 14.2; *2 En.* 61.23; *T. Abr.* A.20.14) and come to earth, dwellings need to be made for them (see Marshall, *The Gospel of Luke*, pp. 386-87).

41. For the 'Peter-rock-church' emphasis and a defence of the historicity of this passage see B.F. Meyer, *The Aims of Jesus* (London: SCM Press, 1979), pp.185-97; O. Cullmann, *Peter: Disciple, Apostle, Martyr* (London: SCM Press, 1952), pp. 158-212; G. Maier, 'The Church in the Gospel of Matthew: Hermeneutical Analysis of the Current Debate', in D.A. Carson (ed.), *Biblical Interpretation and the Church* (Exeter: Paternoster Press, 1984), pp. 45-63; Luz, 'Das Parliament Matthäus', pp. 415-33; H. Balz and G. Schneider, *Exegetical Dictionary of the New Testament*, vol.1, (Edinburgh: T. & T. Clark, 1990), p. 415.

to plant a tender shoot (interpreted in Davidic terms) upon a 'high mountain' (ὄρος ὑψηλὸν [v. 22], the same usage in Mt. 17.1); or Amos 9.11, the promised 'rising of the booth (σκηνή, the same in Mt. 17.4) of David that is fallen', τὴν σκηνὴν Δαυὶδ τὴν πεπτωκυῖαν LXX,—the very passage quoted by James in Acts 15.16-17.

4. It is also possible that it was in this context that Peter (and James and John) viewed the presence of Moses and Elijah, as figures of 'restoration' (Mal. 4.4-6). Certainly in 17.10-13 the ensuing discussion is linked to the restoration Elijah was to bring. Perhaps his appearance in 17.5 encouraged Peter, for he could have taken him as 'the figure of restoration': the official restorer (Mal. 4.5-6) had come and so he was going to do his part. Moreover as I. Abrahams has shown, it is possible that in Judaism the 'tent' idea had acquired messianic and eschatological significance.[42] So, in view of the arguments cited and in the light of

42. Peter's suggestion also needs to be viewed in the light of ideas about 'restoration-eschatology' at the time. Several points are relevant here: (1) I. Abrahams, *Studies in Pharisaism and the Gospels*, (Second Series; Cambridge: Cambridge University Press, 1924), pp. 50-55 has shown that the idea of 'tents' and 'tabernacles' was associated with eschatological messianic hopes (Amos 9.11 (Davidic); Isa. 58.12); and is supported by rabbinic parallels BT *Baba Bathra* 75a; *Pesiqta* 186 a-b. (2) The disciples may have understood Jesus' ministry ('to the lost tribes of Israel' Mt. 15.24; they were sent to 'the house of Israel' 10.5-6) primarily in terms of national restoration (Mt. 19.27 [Peter], 20.20-28; Acts 1.6; Acts 3.19-21 [Peter]), i.e. as promised in Isa. 2.2-3; Jer. 4.23-25; Zech. 8.23). So we must reckon with the possibility that Peter's suggestion to make 'booths' (17.4—to be taken with his understanding of the ἐκκλησία [Mt. 16.18]–βασιλεία [16.19] commission given to him earlier) was mixed with eschatological messianic hopes linked with 'restoration'. For Peter 'the day of fulfilment' had arrived (see Lohmeyer, *Das Evangelium Markus*, p. 176; Ramsey, *The Glory of God*, p. 111); (3) According to Mt. 19.28 however, Jesus looks forward to a 'future' restoration (ἐν τῇ παλιγγενεσίᾳ) which corresponds to ἐν τῇ βασιλείᾳ μου in Lk. 22.30 (omitted in the parallel, Lk. 18.24-30/Mt. 19.23-30, but retained in a different context Lk. 22.28-30). This 'regeneration' motif also needs to be viewed in relation to Jesus' dynamic 'kingdom' (God's reign through Jesus cf. 13.36-43; 16.28) concept (19.28; 25.31-32),—a 'kingdom' which would incorporate the 'Gentiles' (Mt. 24.14; 28.19) who already during Jesus' earthly ministry had responded to him (15.21-39). Perhaps a case could be made that Jewish rejection of Jesus' message (offered in 4.17; 10.5-6; 15.24 but rejected 16.1-12; 21.43) that pushed the 'full' realisation of this kingdom/restoration more to the future than its culmination as a present reality.

That 'restoration eschatology' was one of the prominent influences on first century Palestine see: G.B. Caird, *Jesus and the Jewish Nation* (London: Athlone Press, 1965); B.F. Meyer, *The Aims of Jesus*, esp. pp. 171-73; M.J. Borg, *Conflict,*

Matthew's Peter emphasis in 16.13–17.8 (esp. 16.16-19, 22-23, 17.1, 17.4) I suggest that at a deeper level Matthew is associating the Peter-σκηνή motif in 17.4 with (a) the Jesus-Peter-ἐκκλησία, Jesus-new Temple motif in 16.18, and also (b) with the Jesus-Moses-Sinai-tabernacle motif (Exod. 25.10–31.18; 33.7-11).

5. Matthew's Peter motif however does not negate Matthew's portrayal of Jesus' 'Lordship' of the church, for (a) in 16.18 it is 'my' (Jesus') church, which 'I' (he) will build: οἰκοδομήσω μου τὴν ἐκκλησίαν. So it is Jesus who is the builder, but with Peter having a key part in it. (b) In 21.42, in the Temple premises, Jesus directly applies the 'stone' testimonia passage from Ps. 118.22-23 (with its Israel connotations, cf. Acts 4.11; 1 Pet. 2.4, 7) to himself.[43] It is also interesting to note that in 21.42 οἰκοδομοῦντες is used of the Jews who reject him. In contrast, in 16.18 οἰκοδομήσω is used of Jesus who will build his (μου) church on 'this rock' ἐπὶ ταύτῃ τῇ πέτρᾳ.[44] For Matthew, Jesus is very much 'involved' in the building, as λίθος (21.42) and οἰκοδόμος (16.18), but Peter is to play a definite role. (c) There are also several features in the passage (17.5) where Matthew by redaction confirms this Jesus-Peter relationship, one that is based on Jesus' 'Lordship': (i) In the transfiguration setting, the use of κύριε for Mark's ῥαββί is more than stylistic; (ii) εἰ θέλεις: Peter's request is subject to Jesus' approval.

6. Matthew's ἔτι links the voice motif (17.5) to Peter's comments, the voice functions as a corrective to Peter's too narrow political-messianic and Zion perspective. It functions as a reminder that Jesus is the builder, with Peter however playing a crucial part in it. ἀκούετε αὐτοῦ of 17.5 signifies the call to a radical commitment and obedience to Jesus'

Holiness & Politics in the Teachings of Jesus (New York: Edwin Mellen, 1984), E.P. Sanders, *Jesus and Judaism* (Philadelphia: Fortress Press, 1985). That for Matthew the church is the continuation of the consciousness of the national community of Israel see K. Tagawa, 'People and Community in the Gospel of Matthew', pp. 149-62. On the powerful influence of Jewish Christianity in the first century see J. Jervell, 'The Mighty Minority', *ST* 34 (1980), pp. 13-38.

43. But note the use of λίθον instead of πέτρα (in 16.18 for Peter).

44. It is in this capacity that he calls into being a new community. According to Matthew, '*this generation*', the nation of Israel, failed to be the 'people of God' by failing to respond to God's call through Jesus (11.16-24; 12.38-45; 16.4; 17.17) and so judgment was imminent (3.11-12, 23.29-36). But Jesus was the true Israel (Mt. 2.15–Hos. 11.1; Mt. 4.1-11; 21.33-43) and those who respond to him, (7.21-27; 13.11) would form the reconstituted new Israel (8.10-13; 23.14; 28.20).

words—the messianic teachings on which one was to 'build' (cf. Mt. 7.24-27, note the use of λόγους...ᾠκοδόμησεν...τὴν πέτραν)—and to his commands ἐνετειλάμην 28.20. The latter also needs to be seen in relation to the consistent use of ἐνετείλατο in Deuteronomy, representing Yahweh's commands through Moses.

7. Finally, Matthew omits Mark's οὐ γὰρ ᾔδει τί ἀποκριθῇ ἔκφοβοι γὰρ ἐγένοντο. For Mark, Peter's statement and suggestion to build three booths (9.5) was due to his being unable to come to terms with the unusual circumstance that they were in, and due to fear (ἔκφοβοι γὰρ ἐγένοντο). Matthew, however, uses the 'fear' motif differently (as we shall shortly see in v. 9). Here by omitting the fear motif he is not merely more charitable about Peter's reaction: he perhaps implies that Peter meant what he said, even though he was mistaken.

So I suggest that it is probable that Matthew has linked the Peter-building motif in 17.4 with a similar motif in 16.17-20. In 16.16 however, Peter confesses Jesus as Christ and Son of God, and this is followed by the dominical word about Peter and the building of the church; in 17.1-8 Peter suggests 'building', and the affirmation of Jesus' sonship by the divine voice functions as a corrective to Peter, as I will shortly show.

5. *Matthew 17.5 and Mark 9.7*

Mt. 17.5   ἔτι αὐτοῦ λαλοῦντος ἰδοὺ νεφέλη φωτεινὴ ἐπεσκίασεν αὐτούς, καὶ ἰδοὺ φωνὴ ἐκ τῆς νεφέλης λέγουσα· οὗτός ἐστιν ὁ υἱός μου ὁ ἀγαπητός, ἐν ᾧ εὐδόκησα· ἀκούετε αὐτοῦ.

Mk 9.7   καὶ ἐγένετο νεφέλη ἐπισκιάζουσα αὐτοῖς, καὶ ἐγένετο φωνὴ ἐκ τῆς νεφέλης· οὗτός ἐστιν ὁ υἱός μου ὁ ἀγαπητός, ἀκούετε αὐτοῦ.

ἔτι αὐτοῦ λαλοῦντος

Matthew's genitive absolute construction ἔτι αὐτοῦ λαλοῦντος is not in Mark, and is designed to produce grammatical flow. Similar insertions are seen in Mt. 12.46 = Mk 3.31 and Mt. 9.18 = Mk 5.21, and in both these passages the clause is placed at the beginning of a section as a connecting link. But here perhaps it also functions once again to focus on Peter—it was while Peter was speaking that the voice was heard. Matthew's use of ἔτι makes this point,[45] and in context the voice has

---

45.   Also cf. Mt. 12.46; 26.47 and Arndt and Gingrich, *Lexicon*, pp. 315-16.

special relevance for Peter. Moreover, Matthew's omission of Mk 9.6, suggests that for Matthew, Peter meant what he said. If this is recognised, then Matthew seems to suggest that ἀκούετε αὐτοῦ at the end of v. 5 is specially applicable to Peter; and functions both positively in highlighting Peter and also as a corrective to Peter's suggestion.

Matthew 17.5 in View of 17.3

Mark's ἐγένετο is replaced by ἰδού. In v. 3 we noted the theophanic significance which ἰδού and its semitic equivalents often carried, and the same could be said here. Moreover, in the previous chapter we have seen that the occurrence of ἰδού has a significant parallel in καὶ ἰδού in Dan. 7.13 (also 7.2). Also note the use of ὅραμα in Dan. 7.13 (in contrast to αἰ ὁράσεις used twice in the same chapter, at 7.1; 7.15), which is to be compared with τὸ ὅραμα in Mt. 17.9.

νεφέλη φωτεινὴ

These apocalyptic motifs are strengthened by Matthew alone adding φωτεινὴ to Mark's νεφέλη. This apocalyptic motif functions as a counterpart to motifs such as ὡς ὁ ἥλιος...ὡς τὸ φῶς in v. 2. In the Old Testament and in intertestamental Judaism the 'cloud' is associated with 'divine presence' (Exod. 24.15-18; 40.34-38; Ps. 97.2) that gives protection (Isa. 4.5-6). In certain contexts it is also associated with the theme of judgment (Ezek. 30.3; Zeph. 1.15; *2 Bar.* 53.1-12), and also with eschatology (Mt. 24.30/Mk 13.26/Lk. 21.27; Mt. 26.64/Mk 14.62; 1 Thess. 4.17; *4 Ezra* 13.3). In *2 Macc.* 2.8 the appearance of the 'cloud' and the 'glory of the Lord' were expected in the days of the Messiah. In view of Matthew's Son of Man *inclusio*, and also, since in Mt. 24.30 (and par. Mk 13.26; Lk. 21.27) and 26.64 (and par. Mk 14.62) Jesus the 'Son of Man' is associated with 'clouds' (as in Dan. 7.13),[46] it may be that here too νεφέλη has messianic significance.

The Blending of Moses-Sinai and Danielic Motifs

Matthew's ἐπεσκίασεν, a rare verb in Greek,[47] also recalls the

---

46.   Perhaps the plural 'clouds' and singular 'cloud' need not be made much of since contra Mt. 24.30; Mk 13.20 (also Dan. 7.13; 26.64) Luke has the singular 'cloud' in 21.27. So it is perhaps arguable that for Matthew, with his Danielic 'Son of Man' *inclusio*, the 'cloud' in 17.5, in addition to allusion to Exodus 19–34, also symbolises the 'clouds' in Daniel 7.

47.   On ἐπισκιάζω, see Arndt and Gingrich, *Lexicon*, p. 298. In the New Testament, it is found only in Mk 9.7; Mt. 17.5; Lk. 9.34. In Lk. 1.35 καὶ δύναμις

language of the Exodus theophany (cf. Exod. 40.35) where the cloud overshadowed (ἐπεσκίαζεν) the tent of meeting. Matthew's main verb ἐπεσκίασεν (compare Mark's participle ἐπισκιάζουσα), is emphatic, and taken with his suggestive ἰδού, Matthew intends νεφέλη to be taken in its Old Testament and apocalyptic sense.

So, the 'cloud' points not only to the Danielic Son of Man idea, but Matthew by his distinctive 'bright cloud' νεφέλη φωτεινή also emphasises the *shekinah* concept of the visible glory of God.[48] We are reminded of the cloud in the Sinai theophany: thus in Exod. 34.5 καὶ κατέβη Κύριος ἐν νεφέλη (see also Exod. 19.9, 16; 24.15, 16, 18, 40.34), we are reminded of the association of the cloud and glory with the tent of meeting: Exod. 40.34 καὶ ἐκάλυψεν ἡ νεφέλη τὴν σκηνὴν...καὶ δόξης Κυρίου ἐπλήσθη ἡ σκηνή. In Exod. 40.35 the verb ἐπεσκίαζεν (ἐπ' αὐτὴν ἡ νεφέλη) is used, which parallels Matthew's ἐπεσκίασεν, and also is associated with δόξης Κυρίου. This passage is significant since the word *shekinah* derives from the Hebrew שכן, which is translated by the Greek ἐπεσκίαζεν, which is the same verb used here ἐπεσκίασεν (also Mk 9.7; Lk. 9.34). It is interesting to note that Isa. 4.5 alludes to Exod. 40.38 in describing the *shekinah* cloud-glory, which as in the Israel-wilderness setting is to appear during a future time of rest under the Messiah.[49]

If this line of argument is accepted, then here once again Matthew has blended Moses-Sinai, Daniel 7 and apocalyptic motifs. The implication is that like Moses and Elijah at Sinai, the three disciples who are the nucleus of the new Israel, behold a similar new Sinai theophany, associated with the idea of the 'coming of God.' For Matthew, I have suggested, the 'coming of God' in the transfiguration functions as a prolepsis of the 'coming of God–coming of the Son of Man' motifs in passages such as 13.36-43; 16.27, 28; 25.31-46.

Matthew 17.5 and Matthew 3.17

Matthew's second use of ἰδού too will prove to be more than stylistic, for by its insertion and ἐν ᾧ εὐδόκησα, he has made 17.5 correspond almost identically with 3.17.

ὑψίστου ἐπισκιάσει σοι (Mary), and in Acts 5.15 Peter's shadow overshadowed some (ἐπισκιάση). The same idea however, but with a different metaphor may be seen in Jn 1.14 (ἐσκήνωσεν); 2 Cor. 12.9 (ἐπισκηνώση) and Rev. 7.15 σκηνώσει (also see McNeile, *Matthew*, p. 250).

48.   On *Shekinah* see Davies and Allison, *St Matthew*, II, p. 701.
49.   Also cf. *2 Macc.* 2.8.

Mt. 17.5   Mt. 3.17

καὶ ἰδοὺ φωνὴ ἐκ τῆς νεφέλης   καὶ ἰδοὺ φωνὴ ἐκ τῶν οὐρανῶν
λέγουσα· οὗτός ἐστιν ὁ υἱός μου   λέγουσα· οὗτός ἐστιν ὁ υἱός
ὁ ἀγαπητός, ἐν ᾧ εὐδόκησα·   μου ὁ ἀγαπητός, ἐν ᾧ εὐδόκησα·
ἀκούετε αὐτοῦ.

Except for ἐκ τῆς νεφέλης (17.5) and ἐκ τῶν οὐρανῶν (3.17) it is identical. These two phrases are arguably synonymous ways of referring to the divine presence. I have argued this for ἐκ τῆς νεφέλης (see section above); as for ἐκ τῶν οὐρανῶν, it is commonly used in this sense in apocalyptic literature (Dan. 4.31; *1 En.* 13.8; 65.4; *2 Bar.* 13.1; 22.1; Rev. 10.4; 11.12; 14.13).[50] And it is striking that in the independent witness to the transfiguration in 2 Pet. 1.16-18, the voice comes ἐξ οὐρανοῦ ἐνεχθεῖσαν (v. 18).

Two other factors make the parallel between 3.17 and 17.5 more striking: (1) In contrast to the second person rendering in Mk 1.11 and Lk. 3.22, in Matthew alone it is in the third (3.17) and hence is identical to 17.5. (2) καὶ ἰδοὺ (Mt. 3.17) is absent in Mk 1.11 (καὶ φωνὴ = Lk. 3.22).

This suggests a significant Matthean redaction; the only issue is, did Matthew redact 17.5 to correspond with 3.17 or 3.17 to suit 17.5? Perhaps it may be argued both ways: for (1) it may be that by adding ἐν ᾧ εὐδόκησα—not found in Mk 9.7; Lk. 9.35, but in the baptism-voice Mk 1.11 = Lk. 3.22 (ἐν σοὶ εὐδόκησα)—Matthew has aligned 17.5 with 3.17. (2) But Matthew has ἐν ᾧ εὐδόκησα in 3.17, this in contrast to Mk 1.11 = Lk. 3.22. So it appears that Matthew has redacted both 3.17 and 17.5 in order that they may correspond with each other! The insertion of καὶ ἰδοὺ in 3.17 increases the parallelism.

So I suggest that by this deliberate correspondence Matthew has theologically and redactionally firmly linked the baptism with the transfiguration. For the baptism with its 'coming of God' and 'Exodus' motifs[51] compares well with the transfiguration. Moreover, just as Jesus' baptism with its 'vision-epiphany' motif may be taken as a parallel to the call of Old Testament prophets (Isa. 6.1-8, Jer. 1.11-19, Ezek. 1.4-28, etc.) so is 17.1-8 (1) a confirmation of Jesus' call, and also (2) as I have already argued, a re-affirmation of the disciples' call to follow him (cf. Mt. 4.18-22; 16.13-20).

50. Bauckham, *Jude, 2 Peter*, p. 206.
51. This will be discussed further in ch. 6.2.

Matthew 17.5 and Matthew's Son of God Christology
One further point needs to be noted: The 'voice from the cloud' also
goes on to present the Son of Man as the Son of God. This verse with
its 'Son' Christology—οὗτός ἐστιν ὁ υἱός μου ὁ ἀγαπητός, ἐν ᾧ
εὐδόκησα; ἀκούετε αὐτοῦ—undoubtedly is the climax of Matthew's
τὸ ὅραμα, and functions in several, but interrelated, ways.

1. I have already commented on its links with the baptism-voice in
3.17. (2) It affirms the disciples' confession at the lake side ἀληθῶς
Θεοῦ υἱὸς εἶ (14.33). (3) Closer to the transfiguration pericope, it
affirms Peter's confession in 16.16 (ὁ υἱὸς τοῦ Θεοῦ τοῦ ζῶντος in
Matthew alone), where in addition to the 'Son of God' motif of 14.33 is
found Χριστὸς (as in Mk 8.29 and Lk. 9.20—who adds τοῦ Θεοῦ).
This ὁ Χριστὸς /ὁ υἱὸς τοῦ Θεοῦ combination is also paralleled in the
high priest's words in 26.64, where by use of σὺ εἶπας and the tactful
use of 'Son of Man' Jesus seems to avoid the misunderstood title
'Christ' while accepting its application to him.[52] Here again, albeit
indirectly, Matthew (also Mark and Luke) presents the Son of Man as
Son of God. (4) It is also a further answer to Jesus' question about the
'Son of Man' (in Matthew's redaction alone) in 16.13. Coming in a
bracket of Son of Man sayings, 17.5 (like 16.16-17) presents the Son of
Man as Son of God. (5) The 'Son' theme in 17.6 also compares well
with the 'Son' theme in 27.54, and since 17.6 and 27.54 are the only
two places where Matthew uses ἐφοβήθησαν σφόδρα, it seems very
likely an intentional linking of the two events.[53] (6) Finally this verse
contributes towards Matthew's prominent Son of God Christology.[54]

52.   Cf. D.R. Catchpole, 'The Answer of Jesus to Caiaphas (Mtt. XXVI.64)',
NTS 17 (1970–71), pp. 213-26, esp. p. 226 though 'reluctant or circumlatory in
formulation' (also see 27.11). This is due to (1) Jesus' disapproval of the oath
formula in v. 63 and (2) political implications of such a question.

53.   On this see Davies and Allison, *St Matthew*, II, pp. 706-707.

54.   J.D. Kingsbury, *Matthew: Structure, Christology, Kingdom* (Philadelphia:
Fortress Press, 1975), pp. 40-127; 'The Figure of Jesus in Matthew's Story: a
Literary-Critical Probe', *JSNT* 21 (1984), pp. 3-36, while rightly highlighting
Matthew's 'Son of God' Christology, he overstates himself by (1) trying to argue
that all other Christologies are subsumed under it, and (2) pitting one Christology
against another. For a critique on Kingsbury's position see D. Hill, 'The Figure of
Jesus in Matthew's Story: a Response to Professor Kingsbury's Literary-Critical
Probe', *JSNT* 6 (1980), pp. 2-16; France, *Matthew–Evangelist*, pp. 292-98; D.J.
Verseput, 'The Role and Meaning of the "Son of God" Title in Matthew's Gospel',
NTS 33 (1987), pp. 532-56. On the danger of attaching too much significance to

The background of οὗτός ἐστιν ὁ υἱός μου ὁ ἀγαπητός, ἐν ᾧ εὐδόκησα· ἀκούετε αὐτοῦ however has been much debated. Scholars have seen echoes of various Old Testament passages, or a combination of them. For example the Markan rendering of the voice at Jesus' baptism (Mk 1.11): σὺ εἶ ὁ υἱός μου ὁ ἀγαπητός, ἐν σοὶ εὐδόκησα, is generally taken: (1) as a conflation of Isa. 42.1 and Ps. 2.7.[55] But this is by no means certain, for (2) Jeremias, Fuller, Cranfield and Hahn deny any allusion to Ps. 2.7.[56] (3) P.G. Bretscher sees the influence of Exod. 44.22-23 and hence an Israel typology.[57] (4) G. Vermes, C.H. Turner, E. Best, R.J. Daly, W.L. Liefeld, C. Rowland see the influence of Gen. 22.2, 12, 16 and an Isaac typology.[58]

Christological 'titles' see L.E. Keck, 'Toward the Renewal of New Testament Christology', *NTS* 32 (1986), pp. 362-77.

55.　Cf. Marshall, *Gospel of Luke*, pp. 154-57; 'Son of God or Servant of Jahweh?—A Reconsideration of Mark 1.11', *NTS* 15 (1968–9) pp. 326-36; Gundry, *The Use of the Old Testament*, pp. 29-31; Meier, *The Vision of Matthew*, p. 28; France, *Matthew*, p. 96; *Matthew–Evangelist*, p. 293; F.W. Beare, *The Gospel according to Matthew* (Oxford: Basil Blackwell, 1981), pp.101-104; McNeile, *Matthew*, pp. 32-33, also cites Gen. 22; Amos 8.10; Jer. 6.26. One needs to reckon with the western rendering of Lk. 3.22 which simply cites LXX Ps. 2.7 (υἱός μου εἶ σύ, ἐγὼ σήμερον γεγέννηκά σε, D it, Ju [C1] Or *Meth. Hil. Aug.*: see *SQE* p.27) but this reading is secondary (see Marshall, *Luke*, pp.154-55).

56.　J. Jeremias, *The Servant of God* (London, 1957), pp. 80-81; *TDNT*, V, p. 701; O. Cullmann, *Christology of the New Testament*, p. 66; *Baptism in the New Testament* (London: SCM Press, 1958), pp. 16-17; R.H. Fuller, *The Foundations of New Testament Christology* (London: Collins, 1969), p.170; Cranfield, 'The Baptism of our Lord', pp. 60-61; F. Hahn, *The Titles of Jesus in Christology* (London: Lutterworth, 1969), p. 336. Jeremias notes that the voice at the baptism and the transfiguration vacillates between ἀγαπητός [Mk 1.11; Mt. 3.17; Lk. 3.22; Mk 9.7; Mt. 17.5; Lk. 9.35 (in C A D W Φ *pl* lat sy(ᶜ)ᵖ) and 2 Pet. 1.17] and ἐκλελεγμένος (in P⁴⁵ P⁷⁵ ℵ B L Ξ 892 1241, and the variant ὁ ἐκλεκτός in Θ f 1365). According to Jeremias, these are alternative renderings of בחירי MT Isa. 42.1, which is sometimes translated as ἐκλεκτός (LXX Σ Θ), which also occurs in a version of the baptismal voice in Jn 1.34 (𝔓⁵ᵛⁱᵈ ℵ* beff²* syˢᶜ· Ambrose).

57.　P.G. Bretscher, 'Exodus 4.22-23 and the Voice from Heaven', *JBL* 87 (1968), pp. 301-311.

58.　G. Vermes, *Scripture and Tradition* (Leiden: Brill, 1973), pp. 222-23; C.H. Turner, 'Ο ΥΙΟΣ ΜΟΥ Ο ΑΓΑΠΗΤΟΣ', pp.113-29; E. Best, *The Temptation and Passion: The Markan Soteriology* (Cambridge: Cambridge University Press, 1965), pp. 169-72; R.J. Daly, 'The Soteriological Significance of the Sacrifice of Isaac', *CBQ* 39 (1977), pp. 68-71; Liefeld, 'Theological Motifs', pp. 162-79, esp. pp. 175-78; Rowland, *The Open Heaven*, p. 367.

Since the link between the baptismal voice and the transfiguration voice has been generally recognised both events have been drawn into the discussion.[59] Some of the difficulties faced in this debate are as follows: Taking views (1) and (2) above, the first part of Ps. 2.7 LXX υἱός μου εἶ σύ resembles Mark's σὺ εἶ ὁ υἱός μου (but note the change in word order), but the rest ἐγὼ σήμερον γεγέννηκά σε has no link with Mark's ὁ ἀγαπητός, ἐν σοὶ εὐδόκησα. On the other hand, Mark's ὁ ἀγαπητός and εὐδόκησα are unparalleled in Isa. 42.1 LXX Ἰακὼβ ὁ παῖς μου, ἀντιλήμψομαι αὐτοῦ. Ἰσραὴλ ὁ ἐκλεκτός μου, προσεδέξατο αὐτὸν ἡ ψυχή μου, but are paralleled in the version of Isa. 42.1 quoted in Mt. 12.18 ἰδοὺ ὁ παῖς μου ὃν ᾑρέτισα, ὁ ἀγαπητός μου εἰς ὃν εὐδόκησεν ἡ ψυχή μου. The matter is further complicated by the baptism-voice in Jn 1.34, where ὁ υἱός is rendered ὁ ἐκλεκτός in some manuscripts (𝔓[5vid] ℵ* beff[2*] sy[sc,] Ambrose), being, according to Jeremias, Brown, Schnackenburg, Davies and Allison, the most primitive reading.[60] If this reading is accepted, then the independent version of the baptismal voice alludes to Jesus as ὁ ἐκλεκτός (recalling Isa. 42.1 LXX) and Ps. 2.7 plays no role.[61]

Jeremias argues that both υἱός and ὁ ἀγαπητός are derived from Isa. 42.1, the argument being, (a) Isa. 42.1 speaks of God's עבד. This was rendered by the Greek word παῖς (in the pre-Markan tradition attested in Mt. 12.18). And this in turn became υἱός as now in Mark.[62] (b) ἀγαπητός is a translation of בחירי, which the LXX renders as ὁ ἐκλεκτός. But this perhaps leans too heavily on Mt. 12.18,[63] for, as Gundry[64] has argued, ὁ ἀγαπητός in Mt. 12.18 may be due to Matthew redactionally conforming the Isaiah citation there to the baptismal voice (3.17) and, by anticipation, to the voice at the transfiguration (17.5). I shall return to Isa. 42.1 a little later, but here suffice to note that although Jeremias may have pressed his case too far, yet the importance of Isa. 42.1 for Matthew can hardly be doubted in the light of his 12.18.

59.   See Davies and Allison, *St Matthew*, I, pp. 336-43; II, pp. 701-702.
60.   Cf. Jeremias, *TDNT*, V, p. 701; R.E. Brown, *The Gospel according to John*, I (New York: Doubleday, 1966), p. 57; R. Schnackenburg, *The Gospel according to St John*, I (London: Burns & Oates, 1968), pp. 305-306; Davies and Allison, *St Matthew*, I, p. 338.
61.   Davies and Allison admit this in *St Matthew*, I, p. 338.
62.   Jeremias, *The Servant of God*, pp. 80-81; Hahn, *The Titles of Jesus in Christology*, p. 307.
63.   See Bauckham, *Jude, 2 Peter*, p. 208.
64.   Gundry, *Matthew*, p. 229.

The thing that points most clearly to the influence of Ps. 2.7 in the baptismal voice is the phrase σὺ εἶ (Mk 1.11, Lk. 3.22), but Matthew does not have σὺ εἶ at the baptism (3.17) nor at the transfiguration (17.5).[65] While the influence of Psalm 2 in Judaism should not be underestimated,[66] some of the arguments put forward particularly in relation to Mt. 3.17 and 17.5 are tenuous. For example, Gundry argues that ὁ ἀγαπητός is derived from the Targum to Ps. 2.7, but as E. Lohse, followed by R.J. Bauckham,[67] has pointed out, the Targum to Ps. 2.7 in fact is reaction against the Christian doctrine, and is an attempt in rabbinic Judaism to play down the idea of divine sonship and reduce it to a mere comparison; and so it is counter-productive to build on this passage.

Thus, it needs to be asked if the term 'Son' in Mt. 17.5 (Mk 9.7; Lk. 9.35) needs to be *restricted* to a messianic meaning suggested by Psalm 2 (or Isa. 42.1-2),[68] or whether something more is intended. This takes us (1) to Bretscher's view where he suggests the influence of Exod. 4.22 and (2) the influence of Genesis 22 cited by Liefeld and others.

P.G. Bretscher,[69] argues that the original form of the heavenly voice is based on a literal rendering of Exod. 4.22 MT בני בכרי ישראל which he translates as ὁ υἱός μου ὁ πρωτότοκός μου 'Ισραήλ (ἐστιν). This rendering compares well with the version of the heavenly voice (at transfiguration) in 2 Pet. 1.17: ὁ υἱός μου ὁ ἀγαπητός μου οὗτός ἐστιν, with ἀγαπητός supplanting ὁ πρωτότοκός, and οὗτός for 'Ισραήλ. But against this Bauckham points out that it is doubtful if Bretscher has provided sufficient reasons why בכרי should be translated as ἀγαπητός.[70] Bretscher's view links Israel's sonship in Exod. 4.22 with Jesus' sonship, and this Jesus-Israel-God's Son identification is seen

---

65.   Hence I cannot understand the logic behind the plain acceptance of the influence of Psalm 2 in Mt. 3.17 and 17.5 by Davies and Allison, *St Matthew*, I, p. 338.

66.   Psalm 2 may have been interpreted in a messianic sense in pre-Christian Judaism, but this is far from certain. See Davies and Allison, *St Matthew*, I, p. 339; Liefeld, 'Theological Motifs', p. 176; J.A. Fitzmyer, *A Wandering Aramean* (Missoula: Scholars Press 1979), pp. 675-77.

67.   E. Lohse, *TDNT*, VIII, p. 362; Bauckham, *Jude, 2 Peter*, p. 207.

68.   This question is rightly asked by Liefeld, 'Theological Motifs', p. 176. On the (debated) issue of Isa. 42.1 being used messianically see Davies and Allison, *St Matthew*, I, p. 339.

69.   Bretscher, 'The Voice From Heaven', pp. 301-312.

70.   Bauckham, *Jude, 2 Peter*, p. 208.

in Mt. 2.15 (cf. Hos. 11.1),[71] but we shall soon see that the idea of Genesis 22 influence has much to commend it.

Genesis 22.2, 12, 16
It is significant that the closest verbal parallel to Mt. 17.5 (Mk 9.7) is found in Gen. 22.2. The texts may be set out as follows:

MT	קח־נא את־בנך את־יחידך אשר־אהבת
Gen. 22.2	λάβε τὸν υἱόν σου τὸν ἀγαπητόν, ὃν ἠγάπησας
Mk 9.7	οὗτός ἐστιν ὁ υἱός μου ὁ ἀγαπητός
Mt. 17.5	οὗτός ἐστιν ὁ υἱός μου ὁ ἀγαπητός
Lk. 9.35	οὗτός ἐστιν ὁ υἱός μου ὁ ἐκλελεγμένος

In the LXX ἀγαπητός and μονογενής are used to translate יחיד MT, and Liefeld, citing De Kruif, argues that in Amos 8.10, Zech. 12.10, Jer. 6.27, the focus is on an only child, and in these examples ἀγαπητός is used (translating the Hebrew יחיד).[72] In Judg. 11.34, however, where too the focus is on Jephthah's 'only child' (his daughter), μονογενής is used. It is significant that in each of these examples the referent is a 'son or daughter who has either died or is in mortal danger', a point that well fits both Isaac in Gen. 22.2 and also Jesus.[73] Thus, (1) since among other things the transfiguration pericope needs to be set in the context of Jesus' passion predictions (Mt. 16.21 and par.; 17.23 and par.) and (2) since Matthew seems to link the 'Son of God' theme at the transfiguration (17.5-6) with the 'Son of God' theme in the passion narrative (27.54) (the only two places where Matthew uses ἐφοβήθησαν σφόδρα), it is arguable that an *Akedah*–Genesis 22 echo lies behind

71. Gundry notes that Exod. 4.22 itself may provide a broad base for the messianic use of Ps. 2.7 (Bretscher has argued for the same in Hos. 11.1), and T.W. Manson, 'The Old Testament in the Teaching of Jesus', pp. 323-24, cites a midrash on Ps. 2.7 which illustrates the text 'thou art my son' from the law (Exod. 4.22-24), the Prophets (Isa. 42.1) and the Hagiographa (Ps. 110.1).

72. Liefeld, 'Theological Motifs', p. 176.

73. Liefeld, 'Theological Motifs', p. 176 points out that this theme is expressed in the New Testament especially by Luke: see 7.12 (the only son of the widow of Nain); 8.42 (Jairus' only daughter); 9.38 (the incurable son (soon after the transfiguration). Also see Jn 3.16; Heb. 11.17.

Mt. 17.5. Moreover, perhaps the 'mountain' context of Genesis 22 and Matthew 17 adds to this parallelism.[74]

So I conclude that (1) the influence of Genesis 22 on Mt. 17.5 is quite probable. (2) By his distinctive ἐν ᾧ εὐδόκησα (in contrast to Mk 9.7; Lk. 9.35) Matthew makes the agreement with the baptism voice perfect (3.17), and he also alludes to Isa. 42.1 (see his 12.18).[75] And Jesus's identification with עבד is quite fitting in a pericope so influenced by Mosaic motifs, for Moses himself was עבד par excellence. (3) Since

---

74. On the significance of the 'Binding of Isaac' in Judaism and its relevance for New Testament Christology see Liefeld, 'Theological Motifs', pp. 177-78; Vermes, *Scripture and Tradition*, (1973), p. 195; J.E. Wood, 'Isaac Typology and the New Testament', *NTS* 14 (1967–68), pp. 583-89. The New Testament passages usually associated with the Jesus-Isaac typology are Rom. 8.32; Jas 2.20; less clearly in Jn 1.29; 1 Pet. 1.19; Jn 3.16; Jn 8.56; 1 Cor. 15; Gal. 3.16; see H.W. Attridge, *The Epistle to the Hebrews* (Philadelphia: Fortress Press, 1989, pp. 333-34; F.F. Bruce, *The Epistle to the Hebrews* (Grand Rapids: Eerdmans, 2nd edn, 1988), p. 308, n.135, p. 309, nn. 142, 143; McCurley, "And after Six Days", p. 78; Ridderbos, *The Epistle of Paul to the Churches of Galatia*, pp. 132-34; D.A. Hagner, *Hebrews* (Peabody: Hendrickson, 1983), pp. 197-98 n. 31. On Isaac typology in early Christian literature see P.E. Hughes, *A Commentary on the Epistle to the Hebrews* (Grand Rapids: Eerdmans, 1977), pp. 484-85; Daly, 'The Sacrifice of Jesus', pp. 45-75. P.R. Davies and B.D. Chilton, 'The Aqedah: A Revised Tradition history', *CBQ* 40 (1978), pp. 514-46 argue that the 'expiatory value' was first attributed to the sacrifice of Isaac after AD 70, but allow for the possible echo of Genesis 22 in Jn 3.16; 1 Jn 4.9 (p. 531). For a comprehensive treatment see J. Swetnam, *Jesus and Isaac* (Rome: Biblical Institute Press, 1981). For New Testament references see Swetnam, *Jesus and Isaac*, pp. 80-85. It is true that the expiation of sins achieved through Jesus' death may be contrasted with the *Aqedah* where it was not achieved, but this goes to show that Jesus is greater than Isaac, and need not deny the 'typology' as such, especially if such an '*aqedah*' typology was important for the Jews (see Swetnam). So a case could be made that Genesis 22 had a reasonable influence on New Testament Christology.

75. It is only the transfiguration-voice of Mt. 17.5 and 2 Pet. 1.17 that have the clause 'with whom I am well pleased'. Bauckham, *Jude, 2 Peter*, pp. 209-210, while arguing against 2 Peter being dependent on the Matthean redaction of the transfiguration, compares the εἰς ὅν constructions in Mt. 12.18 and 2 Pet. 1.17 and suggests that the tradition behind the phrase ὁ ἀγαπητός μου εἰς ὃν εὐδόκησεν ἡ ψυχή μου in Mt. 12.18 depends on a tradition of the words of the voice different from that used in Mt. 3.17; 17.5; but related to the tradition in 2 Pet. 1.17. Conversely, since, as Gundry, *Matthew*, p. 229 has drawn attention to the possible redactional link that Matthew makes between 3.17, 12.18 (= Isa. 42.1) and 17.5, my point is that 'Isa. 42.1' influence is strong in Mt. 17.5.

Matthew does not have the phrase σὺ εἶ (see Mk 1.11; Lk. 3.22) which is crucial to reading Ps. 2.7 in the baptismal voice and hence by implication in the transfiguration voice, it is doubtful if Matthew is intending to press for a Davidic Christology at the transfiguration.[76]

ἀκούετε αὐτοῦ

Finally, Matthew retains ἀκούετε αὐτοῦ, with its distinctive echo of αὐτοῦ ἀκούσεσθε of Deut. 18.15.[77] Given the Mosaic motifs in Mt. 17.1-8, it is highly likely that Matthew is reproducing themes from the context of Deuteronomy 18. We have seen that the Samaritans used Deut. 18.5 as a messianic proof text: it was attached to their version of the Decalogue, and the *Taheb*-Messiah was to be a teacher (cf. Jn 4.25). It is applied to Jesus in Act 3.22-23, 7.37. Matthew's retention of it in 17.5, viewed in the light of his Moses motifs, heightens the Moses-Jesus parallelism. The full significance of the Deut. 18.15-19–Jesus link has not been adequately exploited.

1. According to v. 16 the prophet-like-Moses was to have the same honour as Moses at Sinai: 'just as you desired of the Lord your God at Horeb on the day of the assembly...' It is perhaps also worth noting the 'assembly' theme (הקהל, ἐκκλησίας LXX) in v. 16, since the ἐκκλησία is important for Matthew (Mt. 16.18; 18.17). So Moses, Sinai and the assembly are important themes in Deut. 18.16, which fits well with Matthew's Moses-Sinai-Jesus link, and also by implication with Jesus' relation to the new Israel represented by the three disciples. For it is arguable that just as Jesus is the essential Israel, the chosen three disciples themselves, on this new Sinai event, represent the new Israel, who are to ἀκούετε αὐτοῦ Jesus, the new and greater Moses, the Son of Man who is Son of God, and like Moses one who is עבד par excellence.

2. The words of Deut. 18.18 too are of significance:

---

76.   In ch. 6.7 I shall evaluate Matthew's Davidic Christology (cf. 1.1, 6, 17, 20; 12.23) especially in the context of healings (cf. 9.27; 15.22; 20.30, 31; 21.9, 15) and the 'apparent' rejection of the title in 22.41-45. But here suffice to note that it is highly muted in 3.17 and 17.5.

77.   Davies and Allison, *St Matthew*, II, pp. 702-703 following C L W Θ *f¹³* Maj lat sy Chr PsAug Cyp Hil Ephr mae have αὐτοῦ ἀκούετε. The Nestle-Aland text following ℵ B D *f¹* 33 ff¹ r² Hip Or sa bo have the reverse order. Davies and Allison point out that the imperative ἀκούετε echoes the Hebrew שמע meaning obey (Exod. 6.12; 2 Chron. 28.11) and the same holds true on occasion for ἀκούω in Mt. 18.15-16; Lk. 16.29, 31; Jn 5.25; 8.47; Acts 28.28.

and I will put my words in his mouth, and he will speak to them all that I command him. And whoever will not give heed to my words which he shall speak in my name, I myself will require of him.

This is highly reminiscent of what the Jesus of Matthew taught about his 'words' (Mt. 13.9-23; 24.35) and 'teachings' (4.23; 9.35; 21.23; 26.55). They were 'words' of the kingdom (13.19), the kingdom of the (my) Father (26.29) and the Son of Man's kingdom (16.28). Most significant is the 'Q' passage of Mt. 7.24-27: 'Every one then who hears (ἀκούει, to be compared with ἀκούετε αὐτοῦ of 17.5) these words of mine and does them will be like a wise man who built (ᾠκοδόμησεν) his house upon the rock' (τὴν πέτραν, which makes an interesting comparison with 16.18). And every one who 'hears' and does not heed these words builds his house on the sand and is a sure candidate for judgment. The teaching is reminiscent of Deut. 18.18.

The ἀκούει...ᾠκοδόμησεν...τὴν πέτραν combination in Mt. 7.24, makes an interesting comparison not only with similar words in Mt. 16.18 (πέτρᾳ, οἰκοδομήσω) but also with Peter's suggestion in 17.4 and the command to 'hear' ἀκούετε αὐτοῦ in 17.5. For just as Peter was to be the πέτρα on which the ἐκκλησία (note parallel with Sinai-'assembly' idea in Deut. 15.16) was to be built (οἰκοδομήσω), it was also to be built on the words and teachings of Jesus (e.g. 7.24). This is in keeping with Matthew's prominent emphasis on Jesus' teaching, for example, note the final words in Matthew's gospel διδάσκοντες αὐτοὺς τηρεῖν πάντα ὅσα ἐνετειλάμην ὑμῖν (Mt. 28.20). It is with these associations in mind, and the Sinai framework within which Deut. 18.15-19 is set, that Matthew's ἀκούετε αὐτοῦ in 17.5 needs to be understood.

Jesus-Son of God Motif in Matthew 17.5 in the Light of Moses-Sinai and Son of Man-Daniel 7 Themes in Matthew 17.1-8
How does the 'Son' motif in 17.5 compare with the Moses-Sinai and Danielic framework that Matthew has given the transfiguration pericope? Considering Matthew's Moses emphasis, how does the figure of Moses fit in to all this? Given Matthew's Moses emphasis, since the prophet-like-Moses motif (Deut. 18.15-19) occurs prominently in the last phrase of the voice, ἀκούετε αὐτοῦ (17.5), it may be argued that this key phrase acts as an hermeneutical control over the whole statement, including the Jesus-Son of God identification. But apart from this, the following points are worth considering:

1. We have seen that *Jesus-'ebed-Yahweh* (Isa. 42.1), and *Jesus-*

obedient son (Gen. 22.2) themes are the most relevant to the son motif in Mt. 17.5.

2. The *'ebed-Yahweh* (Isa. 42.1) and Israel-obedient-son (Gen. 22) Christologies link well with the theme of Jesus' suffering and death in the immediately preceding 16.21-28 and also 17.22-23. But it is instructive also to realise that Moses is consistently called God's servant, עבד (Exod. 4.10; 14.31; Num. 12.7, 8; Deut. 3.24; Jos. 1.2, 7; 9.24; 11.15). He is *'ebed-Yahweh* (עבד-יהוה) in Deut. 34.5; Josh. 1.1, 13, 15; 8.31, 33; 11.12; 12.6; 13.8; 14.7; 18.7; 22.2, 4, 5.[78] Given the Moses emphasis of the time, and given Matthew's Moses emphasis in 17.1-8 and elsewhere, this Moses-*'ebed-Yahweh* motif makes an interesting comparison with the Jesus-*'ebed-Yahweh* motif in 17.5 (3.17).

3. Finally, given the Mosaic themes in Mt. 17.1-8, it is interesting to compare the Jesus-Sonship motif in Mt. 17.5 with the Moses-Son of God motif in certain Jewish writings.

(a) *Moses and Sonship Language:* In Jewish literature Moses too has been called God's son, God's chosen one, God's beloved. For example in the 175–150 BCE Sir. 45.1 he is called the Beloved of God, and he that was made glorious as God (v. 2), God had chosen him out of all flesh (v. 4). In the first century CE *Liv. Proph.* 2.14-15, he is God's chosen one. In the pre-Christian Ezekiel the Tragedian, v. 100, God addresses Moses: 'Take courage, son, and listen to my words.'[79]

(b) *Sonship and Divinity:* It is also significant that language and motifs bordering on 'divinity' or quasi-divinity have been applied to Moses. In Philo, God appointed him (Moses) as god (*Sacr.* 9), Moses is almost divinised in Philo's writings (cf. *Mos.* 2.288). At Sinai Moses and Israel 'see' God at Sinai, receive 'second birth' and become 'sons of God' (*Conf. Ling.* 146, *Leg. All.* 1.4). Josephus, while not going as far as Philo, describes Moses as θεῖον ἀνδρα (*Ant.* 3.180). According to the first to second-century BCE Artapanus, Moses was worthy to be honoured like a god and to have been named as Hermes by the Egyptian priests,[80] and the first-century CE *T. Mos.* 1.14 seems to ascribe pre-

78. Als cf. 2 Kgs 18.12; 2 Chron. 1.3; 24.6. In 1 Chron. 6.49; 24.9 he is *'ebed-Yahweh.*

79. In the second- to ninth-century CE *Greek Apocalypse of Ezra* 6.5-13, Ezra is assimilated to Moses, and in this setting is 'tempting' to take God's address to his only begotten son: "Go down, my beloved son..." (see *OTP*, vol. 1, p. 577) as referring to Moses'.

80. Cf. Tiede, *Charismatic Figure*, pp. 317-24.

existence to Moses. He was the Hebrew par excellence, the model for all Israel, prophet-priest-king-mediator, law-giver, God's beloved, God's son; see, Sir. 44.23-45.5; *Jub.* 1.4; Ps.-Philo. 12.1; *T. Mos.* 1.14-15; *Liv. Proph.* 2.14-15; the one like the son of man cf. Ezek. Trag. 68–89.

So I conclude that, since this idea of 'divinity' is also closely related to the idea of sonship, which along with the ''*ebed-Yahweh*' title had been applied to Moses, and, given the Moses emphasis of the time, Matthew has used Moses-Sinai categories in his transfiguration pericope to present Jesus as the greater Moses, and he is presenting Jesus as Son of God far superior to any current conceptions of Moses as son of God.[81]

6. *Matthew 17.6-7*

Mt. 17.6-7   καὶ ἀκούσαντες οἱ μαθηταὶ ἔπεσαν ἐπὶ πρόσωπον αὐτῶν
καὶ ἐφοβήθησαν σφόδρα. καὶ προσῆλθεν ὁ Ἰησοῦς καὶ
ἁψάμενος αὐτῶν εἶπεν· ἐγέρθητε καὶ μὴ φοβεῖσθε.

17.6 and 7 are unique to Matthew. They are thus particularly valuable material for unlocking Matthew's understanding of the transfiguration: (1) It is plain that καὶ ἀκούσαντες refers to hearing the voice from the cloud (v. 5), which also includes the specific command ἀκούετε αὐτοῦ with its Deuteronomy 18 echoes.

2. In response to this hearing: οἱ μαθηταὶ ἔπεσαν ἐπὶ πρόσωπον αὐτῶν καὶ ἐφοβήθησαν σφόδρα. We have earlier noticed that by contrast with Mk 9.6 (Lk. 9.34) Matthew has no fear motif in the parallel 17.4, but introduces it only in 17.6. This is because it functions

---

81.   Issues related to the 'development' of the 'Son of God' in New Testament has been widely discussed: see G. Vermes, *Jesus the Jew* (London: SCM Press, 3rd edn, 1989), pp. 192-222; F. Hahn, *The Titles of Jesus in Christology*, pp. 336-37, and it is well known that angelic beings (Gen. 6.2, 4; Deut. 32.8; Pss. 29.1; 89.7; Dan. 3.25), Israelites/Israel (Exod. 4.22; Deut. 32.5-6; Jer. 31.20; Hos. 11.1; 18-19), the Kings of Israel (2 Sam. 7.14; Pss. 2.7; 89.26-7), 'the righteous' (Sir. 4.10; *Wis.* 2.17-18; *Jub.* 1.24-25 etc.) have been 'sons of God'. And hence Moses, could be placed under the category of 'righteous'. But given the emphasis in Ezek. Trag. v. 100 (Daniel 7 and Sinai setting, see ch. 3); *Assumption of Moses* 1.14 (where he is ascribed pre-existence), 12.6 where Moses enjoys the role of intercessor, it is not impossible that the Moses-God's son may have acquired special significance. However, Matthew's Jesus-Son of God association (2.21-23; 2.15; 4.3, 6; 14.33; 16.16; 17.5; 21.37; 27.54, further see ch. 6.7), coupled with the idea that Jesus was greater than the Temple, Jonah, Solomon (Mt. 12.6, 41, 42), perhaps challenges any current conceptions of Moses as Son of God.

differently for him. Mark associates the fear with Peter's ill-thought out suggestion in 9.5, and both are in response to the transfiguration event itself. But Matthew has specifically associated it with the disciples' response to the voice from the cloud. So the fear is in response to both (a) the transfigured Jesus whom they should 'hear' and obey (ἀκούετε αὐτου) and (b) the voice from heaven, for it is on hearing this (ἀκούσαντες) voice that they 'fell on their faces' (17.6).

3. The response of 'fear and prostration' placed here also corresponds to the typical response to visions in such apocalyptic passages as Ezek. 1.28; 2.1; 40–48; Rev. 1.12-20, particularly Dan. 7.15, 28; 8.17, 18; 10.7-9, 15-19. These visions are similar in form to Matthew's presentation of the transfiguration as τὸ ὅραμα (17.9)

Prostration (ἔπεσαν ἐπὶ πρόσωπον) is also found in Exod. 3.6, where, after seeing the 'vision' (τὸ ὅραμα 3.3 LXX) at Horeb/Sinai, Moses turned his face away (ἀπέστρεψε δὲ Μωυσῆς τὸ πρόσωπον αὐτοῦ...). A similar reaction by Moses is also seen at the second giving, or renewal, of the covenant in Exod. 34.8 LXX καὶ σπεύσας Μωυσῆς, κύψας ἐπὶ τὴν γῆν προσεκύνησε, when the 'Lord passed before his face' (also cf. Exod. 33.11, Deut. 34.10). In addition Israel feared when they saw the transfigured face of Moses (καὶ ἐφοβήθησαν ἐγγίσαι αὐτῷ Exod. 34.30, compare ἐφοβήθησαν in Mt. 17.6), and earlier on in Exod. 20.18 where Israel 'were afraid and trembled' at the Sinai theophany. So here, the disciples' response to the vision has significant points in common with the 'vision-response' pattern in Exod. 3.3-6; Dan. 8.1-17, 18; 10.7-9.

4. The Matthean καὶ προσῆλθεν ὁ Ἰησοῦς καὶ ἁψάμενος αὐτῶν εἶπεν· ἐγέρθητε καὶ μὴ φοβεῖσθε may be interpreted in a natural way: (a) the disciples are terrified due to this supernatural experience, and (b) their fear is relieved by Jesus' assurance μὴ φοβεῖσθε (also 14.27). But there are other features that invite us to discern the significance of 17.7 at a deeper level.

(a) In Matthew, only here (προσῆλθεν) and in 28.18 (προσελθὼν) is Jesus spoken of as approaching someone; in every other instance it is others who approach him. This usage is peculiar to Matthew, and on both occasions Jesus is portrayed in an extraordinary setting: in Matthew 17 it is the transfiguration, and in 28.18 it is the resurrected Jesus who comes. On both occasions there is a response of reverence (cf. προσεκύνησαν 28.17). It may well be that Matthew intends to make a link between the transfiguration and another 'Galilee' mountain event in 28.16-20.

(b) The 'touch' motif ἀψάμενος (Mt. 17.7) compares well with similar motifs in Dan. 8.18 (ἥψατό), 10.10 (ἀπτομένη μου) 10.16 and 18 (ἥψατο).

(c) The command μη φοβεῖσθε (echoed also in 14.27) compares with Dan. 10.12 μὴ φοβοῦ Δανιήλ (also v. 19 μὴ φοβοῦ ἀνὴρ ἐπιθυμιῶν). It is also significant to note that in the Sinai setting of Exod. 34.30, when the people are 'afraid to come near the transfigured Moses', it is Moses who speaks to them (v. 31-32). And in 21.20 he strengthens Israel saying 'Do not fear'. So in this verse too there are Sinai and Danielic themes, and it is not inconceivable that Matthew was sensitive to this.

7. *Matthew 17.8 and Mark 9.8*

Mt. 17.8   ἐπάραντες δὲ τοὺς ὀφθαλμοὺς αὐτῶν οὐδένα εἶδον εἰ
          μὴ αὐτὸν Ἰησοῦν μόνον.

Mk 9.8   καὶ ἐξάπινα περιβλεψάμενοι οὐκέτι οὐδένα εἶδον ἀλλὰ
          τὸν Ἰησοῦν μόνον μεθ' ἑαυτῶν

Here we return to Matthew's redaction of Mark. (1) Matthew's ἐπάραντες δὲ τοὺς ὀφθαλμοὺς αὐτῶν for Mark's καὶ ἐξάπινα περιβλεψάμενοι is explicable since in Mark's account the three disciples do not fall to the ground. (2) Matthew omits Mark's οὐκέτι, for in his account the disciples had been prostrate on the ground, and had not seen any one for some time. (3) Matthew adds εἰ μὴ and especially αὐτὸν before Ἰησοῦν (for Mark's ἀλλὰ τὸν) for the sake of emphasis on Jesus. (4) He also omits Mark's μεθ' ἑαυτῶν so that the focus and climax of the event may be on none other than Jesus alone: Ἰησοῦν μόνον.[82]

8. *Matthew 17.9; 17.10-13 in the Light of Mark 9.9-10 and 9.11-13*

Matthew 17.9 and 17.10-13 form the other end of the 'Son of Man' double bracket within which Matthew has presented his transfiguration pericope, and so are important for my thesis. Nevertheless, since I have already commented on these verses in the previous chapter, I shall be brief. First some preliminary points need to be made: If Mt. 17.2-6 was the 'vision', and vv. 7-8 the disciples' reaction to the vision, then vv. 9-13 may in some sense be associated with the 'interpretation of the vision'. In 17.9 there is a call to silence about τὸ ὅραμα 'until' ἕως οὗ ὁ υἱὸς τοῦ ἀνθρώπου ἐκ νεκρῶν ἐγερθῇ. Interestingly in Matthew

---

82. On this see Gundry, *Matthew*, p. 345.

this is the fifth and last occasion the disciples are commanded to be silent, the earlier occasions being 8.4; 9.30; 12.16; 16.20. But only on this occasion is it implied that Jesus permits his disciples to speak—in the future after the resurrection. In view of this it is arguable that one key to the interpretation of the transfiguration may lie in the resurrection.

Matthew 17.9 and Mark 9.9-10

Mt. 17.9   καὶ καταβαινόντων αὐτῶν ἐκ τοῦ
ὄρους ἐνετείλατο αὐτοῖς
ὁ Ἰησοῦς λέγων· μηδενὶ εἴπητε τὸ
ὅραμα ἕως οὗ ὁ υἱὸς
τοῦ ἀνθρώπου ἐκ νεκρῶν ἐγερθῇ

Mk 9.9   καὶ καταβαινόντων αὐτῶν ἐκ τοῦ
ὄρους διεστείλατο
αὐτοῖς ἵνα μηδενὶ ἃ εἶδον
διηγήσωνται, εἰ μὴ ὅταν ὁ υἱὸς
τοῦ ἀνθρώπου ἐκ νεκρῶν ἀναστῇ

Mk 9.10   καὶ τὸν λόγον ἐκράτησαν πρὸς
ἑαυτοὺς συζητοῦντες τί
ἐστιν τὸ ἐκ νεκρῶν ἀναστῆναι

1. Matthew has ἐνετείλατο for Mark's διεστείλατο. In 19.7 ἐνετείλατο (par. Mk 10.4) is used in reference to Moses' command, about divorce, superseded by Jesus' λέγω δὲ ὑμῖν...(19.8-9). The only other use in Matthew is 4.6 (ἐντελεῖται) and in some manuscripts in 15.4 (ἐνετείλατο) and in both instances it is with reference to God. So in Matthew it is restricted to God (twice), Jesus (twice) and Moses (once). Due to its restricted usage, and in view of the immediately preceding 'mountain motif' (καὶ καταβαινόντων αὐτῶν ἐκ τοῦ ὄρους ἐνετείλατο...) it is possible that it serves Matthew's paralleling of Jesus with Moses.[83]

2. Matthew's ὁ Ἰησοῦς λέγων (absent in Mark) lays the emphasis on Jesus, and needs to be seen in the light of αὐτὸν Ἰησοῦν μόνον in v. 8.

3. Matthew's description of the transfiguration as τὸ ὅραμα suggests that Matthew sees it as theophanic vision akin to those found in Old Testament and New Testament apocalyptic (see preceding discussion).

4. Matthew omits Mk 9.10 (καὶ τὸν λόγον ἐκράτησαν πρὸς

---

83. So Gundry, *Matthew*, p. 346.

ἑαυτοὺς συζητοῦντες τί ἐστιν τὸ ἐκ νεκρῶν ἀναστῆναι). It has been suggested that, as in 17.4 (contra Mk 9.6), Matthew here presents the disciples as having understanding.[84] But this need not be the case: I shall argue below that Matthew's τί οὖν (17.10) links the resurrection issue in 17.9 with the coming of Elijah; so Mark's question (9.10) is implied in Matthew's τί οὖν.

Matthew 17.10-13 and Mark 9.11-12

Matthew 17.10-13 in comparison with Mk 9.9-13 seems to be so 'independent, though complementary', that some have suggested that he is drawing from a different source.[85] But there are sufficient parallels to suggest that Matthew has redacted Mark, which, however, does not exclude the possibility that he had access to other sources. In this section, I shall only comment on some main Matthean differences and their significance.

It also needs to be noted that Mt. 17.10-13 with its obvious links with v. 9 (which causes the discussion in 10-13) brackets the transfiguration pericope with 16.13-28 and contributes towards the second part of the 'Son of Man' double bracket: 16.27; 16.28—17.1-8—17.9; 17.12.

Mt. 17.10	Καὶ ἐπηρώτησαν αὐτὸν οἱ μαθηταὶ λέγοντες· τί οὖν οἱ γραμματεῖς λέγουσιν ὅτι Ἠλίαν δεῖ ἐλθεῖν πρῶτον
v. 11	ὁ δὲ ἀποκριθεὶς εἶπεν· Ἠλίας μὲν ἔρχεται καὶ ἀποκαταστήσει πάντα·
Mk 9.11	Καὶ ἐπηρώτων αὐτὸν λέγοντες· ὅτι λέγουσιν οἱ γραμματεῖς ὅτι Ἠλίαν δεῖ ἐλθεῖν πρῶτον
v. 12	ὁ δὲ ἔφη αὐτοῖς· Ἠλίας μὲν ἐλθὼν πρῶτον ἀποκαθιστάνει πάντα· καὶ πῶς γέγραπται ἐπὶ τὸν υἱὸν τοῦ ἀνθρώπου ἵνα πολλὰ πάθῃ καὶ ἐξουδενηθῇ

84. By use of λέγων Matthew does not adopt Marks ἵνα clause, but changes it to a more direct quotation.

85. See A. Schlatter, *Der Evangelist Matthäus* (Stuttgart: Calwer, 1963), pp. 530-32.

(a) Matthew has changed Mark's ἐπηρώτων to ἐπηρώτησαν: 'they asked' to go with οἱ μαθηταί.[86] The use of οἱ μαθηταί is significant, for it anticipates v. 13 where they are portrayed as having understood Jesus' point about Elijah being the Baptist.

(b) Matthew also has τί οὖν οἱ γραμματεῖς λέγουσιν...for Mark's ὅτι λέγουσιν οἱ γραμματεῖς. The replacement of Mark's ὅτι (9.11) by τί (Mt. 17.10) may be purely stylistic.[87] But Matthew's use of οὖν is significant; it makes for a closer connection with the preceding v. 9, with its (i) 'vision' motif, which includes their seeing Elijah on the mountain, and (ii) statement on the resurrection (and therefore death). But the meaning of the disciples' query on Elijah's coming has been much debated. Scholars have made several suggestions, for example (i) That the disciples were clarifying, how does Elijah's appearance (17.3) stand in relation to the official position of the οἱ γραμματεῖς?[88] Where is his 'restoration' movement and if we are to take this appearance (17.3) as a fulfilment of his coming, why should we not proclaim your messiahship?[89] (ii) How do we fit the resurrection motif (17.9, and therefore death), with the Elijah motif?[90]

Some Observations

Whether (i) is a valid interpretation of Ἠλίαν δεῖ ἐλθεῖν πρῶτον; is

86.   France, *Matthew—Evangelist*, pp. 261-65, rightly points out that Matthew does not restrict μαθητής to the inner circle of twelve (e.g. 8.21; 10.24-25; 10.42). On Matthew's emphasis on 'disciple-discipleship' see Wilkins, *The Concept of Disciple*; W.F. Albright and C.S. Mann, 'The Disciples', in *Matthew* (New York: Doubleday, 1973), pp. lxxxiv-lxxx; U. Luz, 'The Disciples in the Gospel according to Matthew', in G.N. Stanton, *Interpretation*, pp. 98-128. The view that Matthew presents the disciples as men of understanding needs to be taken with caution, see Mt. 14.31; 16.22 of Peter, 26.50-56, 28.17 for instances where they lacked understanding (but cf. 11.11; 13.11; 14.33).

87.   See Allen, *St Matthew*, p. 186, McNeile, *Matthew*, p. 252; Gundry, *Matthew*, p. 346; it avoids confusion with the exegetical ὅτι in the clause that follows, but it could be purely stylistic.

88.   See Allen, *St Matthew*, p. 186.

89.   Cf. Allen, *St Matthew*, p. 186 followed by France, *Matthew*, p. 264.

90.   On such, and related arguments see Hill, *The Gospel of Matthew*, p. 267; Carson, *Matthew*, pp. 388-89; Allen, *St Matthew*, p.186. But Matthew by his specific use of οὖν links their question with the teaching on the resurrection just mentioned in 17.9.

highly debated. It is true that the 'coming of Elijah' is alluded to quite frequently in Jewish literature, cf. *Apoc. Elij.* 4.7-12;[91] Justin, *Dial.* 8.4; 49.1; *Sib. Or.* 2.185-195; *b. Menah.* 63a; *b. Pesah.* 13a, 20b; *b. Erub.* 43b; *m. Sota* 9.15; *b. Sabb.* 108a; *Midrash Rabbah Deut.* 11.17-18, perhaps *4 Ezra* 7.109; *1 En.* 93.8,[92] and of course Mal. 4.5. But J.A.T. Robinson, J.A. Fitzmyer, and especially M.M. Faierstein,[93] (in contrast to J. Jeremias, G.F. Moore, G. Vermes, D.C. Allison and others)[94] have argued that the generally cited Elijah-forerunner of the Messiah idea does not enjoy much 'early' support in Jewish literature in itself.[95]

Point (ii) however, is of particular importance in unlocking the thorny point in relation to the 'coming of Elijah' motif in Mt. 17.10-13; Mk 9.11-13. In recent years articles by M.M. Faierstein, D.C. Allison, J.A. Fitzmyer and most recently by J. Taylor[96] have vigorously debated the background of Mt. 17.10-13 and Mk 9.11-13. Fitzmyer, I believe correctly, has argued that the scribes' teaching that 'Elijah must come before' (δεῖ ἐλθεῖν πρῶτον) refers to the 'raising of the dead'. He refers, for example, to *m. Sota.* 9.15 where the resurrection of the dead 'shall come through Elijah of blessed memory'. Other texts,

91.   On the comings of Enoch and Elijah see R. Bauckham, 'The Martyrdom of Enoch and Elijah: Jewish or Christian?', *JBL* 95/3 (1976) pp. 447-58.

92.   Also cf. Ginzberg, *The Legends of the Jews*, VI, pp. 106-107, n. 600; p. 339, n.105; J. Klausner, *The Messianic Ideal* (London: Allen & Unwin, 1925), p. 451. For examples of later texts on Elijah as forerunner of the Messiah, cf. Ginzberg, The Legend of the Jews, VI, p. 234; p. 235, ns.114-16; 118-19.

93.   J.A.T. Robinson, 'Elijah, John, and Jesus: an Essay in Detection', *NTS* 4 (1958), pp. 263-81; J.A. Fitzmyer, 'More about Elijah Coming First', *JBL* 104 (1985), pp. 295-96; M.M. Faierstein, 'Why Do the Scribes Say that Elijah Must Come First?', *JBL* 100 (1981), pp. 75-86.

94.   In support of the forerunner theory see Jeremias, *TDNT*, 2.928-41; G.F. Moore, *Judaism in the First Century of the Christian Era* (Cambridge: Cambridge University Press, 1927), p. 357; Vermes, *Jesus the Jew*, p. 94; D.C. Allison, 'Elijah Must Come First', *JBL* 103 (1984), pp. 256-58.

95.   The prominent passage is the late *baraita* in *b.t.Erub* 43 (i.e. of 4th–5th century CE origin), see Fitzmyer, 'More About Elijah Coming First', p. 269; Justin, *Dial.* 49.1, see J.C.M. van Winden, *An Early Christian Philosopher: Justin Martyr's Dialogue with Trypho*, p. 123.

96.   Fitzmyer, 'More About Elijah Coming First', pp. 295-96; J. Taylor, 'The Coming of Elijah, Mt. 17, 10-13 and Mk 9, 11-13. The Development of Texts', *RB*, 97 (1991), pp. 107-119, esp. p. 117; Robinson, 'Elijah, John and Jesus', pp. 275-77.

b.t. Sanh. 113a; *j.t. Sabb.* 3c have also been cited.[97] In the second-century CE *Sibylline Oracles* 2.185b-195 one of the 'three signs' that the 'Thesbite' will display is linked to the resurrection of the dead (2.220b-250).

That this is the background to Mt. 17.10 and parallels is suggested by the immediately preceding context in Mark and Matthew, where the resurrection is mentioned. And we may also recall my earlier discussion of the connection between the Son of Man of Daniel 7 and the 'resurrection' of Daniel 12. Moreover, it makes good sense to see the scribal teaching about Elijah's restoration in the light of the Danielic expectation of the resurrection.

2. Finally, in 17.11, (a) as in 17.4, Matthew's ἀποκριθεὶς εἶπεν for Mark's ἔφη αὐτοῖς is a stylistic change with αὐτοῖς dropping out as redundant, after the preceding reference to οἱ μαθηταὶ (v. 10). (b) Mark's participle ἐλθὼν becomes the finite verb ἔρχεται, and, as in 24.42-44, it may be argued that the present tense could take a future sense (πρῶτον drops out). Gundry has argued that ἔρχεται, contrasts with ἦλθεν as used of the 'historical appearance' of the Baptist in 11.18; 21.32, (and 17.12). Gundry's point is that Matthew is making a difference between the 'coming of Elijah' in the historical appearance of the Baptist (11.18; 21.32) and the 'future' appearance of Elijah. But against this it may be argued that the future tense signifies scribal hope (note γραμματεῖς 17.10) and not Jesus' prediction of a still future coming of Elijah.[98]

---

97. See Davies and Allison, *St Matthew*, 2, p.715, n.22. But they tend to find a 'forerunner' significance in Mt. 17.9 (also see Davies and Allison, *St Matthew*, 1, pp. 313-14; Allison, 'Elijah Must Come First', p. 256). But Davies' position is challenged by Fitzmyer, 'More About Elijah Coming First', pp. 295-96.

98. Cf. Allen, *St Matthew*, p. 186; France, *Matthew*, p.265; Davies and Allison, *St Matthew*, II, pp. 714-15. I have argued that Luke omits Mk 9.11-13 due to his interest in the Elijah-Jesus motif (see Appendix). Matthew, however, is capable of alluding to the 'literal (rabbinic) interpretation' of scripture: see Zech. 9.9 in 21.2,7. On this see C. Deutsch, *Hidden Wisdom and the Easy Yoke* (Sheffield: JSOT Press, 1987), p. 15.

Matthew 17.12-13 and Mark 9.13

Mt. 17.12-13   λέγω δὲ ὑμῖν ὅτι Ἠλίας ἤδη ἦλθεν, καὶ
οὐκ ἐπέγνωσαν
αὐτὸν ἀλλὰ ἐποίησαν ἐν αὐτῷ ὅσα
ἠθέλησαν· οὕτως καὶ
ὁ υἱὸς τοῦ ἀνθρώπου μέλλει πάσχειν
ὑπ' αὐτῶν. τότε
συνῆκαν οἱ μαθηταὶ ὅτι περὶ Ἰωάννου
τοῦ βαπτιστοῦ εἶπεν αὐτοῖς

Mk 9.13   ἀλλὰ λέγω ὑμῖν ὅτι καὶ Ἠλίας
ἐλήλυθεν, καὶ ἐποίησαν.
αὐτῷ ὅσα ἤθελον, καθὼς γέγραπται
ἐπ' αὐτόν

1. Here, Matthew's λέγω δὲ ὑμῖν (contra Mark's ἀλλὰ λέγω ὑμῖν) is in order to produce a μὲν...δέ construction in vv. 11 and 12.[99]

2. Matthew's καὶ οὐκ ἐπέγνωσαν αὐτὸν is emphatic, for it makes the point that though the scribes were right in their expectation (17.11) the reality within which it was being

99. Matthew omits the problematic Mk 9.12b (for where in the Old Testament is it written so?). This perhaps is (1) because the force of Mk 9.12b is already found in Mt. 17.9; which also necessitates a prior suffering and death, or (2), more likely in context, to maintain his μὲν...δὲ construction in vv. 11 and 12. According to Albright and Mann, *Matthew*, p. 204, Mk 9.12 is a question posed by the disciples to Jesus; and according to Gundry, *Matthew*, p. 347, this omission is due to the fact that in Matthew the disciples already are aware that Jesus will suffer. According to W. Wink, *John the Baptist in the Gospel Tradition* (Cambridge: Cambridge University Press 1968), p. 14, Mk 9.11-13 originally referred only to Elijah, and J. Taylor, 'The Coming of Elijah', p. 119 tries to argue that the Son of Man in Mk 9.11 is Elijah who is to suffer. It is true that if 'Son of Man' in Mk 9.11 is to be taken as generic, then it could apply both to Elijah and Jesus, i.e. as those representing this 'suffering' class. This 'suffering' theme also compares with the *'ebed-Yahweh* motif in Mk 9.7 and parallels. To this theme one could also apply Isa. 53.3 (so W.L. Lane, *The Gospel of Mark* [Grand Rapids: Eerdmans, 1974], pp. 325-26 on γέγραπται, and others cite 1 Kgs 19.2-10 in relation to Elijah; but see Allen, *St Matthew*, p. 187). Hooker, *The Son of Man in Mark*, pp. 30-32 points to the Son of Man's identification with the saints suffering in Dan. 7.21-22. In Matthew's redaction however, (more clearly than Mark) the 'Son of Man' seems to be distinguished from Elijah (see οὕτως καὶ ὁ υἱὸς τοῦ...by which Jesus refers to himself); but as in Mark, though more plainly, it also sets out the Jesus-Baptist-Elijah-suffering motif.

worked out (in relation to the coming of John the Baptist, and
also in the light of the Jesus-Baptist relationship) was so very
different from their view of things that 'they did not know him'.

3. In 17:12 Matthew's ἀλλά functions as a contrast with the
previous clause, and just as Matthew omits Mark's γέγραπται
clause (with reference to Jesus, cf. Mk 9.12), he also omits
καθὼς γέγραπται ἐπ' αὐτόν (with reference to John).
Through this Matthew focuses on the Jesus-John parallelism:
οὕτως καὶ ὁ υἱὸς τοῦ ἀνθρώπου μέλλει πάσχειν ὑπ'
αὐτῶν. This addition compensates for his omission of Mk 9.12.
On the other hand, it is also possible that he is simply
rearranging Mk 9.12, placing the Jesus-suffering motif here
rather than in v. 11. Either way, Matthew brings out the
significance of the Elijah-John and John-Jesus relationship—via
the theme of suffering ἀλλὰ ἐποίησαν ἐν αὐτῷ ὅσα
ἠθέλησαν more plainly than Mark.

Conclusions

1. My exegesis of Mt. 17.1-9 confirms my arguments in ch. 4. (a)
Matthew has presented his transfiguration pericope within a 'Son of
Man *inclusio*' and has primarily applied both Moses-Sinai and Daniel 7
apocalyptic categories. Note, for example, the use of apocalyptic-Danielic
language and motifs in 17.2 (cf. Dan. 12.3 = Mt. 13.43), καὶ ἰδοὺ (17.3,
5), use of τὸ ὅραμα (17.9), the skillful use of the fear motif, the
production of a vision-interpretation form and content (b) For Matthew,
the transfiguration portrays the idea of the 'coming of God'. This is seen
in two complementary ways: (i) The 'bright cloud', and 'voice' on the
mountain demonstrates a Sinai type 'coming of God'. (ii) Jesus, the 'Son
of Man' (Mt. 16.27, 28; 17.9, 12; Dan. 7.13) and the new and greater
Moses, goes up the mountain (Exod. 19; Ezek. Trag. 68–82) to meet
with God. He is transformed, is proclaimed as 'Son of God' (Mt. 17.5),
thus the event is also a demonstration that God had 'come in Jesus'.
This is a theme that Matthew has already stressed in 1.23, and 3.3,
where Isa. 40.3 a prophecy about Yahweh's coming is applied to Jesus.
Hence, through the transfiguration, Matthew demonstrates that (i) in
Jesus 'the coming of God' had occurred (cf. 1.23; 3.3; 12.28), attested
by the voice, and by the two heavenly witnesses Moses and Elijah, and
(ii) this will be further attested at his resurrection (26.64; 28.18-20).
In addition, since Matthew in 17.1-8, has blended both Moses-Sinai

and Daniel 7 themes with their associated ideas of the 'kingdom of God', and 'glory', by way of extension, and in a more indirect sense, it is possible also to take his understanding of the transfiguration as in some sense linked to the idea of 'Jesus coming' for judgment (in the near future, 70 CE [cf. 16.28], but not exhausted by it), and at the 'close of the age', once again for judgment (13.38-42; 16.27; 25.31-33, 41-46) and vindication (13.43; 24.29-31; 25.33-40, 46b).

2. Matthew is not unaware that motifs such as kingdom and glory evoked political sentiments (as displayed in Peter's suggestion), but he probably de-politicised these sentiments by muting the Davidic/Zion motif and by amalgamating the Son of Man motif with the Moses motif and the 'servant' motif of Isaiah 42.[100] Matthew has clearly shown in chapter 12 that Jesus was greater than the Old Testament figures and the Old Testament institution of the temple (12.6), Jonah (the prophets), and Solomon (Davidic kings)—the three great pillars of Jewish life and faith. What really needed to be dealt with decisively was the issue of Mosaic authority and the law, an issue which was heightened by the Moses emphasis of the time and also by the dialogue and controversy with the Pharisees and perhaps synagogue that Matthew and his community were probably engaged in at the time.[101] This he had done to some extent in the sermon on the mount, but by presenting the transfiguration

100. Josephus avoids interpreting Daniel 7, which perhaps suggests that he took 'the one like a son of man' of Daniel 7 in 'political' terms. He is also hesitant over revealing the meaning of Daniel 2 (*Ant.* 10.210), since he believed that Daniel wrote about Rome which he took to be the 'fourth empire' (*Ant.* 10.276). But whether this 'political' understanding of the Son of Man motif was representative or whether it was reflected in Jesus' usage is uncertain. In Josephus' case, he was using Daniel to retell the story of Israel, and hence in his interpretation he seems to have found Daniel 2, 7, too direct (against Rome, the fourth empire). So it was expedient for him to be cautious. The evangelists, however, have Jesus freely using the title 'the Son of Man' (which in its Daniel 7 setting does have political connotations) it perhaps did not carry so much of a 'militaristic-political' and anti-Rome significance as seen in Josephus, dictated by his use of the book of Daniel. A pure Josephus-type view, disregards the 'generic' use of the title, and also the 'lowly Son of Man' connotations (Ezek. 2.1; Ps. 8.4-8; cf. Hooker, *The Son of Man*, pp. 30-32) the title could be made to carry.

101. See K. Stendahl, *The School of Matthew*, p.xi; Viviano, 'Where Was the Gospel according to St Matthew Written?', pp. 533-46; L.E. Keck, 'The Sermon on the Mount', in D.G. Miller and D.Y. Hadidian (eds.), *Jesus and Man's Hope*, vol. 2 (Pittsburgh: Pittsburgh Theological Seminary, 1971), pp. 311-22, esp. pp. 320-21. Davies, *The Setting of the Sermon on the Mount*, pp. 256-315, however, proposes a dialogue with Jamnia.

as a new Sinai event, he forcefully demonstrates that Jesus is the new and greater Moses.

Moreover, he achieves this by precisely presenting Jesus at the transfiguration as the Danielic Son of Man and also the Son of God. Like Moses and the 'one like the son of man' (Dan. 7.13), Jesus represents and is new Israel, with the three disciples as its potential nucleus. Heeding Jesus' words (17.5; Deut. 18.15) means heeding God (7.24-26; 28.19), or else meeting the consequences (Deut. 18.19; Mt. 7.26-27). So for Matthew, the transfiguration is a demonstration of King Jesus in his kingdom which has immediate and far reaching consequences.

3. Matthew displays considerable interest in Peter (cf. 4.18-20;14.28-33; 17.24-27; 16.13-20; 19.27-30). At the transfiguration, Matthew (a) positively links Peter's role with Jesus' ἐκκλησία-building in 16.16-19, and (b) negatively highlights Peter's earthly 'restoration' and Zion-political perspective. Jesus had offered his brand of restoration via repentance to Israel, but their rejection (16.1-12 typical), contrasted with Matthew's portrayal of Gentile receptivity (15.21-39), makes the Caesarea Philippi event the turning point. The presence of Elijah and Matthew's portrayal of the Elijah motif in 17.9-13 heighten this 'restoration' motif. But via his redaction of the words of the voice (17.5) and through the command 'listen to him', which in context, is specifically applicable to Peter, he puts this 'restoration' motif in perspective. It was Jesus who was to be the true builder (Mt. 16.18; Heb. 3.3) and hence was to be listened to. This corresponds to a similar emphasis in 19.27-30 where again Peter triggers the teaching. The command 'listen to him', to be taken in conjunction with 16.16-19, also gives Peter a Joshua-Moses-like role, which was appreciated by the new community, though its over-emphasis by the community caused problems for people like Paul.

4. Matthew firmly links the transfiguration with the baptism (3.17) and also Jesus' final earthly appearance in 28.16-20. For the moment, redactional and thematic links with other passages in Matthew's Gospel (e.g. 4.1-11; 5-7; 28.16-20) must wait until ch. 6 where Matthew's Jesus-Moses parallelism elsewhere in his gospel will be evaluated. So the transfiguration pericope occupies a crucial place in Matthew's structure and arrangement.

5. I have shown that it is also possible that Matthew's 'light' motif takes on theological-missiological significance and compares with (a) Jesus as light of the 'Galilee of the Gentiles' (4.15-16), (b) disciples as lights

(5.14-16), (c) 'light and kingdom' (13.43); and (d) anticipates 28.18-20.

In this, Matthew's interest in geography—here Galilee (4.17–16.20; 16.21–18.35; 26.32; 28.10, 16), the 'Galilee of the Gentiles' (4.15)—plays a crucial part. Peter receives his ἐκκλησία-kingdom-commission at the 'waters of Dan', witnesses the transfiguration (with James and John), and in context receives God's command 'listen to him'. For Matthew the implication of all this is that Jesus is the new and greater Moses, the new temple which incorporates both Jews and Gentiles. This is one reason why Matthew redactionally and thematically links 17.1-8 with 28.16-20.

6. Like Mark, but more plainly, Matthew associates the Baptist with Elijah. He also accommodates the Elijah-resurrection/restoration scribal teaching (also cf. *m. Sota.* 9.18; *Sib. Or.* 2.185-195) with Jesus, in the Son of Man's resurrection motif.

By clearly taking care of the Elijah motif, and linking it to the Son of Man's suffering, death and resurrection, Matthew, (more skillfully than Mark) has made the ramifications of the Elijah-Baptist-Jesus association clear. Matthew has left room to exploit (1) the Moses-Sinai motif; note for example his addition of the face-radiance motif and positioning of Moses before Elijah in contrast to Mark, and (2) he has left room also to exploit the Daniel 7 and relevant apocalyptic themes. Both these factors are stressed that he may portray the transfiguration also in terms of the 'coming of God' idea. My exegetical study of various passages in the coming chapter will further elucidate this and bring out the full significance of Matthew's theology and Christology in his understanding of the transfiguration.

Chapter 6

MATTHEW'S TRANSFIGURATION PERICOPE (17.1-13) IN THE LIGHT
OF THE JESUS-MOSES AND EXODUS-SINAI PARALLELISM
ELSEWHERE IN THE FIRST GOSPEL

There is no real consensus on how far Matthew intended to present
Jesus as the new Moses. W.D. Davies in his famous book on the sermon
on the mount comes to the cautious conclusion that Matthew would
have been more explicit if he intended his readers to infer such a Jesus-
Moses parallelism.[1] Scholarship has generally followed Davies' cautious
approach. R.J. Banks[2] is dismissive of any Jesus-Moses parallelism, and
R. Mohrlang[3] is also dismissive of any 'new or second Moses' or 'new-
law' motif but, with Davies and others, concedes that there are 'a
number of parallels between the lives of Jesus and Moses' but that this
parallelism is 'not dominant or exclusive'. D.A. Carson,[4] drawing on
Davies' conclusions, goes on to add that he finds the Moses motif to be
'weak' in Matthew. On Matthew's Moses motif, however, Blair,
Goulder, Gundry, Dunn, France, Allison and Wright are more positive.[5]

1.   Davies, *The Setting of the Sermon on the Mount*, pp. 25-93.
2.   R. Banks, *Jesus and the Law in the Synoptic Tradition* (Cambridge:
Cambridge University Press, 1975), pp. 229-35.
3.   R. Mohrlang, *Matthew and Paul* (Cambridge: Cambridge University Press,
1984), esp. pp. 23-25, who also includes a good survey of scholarship. For judicious
critique of Mohrlang's position and for a qualified acceptance of the Jesus-
eschatological Torah concept (cf. Gal. 6.2; Jn 13.34) see Allison, *The New Moses: A
Matthean Typology* (Minneapolis: Fortress Press, 1993), pp. 320-28.
4.   Carson, *Matthew*, p. 123.
5.   E.P. Blair, *Jesus in the Gospel of Matthew* (New York: Abingdon Press,
1960), pp. 124-37; Gundry, *Matthew* (generally); M.D. Goulder, *Type and History in
Acts* (London: SPCK, 1964), pp. 1-14 (who rightly comments on the role typology
played in the New Testament and the *cumulative* effect of it as intended by a given
New Testament writer, see pp. 2-3); J.D.G. Dunn, *Unity and Diversity in the New
Testament* (London: SCM Press, 1977), pp. 248-49; France, *Matthew—Evangelist*,
pp. 186-89; D.C. Allison, 'Jesus and Moses (Mt. 5.1-2)', *ExpT* 98 (1986–87),

Interestingly, in the light of advances made in the study of 'background' of the New Testament material and of Second Temple Judaism in general, Davies and Allison in their recent commentary give a more positive role to the Jesus-Moses typology in Matthew.[6] Perhaps the positions reached by scholars, who have among other things appealed to and developed Davies' earlier conclusions, also need to be reconsidered. This is hinted in certain works such as that of T.L. Donaldson,[7] who even though pressing for a 'Zion' emphasis in Matthew, is unable to shake off Matthew's Moses motif. Furthermore, in spite of criticisms of B.W. Bacon's other arguments, his five-fold division based on deliberate structural markers in 7.28; 11.1; 13.53; 19.1 and 26.1 still commands respect, and so the gospel structurally fits a Pentateuchal 'model'.[8]

pp. 203-205; *The New Moses*, (for a positive view on intertextuality and typology see pp. 1-8). E. Klostermann, *Das Matthäusevangeliun* (Tübingen: Mohr, 1971), p. 72; W. Grundmann, *Das Evangelium nach Matthäus* (Berlin: Evangelische Verlagsanstalt, 1968), pp. 245-46, compare the ten miracles (Matthew 8–9) with the 'ten plagues' in Exodus 7–12. J.D. Kingsbury, *Matthew: Structure, Christology, Kingdom* (Philadelphia: Fortress Press, 1975), pp. 89-92, subsumes the Jesus-Moses parallelisms under his characteristic 'Son of God' emphasis (see pp. 90-92). Contra Kingsbury's views and critique see Allison, *The New Moses*, pp. 311-19. Wright, *The New Testament and the People of God* (Minneapolis: Fortress Press/London: SPCK, 1992), pp. 386-90 accepting the structural markers (7.28; 11.1; 13.53; 19.1; 26.1), parallels the nine 'beatitudes' in 5.3-11 contrasted by the seven 'woes' in 23.13-33 with the list of *curses* and *blessings* in Deut. 27.15-26, 28.16-17—amplified in 28.20-68—he concludes: 'Matthew has woven this covenantal choice into the very structure of his gospel'.

6.   See Davies and Allison, *Saint Matthew*, I, pp. 190-95 (on the infancy narrative), and pp. 423-24, on the sermon on the mount; also 'Reflections on the Sermon on the Mount', *SJT* 44, No.3 (1991), p. 198. Allison, *The New Moses*, in pp. 298-306 evalutes Davies' earlier work, *The Setting of the Sermons on the Mount*, but points out that now Davies is much more open 'to the Mosaic approach to the First Gospel' (see p. 306 n. 34).

7.   Donaldson, *Mountain*, pp. 98-99, and pp. 72-73, appeals to Davies' *The Setting*, p. 93. For my critique of Donaldson's position and Zion emphasis, see ch. 6.7. Recently also see Allison, *The New Moses*, pp. 324-25.

8.   B.W. Bacon, *Studies in Matthew* (London: Constable, 1930); 'The "Five Books" of Matthew against the Jews', *The Expositor*, 15, 8th series (1918), pp. 56-66. A five-fold 'model' is adopted by Kilpatrick, *The Origins*, pp. 135-36; Davies, *The Setting of the Sermons on the Mount*, p. 93 is cautious, but see Davies and Allison, *Saint Matthew*, I, pp. 58-72. D. Hill, *The Gospel of Matthew* (London: Marshall, Morgan & Scott, 1972), pp. 44-48, too finally ends up with a five-fold outline. Stanton, 'The Origin and Purpose of Matthew's Gospel', p. 1940 finds a

So, the matter of Matthew-Moses relation is an open one. Given our particular interest in the Moses propaganda in first-century Judaism and my suggested analysis of Matthew's transfiguration (within Moses-Sinai and Daniel 7 categories), the purpose of this chapter is to set the transfiguration in the light of the Moses and Daniel 7 motifs elsewhere in the first gospel, to see whether my reading of the transfiguration makes sense in the broader context. Here the following main passages, Matthew 1–2; 4; 5–7 (with 19.3-12; 23.2f.); 26.17-29; 28.16-20 will be discussed; and to a lesser degree, other more obvious Moses type passages: for example Moses manna type feeding miracles of Mt. 14.15-21; 15.32-39. Finally, I shall evaluate the Moses-Jesus parallelism in the light of any Davidic and 'Son of David' categories in Matthew. As a starter to my inquiry I shall begin with the infancy narratives.

1. *Moses and Matthew's Infancy Narrative (Mt. 1.18–2.23)*

The following points are pertinent to my discussion, at the end of which I shall draw some conclusions:

The Importance of Matthew 1–2 for Matthean Christology
The importance of Matthew's infancy narrative as a window into Matthew's (complex!) hermeneutical method has in various ways been set out by K. Stendahl, G.M. Soares Prabhu, R.E. Brown, R.T. France, B.M. Nolan and recently Davies and Allison.[9] In 1.1-17, and via Joseph

---

rigid Bacon view an 'over-simplification'; so also Carson, *Matthew*, p. 50; Kingsbury, *Matthew: Structure*, pp. 7-25 suggests a three-fold theory based on pointers in 4.17 and 16.21, and this is followed by D.R. Bauer, *The Structure of Matthew's Gospel* (Sheffield: Almond Press, 2nd edn, 1989), esp. pp. 21-54.

9.   K. Stendahl, 'Quis et Unde? An Analysis of Matthew 1–2' in W. Eltester (ed.), *Judentum, Urchristentum, Kirche* (Berlin: Töpelmann, 1960), pp. 94-105; reprinted in G.N. Stanton, (ed.), *The Interpretation of Matthew* (London: SPCK, 1983), pp. 54-66; G.M. Soares Prabhu, *The Formula Quotations in the Infancy Narrative of Matthew* (Rome: Biblical Institute Press, 1976); R.E. Brown, *The Birth of the Messiah* (London: Geoffrey Chapman, 1977); R.T. France, 'Herod and the Children of Bethlehem', *NovT* 21 (1979), pp. 98-120; 'The Formula-Quotations of Matthew 2 and the Problem of Communication', *NTS* 27 (1980–81), pp. 233-51; 'Scripture, Tradition and History in the Infancy Narratives of Matthew', in *Gospel Perspectives*, vol. 2, 1981, pp. 239-66; 'The Massacre of the Innocents—Fact or Fiction?' in E.A. Livingstone (ed.), *Studia Biblica*, vol. 2 (1978), pp. 83-94; B.M. Nolan, *The Royal Son of God* (Göttingen: Vandenhoeck & Ruprecht, 1979); Davies and Allison, *Saint Matthew*, I, pp. 190-91.

(by 'adoption', see 1.16, 25; 2.20), Matthew establishes that Jesus is legal 'Son of David', and so has legal rights to messiahship, Χριστός (1.1, 16, 17). Apart from this, in his birth story (1.18–2.23) Matthew also displays geographical interests (Bethlehem, Egypt, Nazareth), which help to unify the chapter.[10] But in view of the concentration of Davidic motifs in Mt. 1.1-17 and its continuation (1.18-25; 2.1-12), it is remarkable that he has juxtaposed these with other typological parallels to which he directs his readers, especially in 1.18–2.23. It is well known that the specific typology used in these pericopes (especially those suggested by three of his five formula quotations cf. 2.5-6, 17-18, 23) has posed considerable difficulty for New Testament scholarship.[11] But I side with those scholars who take it that the key to Matthew's treatment of his infancy narratives lies primarily in his use of both biblical and current haggadic traditions about Moses. This will be borne out by the discussion below.

The Moses-Infancy and Egypt-Exodus Motif: the Most Suitable Framework

P. Winter, R.E. Brown, R.T. France and Davies and Allison[12] have effectively shown that Matthew's infancy narrative reflects a Moses-

10. Cf. Stendahl, 'Quis et Unde?', pp. 95-96; France, 'The Formula-Quotations', pp. 233-34.

11. To take one example, the Old Testament validation for Mt. 2.23 (Nazarene) is problematic (cf. Davies and Allison, *Saint Matthew*, I, pp. 274-81) and seems to reflect Matthean ingenuity. Scholars are also divided on the specific point behind Matthew's use of Ναζωραῖος. For Stendahl, 'Quis et Unde?', it needs to be seen in the light of Matthew's 'christological geography', in terms of Ναζαρέθ (v. 23) (p. 98). This is contested by J.A. Sanders, 'Ναζωραῖος in Matt. 2.23', *JBL* 84 (1965), pp. 169-72, who while linking it to 'inhabitant of Nazareth' (geography) also speaks of Matthew's wordplay, echoing the Samson-Nazarite typology (Judg. 13.7, 16.7), pp. 170-72. So also G. Allan, 'He Shall be Called a Nazarite?', *ExpT* 95 (1983), pp. 81-82. But according to J. Spencer Kennard, 'Was Capernaum the Home of Jesus?', *JBL* 65 (1946), pp. 131-41 Ναζωραῖος was not derived from Ναζαρέθ, and Jesus had no special historical association with the village of Nazareth (also see his 'Nazarean and Nazareth', *JBL* 66 (1947), pp. 79-81). This is challenged by W.F. Albright, 'The Names "Nazareth" and "Nazorean"', *JBL* 65 (1946), pp. 397-401. In view of Matthew's geographical and Christological interest, J.A. Sanders' view seems most appropriate. But the example also illustrates Matthew's creative use of the Old Testament and word play. A pure 'geographical' (so Stendahl) motif is unpersuasive.

12. See P. Winter, 'Jewish Folklore in the Matthean Birth Story', *HeyJ* 53 (1954), pp. 34-42; Brown, *The Birth of the Messiah*, esp. pp. 113-16; France, 'Herod

Jesus parallelism. These writers also go on to show that similar Moses motifs are echoed in the writings of Josephus (*Ant.* 2.205-206), *Exod. R.* 1.18; *Targum Pseudo-Jonathan* to Exod. 1.15, Philo and others.[13] It is pointless to reproduce all the arguments, but the following is a summary of those cited in favour of such Moses-Jesus parallels: (1) in Josephus *Ant.* 2.210-16 Moses' father is ill at ease about his wife's pregnancy and Pharaoh's decree (cf. Exod. 1.15-22), but is exhorted by God; compare Mt. 1.18-21. (2) Pharaoh wants to rid himself of a rival (*Ant.* 2.205-209); compare Herod in Mt. 2.2-18. (3) Pharaoh learns of a future deliverer from ἱερογραμματέων (*Ant.* 2.205, 234); compare ἀρχιερεῖς and γραμματεῖς in Mt. 2.4-6. (4) Moses leaves his land of birth for protection (Exod. 2.15); compare—in reverse parallelism—how providentially Jesus is taken from his land of birth to Egypt (Mt. 2.13-14). (5) Moses is protected as a child (Exod. 2.1-10; Philo, *Mos.* 1.12; Josephus, *Ant.* 2.217-27; so is Jesus (Mt. 2.13-15, 22-23). (6) Moses is commanded by God to return to Egypt (Exod. 4.19). In comparison, after Herod's death, Joseph is commanded by the angel to return to Israel, his place of birth (Mt. 2.19-20).

On point (4) it has been observed that both commands are almost identical: τεθνήκασιν γὰρ οἱ ζητοῦντες τὴν ψυχὴν τοῦ παιδίου (Mt. 2.20) with τεθνήκασιν γὰρ πάντες οἱ ζητοῦντές σου τὴν ψυχήν (Exod. 4.19). And of special significance is Matthew's use of the plural οἱ ζητοῦντες though Herod is the immediate referent (4.19). There are also other verbal parallels: (a) τελευτήσαντος in Mt. 2.19 and ἐτελεύτησεν in Exod. 4.18, (b) (ἄγγελος) κυρίου...(λέγων) in Mt. 2.19 and (εἶπεν δὲ) ὁ κύριος in Exod. 4.19, and perhaps less direct similarities like (c) τὸ παιδίον in Mt. 2.21 and τά παιδία in Exod. 4.20. Moreover, when one recalls Matthew's creative use of Old Testament typology, νυκτὸς καί ἀνεχώρησεν (Mt. 2.14) too may suggest an Exodus motif (Exod. 12.41). Perhaps another parallel is that just as Matthew presents Jesus as true 'king' of Israel (2.2) in contrast to Herod (2.9), Moses too, in Jewish tradition, was considered 'king', and may be contrasted with Pharaoh.[14] From these midrashic traditions

and the Children of Bethlehem', esp. pp. 105-106, 108-109; Davies and Allison, *Saint Matthew*, I, pp. 190-95. That Mt. 1.18–2.23 is 'programatic' for Matthew's Moses-Exodus typology in the First Gospel see Allison, *The New Moses*, pp. 140-65.

13.   See M.M. Bourke, 'The Literary Genus of Matthew 1–2', *CBQ* 22 (1960), pp. 160-75.

14.   Cf. Philo, *Mos.* 1.1, 8-9; 18-32, 48; 158; Ezekiel the Tragedian 68–82.

circulating in the first Christian century one could confidently conclude that Matthew's presentation has been influenced by these Moses motifs. It is arguable that he was thus deliberately addressing the Moses ideology of the time.

Some Arguments Against

B.M. Nolan[15] represents those who dismiss any Moses motif in Matthew's infancy narrative. He argues, among other things (1) that the reference to 'Egypt' (2.13) in itself does not suggest a Moses parallelism; Moses flees from Egypt, and does not go there for refuge. Others sought refuge in Egypt (1 Kgs 11.40; Jer. 26.21). (2) Herod's evil intent is commonplace in those seeking to get rid of their rivals (Judg. 9.1-6; 2 Kgs 10.1-11; 2 Chron. 21.2-4; 2 Kgs 11.1-2), and is not necessarily an allusion to Pharaoh. These arguments have some weight, but in the area of Old Testament typology a one-to-one correspondence is not the norm.[16] Moreover, Nolan's overall case is unpersuasive, not least when he offers the peculiar explanation that, although there are no verbal contacts between Matthew 2 and biblical tales of violence at court, 2.13-15 echoes Solomon's malevolence against Jeroboam, who had tried to take refuge in Egypt until the monarch's death cf. 1 Kgs 11.40 (p. 40). But it is hardly conceivable that Matthew would have paralleled Jeroboam, who eventually formed a breakaway and apostate kingdom, with Jesus. Nolan perhaps senses this and is forced to concede that 'This passage most resembles Matthew in content, but the terminology of Exod. 2.15 is closer to the Gospel'.[17] This 'concession' itself shows that he is unable to dismiss the Moses-exodus motif.

So, while through his five-formula quotations (1.22-3; 2.5-6, 15, 17-18, 23), Matthew presents Jesus as (1) the Messiah who 'fulfils' Scripture, (2) the representative of Israel (2.15, 18), and (3) 'son of David' (1.1-17; 2.20; 21.9, 15). It is striking that this Davidic-Christology is juxtaposed with (1) a Moses-Jesus typology and (2) as I shall discuss later a 'Son of God' Christology (cf. Mt. 2.18, 20-25).

15.   Nolan, *The Royal Son of God*, pp. 236-37.

16.   France, *Jesus and the Old Testament*, pp. 38-43, 76-80; *Matthew–Evangelist*, pp. 186-91; J. Goldingay, *Approaches to Old Testament Interpretation* (Leicester: IVP, 1981), pp. 97-115; Allison, 'Jews and Moses', pp. 203-205. For other, but less prominent, parallelisms in the infancy narrative (e.g. Joseph, Samson typologies) see: Brown, *The Birth of the Messiah*, pp. 224-25, 376-77; Soares Prabhu, *The Formula Quotations*, pp. 205-207.

17.   Nolan, *The Royal Son of God*, p. 40.

2. The Baptism Narrative (Mt. 3.13-17)

I have already dealt with this passage in the previous two chapters, and hence my comments here will be brief. Matthew in his baptism pericope heightens the Jesus-Moses, Jesus-Israel and also Moses-exodus and Sinai motifs and the following points will elucidate this:

John and the Messiah's New-Exodus Ministry

It may be argued, not least in the light of Matthew's geographical interests, that ἐν τῇ ἐρήμῳ (3.1, 3) itself evokes a Israel-wilderness-exodus motif,—a motif not uncommon in first century Palestine, as demonstrated by the wilderness retreat by Qumran-covenanters and certain messianic pretenders. But in Mt. 3.3, the Baptist in his 'wilderness' ministry and as forerunner prepares τὴν ὁδὸν κυρίου. This function of the Baptist is interpreted by Matthew in terms of Isa. 40.3 with its new-exodus associations. Since Matthew simultaneously applies this new-exodus-coming of God motif of Isa. 40.3 directly to Jesus (thus transferring the function of Yahweh to Jesus), here John is portrayed as playing a role in inaugurating the Messiah's new-exodus ministry, and this ἐν τῇ ἐρήμῳ.[18]

Malachi 3.1 and Exodus 23.20

This John-Jesus-exodus motif is further stressed by Matthew's redaction in 11.10, where Matthew has Jesus combining Mal. 3.1 with Exod. 23.20 and (1) applying it to John, but (2) also conveying something about the Jesus-Yahweh relationship. This dual emphasis is demonstrated in the following manner. (1) By adding πρὸ προσώπου σου taken from Exod. 23.20 to τὸν ἄγγελόν—which itself in the Hebrew מלאך is the identical usage in Exod. 23.20 and Mal. 3.1—Matthew gives the Baptist an exodus-wilderness significance. But (2) in addition to πρὸ προσώπου σου from Exod. 23.20, in the second line (Mt. 11.10) Matthew changes 'before me' (ὁδὸν πρὸ προσώπου μου Mal. 3.1) to 'before you' (τὴν ὁδόν σου ἔμπροσθέν σου Mt. 11.10), and has Yahweh himself addressing the Messiah, something not seen in any reading of Mal. 3.1.

---

18. Though according to Mt. 11.11 John is 'outside' the 'kingdom of heaven' (properly understood). For Matthew's presentation of the Baptist, his explicit John-Elijah association, see R.L. Webb, *John the Baptist and the Prophet* (Sheffield: JSOT Press, 1991), pp. 55-60.

So the thrust of Mt. 11.10-15 is that if the Baptist (as Elijah) prepares the way for Yahweh (3.3/Isa. 40.3) and the 'day of Yahweh' (Mal. 3.1-2; 4.5-6), then Jesus is the manifestation of Yahweh and ushers in the eschatological day of Yahweh. Since it is arguable that certain Jewish traditions and schools of thought took it that the exodus-Sinai events would be re-enacted in the 'last days' and this ἐν τῇ ἐρήμῳ, Matthew may well be seeking to portray both John's and Jesus' 'eschatological' ministry with exodus symbolism. For this exodus motif is seen in statements about the Baptist in both Mt. 3.3 and 11.10.

Having looked briefly at John and hence indirectly at Jesus, it is profitable to turn to Matthew's portrayal of Jesus himself at the baptism.

The Baptism and the Coming of God Motifs
The Jesus-exodus-Israel motif may also be seen in relation to some of the coming of God motifs seen at the baptism itself. Before I comment on this further, it must also be recognised that the baptismal setting also evokes apocalyptic themes, which contributes to my arguments that Matthew has specifically linked the baptism with the transfiguration. And in the general wilderness setting of the baptism, it is arguable that some of these apocalyptic motifs too contribute to a wilderness-exodus and at times Sinai type motif. Hence I shall begin with some apocalyptic motifs:

1. *Apocalyptic motifs:* In 3.16 Matthew (with Mk 1.10; Lk. 3.21) tells us that καὶ ἰδοὺ ἠνεῴχθησαν οἱ οὐρανοί. Here the theme of the 'riverside' (Jordan) and the 'opened heaven' makes an interesting parallel with Ezekiel's riverside vision of Ezek. 1.1 (καὶ ἠνοίχθησαν οἱ οὐρανοί, καὶ ἴδον ὁράσεις Θεοῦ), and perhaps in a lesser degree with Daniel's riverside (Ubal) vision in Dan. 8.3. ἠνεῴχθησαν οἱ οὐρανοί in Mt. 3.16 has to be seen in relation to φωνὴ ἐκ τῶν οὐρανῶν in 3.17, which too echoes similar motifs seen in apocalyptic literature (Dan. 4.31; *1 En.* 13.8; 65.4; *2 Bar.* 13.1; 22.1; Rev. 10.4; 11.12; 14.14).[19] So ἠνεῴχθησαν οἱ οὐρανοί...φωνὴ ἐκ τῶν οὐρανῶν suggests an apocalyptic background for the baptismal setting, as for Matthew's presentation of the transfiguration. This contributes to Matthew's linking of 17.5 with 3.17.

2. *Exodus-Sinai type motifs in Isa. 63.19 and the baptism accounts:* ἠνεῴχθησαν οἱ οὐρανοί is perhaps also consciously reminiscent of Isa. 63.19 [64.1]. In Isa. 63.19 [64.1] the prayer of the prophet is for

---

19. See Bauckham, *Jude, 2 Peter*, p. 206.

Yahweh 'to rend (קרעת MT, ἀνοίξῃς LXX) the heavens and come down'. It has been pointed out that Mark's σχιζομένους, perhaps more emphatically than Matthew or Luke, takes after the MT קרעת of Isa. 63.19 [64.1], and so alludes to a similar Isa. 63.19 [64.1] setting.

Given the wilderness setting of the baptism, and given Mark's symbolic use of the wilderness motif, the possibility of this theory is strengthened by recognising that Isa. 64.1-2 alludes to exodus-type motifs (more particularly exodus-Sinai and coming of God motifs).[20] These wilderness and Sinai-type themes may be inferred from the following comparisons: (1) 'mountains quake at thy presence' (64.1, compare Exod. 19.18); (2) 'as when fire kindles brushwood' (64.2), compare Exod. 19.16, 18; 20.18; 24.17; Deut. 33.2. (3) In 64.2 the motif of people's 'trembling' at the 'coming of God' may be paralleled with Israel's trembling at the Sinai theophany (Exod. 19.16; 20.18). (4) Exod. 24.17 attributes the cataclysmic happenings on the mountain to the 'appearance of the glory of the Lord'. And several Isaiah commentators, J. Young, J.D.W. Watts, R.N. Whybray, and G.W. Wade, have suggested that Isa. 64.3 echoes Sinai-type themes when it renders 'whenever you work gloriously [ἔνδοξα] trembling from thee shall take hold upon the mountains'—thus associating the writer's request for the 'coming of God' (64.1) with the idea of Sinai-glory.[21] (5) There are also some verbal similarities between Isa. 63.19 [64.1] and the exodus-Sinai event, for in both instances the Hebrew ירד (cf. Exod. 19.18, 20) is used to describe the 'coming of God.' This suggests the expectation of a Sinai-type 'coming of God' in Isa. 64.3.

The verbal parallelism is closest to Mark with his σχιζομένους. But Matthew's ἠνεῴχθησαν, and similarly Luke's ἀνεῳχθῆναι, probably reflect the LXX ἀνοίξῃς (Isa. 63.19 [64.1]).[22]

---

20.   For Mark's emphasis on wilderness-exodus motif see Mauser, *Christ in the Wilderness*, pp. 77-103; Lane, *Mark*, pp. 12-13; W.M. Swartley, 'The Structural Function of the Term "Way" (Hodos) in Mark's Gospel', in H. Charles (ed.), *The New Way of Jesus* (Kansas: Faith & Life, 1980), pp. 73-86. On Luke: D.P. Moessner, 'Jesus and the "Wilderness Generation": The Death of the Prophet Like Moses According to Luke', in K.H. Richard (ed.), *SBLSP* 1982 (Chico: Scholars Press, 1982), pp. 339-40; J. Manek, 'The New Exodus in the Books of Luke', *NovT* 2 (1958), pp. 8-23.

21.   See J. Young, *The Book of Isaiah*, vol. 3 (Grand Rapids: Eerdmans, 1981), p. 490; J.D.W. Watts, *Isaiah 34–60* (Waco: Word Books, 1987), p. 335; R.N. Whybray, *Isaiah 40–66* (London: Oliphants, 1975), p. 262.

22.   For comments on the general religious significance attached to the area, and

3. *Israel-baptism parallelism:* Finally, another possible exodus-parallel is that between Moses/Israel crossing the Red Sea and Jesus being baptised in the Jordan (1 Cor. 10.1-5). W.D. Davies, citing W.L. Knox, suggests that, like proselyte baptism, John's baptism typified the 'coming out of Egypt, passing through the Red Sea into the promised land'.[23] It was eschatological, in that it paralleled the creation of the universe with the creation of a 'new people' Israel at the exodus (cf. Isa. 43.16-20). Davies, though cautious in his treatment of Matthew's presentation of Jesus' baptism, nevertheless concludes that it is not impossible that the new exodus motif is to be discovered in the ministry of John the Baptist. Furthermore, Davies, developing Lohmeyer's suggestion, holds out the possibility that Jesus as King-Messiah and Servant identifies with new (renewed) Israel, and undergoes a 'new baptism' corresponding to that of the first exodus (p. 44).

The case for recognizing an Israel-exodus typology in the baptism story is strengthened by the similar Jesus-Israel-God's Son-(exodus-Egypt) typology seen already in Mt. 2.15, and, as I shall show, in 4.1-11.

So the cumulative force of the following parallels: (1) the Baptist-exodus parallelism (Mt. 3.3/Isa. 40.3; Mt. 11.10/Exod. 23.20), (2) Jesus-Yahweh-new-exodus parallelism (3.3, 11.10), (3) Jesus-opened heavens-Isa. 64.1, wilderness-Sinai and 'coming of God' parallelism (Mt. 3.16), (4) Jesus-Israel-baptism parallelism, suggest that just as in Matthew 1–2, at the baptism too there is a Jesus-exodus-Sinai, and hence new-Moses parallelism.

3. *The Temptation Narrative and the Jesus-Exodus-Israel Parallelism (Mt. 4.1-11)*

The Link Between Matthew 4.1-11 and 3.13-17

It has been rightly pointed out by B. Gerhardsson, G.H.P. Thompson, A.B. Taylor, J.A.T. Robinson and others that the phrase εἰς τὴν ἔρημον

---

their relation to the 'waters of Dan' which fed the Jordan see G.W. Nickelsburg, 'Enoch, Levi and Peter', pp. 575-600; J. Allegro, *The Dead Sea Scrolls* (Harmondsworth: Penguin Books, 1956), pp. 142-43; Milik, 'Le Testemant de Lévi', p. 430.

23.   The extent to which the practice and understanding of proselyte baptism influenced the baptism of John and early Christian baptism is a much debated question, *DNTT*, vol. 1, p. 145.

(4.1) in the temptation narrative links it to the baptism narrative.[24] Moreover, two of the temptations are directly associated with the motif of 'Sonship' (εἰ υἱὸς εἶ τοῦ Θεοῦ Mt. 4.3, 6/Lk. 4.3, 9), and this continues the Sonship motif in Mt. 3.13-17 (Mk 1.9-11; Lk. 3.21-22), also in 2.15 (Israel-Son of God). These links and the primary focus of the temptation narratives on Deuteronomy 6–8 (quoted three times by Jesus, Mt. 4.4/Deut. 8.3; Mt. 4.7/Deut. 6.16; Mt. 4.10/Deut. 6.13, passages connected with Israel's testing in the wilderness, Deut. 8.2, 5) suggest that Jesus' experience (as Israel) ἐν τῇ ἐρήμῳ is seen to be parallel to Israel's testing in the wilderness (Deut. 6–18).[25]

This position is quite persuasive: in the temptation narrative, where Israel of old failed, the new Israel, embodied in Jesus, has triumphed.[26] In this, however, the role of Moses is disputed. For, as Davies and Gerhardsson[27] followed by others have concluded, in 4.1-11 Jesus is associated with Israel and not Moses as such. However, as on previous occasions, there are certain nuances peculiar to Matthew's text which may suggest a Moses-exodus-Jesus parallelism.

---

24.   B. Gerhardsson, *The Testing of God's Son* (Lund: Gleerup, 1966), pp. 19-20, who takes it as an elaborate midrash; G.H.P. Thompson, 'Called–Proved–Obedient', *JTS* 11 (1960), p. 9; A.B. Taylor, 'Decision in the Desert: The Temptation of Jesus in the Light of Deuteronomy', *Int* 14 (1960), pp. 300-309; J.A.T. Robinson, *Twelve New Testament Studies* (London: SCM Press, 1962), pp. 53-60. For a recent survey of scholarship, issues of debate, see Donaldson, *Mountain*, pp. 87-104 (see text for my evaluation on Donaldson's Zion perspective).

25.   Gerhardsson, *The Testing of God's Son*, pp. 19-20; Robinson, *Twelve New Testament Studies*, pp. 53-60; France, *Matthew*, pp. 96-100; *Jesus and the Old Testament*, pp. 50-53.

26.   Cf. J.A. Kirk, 'The Messianic Role of Jesus and the Temptation Narrative: A Contemporary Perspective', *EvQ* v. 44, No.1, (1972), pp. 11-29 continued in vol. 1, 44, 2, (1972), pp. 91-102. He argues that there was a close link between the desert and popular messianic expectations (cf. Josephus *Ant.* 20, 97, Acts 5.36-37, p. 19). Jesus was 'tempted' by Satan to act as a Davidic-Saviour-Messiah figure, especially at the 'Temple' temptation, which Kirk links to Matthew's 'holy city' idea (4.5; 27.53, *contra* Luke's Jerusalem 4.9). If this is accepted, then Matthew specifically has Jesus refusing to act as a new-David of popular expectation (pp. 93-94).

27.   Davies, *The Setting of the Sermon on the Mount*, pp.45-48; Gerhardsson, *The Testing of God's Son*, pp. 43-44. That the evangelist overlaid the existing Israel typology with Mosaic motifs (especially against the backdrop of Nebo) see Allison, *The New Moses*, pp. 165-72.

A Case for Moses-Jesus Parallelism

The following factors favour the combination of a Moses and Israel typology.

1. The addition καὶ νύκτας τεσσεράκοντα is peculiar to Matthew (contrast Mk 1.13; Lk. 4.2). This may recall the experiences both of Elijah (1 Kgs 19.8) and Moses (Exod. 34.28; Deut. 9.9, 18), with εἰς ὄρος ὑψηλὸν λίαν (Mt. 4.8) reinforcing such wilderness-Sinai allusions.[28] But against such a Moses (Elijah) parallelism, it has been argued that, in view of the Israel-Deut 6–8 theme throughout Mt. 4.1-11, the forty days symbolise Israel's forty years hunger in the wilderness (Deut. 8.1-10). And since Israel itself is spoken of as 'son' in 2.15, this could be said to lend itself to such a Jesus-Israel-Son association. But 'forty days and nights' are not equal to 'forty years', except symbolically. And though Israel was 'humbled, tested' and at times 'hungered' for 'forty years' in the wilderness, she never 'fasted' but was always fed (Deut. 8.2-3). Moreover, in Exod. 34.28 it was not Israel who fasted forty days and forty nights, but its representative, Moses.

2. Attention also has been drawn to Matthew's use of the plural οἱ λίθοι...ἄρτοι (4.3) in contrast to Luke's τῷ λίθῳ...ἄρτος (4.3) and it has been argued that the devil was prematurely suggesting an exodus-manna miracle as at Exod. 16.4-5—an expectation, associated with the arrival of the messianic age, the introduction of the eschatological conditions on the pattern of the Mosaic age.[29] Davies, Gerhardsson, and recently Davies and Allison,[30] dismiss this on the grounds that (a) Matthew frequently has plurals where Mark and /or Luke have singulars, (b) manna-producing was to be a public miracle, (c) it is Jesus who is hungry not the crowd, (d) manna was 'bread from

---

28. For the significance of the concept 'forty days' in Jewish literature, see Davies and Allison, *Saint Matthew*, 1, pp. 358-59.

29. Perhaps the crowd took it to be so in 14.13-21, and the idea of the Messiah's manifestation in the desert is seen in Mt. 24.26; Acts 21.38. J. Nolland, *Luke 1–9.20* (Dallas: Word, 1989), p. 179, finds Luke's singular 'loaf' and 'stone' a more appropriate response to hunger than Matthew's 'loaves' and 'stones'.

30. Davies, *The Setting of the Sermon on the Mount*, pp. 361-64; Gerhardsson, *The Testing of God's Son*, pp. 43-44; Davies and Allison, *Saint Matthew*, I, pp. 361-62.

above' not from stones. But Matthew does record 'feeding' miracles in Mt. 14.15-21 (Mk 6.35-43; Lk. 9.12-17; Jn 6.5-14, 31-32), Mt. 15.32-39 (Mk 8.1-10), which according to 14.22 (and Mk 6.45, clearly in Jn 6.14-15, 31-32) the crowd may have interpreted as a Moses-manna-miracle. In view of this it is not unlikely that Matthew in some sense links 4.3 with these Moses-type feeding/manna miracles. Moreover, the fact that after the temptations 'angels came and ministered to him' (Mt. 4.11; Mk 1.13), where διηκόνουν (as in Mt. 8.15; 25.44) takes on the meaning of 'to give to eat', suggests both an Elijah (1 Kgs 19.5-8) and a Moses-Israel-manna (angel food) feeding motif. Hence it may be argued that Jesus, the new Moses, not willing to use God-given powers for 'himself' (a motif reflected in Moses' attitude to his vocation, Exod. 32.9-10), qualifies as new Israel's true leader.

Pseudo-Sinai (Mt. 4.8-10) and the New Sinai

Only here (4.8) and in the transfiguration (17.1) does Matthew speak of εἰς ὄρος ὑψηλὸν (contrast to Luke's less specific καὶ ἀναγαγὼν αὐτὸν 4.5). This may suggest a redactional link between the two mountains. It is well known that in this Q passage, Matthew's order differs from Luke's: while Matthew's final temptation is on the mount, Luke climaxes his temptation narrative with the temple pinnacle (4.9-12). It is disputed which is the more original order,[31] but, given (1) Matthew's special interest in the mountain motif, and (2) the lack of any explicit 'Sonship' theme in the mountain-temptation, it is conceivable that Matthew (an imaginative scribe, as he proves to be) has arranged his material in order (a) to associate the two Sonship-temptations (Mt. 4.3, 6) and (b) to climax his narrative with the mountain-temptation motif (4.9). In the light of this redactional link, two points are of significance here, one based on Satan's statement (Mt. 4.9) and the other on Jesus' answer (4.10).

1. *A comparison with the exodus-golden calf and idolatry motif:* Considering, first, Jesus' final answer (4.10) where he cites Deut. 6.13, J.A.T. Robinson has made the important observation that the real issue behind Deut. 6.13-15 is suggested by the parallel Exod. 34.11-17, since in these related passages there is the strict injunction against idolatry and

31.   See discussion in Marshall, *Luke*, pp. 166-67. The opinions are finely balanced.

going after other gods (as they had already done with the golden calf Exod. 32).[32] For Israel's Lord is a jealous God (v. 14), who alone must be the object of his people's worship v. 17. It is significant that Exodus 34 is a Mount Sinai passage, and I conclude that Jesus' answer in Mt. 4.10 echoes both Deut. 6.13-15 and Exod. 34.11-17 and reflects the anti-idolatry/false gods theme, stressed by God's words given to Moses (and Israel) at Sinai.[33]

In the light of this illuminating parallel, it may be that in this passage Satan's suggestion reflects a golden calf or idolatry/false god motif, with Satan himself soliciting such reverence. But Jesus, as God's Son (4.3, 6) and true Israel and new Moses, rejects compromise in exchange for the 'kingdom' and 'glory' that he is promised. It must be noted that while in Mt. 4.8-9 Satan is portrayed as possessing this kingdom-glory, the point behind the temptation pericope is that Jesus has come to contest Satan's dominion.[34] For Matthew's Jesus recognises that it is God who gives or 'delivers' all things (πάντα) to his Son (Mt. 11.27, compare use of πάντα here with 4.9; and 28.20); and this is in keeping with Danielic emphasis where it is God who 'gives' the kingdom (Dan. 2.37; 7.14), a motif also clearly demonstrated in 28.18 ἐδόθη μοι.[35]

It is significant that this offer of kingdom and glory itself has connections with both Sinai and Daniel 7 concepts (see ch. 4 and the table there). Could then Matthew in some sense be linking 17.1-8 with 4.1-11? It is arguable that what Jesus rejects from Satan is what he proleptically receives at the transfiguration. So, just as there is a deliberate link between Mt. 4.1-11; 17.1-8 and 28.16-20 (linked by the common 'mountain' and Sinai/Daniel 7 kingdom-glory associations), Matthew perhaps portrays the devil's offer of βασιλεία-κόσμος-δόξα to Jesus on this εἰς ὄρος ὑψηλὸν (4.8 with 17.1) in terms of a false/pseudo-Sinai, and pseudo-Daniel 7.

Jesus the Victorious New Moses in Contrast to Moses' Failure
Perhaps one other Moses-Jesus-exodus parallel, and one that links with my previous point, is that in Num. 27.12-14; Deut. 3.23-28; 32.48-52 and Deut. 34.1-4 Moses views the promised land but does not enter due

32. Robinson, *Twelve New Testament Studies*, p. 57.
33. In support of the Jesus-Deuteronomy parallelism see Hill, *Matthew*, p. 101, who shows certain verbal similarities between Deut. 34.1-4 and Mt. 4.8-11.
34. See France, *Matthew*, p. 99.
35. See Chapter 6.6. below.

to previous disobedience (Num. 20.12). Both Moses' failure, and the failure of old Israel is precisely identified with Jesus' own disciples' failure in Mt. 17.17 (ᾧ γενεὰ ἄπιστος καὶ διεστραμμένη); Deut. 32.5 (γενεὰ σκολιὰ καὶ διεστραμμένη); Deut. 32.20 (γενεὰ ἐξεστραμμένη; also note γενεὰ πονηρὰ in Mt. 12.39). In contrast, however, in Mt. 4.8-10 Jesus, Son of God-true Israel, views...πάσας τὰς βασιλείας τοῦ κόσμου καὶ τὴν δόξαν αὐτῶν (Mt. 4.8), but (unlike Adam) forbids the premature hastening of events. By refusing premature messianic power (but anticipating 28.16) and being an obedient 'Israel-Son of God' he is portrayed as greater than Moses and disobedient Israel.

So we have seen that (1) by linking the temptation pericope with the baptism pericope, and (2) by redactionally and theologically also linking it with the transfiguration (17.1-8) and final commission (28.16-20) pericopes, Matthew continues his Moses-exodus-Israel, Moses-Jesus parallels. It is also possible that, by his redaction and arrangement of material, Matthew presents his Jesus as rejecting pseudo-Sinai and Daniel 7 motifs ('glory' and a 'kingdom' offered by Satan) in anticipation of Mt. 17.1-8, 28.16-20 and also 16.27-28; 19.28; 24.30-31; 25.31-32; 26.64. In effect, the cumulative thrust of my argument is: (1) It is possible that for Matthew εἰς ὄρος ὑψηλον functions as a false and pseudo-Sinai, which Jesus overcame. (2) Matthew by redaction and arrangement (in contrast to Luke) climaxing with εἰς ὄρος ὑψηλον anticipates the new Sinai at 17.1-8, a motif which I shall show is alluded to in the sermon on the mount (Mt. 5–7) and reinforced in 28.16-20.

4. *The Sermon on the Mount (Matthew 5–7)*

In the previous chapter I have argued that Matthew has probably linked 17.2 and 5.14-15 both theologically and redactionally. Here, however, I shall be viewing Matthew 5–7 as a whole with special reference to the issue of the law.

A Case for a Moses Typology

Matthew 5–7 have received considerable scholarly attention, and B.W. Bacon has argued that in his sermon on the mount, Matthew has produced a Christian Torah, or 'new Torah' with Jesus as the new Moses and the mountain motif as an anti-type to Sinai.[36] This Matthew 5–7/

36.   B.W. Bacon, 'The "Five Books" of Matthew against the Jews', pp. 56-66;

Moses-Sinai motif is supported by Lohmeyer, recently Gundry, Dunn and others,[37] but has been criticised by, among others, R.J. Banks.[38] In his earlier work, *The Setting of the Sermon on the Mount*, W.D. Davies, after a lengthy analysis of possibilities, concluded that Matthew could have been more explicit if he really wanted to stress a new Moses motif.[39] But later goes on to add 'Matthew presents Jesus as giving a Messianic law on a Mount, but avoids the express concept of a New Torah and a New Sinai...he avoids the express ascription to him of the honorific "a new Moses"'.[40]

Davies is cautious, but there is no dismissal of the Moses-Sinai parallelism as such—a point that has been repeatedly made in his recent writings in association with D.C. Allison.[41] It is true that (unlike Mt. 17) the mountain in Matthew 5 does not appear to be a place of divine theophany like Sinai, but certain factors favour a Sinai symbolism: (1) It is instructive to note that Matthew 5–7 is the first of the five blocks of teaching (5–7; 9.36–10.42; 13.1-52; 17.22–18.35; 23–25), and Dunn finds it hardly a coincidence that Matthew specifically associates Jesus' first block of teaching with a mountain setting (whereas Luke speaks of a level place).[42] (2) Gundry, Davies and Allison have pointed out that (a) Matthew's ἀνέβη εἰς τὸ ὄρος (cf. 14.23; 15.29) is similar to the LXX ἀναβαίνω + εἰς τὸ ὄρος construction which is mostly used of Moses' ascent of Mount Sinai: Exod. 19.3, 12, 13; 24.12, 13. (b) Jesus' sitting position καὶ καθίσαντος αὐτοῦ (Mt. 5.1) may be paralleled in Moses' posture (אשב MT) of Deut. 9.9, since this verb, in addition to the sense of 'dwelling', can also mean sitting (so *b.t. Meg.* 21a; *b.t. Sota* 49a).[43]

Studies in Matthew, pp. 81-82, p. 177; *The Sermon on the Mount*, p. 23; 'Jesus and the Law: A Study of the First "Book" of Matthew (Mt. 3–7)', *JBL* 47 (1928), pp. 203-231. Here Bacon refers to the 'new and higher Torah', pp. 215, 229, but does not develop the Moses-Sinai typology as such.

37. Lohmeyer, *Das Evangelium des Matthäus*, p. 76; Gundry, *Matthew*, p. 66. For others advocating new Moses, new law motif see examples in Mohrlang, *Matthew and Paul*, p. 147 n.161.

38. Against Bacon, see Banks, *Jesus and the Law*, pp. 229-35, esp. pp. 230-31 especially for excluding prologue and epilogue.

39. Davies, *The Setting of the Sermon on the Mount*, p. 93.

40. Davies, *The Setting of the Sermon on the Mount*, p. 108.

41. See recently, W.D. Davies and D.C. Allison, 'Reflections on the Sermon on the Mount', *SJT* 44, no. 3 (1991), pp. 298-99.

42. Dunn, *Unity and Diversity*, p. 248.

43. Gundry, *Matthew*, p. 66; Davies and Allison, 'Reflections', (1991), pp. 298-

A contributing argument is that, in Matthew, only once (15.29) does Jesus sit without teaching and ministering. This perhaps suggests that Jesus' posture, sitting and teaching/ministering (13.1, 2; 15.29; 24.3-4; especially in 5.1), was important for Matthew. There may also be a polemic against those who 'sat' on Moses' seat: for in Mt. 23.2 it is the scribes and the Pharisees who sit (ἐκάθισαν) on Moses' seat. Matthew's frequent portrayal of Jesus' sitting/teaching-ministering may perhaps also be a subtle polemic against the supposed 'authority' (with regards to the law of Moses) of the scribes and Pharisees.[44] It is with this in view that one needs to approach the much vexed problem of Jesus and the law, especially in Mt. 5.18-20, 20-48; 7.12-27; 11.13, and such law-related passages.

Jesus-Moses and the Law in Matthew 5–7 and its Relevance to Matthew's Transfiguration Pericope
The complexities with regard to the vexed issue of Jesus and the law in Matthean, Pauline and New Testament studies are well known, and despite the number of articles and writings that have emerged in recent years, there is no real consensus on the matter.[45] It would be naive to

99; Allison, *The New Moses*, pp. 179-80, also pp. 172-94 for positive discussion on Moses-Jesus parallels in Matthew 5–7.

44.   In the light of Jesus' attack on scribal tradition (15.1-20), Pharisees' teaching (16.6-12), the dispute on sabbath (12.1-4), divorce (19.3-9), Banks, *Jesus and the Law*, pp. 175-77; France, *Matthew*, p. 324 suggests that 23.2-3, may be a 'tongue in cheek comment'.

45.   For the view (1) that Jesus 'fulfils' and transcends the law: see Banks, *Jesus and The Law*; 'Matthew's Understanding of the Law: Authenticity and Interpretation in Matthew 5.17-20', *JBL* 93 (1974), pp. 242f. In general agreement with this view: R.A. Guelich, *The Sermon on the Mount* (Waco: Word, 2nd edn, 1983), esp. pp. 138-42, 164f.; D.J. Moo, 'Jesus and the Authority of the Mosaic Law', *JSNT* 20 (1984), pp. 3-49; G.N. Stanton, 'The Origin and Purpose of Matthew's Sermon on the Mount', in G.F. Hawthorne and O. Betz (eds.), *Tradition and Interpretation in the New Testament* (Grand Rapids: Eerdmans; Tübingen: Mohr [Paul Siebeck] 1987), pp. 181-92, esp. p. 188. (2) That Jesus establishes the law, G. Barth, 'Matthew's Understanding of the Law', in G. Bornkam, G. Barth and H.J. Held (eds.), *Tradition and Interpretation in Matthew* (London: SCM Press, 1960), pp. 58-164, who also comes out in favour of the love commandment as the controlling factor in Jesus' attitude to the law (p. 69). Similarly, U. Luz, *Matthew 1–7* (Edinburgh: T. & T. Clark, 1989), pp. 268-69, argues that the *primary* point is obedience to the law, praxis prior to teaching (p. 265), but does not rule out subsidiary motifs. (3) According to J.P. Meier, *Law and History in Matthew's Gospel*, p. 165, Jesus' 'death and

think that one could do justice to all the relevant issues in a few paragraphs. But since the Moses typology is crucial in Matthew's presentation of the transfiguration—with the climaxing ἀκούετε αὐτοῦ (17.5) along with τηρεῖν πάντα ὅσα ἐνετειλάμην ὑμῖν (28.20) stressing the vital importance of Jesus' words to Matthew's community (also 7.24-27, 11.25-30)—the study of the possible Moses themes in Matthew 5–7 and a comparison of this with themes arising from Mt. 17.1-8 are important for this thesis. For I shall show that Matthew, by what he conveys about Jesus and the law, and the law in relation to Jesus' teaching, anticipates the transfiguration. In order to bring this out several points need to be made.

1. *Matthew's concern for the law:* It is clear from passages like 6.1-6, 16-18; 23.2, that Matthew's community is concerned with issues about the law, and is perhaps 'reviled' (ὀνειδίσωσιν 5.11) and also 'persecuted' by the Jews on account of it (5.10-12). So Matthew is dispelling the belief that his community and its founder were antinomians (the issue probably raised by his supposed sabbath-breaking 12.1-14 and eating with sinners Mt. 9.10-13, 11.19) and presents Jesus himself as 'law-abiding' (5.17-20). This applies also to the disciples, for according to 5.19-20 'law-abiding' has ramifications for one's place in the kingdom. This suggests Matthew's loyalty to the law, and in fact he categorises those who disobey Jesus and his words as workers of τὴν ἀνομίαν (7.23).[46] It is also suggested by (a) Matthew's fondness for δικαιοσύνη, used in 5.20 in terms of keeping the law (as interpreted by Jesus).[47] (b) Mt. 15.17-20/Mk 7.18-23, Matthew by omitting Mark's καθαρίζων πάντα τὰ βρώματα seems to be less willing to abandon the dietary laws.[48]

---

resurrection' is the turning point for Matthew's 'salvation-history perspective', at which 'the binding force of the Mosaic law as an inviolable whole and *qua* Mosaic has passed with the passing of the old creation. What stands in its place are the words of Jesus.'

46.   Also see 23.28; 24.12.

47.   See 3.15; 5.6, 10, 20; 6.1, 33; 21.32; in the gospels it is found only in Lk. 1.75 and Jn 16.8, 10.

48.   See Dunn, *Unity and Diversity* , p. 248; C.E. Carlston, 'The Things that Defile (Mk 7.14) and the Law in Matthew and Mark', *NTS* 15 (1968–69), pp. 57-69. The authenticity of καθαρίζων πάντα τὰ βρώματα is disputed, but it enjoys good manuscript support (see *UBS* p. 150). R.A. Guelich, *Mark 1–8.26* (Dallas: Word, 1989), pp. 377-79, while allowing that 'this view point may well have been shared by Mark's community' suggests that it may have been introduced into the story.

2. *Matthew and the law in Mt. 5.17-19:* Further to these somewhat general comments, any discussion on Matthew's attitude to the law needs to come to terms with his enigmatic 5.17-19 and the antitheses in vv. 21-48. Certain factors govern any discussion on 5.17-20: (a) arguments based on its immediate context, vv. 16, 20, (b) some pregnant words and phrases, like πληρῶσαι (5.17) and ἕως ἂν πάντα γένηται (5.18), and (c) the wider setting, especially of the antitheses in 5.21-48. I shall take them in order:

(a) *The scope of Mt. 5.17-20:* In view of its immediate context, v. 16 and v. 20, D. Wenham, claims that Mt. 5.17-20 'is not a detailed statement concerning every single aspect of the Christian's relationship to the Old Testament law'.[49] For in this passage Matthew is addressing specific issues, for example, defending Jesus against the accusation that he was antinomian, and hence 5.17-20 is not to be taken as programmatic about every aspect of the Old Testament law.[50] This argument gives weight to the immediate context (vv. 16, 20), limits the scope of 5.17-20, and so has much to commend it.

(b) *Matthew's use of πληρῶσαι (5.17), and γένηται (5.18):* Matthew in 5.17-20 introduces key motifs, words and phrases. Matthew's use of πληρῶσαι has been taken variously to mean (i) establish, accomplish, obey,[51] (ii) to bring out inner and full meaning,[52] (iii) (following on from this) to bring to eschatological fulfilment, bringing the τέλος which the Torah anticipated.[53] But πληρῶσαι also needs to be set against the

49.   D. Wenham, 'Jesus and the Law: an exegesis on Matthew 5.17-20', *Themelios*, 4 (1979), pp. 92-99.

50.   But antinomianism as a concept itself is condemned by Jesus in Mt. 13.41, where τὴν ἀνομίαν will be judged (v. 42), also cf. 25.32-33.

51.   Barth, 'Matthew's Understanding of the Law', pp. 66-69; Wenham, *Themelios*, 4 (1979), p. 93; Luz, *Matthew 1–7*, pp. 268-69; C. Brown, *DNTT*, vol. 3, pp. 181-85; Davies and Allison, *Saint Matthew*, I, p. 485 n. 9.

52.   Cf. W.C. Allen, *A Critical and Exegetical Commentary on the Gospel According to St Matthew* (ICC, Edinburgh: T. & T. Clark, 1921), p.45; A. Plummer, *An Exegetical Commentary on the Gospel according to St Matthew* (London: Robert & Scott, 1915), p. 76; A.H. McNeile, *The Gospel According to St Matthew* (London: MacMillan, 1955), p. 58.

53.   Banks, *Jesus and the Law*, pp. 207-219; Meier, *Law and History*, pp. 73-82, 162; Moo, 'Jesus and Mosaic Law', pp. 3-49; Davies and Allison, *Saint Matthew*, I, pp. 484-87; France, *Matthew–Evangelist*, pp. 191-97, esp. pp. 194-95, is in sympathy of Bank's position, consistent with the regular use of πληρόω in Matthew (p. 195); so also Moo, 'Jews and Mosaic Law', pp. 24-26. See Davies, *The Setting of the Sermon on the Mount*, pp. 183-90 for the argument that the Messiah's role would

equally enigmatic ἕως ἂν πάντα γένηται of 5.18.

It has been argued that the phrase ἕως ἂν πάντα γένηται sets a limit on the concept of the inviolability of the Torah. This is important when it is recognised that this phrase does not occur in the parallel in Lk. 16.17, and hence is probably Matthew's redaction of a common ('Q') source. The actual meaning has been disputed. For example, (1) it has been taken synonymously with the previous ἕως ἂν clause: 'till heaven and earth pass away' (5.18) and hence as 'until the end of the earth'.[54] On the other hand (2) it has been argued that the second ἕως ἂν clause is more subtle, it is noted that (a) πάντα has no antecedent, and (b) that γένηται means literally 'happens' and is used of events (1.22; 21.4; 26.54-56), not of things 'being done', or obeying the law.[55] So it is suggested Mt. 5.18 means until what it looks forward to arrives, or according to Davies, the law remains valid until it reaches its 'destined end'.[56] This 'culmination' is already (for Matthew) happening in the ministry and teaching of Jesus.

This is an attractive view, but it is difficult to pin down what πάντα γένηται points to. For Meier[57] it points to the resurrection, and since 'resurrection' is a key theme in Matthew (16.21; 17.10; 23; 26.64; 27.52-53; 28.18) it fits Matthew's theology well. But since the first gospel is a post-resurrection work, the resurrection hypothesis does not explain why Matthew was less willing to abandon the dietary laws (Mt. 15.17 in contrast to Mk 7.19), advocating the keeping of the law (5.19; 23.3).

In 24.34 πάντα...γένηται is used in the context of the events of 70 CE, the demise of the Temple, which leads us to speculate as to whether Matthew stands firmly within the mainstream of Jewish Christianity in wanting to retain the 'whole' law until the 'event' of 70 CE; the

include the definitive exposition of the law, at times coming close to the promulgation of a new law, cf. also W.D. Davies, *Torah in the Messianic Age and/or the Age to Come*, SBLMS 8 (Philadelphia, 1952).

54. Wenham, *Themelios* 4 (1979), p. 93; Dunn, *Unity and Diversity*, p. 246; Davies and Allison, *Saint Matthew*, 1, pp. 490, 494-95, who cite 24.34 as an example of the 'eschatological consummation'. On this see D.C. Allison, *The End of the Ages has Come* (Philadelphia: Fortress Press, 1985).

55. Cf. Banks, *Jesus and the Law*, pp. 215f.; Meier, *Law and History* , pp. 53-57; Carson, *Matthew*, p. 145; France, *Matthew*, p. 115; Moo, 'Jesus and Mosaic Law', p. 27; Davies and Allison, *Saint Matthew*, I, pp. 494-95 ('a definite end to the law is set forth').

56. Davies, *The Setting of the Sermon on the Mount*, p. 100.

57. Meier, *Law and History*.

destruction of the law-related function of the temple, temple-cult.[58] Whether or not this is correct, what is sufficiently clear in Matthew is that in spite of his interest in the law, he also seems to suggest that the law's restatement (hence a new and greater Moses function) had already begun in Jesus' life and ministry, for this is demonstrated in the antitheses in 5.21-48, his interpretation of the Torah in 12.1-8, 9-14, and generally in his teaching 11.25-30, and instruction on the kingdom 13.1-52.

(c) *The antitheses: an affirmation of Matthew's fulfilment and restatement emphasis, suggesting Jesus the transformer of the law:* Principally I wish to cite two points that demonstrate that for Matthew the law was reaching its fulfilment or realization already in the ministry and teaching of Jesus:

(i) It is significant to compare Mt. 5.17-18 with the parallel passage in Lk. 16.16-17. Lk. 16.17 is a statement of the abiding validity of the law (compare Mt. 5.18), which is immediately followed by the teaching on divorce (16.18). The same sort of 'sequence' is seen in Matthew, where while stressing Jesus' loyalty to the law, he also hints that the law is valid so long as it is restated and taken up in Jesus. This perspective on the law fits well with Matthew's polemic against the scribes and the Pharisees,[59] where he (1) defends Jesus and his community against antinomianism and (2) also portrays Jesus as the new and greater Moses.

(ii) This restatement for example is well demonstrated in Matthew's antitheses (Mt. 5.21-48). In view of the positive statement about the law in 5.17-20, it is striking that Jesus' teaching on certain aspects of the law (including the moral law, 5.21, 27), while not 'abolishing' it (καταλῦσαι 5.17) in a real sense, revises, intensifies and in a qualified sense transcends the Mosaic law. Interestingly, a similar technique is also adopted in Mt. 23.1-39, where after an apparent endorsement of the Mosaic teaching of the scribes and Pharisees (v. 3), their practices and excessive teachings are condemned. In the light of this remarkable juxtaposing of material, whatever the weaknesses in certain of R. Banks' other arguments, at least with respect to 5.21-48, it may be said that 'It is only in so far as it (the law) has been taken up into that teaching and

---

58. Dunn, *Unity and Diversity*, p. 250.

59. For Matthew's polemic against the Pharisees see Stendhal, *The School of Matthew*, p.xi; Viviano, 'Where Was the Gospel according to Saint Matthew Written?', pp. 533-46.

completely transformed that it lives on.'[60] This restatement of the law includes showing the roots from which the old commandments stem, making some of them more comprehensive,[61] and, in view of the kingdom ethic, making some of them redundant. The implication is that the Old Testament law continues as it is restated in a new way.

So (1) The discussion above suggests two basic points: (a) Matthew's loyalty to the law (e.g. Mt. 5.19; 15.17-20/Mk 7.18-20; 23.2-3, 23), and (b) his emphasis on fulfilment, Jesus' interpretation (12.1-8, 9-14) and restatement of the law (5.21-48; 5.32; 19.9; 23.5-22). The latter point confirms the special place and authority the teachings of Jesus have in the first gospel (7.24-27, 28-29; 11.28-30; 13.1-52, 54; 28.18-20).

2. Holding the balance between points (a) and (b) is important to the *writer* of the first gospel since he firmly stands within the mainstream of Jewish Christianity,[62] and understands Jesus' teachings as loyal to and (in view of the 'fulfilment'[63] situation) as restating the law first given through Moses. This 'creative tension' is also illustrated by the fact that, while on the one hand Matthew warns his community against antinomianism (5.20, 7.15-23), on the other he fights against rigid legalism advocated by the Pharisees (5.12-14; 16.12; 23.1-36), giving emphasis to 'love' as in Hos. 6.6 (5.43-48; 12.7).

3. That Matthew presents Jesus as the fulfilment of Old Testament revelation is clearly seen in the formula quotations[64] but it is also arguable that Matthew sees Jesus' teaching as the climax of the prophetic interpretation of the law.[65] This is seen in passages like 5.17; 7.12; 11.13; 22.40 where Matthew speaks of the 'law and the prophets', and particularly in 11.13 where Jesus as a person and his words/teaching emerge as

60. R. Banks, 'Matthew's Understanding of the Law: Authenticity and Interpretation in Matthew 5.17-20', *JBL* 93 (1974), p. 242

61. On this see Goulder, *Midrash and Lection in Matthew*, p. 284. That Matthew's Gospel also presents us with the nomos of the Messiah—if not in terminology then in substance, Jesus as the new lawgiver, the eschatological revealer and interpreter of Torah, the one who brought end-time revelation (for the heart as in Jer. 31.31-34) see Allison, 'The New Moses', pp. 187, 190, 172-90.

62. So Mohrlang, *Matthew and Paul*, pp. 7-26, 42-47; Dunn, *Unity and Diversity*, pp. 248-49.

63. France, *Matthew—Evangelist*, p. 196; makes a distinction between the authority and function of the law in the pre- and post-fulfilment situation.

64. See 1.22-23; 2.5-6; 15-16; 17-18; 23-24; 4.14-16; 8.17; 12.17-21; 13.35; 21.4-5; 27.9-10.

65. See Dunn, *Unity and Diversity*, p. 248.

that to which the law and the prophets in their prophetic role look forward (note the use of ἐπροφήτευσαν in 11.13).[66] If this is so, this gives Jesus a new Moses role; for (a) by his 'loyalty' to the law (5.17-20; 23.1-2; 23), but (b) also by his restatement of it (5.21-48; 12.1-8; 9-14; 23.4-22), Jesus functions as a new but greater Moses.[67] That is to say that Matthew is interested in the Mosaic law but he sees the law taken up in Jesus, the new Moses.

4. The implication of all this is that for Matthew the law abides and is authoritative, but its function has changed. Its literal and simple observance could no longer regulate Christian conduct; decisive now is Jesus' interpretation of it along with his 'new' words and 'authoritative' teaching (7.23-29; 11.25-30; 17.5; 28.20). The fundamental importance Matthew attaches to the 'words' and 'teachings' of Jesus is well brought out by G.N. Stanton,[68] who points out that while Matthew 5–7 portray Jesus as 'Messiah of Word', (in comparison with 'Messiah of Deed' in chs. 8 and 9), for the evangelist it is only the first of five discourses to which he attaches *equal* importance. This is made clear at 26.1 the verse which follows the final discourse, for while earlier discourses finish with the transitional verse καὶ ἐγένετο ὅτε ἐτέλεσεν ὁ Ἰησοῦς τοὺς λόγους τούτους (7.28; 19.1; with modifications 11.1 and 13.53), in 26.1 Matthew makes the important addition πάντας to read: Καὶ ἐγένετο ὅτε ἐτέλεσεν ὁ Ἰησοῦς **πάντας** τοὺς λόγους τούτους.

In addition, taking the underlying Q logion behind Mt. 7.21 and Lk. 6.46, from which perhaps both evangelists drew independently, Matthew has the paraphrase ἀλλ' ὁ ποιῶν τὸ θέλημα τοῦ πατρός μου τοῦ ἐν τοῖς οὐρανοῖς (7.21) for Luke's καὶ οὐ ποιεῖτε ἃ λέγω (6.46).

---

66. The phrase τὸν νόμον ἢ τοὺς προφήτας has been understood variously: as 'scripture' in its entirety, forming an *inclusio* with 7.17; so: Carson, *Matthew*, p. 144; Guelich, *The Sermon on the Mount*, p. 142.

67. The fact that the first gospel was favoured by the Ebionites who saw Moses and Jesus as the two greatest prophets perhaps supports the presence of a Moses Christology, and also Matthew's conservative attitude towards the law which attracted them. On this see Dunn, *Unity and Diversity*, pp. 240, 248-49; W.W. Wessel, 'Ebionites', in *The International Standard Bible Encyclopedia*, vol. 2 (Exeter: Paternoster Press, 1982), pp. 9-10.

68. Stanton, 'The Origin and Purpose of Matthew's Sermon on the Mount', pp. 181-92. The Jesus-wisdom-teaching/Torah motif is emphatically seen in Mt. 11.25-30; see C. Deutsch, *Hidden Wisdom and the Easy Yoke*; M.J. Suggs, *Wisdom Christology and the Law in Matthew's Gospel* (Cambridge, MA: Harvard University Press, 1970); France, *Matthew—Evangelist*, pp. 271-72, 304-305.

Considering the emphasis on Jesus' words and teaching in both Matthew's sermon on the mount (5–7) and Luke's sermon on the plain (Lk. 6.20-49), it is probable that Luke's ἃ λέγω is closer to Q than Matthew.[69] Whatever the case, this comparison implies a solidarity between Jesus' word and God's will. If Matthean redaction is accepted, then for him doing Jesus's words (clearly seen in 7.24 ἀκούει μου τοὺς λόγους τούτους καὶ ποιεῖ αὐτούς) is the same as 'doing the will of my father in heaven' (7.21).

Therefore the words of Jesus are of fundamental importance, and significantly τηρεῖν πάντα ὅσα ἐνετειλάμην ὑμῖν are Matthew's Jesus' final 'words' to his community (28.20). Matthew takes pains to emphasise the 'authority' (ἐξουσία 7.29, also cf. 28.18) of Jesus' words and teachings (5.1–7.29; especially note 7.24-27; 11.25-30; 13.1-53; 16.21-28; 17.22-27; 18.1-35; 19.3-12; 19.23-28; 24.1-25.46, and other interspersed sections). This is recognised by the ὄχλοι (7.28) who are ἐξεπλήσσοντο οἱ ὄχοι ἐπὶ τῇ διδαχῇ αὐτοῦ (7.28), for it had 'authority' (ἐξουσία 7.29). And this separated Matthew's Jesus 'from their scribes'—καὶ οὐχ ὡς οἱ γραμματεῖς αὐτῶν (7.29).[70]

I have already shown that in 17.1-9 Matthew portrays Jesus as the new and greater Moses, and in 17.5 he also alludes to the authority of the prophet-like-Moses (ἀκούετε αὐτοῦ compare Deut. 18.15-20). In this passage, the prophet's words are comparable with those of Yahweh's. For it is Yahweh's words ('ρήματα LXX, דברי MT) that are put 'in his mouth' (v. 18), and he shall speak all that Yahweh shall command him (ἐντείλωμαι αὐτῷ). It is with such associations in view that (a) Matthew's emphasis on Jesus' words/teaching, and (b) his new-Sinai portrayal at the transfiguration need to be understood.

5. So I conclude that Matthew 5–7 is suggestive of the Moses-Sinai theme, and in this capacity it anticipates the transfiguration pericope of 17.1-9 with its clearer Jesus-new-Sinai/new-Moses emphasis. Hence Matthew 5–7 is another occasion where Matthew presents Jesus in a new Moses framework.

---

69.   See Davies and Allison, *Saint Matthew*, I, p. 712, n.29.

70.   Banks, *Jesus and the Law*, p. 226, Stanton, 'The Origin and Purpose of Matthew's Sermon on the Mount', pp.181-92. Matthew's Jesus-Word/teaching is consistent with a similar emphasis found elsewhere in the New Testament, particularly see Jn 1.1-11; Col. 3.16; Heb. 1.1; 1 Pet. 1.23-25; Rev. 19.13.

5. *The Last Supper (Mt. 26.17-29)*

The links between the exodus, the passover and the last supper are obvious, and whatever the theories concerning the dating of the last supper and its relation to the account in the fourth Gospel,[71] it is evident that Jesus was doing something innovative with the passover.[72] The event, of course, is not peculiar to Matthew, but I shall show that Matthew's treatment heightens the Moses-Israel-exodus and Sinai-Jesus typology.

The Significance of the Moses-Sinai Blood-Covenant of Exodus 24.3-8
While the influence of Jer. 31.31-34 and Isa. 53.10, 12[73] has been seen in the last supper, for my purposes it is important to note that τὸ αἷμά μου τῆς διαθήκης (Mt. 26.28) not only links with the passover context of Exodus 12, as the general setting (Mt. 26.17-29 and par.) demands, but also recalls Exod. 24.3-8, the covenant sealing ceremony at the foot of Mount Sinai.[74] In Exod. 24.3-8, sacrifice is made on a twelve-pillar

---

71. For various theories see Carson, *Matthew*, pp. 528-32. No real solutions are forth coming, and attempts to harmonise them are beset with difficulties. Even Josephus seems confused about 'unleavened bread' and 'passover', see: Gundry, *Matthew*, p. 524.

72. Cf. Hill, *Matthew*, p. 340; Viviano, 'Matthew', p. 670; G.E.P. Cox, *The Gospel of St Matthew* (London: SCM Press, 1952), p. 150; A.W. Argyle, *The Gospel According to Matthew* (Cambridge: Cambridge University Press, 1963), p. 200; H.A.W. Meyer, *Kritisch-exegetischer Handbuch über das Evangelium des Matthäus* (Göttingen: Vandenhoeck & Ruprecht, 1844), p. 216; J. Schniewind, *Das Evangelium nach Matthäus* (Göttingen: Vandenhoek & Ruprecht, 1968), p.260; Trilling, *The Gospel According to St Matthew*, vol. 2, p. 468; France, *Matthew*, p. 369; Carson, *Matthew*, p. 537.

73. Schniewind, *Das Evangelium nach Matthäus*, p. 260; France, *Matthew*, p. 369; Carson, *Matthew*, p. 537.

74. On Exod. 24.4-8, cf. Lohmeyer, *Matthäus*, pp. 356-57; Grundmann, *Matthäus*, p. 536; Viviano, *Matthew*, p. 670, who also cites Lev. 17.11; Cox, *The Gospel of St Matthew*, p. 150; Argyle, *Matthew*, p. 200; Plummer, *Commentary*, p. 364; Meyer, *Commentary*, p. 216; Schniewind, *Das Evangelium nach Matthäus*, p. 260; Trilling, *The Gospel According to St Matthew*, vol. 2, p. 468; France, *Matthew*, p. 369; R.H. Gundry, *The Use of the Old Testament in St Matthew's Gospel* (Leiden: Brill, 1975), pp. 57-58; Carson, *Matthew*, pp. 537-39. B. Lindars, *New Testament Apologetic* (London: SCM Press, 1961), pp. 132-33, cites Zech. 9.11, in favour of Exod. 24.8, since he thinks Exod. 24.8 would imply a typological exegesis not used so early in the tradition, but Lindars fails to recognise the typology in Qumran (cf.

altar, symbolising all Israel, and the covenant is sealed in blood—with Moses acting as mediator.[75] Given Matthew's Moses emphasis, it is arguable that just as Moses (1) was the human initiator of the passover, and (2) mediated the blood covenant ceremony at Sinai; so Matthew's Jesus, as the new and greater Moses, radically reinterprets the themes at Exodus 12 and 24.

The Messianic Banquet and Sinai

In Mt. 26.29 Matthew's Jesus predicts that he will πίνω μεθ' ὑμῶν καινὸν ἐν τῇ βασιλείᾳ τοῦ πατρός μου. The idea of a future banquet is of course seen in passages like Isa. 25.6; Ezek. 39.17-20; *1 En.* 62.14; *2 En.* 42.5.[76] But while these passages exist, it is remarkable to note that it was at Sinai that Moses and the elders of Israel (representing the people) 'beheld God', and in the setting of a covenant meal (Gen. 31.46, 54; Exod. 18.12) 'ate and drank' (Exod. 24.11). Moreover, whatever the tradition-history of Exod. 24.11, as the text stands, this was soon after Moses had sacrificed and celebrated the blood covenant at the base of Sinai (Exod. 24.3-8). Since Exod. 24.8 has already been echoed in Mt. 26.27-28, it is natural to assume that the very next verse which predicts a messianic banquet (v. 29) echoes the Moses-Sinai-meal motif of Exod. 24.9-11. Hence I wish to suggest that in the context of the last supper Exod. 24.9-11 is the precedent for the anticipated messianic banquet, a motif that may be alluded to also in Mt. 8.11; Lk. 13.29.

Carson, *Matthew*, p. 537), and as Gundry, *Use of the Old Testament*, pp. 57-58, has pointed out, textual affinities favour Exod. 24.8. Also R. Pesch, *Das Markusevangelium*, vol. 2 (Freiburg: Herder, 1977), pp. 358-59 for the parallel Mk 14.24 where he cites Exodus 24 typology and Isa. 52.13–53.11; also Allen, *St Matthew*, pp. 276-77.

75.   On this cf. M. Noth, *Exodus* (London: SCM Press, 1972), pp. 194-99; B.S. Childs, *Exodus* (London: SCM Press, 1974), pp. 499-511. Traditio-historical issues pertaining to vv. 1-2, 9-11, are recognised; Childs in particular has stressed the importance of this passage for the New Testament context, Heb. 9.8-21, last supper (pp. 509-511). On Mark see Pesch, *Das Markusevangelium*, vol. 2, pp. 358-59; Lane, *Mark*, p. 507. In general support of Moses typology see Allison, *The New Moses*, pp. 256-61.

76.   Cf. Gundry, *Matthew*, p. 70, sees the banquet idea also in Mt. 5.6; 22.1-10, 1Qsa, 4QpPs. 37. Luke perhaps hints at it also in 13.28-29. Other relevant passages are Rev. 2.17; 19.9. *2 Bar.* 29.4 and *4 Ezra* 6.49-50 have the idea of God's enemies becoming food for its conquerors, reminiscent of Ezek. 39.17-20, see Marshall, *Luke*, p. 568.

So my arguments show that, in view of Matthew's Moses-Sinai, exodus-Israel emphasis, these motifs are also seen in his 'last supper' discourse. For here one sees the influence of both (1) the Exodus-passover (Exod. 12) motif, and (2) the Moses-Sinai-covenant-blood (Exod. 24.1-8) motif and (3) the covenant-meal (Exod. 24.12-14). Here too Matthew presents Jesus as the new Moses, who radically reinterpreted the Old Testament tradition.[77]

6. *Jesus' Moses-Type Farewell Discourse* (*Mt. 28.16-20 and Deut. 1–34*)

The final passage in my inquiry is Matthew's concluding and climaxing pericope, Mt. 28.16-20. My discussion on the last supper in some sense leads up to it, since there Matthew's addition μεθ' ὑμῶν (26.29) not only recalls μεθ' ἡμῶν of 1.23, but also veiledly points to ἐγὼ μεθ' ὑμῶν εἰμι of Mt. 28.20.

It is significant that Matthew brings his gospel to a climax with a 'mountain' pericope, which, as I have already shown, has certain parallels in the mountain pericopes in 4.8; 5.1 and 17.1-9. Questions about the tradition and history of this passage are well known, and scholars have found it difficult to align this section with any particular literary genre.[78] The fact that the first gospel climaxes with this 'neat' section is strongly suggestive of the work of a literary artist—a picture that well fits Matthew, who has throughout his gospel proved to be capable of such workmanship.[79] For our purposes, and taking the text as it stands, I shall proceed to determine if this passage echoes any Moses motifs. The following factors are pertinent:

77.   While reading the draft of this thesis, Dr N.T. Wright brought to my attention that if Daniel 7 is about the suffering people of God who are then vindicated by God, then the whole passion narrative comes into play. The Jewish leaders who are initially responsible for Jesus' death, and the Romans who carry it out, are together seen as the forces of chaos oppressing the true Israel. Since the whole episode is also linked to the passover event, here then (as I have argued for the temptation narrative [Mt. 4.1-11], the transfiguration [17.1-8], and will do in the case of the final commissioning in 28.18-10) there is a Daniel-Moses typology.

78.   Cf. B.J. Malina, 'The Literary Structure and Form of Matthew 28.16-20', *NTS* (1970–71), pp. 87-103; J.P. Meier, 'Two Disputed Questions in Mt. 28.16-20', *JBL* 96 (1977), pp. 407-424; Carson, *Matthew*, pp. 591-92; for a good survey of scholarship see Donaldson, *Mountain*, pp. 170-90.

79.   On this see France, *Matthew–Evangelist*, pp. 312-17.

Redactional and Thematic Links

The link between πᾶς οὖν ὅστις ἀκούει μου τοὺς λόγους τούτους καὶ ποιεῖ αὐτούς 7.24, ἀκούετε αὐτοῦ 17.5, and διδάσκοντες αὐτοὺς τηρεῖν πάντα ὅσα ἐνετειλάμην ὑμῖν in 28.20, have already been noted; for in all these passages, the new (renewed) Israel's obedience to Jesus' words is in focus. Moreover (1) both 17.1-8 and 28.16-20 are linked by mountain motifs away from Judea, and (2) only in 17.7 (προσῆλθεν) and 28.18 (προσελθών) is Jesus said to have 'approached' someone, for it is always others approaching him. Hence this use of προσέρχομαι possibly suggests a redactional link.

Daniel 7-Sinai Links

Mt. 28.18 echoes 11.27, but goes beyond that, and several scholars, including O. Michel, E. Lohmeyer, M.J. Lagrange, W.D. Davies, J. Schniewind, W. Grundmann, Albright and Mann, and W. Trilling have detected the influence of Dan. 7.14 in Mt. 28.18.[80] It was O. Michel who

---

80.   O. Michel, 'The Conclusion of Matthew's Gospel: a Contribution to the History of the Easter Message (1950)', in G.N. Stanton (ed.), *The Interpretation of Matthew* (Philadelphia: Fortress Press; London: SPCK, 1983), pp. 30-41; Lohmeyer, *Matthäus*, p. 416; M.J. Lagrange, *Évangile selon saint Matthieu* (Études Bibliques; Paris: Gabalda, 1923), p. 544; Davies, *The Setting of the Sermon on the Mount*, pp. 197-98 speaks of the 'enthronement of the Son of Man'; Schniewind, *Das Evangelium nach Matthäus*, 1956, p. 279; W. Grundmann, *Das Evangelium nach Matthäus*, pp. 577-78; W.F. Albright and C.S. Mann, *Matthew* (New York: Doubleday, 1971), p. 362; W. Trilling, *Das wahre Israel* (Munich: Kösel, 1964), pp. 21-50. Also see Meier, *The Vision of Matthew*, pp. 369-70; Viviano, 'Matthew', p. 678, who speaks of the 'authority of the Son of Man as the authority of the kingdom of God', Mt. 6.10. Hill, *Matthew*, cites Dan. 7.14, but with Barth, 'Matthew's Understanding of the Law', p. 133, is in favour of an 'exaltation' motif more than resurrection, hence cites Phil. 2.9.

Those who do not cite Daniel 7 are Plummer, who cites Eph. 1.21, Col. 1.16-21; Phil. 2.9-10, pp. 428-29; Argyle, *Commentary*, p. 221 (Phil. 2.9). Those who associate the 'Son of Man'-Daniel 7 link in Matthew only with parousia contexts, deny it here. Gundry, *Matthew*, p. 595, followed by Donaldson, *Mountain*, p. 177, denies it on the grounds that there is no Son of Man title. But as Keck, 'Towards the Renewal of New Testament Christology', *NTS* 32 (1986), pp. 362-77 has well argued, 'titles' are not the be all and end all of determining christological motifs. Considering the force of ἀπ' ἄρτι in association with 'Son of Man' with its clear Daniel 7 association in 26.64, which need not be associated with the parousia but the 'events' of the next few weeks' (this is what ἀπ' ἄρτι here signifies, i.e. the inauguration of a 'new period', cf. Trilling, *Das Wahre Israel*, pp. 86-87, Meier, *Law*

four decades ago in an influential article showed the linguistic and thematic parallels between Dan. 7.14 and Mt. 28.18.[81] This has in more recent times been developed by other scholars.[82]

Linguistic and Thematic Links: The themes of (1) ἐξουσία v. 18, (ἡ ἐξουσία αὐτοῦ Dan. 7.14), (2) πάντα τὰ ἔθνη v. 19 (καὶ πάντες οἱ λαοί, φυλαί, καὶ γλῶσσαι αὐτῷ δουλεύσουσιν Dan. 7.14), (3) the authority πᾶσα ἐξουσία ἐν οὐρανῷ καὶ ἐπὶ [τῆς] γῆς (v. 18), and permanency of Jesus' presence ἐγὼ μεθ' ὑμῶν εἰμι πάσας...ἕως τῆς συντελείας τοῦ αἰῶνος v. 20, (ἐξουσία αἰώνιος, ἥτις οὐ παρελεύσεται, καὶ ἡ βασιλεία αὐτοῦ οὐ διαφθαρήσεται Dan. 7.14) are all strongly reminiscent of Dan. 7.13-14. Moreover, ἐδόθη in Mt. 28.18, parallels the idea in Dan. 4.14, 22, 29 and 5.21 (LXX ὅτι κυριεύει ὁ Θεὸς ὕψιστος τῆς βασιλείας τῶν ἀνθρώπων, καὶ ᾧ ἂν δόξῃ δώσει a repeated motif) where it is God who bestows authority. And it also parallels Dan. 7.13-14 with its reference to ὡς υἱὸς ἀνθρώπου who 'receives' authority from God (7.14 ἐδόθη; and the 'saints' [ἐδόθη] 7.27). So, it is God who has bestowed divine authority on Jesus as Son of Man. This authority is that of the kingdom of God and its 'glory' (יְקָר, Dan. 7.14) associated with God's honour.

While these motifs are in Daniel 7, I have shown previously that they are also precisely what was demonstrated at Sinai, the coming of God associated with God's kingdom and glory. So, while Mt. 4.8, 5.1 look forward to 17.1-8, Matthew's new Sinai, 28.16-20, looks back to it. In addition, I shall show below, the mountain motif in 28.16 contributes to a Moses/Deuteronomy 34 farewell motif (where Deuteronomy itself looks back to Sinai, in relation to the 'second' giving of the law).

If the influence of Daniel 7, Sinai-kingdom-glory and other related motifs in Mt. 28.16-20, is accepted, then what was proleptically demonstrated in Mt. 17.1-8 and predicted by Jesus in 26.64 is voiced by him in 28.18-20.

---

and History, p. 370, also 23.39; 26.29), climaxing in the resurrection (hence applicable to 28.16-20), Gundry's argument is untenable.

81.   O. Michel, 'The Conclusion of Matthew's Gospel', pp. 30-41.

82.   Trilling, *Das Wahre Israel*, pp. 21-50, like Davies, speaks of a proleptic parousia. He links 13.41-43; 16.27-28, 19.28; 24.30-31; 26.64; specially 25.31-46 (p. 314), the eschatological glory and authority of the Son of Man glimpsed in these passages is now already, after the resurrection, a present reality. Also see France, *Jesus and the Old Testament*, pp. 142-43, *Matthew*, pp. 413-14; *Matthew— Evangelist*, pp. 312-17; Carson, *Matthew*, p. 595.

The Blending of Danielic and Mosaic Motifs

Two factors are crucial in this section: (1) The recognition of the influence of Daniel 7 and Sinai motifs, which I have suggested above, and (2) the blending of this with a Moses-farewell motif, similar to that seen in the book of Deuteronomy. K. Stendahl and B.T. Viviano have rightly observed that Mt. 28.18-20 resembles a farewell discourse. Stendahl points out that 28.20 in particular fits the pattern of a testament or farewell speech.[83] I agree with this form critical judgment, but wish to add that it specifically and remarkably parallels a Moses-farewell discourse. Note:

1. Deuteronomy 33.1-29 recount Moses' farewell addresses to the twelve tribes of Israel. This may be compared with Jesus' specific appearance and commission to his circle of disciples (Mt. 28.16) which, according to Matthew's arrangement, functions as his farewell address to the nucleus of the new (renewed) Israel.

2. Moses' farewell speech anticipates the conquest of the land. In Deut. 34.1, he goes up Mount Nebo and then to Pisgah to view the land that Israel was to conquer. Just as Moses anticipated the establishment of the (albeit earthly) kingdom of God in his farewell discourse, so in Mt. 28.18-20 Matthew's Jesus anticipates world-wide mission, making disciples of all nations, that is, the establishment of the kingdom of God, a prominent theme in Matthew (with its Peter-ἐκκλησια-kingdom ramifications, cf. 16.16-19).

3. It is significant to note that Matthew's use of ἐνετειλάμην is used in Exod. 7.2, 29.35 (ἐντέλλομαι) and consistently in the LXX of Deuteronomy, of what Yahweh has 'commanded', (Deut. 1.3; 30.11; 4.2, 13, 40; 6.1, 2, 17, 25; 7.11; 8.1; 10.13; 11.8, 13), his commands (ἐντολὴ 4.2, 40; 5.29, 31; 6.2, 17; 7.9; 8.2, 6, 11; 10.13; 11.1; 17.20) and also Yahweh's 'words' (τῷ ῥήματι Κυρίου 1.26, 43; 9.23) given to Israel through Moses. Since Matthew has exclusively used ἐντέλλομαι denoting God's commands (15.4) and in 19.7 of Moses' command (ἐνετείλατο) it is remarkable that Matthew in his final pericope uses it of Jesus.

83.   Stendahl, 'Matthew', in M. Black and H.H. Rowley (eds.), *Peake's Commentary on the Bible*, p. 798; Viviano, 'Matthew', p. 674.

4. Finally, a point, perhaps of lesser value but nevertheless worth noting, is that the other time that Matthew uses ἐντέλλομαι of Jesus, is in the transfiguration context of 17.9. It is true that here it is in relation to 'silence' μηδενὶ εἴπητε. But it was silence in relation to τὸ ὅραμα only until the resurrection. Perhaps it is over-subtle to say that ἐνετείλατο in 17.9 alludes in a veiled manner to a Moses-Jesus parallelism, and that it also anticipates 28.20. But it may be argued that the transfiguration event itself was to *function* as a 'teaching event', and hence links with 28.20.[84]

So it is arguable that (1) just as, after Moses' farewell discourse (Deut. 33), Joshua (Josh. 1.1-9) and every prophet that arose took after Moses (Deut 18.15-22), so Matthew in 28.16-20 portrays the disciples as continuing the teaching of Jesus the new and far greater Moses. (2) Since Mt. 28.18 echoes Daniel 7, here too a good case can be made for concluding that Matthew has blended Danielic and Moses-exodus motifs. The Mosaic motifs in 28.16-20 are reminiscent of a Moses-Israel farewell speech or testament, paralleled here by Matthew's portrayal of final words to his new and renewed Israel (the disciples). (3) Matthew's signing off his gospel with διδάσκοντες αὐτοὺς τηρεῖν πάντα ὅσα ἐνετειλάμην ὑμῖν (28.20) once again stresses the importance he places on Jesus' words and teachings. This motif recurs throughout Matthew, for example in 5–7, and especially 7.24-29. In 11.25-30 wisdom categories are applied to Jesus,[85] and in 17.5 the disciples were to ἀκούετε αὐτοῦ. (4) In view of these points it may be concluded that, just as Moses in his farewell speech reminded Israel of the law of God, given through him and left behind for them strictly to follow, so Jesus is presented by Matthew at the climax of his Gospel as the new and greater Moses, who in a similar 'farewell' speech leaves behind 'all' that he has 'commanded' (ἐνετειλάμην), and is the final norm against which even the Mosaic law needs to be evaluated.[86]

---

84. Remarkably Mt. 17.1-8 in the general setting of 16.21–18.35 is surrounded by six teaching blocks, 16.21-23; 16.24-20; 17.9-13; 17.14-20; 17.22-23; 17.24-27.

85. On Mt. 11.19; 25-30; that (1) Matthew like other New Testament writers drew on 'wisdom literature' and that (2) Jesus is the one in whom God's wisdom speaks, see: Suggs, *Wisdom*; C. Deutsch, *Hidden Wisdom*; France, *Matthew— Evangelist*, pp. 302-306.

86. My arguments are further substantiated by Allison's treatment of

I have traced Matthew's use of the Moses-exodus and Moses-Sinai themes in (1) the infancy narrative, (2) the baptism story, (3) the temptation narrative, (4) the sermon on the mount, (5) the last supper, (6) the final commission, and, of course, the transfiguration. I shall now comment on some possible objections to my thesis and finally draw some overall conclusions.

7. Matthew's Moses-Jesus Typology in the Light of Son of David Themes and Zion Theology

In this section I wish to address two possible objections to my thesis: (1) How does Matthew's Moses-Jesus typology fare with his Son of David themes? And (2) how does the Moses-Sinai emphasis I have argued in relation to Mt. 17.1-8 fare in comparison with recent discussion (especially as set forth by T.L. Donaldson) on Zion theology and Matthew's Gospel? I shall take them in order.

Matthew's Moses Motif in Comparison with Davidic and Son of David Motifs

One key objection that could be raised concerning this thesis is: how does the Moses emphasis at the transfiguration, and the general framework I have argued for in the first Gospel, fit with Matthew's use of the Son of David motif? This is a real issue, and in this section I shall prove that while for Matthew Jesus is the 'Son of David', he did not frame his Gospel within Davidic categories. But in the light of (1) the Moses emphasis of the day, and (2) his polemic against the scribes and the Pharisees who emphasised Moses and the law, and (3) his stance within earliest Jewish Christianity, Matthew found Moses categories quite adequate and appropriate to frame his Gospel with. The following discussion will elucidate this:

A Survey of Views

There is no consensus of opinion about Matthew's use of the Son of David motif. For example according to D.J. Verseput, the Davidic category is of 'primary concern to Matthew' and 'propels the narrative from birth to the crucifixion...'[87] But a completely opposite view is

Mt. 28.16-20 in *The New Moses*, pp. 262-66; and Wright, *The New Testament and the People of God*, pp. 388-89.

87. D.J. Verseput, 'The Role and Meaning of the "Son of God" Title in Matthew's Gospel', *NTS* 33 (1987), pp. 532-56.

argued by J.M. Gibbs, according to whom 'Matthew emphatically lays aside the title "Son of David" as *inadequate* in the face of recognition of Jesus as the Son of God (xxii 41-46).'[88]

A similar line is adopted by J.D. Kingsbury,[89] who attempts to show that 'Son of David' (as all other Christological titles in Matthew) is subsumed under Matthew's Son of God motif. On the other hand, D.C. Duling,[90] recently followed by J. Brady,[91] has associated the title 'Son of David' with Solomon, who according to Josephus *Ant.* 7, 45-49, and other Jewish writers, was considered an exorcist and healer. Duling and Brady view Jesus-Son of David within this 'Solomon-therapeutic' pattern.

A Study of Matthew's Use of the Son of David Title and Categories
It may be said generally that Jesus' Davidic origin was a feature of early Christian preaching (Acts 2.29-36; 13.22-23; Rom. 1.3; 2 Tim. 2.8; Heb. 7.11-17,[92] Rev. 5.5; 22.16), though references to it are not in abundance. My purpose, however, is to determine how Matthew in particular has conceived it, which must be done by a study of Matthew's text and not by looking at Matthew through the eyes of Paul (Rom. 1.3; 2 Tim. 2.8), Luke-Acts (Lk. 1.27, 32, 69; 2.4, 11; Acts 2.29-36; 13.22-23) or anyone else (Rev. 5.5; 22.16).

1. *Supposed Davidic Motifs:* In Matthew, the title υἱοῦ Δαυὶδ stands alongside Ἰησοῦ Χριστοῦ in Mt. 1.1, and David (as king in 1.6) features prominently in Matthew's 3 × 14 generation/genealogy schema. From vv. 6-11 it is David's kingly line that is being traced, though whether this could be said of vv. 12-16 is of course debated,[93] for

88.   J.M. Gibbs, 'Purpose and Pattern in Matthew's use of the Title "Son of David"', *NTS* 10 (1963–64), pp. 449-50.

89.   J.D. Kingsbury, 'The Title "Son of David" in Matthew's Gospel', *JBL* 95/4 (1976), pp. 591-602; *Matthew: Structure*, pp. 40-83.

90.   D.C. Dulling, 'Solomon, Exorcism, and the Son of David', *HTR* 68 (1975), pp. 235-52; 'The Therapeutic Son of David: An Element in Matthew's Christological Apologetic', *NTS* 24 (1977–78), pp. 392-410.

91.   J. Brady, 'The Role of Miracle-Working as Authentication of Jesus as "The Son of God"', *Churchman*, 103 No.1 (1989), pp. 32-39.

92.   In Heb. 7.11-17 it is via the royal priesthood of Melchizedek, Ps. 110.4; Gen. 49.10; so: Nolan, *The Royal Son of God*, p. 152.

93.   Gundry, *Matthew*, argues that certain names in Mt. 1.13-15 (Zadok, Eleazar) suggest links with the tribe of Levi, derived from 1 Chron. 6.3-14, and that 'certain names from Luke's list "catch the evangelist's eye"'. Whether Matthew knew of Luke's list is conjectural, but on the other hand, no concrete solutions have been

according to Jer. 22.28-30 none of Coniah's ('Ιεχονίας Mt. 1.12)
offspring were to 'sit on David's throne nor rule Judah again.'[94]
Nevertheless, the general thrust of Mt. 1.1-17 emphasises Jesus' legal-
Davidic connections. The following points are in favour of this:

(a) Matthew insists that (i) Joseph was a Davidid (1.16, 20)—a motif
underlined by the angel (1.20). (ii) In Matthew, it is Joseph who was to
name the child Jesus (1.21), and this in contrast to Lk. 1.31 where this
task is given to Mary. By this Matthew seems to allude to the Old
Testament and Jewish practice whereby it is acknowledgment by the
father which makes a child his son, rather than physical procreation *per
se* (as in Graeco-Roman culture).[95] (b) Matthew by his 3×14 genealogy
(1.17) stresses that in Jesus the Davidic Messiah has come.[96]
(c) Moreover, geography is important for Matthew, and by it he
highlights the Davidic motifs associated for example with the royal birth
place, 'Bethlehem of Judah' (2.12/Mic. 5.2 and 2 Sam. 5.2). (d) The
'star' (Mt. 2.2) too may be reminiscent of Num. 24.17 with its implied
reference to the Messiah;[97] Matthew however does not cite this passage.

---

offered (see Davies and Allison, *Saint Matthew*, I, pp. 181-82). Other factors to be
considered are (1) the links between the tribes of Judah and Levi: in the early *Targum
Neofiti* on Exod. 1.15, Miryam (Moses' sister, and also the Hebrew form of Mary's
name) of the tribe of Levi was considered to have received the crown of royalty, for
she was to be the ancestor of David (cf. Brown, *The Birth of the Messiah*, p. 116
n.45). (2) In this connection it is significant to note that it is not at all certain if Mary
was a Davidid, who, in Elisabeth had a συγγενής, a female relative, not necessarily a
cousin (Lk. 1.36). Elisabeth was ἐκ τῶν θυγατέρων 'Ααρών—which corresponds
to the rabbinic 'daughter of a priest' and is analogous to 'son of Aaron' (Marshall,
Luke, p. 52). Mary's relationship to Elisabeth suggests that she too may have been
from priestly descent (Marshall, *Luke*, p. 71). Whether Matthew was sensitive to these
elements, it is hard to say. But this Judah-Levi connection, which also may impinge
on the John (of the tribe of Levi, cousin of Jesus?) forerunner of Jesus association.

94. The differences between the genealogies of Luke and Matthew are hard to
harmonise, Marshall, *Luke*, pp. 157-65.

95. Gibbs, 'Purpose and Pattern', pp. 446-64, esp. p. 448, also n.1.

96. For the theory that the Hebrew letters in the name David add up to 14, see
Gundry, *Matthew*, p. 19.

97. Like Stendahl, 'Quis et Unde?', p. 59, Davies and Allison, *Saint Matthew*, I,
p. 235 point out that since Matthew's main interest in the formula quotations
(Matthew 1–2) is geographical; Num. 24.17 is not explicitly cited. But Bourke
suggests that in Jewish literature the 'star' functioned as a symbol of the person
himself (*T. Jud.* 24.1; CD 7.18-19) and not of his coming, which may be behind
Matthew's omission (or was Matthew not intending to over-emphasise his Davidic

(e) The motif of 'homage' by the gentile Magi perhaps echoes 1 Kgs 10.1-13. But here it needs to be noted that Sheba's Queen pays homage to Solomon not David. Moreover the 'gentile-homage' motif may also echo Gen. 12.3; 18.18; 22.18; 26.4 (since Jesus is also υἱοῦ 'Αβραάμ 1.1, in whom the nations of the earth find blessing) and/or recall the pilgrimage of nations foretold in Isa. 60.3 and Ps. 72.8-11. (f) The 'shepherding' motif: ὅστις ποιμανεῖ τὸν λαόν μου τὸν 'Ισραηλ (2.6) may also suggest David-shepherd associations (cf. 2 Sam. 5.2). This too is inconclusive, for the 'shepherding' motifs also fit Moses. According to Philo, Moses was the 'ideal' shepherd-king, precisely due to his experience in Midian.

In general it is clear that Davidic themes are to be seen in Matthew's infancy narrative.

2. *The Son of David concept needs to be set in relation to the Son of God motif:* While recognising Matthew's Son of David theme in his infancy narrative, this motif needs to be set in perspective, in view of the 'Son of God' motif. For if Matthew's motif of virginal conception, clearly suggested in 1.25, is given its rightful place, then Jesus is 'Son of David' (through Joseph cf. 1.16, 20) by adoption (legal not physical) and 'Son of God' by divine conception. In relation to this 'perspective' the following points need to be recognised:

(a) J.D. Kingsbury,[98] developing R. Pesch's observations,[99] argues that Matthew's passive ἐγεννήθη (Mt. 1.16, Jesus born by the special act of God) alludes to divine sonship and points forward to the passive participle γεννηθὲν ('that which is conceived') of 1.20, which too alludes to divine activity. By this and through the statements about conception by the Holy Spirit (1.18, 20) and about Joseph's abstinence in 1.25, Matthew asserts that Jesus the Messiah, born of Mary, is Son of God. His origin is in God, and in 'Εμμανουήλ (1.22-23); God dwells with his people (p. 594).

(b) It is true that one needs to take into consideration that according

---

motif?). That the 'star' and 'light' motifs at infancy, and at other times, have also been attached to other important figures see Davies and Allison, *Saint Matthew*, I, pp. 233-34. This includes Moses who is supposed to have illuminated the place of his birth cf. *b. Meg.*14a, *Exod. Rab.* on 2.4, also Abraham (see Bourke, 'The Literary Gems of Matthew 1–2', p. 169).

98. Kingsbury, '"Son of David"', pp. 591-602.

99. R. Pesch, 'Der Gottessohn im matthäischen Evangelienprolog (Mt. 1–2): Beobachtungen zu den Zitationsformeln der Reflexionszitate', *Bib* 48 (1967), esp. pp. 411, 413-14, 416-18.

to Jewish law the father's 'naming' (adoption) and not procreation is the main factor in adoption into the family (already emphasised in 1.21), but the point made by Pesch and Kingsbury that *Matthew* links the idea of virginal conception with the 'Son of God' theme has much to commend it. For irrespective of one's views on the virginal conception, as the text stands, Matthew plainly refers to it in his infancy narrative, and Davies and Allison have rightly captured this in their heading to section 1.18-25: 'Conceived of the Holy Spirit, Born of a Virgin, Implanted into the Line of David.'[100]

(c) This 'Son of God' emphasis in 1.20-25, finds support in Matthew's particular stress on Jesus' filial relationship with 'his Father'. For (i) Jesus repeatedly refers to God as 'my Father' cf. 7.21; 10.32-33; 12.50; 15.13; 16.17; 18.10, 14, 19, 35; 20.23; 25.34; 26.29, 42, 53—all without Synoptic parallel. (ii) Jesus' sonship is highlighted by the way that Matthew alone of the synoptics distinguishes between 'my (μου) Father' (Jesus') and 'your (ὑμῶν) heavenly Father' (disciples' 23.9). (iii) Jesus in Matthew was 'sent' (ἀποστείλαντα 10.40; ἀπεστάλην 15.24), and is plainly called 'Son' (of God) cf. 2.15; 3.17; 4.3, 6; 14.33; 17.5; 27.54; 28.19, (some of these passages also echoing a Jesus-Israel-son relation cf. 2.15; 3.17; 4.3, 6; 17.5). (iv) In the parable of the 'wicked tenants' (21.33-46), Jesus' reference to 'son' (21.37-38) points to his own relation with God, his Father.[101] It is the first public claim by Jesus to be Son of God in Matthew, and it may well lie behind Caiaphas' charge in 26.63.[102]

So, as Matthew has presented it, the Jesus-son motif is not merely to be taken in the way that Son of God appellations are applied to the faithful 'righteous man' in *Wis.* 2.16, 18; 5.5; *Pss. Sol.* 13.8; Sir. 4.10[103]

---

100.   Davies and Allison, *Saint Matthew*, I, p. 196. Verseput's ('Meaning of the "Son of God" Title', p. 532) attempt to dismiss this as a 'backward development' in the historical evolution of Christology is unpersuasive. On the other hand Nolan, *The Royal Son of God*, pp. 43-46, makes much of τό παιδίον and παιδίον μετὰ...τῆς μητρός in terms of the 'great lady/Mother' concept which is equally subjective.

101.   J. Ramsey Michaels, *Servant and Son: Jesus in Parable and Gospel* (Atlanta: John Knox, 1981), has argued that Jesus identified with his parables, which included the 'son' motif. The parables are 'images of the kingdom', and Jesus acts as 'son' since parables are 'stories his Father told him' (p. 101). At times Michaels comes close to psychologising, but his arguments on the 'son' motif, and that Jesus indentified with certain of his parables (in our case, Mt. 21.33-41) merits attention.

102.   So France, *Matthew*, pp. 309-309.

103.   Cf. M. Hengel, *The Son of God* (Philadelphia: Fortress Press, 1976), pp. 43-4; G. Vermes, *Jesus the Jew* (London: SCM Press, 3rd edn, 1989), pp. 195-

who experiences God's fatherly love (though this motif is not foreign to Matthew's Jesus who is obedient 'son' cf. 3.17; 4.3-6; 26.39, 42/Mk 14.36; Lk. 22.42; Mt. 27.43);[104] it points rather to a special relationship with his Father. Hence if Matthew's motif of virginal conception is given due recognition, then the 'Son of David' motif in his infancy narrative needs to be set in perspective of his Son of God motif.

3. *Matthew's use of the title 'Son of David' elsewhere in his Gospel is more 'Solomonic' than 'Davidic':* With the above discussion in view, it is important to ascertain how Matthew has used the 'Son of David' title elsewhere in his Gospel. The following considerations are worth noting:

(a) Jesus nowhere uses it of himself, and introduces it only to question its adequacy (22.41-45). (b) In 21.15-16, he was willing to defend its use by others of him, against religious authorities. (c) Almost every use of the title in Jesus' ministry is directly related to his healing ministry, in the context of (i) a request for healing (9.27; 15.22; 20.30-31) or (ii) people's query (12.22-23); or (children's) praise (21.14-15) after healings (21.15). In view of this it may be argued that people were interpreting Jesus' healings in the light of a popular Son of David-Solomon-therapeutic pattern (e.g. Josephus *Ant.* 7.45-49).[105]

It must be noted that not all healing-miracles in Matthew are explicitly associated with the Son of David (hence Solomon), for example 9.35; 15.30-31. But certain factors suggest a Son of David (Solomon)-healing association: (a) a call for 'mercy' (ἐλέησόν) occurs in every instance where people request healing from the 'Son of David' (Jesus), see 9.27; 15.22; 20.30. This is unique to Matthew, and shows that he associates Jesus as Son of David particularly with acts of mercy (contrast to Mk 10.47/Lk. 18.38 (Mt. 9.27 and 20.30); Mk 7.25—no Son of David [Mt. 15.22]). (b) This is confirmed in 11.2-6, where τὰ ἔργα τοῦ Χριστοῦ

97; Verseput, 'Meaning of the "Son of God" Title', p. 538.

104.   Verseput, 'Meaning of the "Son of God" Title', pp. 532-56, sees an analogy to *Wis.* 2.6-20 in this passage, p. 538.

105.   D.C. Dulling, 'The Therapeutic Son of David: An Element in Matthew's Christological Apologetic', *NTS* 24 (1977–78), pp. 392-410, also his earlier, 'Solomon, Exorcism, and the Son of David', *HTR* 68 (1975), pp. 235-52. Stanton, 'The Origin and purpose of Matthew's Gospel', pp. 1923-24 states that it is 'something of an enigma'. In Matthew alone the cry for 'mercy' precedes the title 'Son of David' (Mt. 9.27; 15.22; 20.30, 31 contra Mk 10.47, 48; Lk. 18.38, 39), see H.J. Held, 'Matthew as Interpreter of the Miracle Stories', in G. Bornkam, G. Barth and H.J. Held (eds.), *Tradition and Interpretation in Matthew*, p. 226; Nolan, *The Royal Son of God*, pp. 158-215.

are quite specifically works of healing and mercy (11.5).

The above arguments suggest that Matthew himself intended his readers to understand Jesus' healings/exorcisms and ministry in terms of works of the Son of David, this title having Solomonic overtones. Significantly the healings, as Kingsbury has noted, were done among people of 'no-account', the blind, lame, dumb, the Canaanite woman, and they function as a critique of Israel, especially of its leaders who are blind to his (Davidic 1.1, 16) Messiahship (11.25; 21.42-46; 21.23-23.39). It is conceivable also that by this Son of David as healer association, Matthew was rejecting the popular nationalistic concept of 'Son of David'.

Matthew's Cautious Use of the Son of David Motif Suggests its Inadequacy as an Over-Riding Framework for his Gospel

A few other passages, as I shall show, support the argument that Matthew wished to correct the politically charged 'Son of David' concept of popular understanding.

1. Even though the Galilean ὄχλοι[106] acclaim him as τῷ υἱῷ Δαυίδ (21.9), on inquiry (21.11) they introduce him to those in the 'city of Jerusalem' as ὁ προφήτης Ἰησοῦς ὁ ἀπὸ Ναζαρὲθ τῆς Γαλιλαίας (21.11). This is remarkable, and seems to mute the messianic force of the earlier τῷ υἱῷ Δαυίδ, at least in Matthew's redaction and arrangement of his material. Moreover, ὁ προφήτης echoes the prophet-like-Moses motif of Deut. 18.15-18, which in relation to ἀκούετε αὐτοῦ in 17.5, and other Moses-Jesus parallelisms in Matthew, is in keeping with the Moses-eschatological expectations of the time (e.g. οὗτός ἐστιν ἀληθῶς ὁ προφήτης ὁ ἐρχόμενος εἰς τὸν κόσμον Jn 6.14). If this is accepted, then here again Matthew has played down the crowd's Davidic-political and nationalistic messianism in favour of a prophet-like-Moses Christology.

2. In 21.14 it is the children who attribute the title 'Son of David' to Jesus, and this in the context of the only recorded healing by Jesus in the temple. Several factors are important here: (a) What Jesus does in the temple in itself is a contrast between him and David who banned the very category of people Jesus healed, from the 'house' in Jerusalem

---

106. On Matthew's use of ὄχλοι (Galilean) in distinction to λαός see Gibbs, 'Purpose and Pattern', pp. 450-51. (1) ὄχλοι are generally 'receptive' in contrast to the 'leaders of the nation'. (2) In 21.11 it is they who introduce Jesus to those in the 'city of Jerusalem'. (3) In 26.47 it is probably they (ὄχλος) with the 'elders of the people' (λαός) who turn against him.

(2 Sam. 5.8). (b) True, Jesus is willing to defend its use (21.16), but he does so by appealing to the LXX version of Ps. 8.2. Significantly Psalm 8 is a psalm praising God and not any man (not even the enigmatic 'son of man' (v. 4) who, in view of vv. 5-8 could be interpreted messianically). Since Matthew has Jesus applying it to himself, it implies a status higher than the 'Son of David' title attributed to him in 21.14. Hence (i) Jesus' non-Davidic temple-healing action (in contrast to 2 Sam. 5.8) and (ii) Jesus' application of Ps. 8.2 strongly suggest that Matthew intended his readers to understand that Son of David categories are *inadequate* to define Jesus.

3. *The significance of Mt. 22.41-46:* It is with the above arguments in view that I come to reject the 'Son of David' title (not to be used again in Matthew) in the enigmatic Mt. 22.41-46. J.A. Fitzmyer, followed by others, has argued that Jesus' method of argument here is in the form of scribal debate where an antinomy is set up in order to seek a solution.[107] But the point is that in the synoptics (Mt. 22.41-46; Mk 12.35-37; Lk. 20.41-44) only the antinomy (David's son/David's Lord) is recorded and not the solution, which however needs to be inferred from what each evangelist has done with his tradition. So one will be able to understand Matthew's particular interest in this issue only by looking at his redaction of the tradition, and especially his expansion of it. The following distinctive Matthean points need to be noted:

(a) In Matthew alone the discussion is specifically addressed to the Pharisees who were 'gathered together', for 'Jesus asked them a question' (22.41, compare Mk 12.35). In Lk. 20.41, the Sadducees (cf. 20.27) seem to be in view.

(b) Matthew alone has two questions; the first τί ὑμῖν δοκεῖ περὶ τοῦ Χριστοῦ? is introductory to the second τίνος υἱός ἐστιν? and this in contrast to Mark's πῶς λέγουσιν οἱ γραμματεῖς ὅτι ὁ Χριστὸς υἱὸς Δαυίδ ἐστιν? (Mk 12.35; with modification Lk. 20.41, e.g. omission of οἱ γραμματεῖς).

(c) Matthew alone elicits an answer *from* the Pharisees, rather than questioning on the belief of οἱ γραμματεῖς in Mk 12.35. The Pharisees answer: λέγουσιν αὐτῷ, τοῦ Δαυίδ (v. 42). The rest of the pericope, with slight modification (of no real importance), follows Mark, but Matthew introduces the 'silence' motif of Mark's previous pericope Mk

107. J.A. Fitzmyer, 'The Son of David Tradition and Mt. 22.41-46 and Parallels', in *Essays on the Semitic Background of the New Testament* (London: Geoffrey Chapman, 1971), pp. 115-21.

12.34 (omitted by Matthew in 22.29, with the whole of Mk 12.32-34), expanding on it in 22.46. Hence by this redaction and arrangement (through which Matthew has introduced the Pharisee-silence theme in 22.46) Matthew, more forcefully than Mark, makes emphatic the point made in 22.41-46 'how is he his [David's] son?'

My conclusion is that Matthew (alone) (i) by addressing the question directly at the Pharisees, (ii) by highlighting the force of the question and doubling it (22.42), (iii) by eliciting an answer from the Pharisees, and also (iv) by introducing the Pharisee's silence specifically at 22.46, has made this pericope his decisive reply to that Jewish understanding of the Messiah (λέγουσιν αὐτῷ· τοῦ Δαυίδ v. 42), which attributed to the Messiah an imperial role and made him a replica of David with an earthly national throne.

4. Matthew's portrayal of Jesus' interpretation of Ps. 110.1: The question is, what exactly is Matthew emphasising in 22.41-46, a pericope, which seems to strike the reader slightly more forcefully than that of Mark or Luke? B.M. Nolan, J.M. Gibbs, J.D. Kingsbury, D.J. Verseput and others have rightly pointed out that τίνος υἱός ἐστιν? suggests that more than one sonship might come into question, for in vv. 41-46 both the issues of Davidic sonship and divine sonship (filial) are set before the reader.[108] But the force of the argument, and this in the light of Jesus' questions, both beginning with πῶς οὖν (22.43), οὖν...πῶς (22.45), seems to focus on the issue of to whom the Christ (that is Jesus to Matthew's readers) owes filial obedience and from whom he receives his sonship.

The Christ according to Matthew's version is the son of someone superior to David, and the one who controls the nature of Jesus' sonship is not David. For Matthew presents Jesus as (1) accepting Davidic authorship of Ps. 110.1 and (2) interpreting the psalm as one addressed to the Messiah.[109] And (3) taking κύριος[110] in 22.45 as superior to

---

108.   Cf. Nolan, *The Royal Son of God*, p. 223; Gibbs, 'Purpose and Pattern', p. 461; Kingsbury, '"Son of David"', pp. 595-96; Verseput, 'Meaning of the "Son of God" Title', pp. 545-46.

109.   Neither of which is accepted by modern scholarship. But that this Psalm became one of the key Old Testament passages for understanding the role of Jesus, see France, *Jesus and the Old Testament*, pp. 163-69; Gundry, *Use of the Old Testament*, pp. 228-29.

110.   Which in the Hebrew text is אדון and is distinct from the previous יהוה in Ps. 110.1.

David, the point being that the Messiah is superior to David. It is possible also (4) that Matthew sees Ps. 110.1 as descriptive of a Messiah whose authority over his enemies is established by divine action and not by human endeavour (in contrast to *Pss. Sol.* 17–18).[111]

The upshot of all this is that while not repudiating Jesus' Davidic rights to messiahship, a point that he establishes in Matthew 1–2, Matthew effectively questions its adequacy. Jesus is more than Son of David. He is David's Lord, and is Son of God.

Summary

This survey of the Son of David title and motifs in the first gospel strongly indicates that Matthew's understanding of this motif is summed up in the word *inadequacy*. Matthew does present Jesus as having legal rights to the title and theme of 'Christ' and 'Son of David', but he is more than Son of David. In the trial narrative, for example, while giving reluctant acceptance (σὺ εἶπας Mt. 26.64) to Caiaphas' question...εἰ ὁ Χριστὸς ὁ υἱὸς τοῦ Θεοῦ (v. 63), in the very next sentence, and quite remarkably, Jesus disregards the title ὁ Χριστὸς (which for Jews like Caiaphas was loaded with politicised Son of David significance, cf. *Pss. Sol.* 17–18) in favour of the title τὸν υἱὸν τοῦ ἀνθρώπου (Mt. 26.64), with its Daniel 7 connotations (Mt. 26.63).

So, my thesis here is that while Matthew found Son of David categories *inadequate*, and this precisely due to the popular but misgiven meaning it had acquired, he found Moses categories quite adequate and appropriate and safe to frame his Gospel with. This is not to say that he is presenting an either/or situation, but (1) he is sensitive to the politically charged nature of the Davidic theme. For example, even in the height of 'Son of David' fervour among the ὄχλοι (21.9) Matthew introduces the ὁ προφήτης motif (21.11) with its Deut. 18.15-18 overtones. (2) Furthermore, to emphasise the Moses typology suits the plot of his

111. Whether *Pss. Sol.* 17–18, and the work in general is militaristic has been disputed. J.H. Charles, 'The Concept of the Messiah in the Pseudepigrapha', *ANRW* II, 19.1 (1979), pp. 188-218, argues that it's Davidic Messiah (17.21-33, 36, 18.5, 7) is subordinate to God (p. 217), and will purge Jerusalem of her enemies not by military conquest, but with the 'word of his mouth'. But surely the work's anti-Gentile emphasis (2.2, 19-25; 7.1-3; 8.23; 17.13-15), portraying them as those having no hope of conversion, expelled from Israel (17), cannot be aligned with (1) Matthew's total picture of the Gentiles (negative in 6.7, 32 etc., but positive in 4.15; 15.21-39, especially 24.14; 28.18-20), nor (2) Matthew's presentation of the Messiah. Also R.B. Wright, 'Psalms of Solomon' in *OTP*, 2, pp. 645-46.

Gospel, and his dialogue with the Pharisees, demonstrating that Jesus is the new and greater Moses.

Matthew's Moses Emphasis in the Light of Recent Discussion on Zion Theology and Matthew's Gospel

In recent years there has been considerable emphasis on Old Testament Zion theology/eschatology and its influence on New Testament writers.[112] In gospel studies, T.L. Donaldson, has applied this to the first Gospel.[113] In his study of Matthew's mountain passages he concludes that the dominant typology at work is not Sinai but Zion, the centre of Israel's theological hope. In Jesus all Zion expectations are fulfilled. Donaldson also views the transfiguration from this perspective.[114] Before looking at that in particular it is profitable to look at some of Donaldson's general arguments.

1. *The importance of Zion:* Donaldson builds on the following premises: (a) Mount Zion, the site of the Temple at the heart of Jerusalem, was associated with lofty theological and eschatological conceptions. It was 'the mountain of the house of the Lord' (Mic. 3.12–4.2) and so the Jerusalem-Zion theme was crucial for Old Testament theology.[115] (b) Old Testament Zion theology is bound up with Yahweh's 'election', Zion as the place of his abode, and so the political and religious centre. This is emphasised by the Psalmist, especially in relation to the Davidic covenant (Pss. 132.11-13, 78.67-71). (c) Israel was conscious that the doctrine of the election of Zion involved a shift from Sinai to Zion (Ps. 68.15-18; Isa. 24.23; 29.6-8). (d) Zion was Yahweh's throne (Ps. 2.6), the place of his sceptre (Ps. 110.2), the throne of David's line (Ps. 132.11-18), and so was inviolable.[116] (e) Prophets, though critical of court and cult, did not disregard Zion theology. They envisaged a restored Zion where (i) scattered Israel was to be gathered, see Jer. 31.1-25; Ezek. 20.33-44; 40–48. (ii) The nations were expected to participate in an eschatological pilgrimage to Zion, see Isa. 29.8; Joel 3.9-21; Mic. 4.11-13. (iii) It would be a place of eschatological blessings. (iv) Zion would also be the scene of a new giving of the law (Isa. 2.2-3). (v) It was to be the place of enthronement, Yahweh's throne, the place of his reign

---

112. For discussion of Old Testament works see J.D. Levenson, *Theology of the Program of Restoration of Ezekiel 40–48* (Missoula: Scholars Press, 1976), pp. 7-49.

113. Donaldson, *Mountain*.

114. Donaldson, *Mountain*, pp. 136-56.

115. Donaldson, *Mountain*, pp. 35-36.

116. Donaldson, *Mountain*, pp. 37-41.

(cf. Isa. 24.23; 52.7; Ezek. 20.33, 40; Mic. 4.6-7; Zech. 14.8-11) and of his messianic king (cf. Ezek. 17.22-24; 34.23-31; Mic. 5.2-4, also see *4 Ezra* 13; *2 Bar.* 40.1-4; *Pss. Sol.* 17.23-51); (vi) and a place from which Yahweh would shepherd his people.[117]

Donaldson has rightly highlighted the Zion motif in the Old Testament, but some of his conclusions are debatable:

(a) On the basis of Isa. 2.2-3, and following up some of Levenson's arguments on Ezekiel, he concludes '...Zion takes over the functions of Sinai, not only succeeding it but even replacing it'. It is true that in Isa. 2.2-3, Zion was to *function* like Sinai for both theological and also geographical reasons, that is, Mount Zion was physically accessible to the Jews and was in their land. But Zion does not displace Sinai altogether: In 1 Kgs 19.7-18 for example, it is clear that Elijah by divine instruction is told to go to Horeb 'the mountain' of God, and this during the monarchy when Zion-Jerusalem had been established! Elijah's pilgrimage to Sinai perhaps functions as a critique of Zion.

(b) Although Sinai motifs have often been applied to Zion, this does not necessarily suggest that Zion has replaced Sinai, but more simply that Sinai themes have been applied to Zion. Recently J.D. Levenson and T.B. Dozeman have shown that Sinai traditions (e.g. Exod. 19–34) themselves may have been redacted by Zion redactors, but, it is not a case of Sinai being set against Zion as it is often portrayed, but rather Sinai motifs being taken into the formulation and expression of Zion traditions, for example, Ps. 50.3; Ps. 78.12-16.[118]

(c) Donaldson also has not given adequate attention to the changes that the mountain motif went through in the intertestamental period, when most of Israel was away from Zion-Jerusalem. R.J. Clifford[119] has pointed out that during this period some of the pre-exilic Mount Zion-Jerusalem emphasis was muted, and he concludes that 'only Mount Hermon seems to be the bearer in intertestamental times of ancient tradition of the Holy mountains'.[120] For the implications of this Mount Hermon motif in relation to the location of the transfiguration, see ch. 4.

117. Donaldson, *Mountain*, pp. 42-48.
118. See J.D. Levenson, *Sinai and Zion* (Minneapolis: Winston Press, 1985), pp. 15-217; T.B. Dozeman, *God on the Mountain* (Atlanta: Scholars Press, 1989), pp. 1-202, also see R.E. Clements, *God and Temple* (Oxford: Basil Blackwell, 1965).
119. R.J. Clifford, *The Cosmic Mountain in Canaan and the Old Testament* (Cambridge: Harvard University Press, 1972), p. 186.
120. Clifford, *The Cosmic Mountain*, p. 189.

(d) This is not to say that Zion theology was unimportant in the first century. Herod's temple-building project for one thing would have helped to elevate Zion and Jerusalem. Moreover, it is not unlikely that it was particularly important to those who were bent on the 'restoration of Israel', the throwing off of the yoke of the Romans, and the establishment and enthronement of the Davidic Messiah to his rightful throne in Jerusalem. Its capture and defence was also on the agenda of some messianic pretenders (*Ant.* 20.167-72; *War* 6.285-88). The Zion-Jerusalem, hence restoration of Israel theme, seen in earlier prophets, now mixed with political-kingdom sentiments, could very well have been part of the hope of certain of Jesus' disciples (Acts 1.6). Peter (Mt. 16.22; Mt. 17.4; 19.27) could well epitomise such a view.[121]

However it is not at all certain if this view was representative, for certainly some had lost confidence in Zion-Jerusalem (e.g. the Qumran community, with their ambiguous view of the Temple). Matthew's emphasis on Capernaum (4.15; 28.10, 16) and his portrayal of the condemnation and destruction of Jerusalem (23.38; 24.2, 15-28) make it doubtful if Zion-Jerusalem played such a programmatic role in his theology as Donaldson has portrayed.

So whether Zion theology was pervasive and representative and whether Matthew was influenced by it is at least debatable. With this in mind I shall now evaluate some of Donaldson's other arguments pertaining to Matthew's Gospel.

2. *The transfiguration and Zion:* Here too Donaldson's over-emphasis on Zion is evident, and his arguments are quite weak. For example, commenting on Mt. 17.2, Matthew's conspicuous insertion of the reference to Jesus' radiant face, Donaldson states: 'the exegesis of the passage goes awry when it is preoccupied with the change in appearance' and that 'this detail has an isolated position in the story'.[122] He concludes 'nothing else in the account depends on it for its meaning', and then he claims 'of itself, it leads only to confusion and misunderstanding, as Peter's misdirected suggestion illustrates'.[123] But against this the following arguments may be made:

---

121. Also see discussion in ch. 5.4.

122. Donaldson, *Mountain*, p. 148; S. Pedersen, 'Die Proklamation Jesu als des eschatologischen Offenbarungsträgers (Mt. xvii.1-13)', *NovT* (1975), pp. 241-64, esp. pp. 241-42.

123. Donaldson, *Mountain*, p. 148; C. Masson, 'La transfiguration de Jésus (Marc 9.2-13)', *RTP* 97 (1964), pp. 1-14, esp. p. 2.

(a) It is clear that in his enthusiasm to focus on 17.5, which he interprets in terms of Psalm 2 and hence Zion, Donaldson has been unable to appreciate Matthew's redaction and particular emphasis. If Matthew (also Luke) has taken the trouble to redact Mark and specifically emphasise the reference to Jesus' face, it was with a purpose, and not merely to associate it with Peter's confusion! Furthermore, it is quite unlikely that Matthew portrays Peter as 'confused', for in view of his Peter emphasis elsewhere, Matthew particularly omits Mark's statement (Mk 9.6) about Peter's ignorance, precisely to bring out the fact that Peter knew what he was suggesting. I have shown that Matthew by his redaction εἰ θέλεις, ποιήσω (17.4) in contrast to ποιήσωμεν (Mk 9.5; Lk. 9.33), links Peter's suggestion with his building-commission in 16.18-19. Moreover, I have also shown that 17.2 is not an insignificant nor, as Donaldson says, an 'isolated' wasted piece of material, but links with other significant Matthean passages like 13.24-30; 36-43; 5.14-16. Mt. 17.2 plays an important role and evokes a Moses-Jesus parallelism which Donaldson uncritically dismisses.

(b) Donaldson sees only the influence of Psalm 2 in Mt. 17.5, which as I have shown, is debatable. The influence of other passages, Isa. 42.1; Exod. 4.22; Gen. 22.2 has been noted, and I have shown that Matthew in particular has muted the influence of Psalm 2 in Mt. 17.5 and also in 3.17. Donaldson fails to cite, let alone discuss the other passages. This is not to say that Psalm 2 exerts no influence on the New Testament, for an explicit Jesus-Psalm 2 association is seen in Acts 13.33; Heb. 1.5; 5.5; and perhaps is to be inferred in Rom. 1.3. Less clearly Heb. 7.28. Rev. 12.5; 19.15 may see Jesus as the ruler of Psalm 2 and in Rev. 2.26-28, Psalm 2 rulership is shared with 'he who conquers'. The influence of Psalm 2 is also seen in 4QFlor. 1.18–2.1; *Pss. Sol.* 17.23-24.[124]

But Matthew has muted the influence of Psalm 2 in 17.5 or 3.17 in view of his other interests, the emphasis on the radiance, the Danielic 'Son of Man' allusions and the presentation of Mk 17.1-8 in relation to Daniel 7.

3. *Matthew's mountain passages:* Donaldson through his discussion of six Matthean mountain passages (4.8; 5.1; 15.29; 17.1; 24.3; 28.16) attempts to show that it is Zion and not Moses-Sinai which is the dominant mountain typology at work. But Donaldson makes much of

---

124. See Bauckham, *Jude, 2 Peter*, pp. 219-20; R.D. Rowe, 'Is Daniel's "Son of Man" Messianic?', in H.H. Rowdon (ed.), *Christ the Lord* (Leicester: IVP, 1982), pp. 72-73.

τὸ ὄρος, and, as France has recently pointed out, it is hazardous to derive so much theology from a simple statement of location, particularly since only three of these passages refer to specific mountains.[125] My evaluation will show that at most points Donaldson has foisted a Zion-mountain-theology on his 'six' passages (I have already discussed Matthew 17 and so it will not feature here).

It is also interesting that Donaldson does not properly consider the one other mountain passage with the similar εἰς τὸ ὄρος in 14.23. In this passage Jesus goes up to pray, and it seems that Donaldson does not give this the same weight as his other six examples because it is less promising for his thesis! Donaldson's thesis is unpersuasive for the following reasons:

(a) Matthew 4.8 refers to an unidentified ὄρος ὑψηλόν. Interestingly, here there seem to be more parallels between Jesus' experience and that of Moses (and Elijah) than indications of a Zion mountain theology.[126] For example in Mt. 4.2 Jesus' fast for 'forty days and forty nights' is comparable to Moses' mountain (Sinai) fasting (Exod. 34.28, Deut. 9.9, 18), and Elijah's (Horeb) fasting (1 Kgs 19.8). Moreover the wilderness motif in Mt. 4.2 compares well with the Exodus-Israel-Moses or Elijah-wilderness setting, rather than any Zion significance.

(b) Matthew 5.1, like 14.23; 15.29, refers to an unspecified mountain. Donaldson has dismissed any new Moses significance in the light of Isa. 2.2-4 (Torah from Zion) and Jer. 31.31-34, giving it a Zion eschatological background.[127] But there is no 'new' law motif in Isa. 2.2-4, nor in Jer. 31.31-34, and there is nothing to suggest there that Sinai-law will be replaced. D.C. Allison has challenged Donaldson's dismissal of Moses motifs in 5.1, and has pointed out that Matthew's use of ἀνέβη (of the 24 times it is used in the LXX, 18 belong to the Pentateuch, particularly to Moses) and particularly καθίσαντος (cf. Deut. 9.9, where Moses 'sat' on Mount Sinai) are reminiscent of Moses-on-Sinai motifs.[128]

(c) Matthew 15.29-31 too refers to an unspecified mountain. Donaldson takes Jesus' healings/feeding on this mountain as a christological fulfilment of the expectations of Zion eschatology. Whilst from a christological point of view there may be some substance to this line of thinking, there

---

125. France, *Matthew—Evangelist*, p. 313.
126. On Mt. 4.8, see Donaldson, *Mountain*, pp. 87-104.
127. Donaldson, *Mountain*, pp. 105-121.
128. 'Jesus and Moses', pp. 203-205 also see Davies and Allison, *Saint Matthew*, 1, pp. 423-25.

is nothing in the general use of εἰς τὸ ὄρος in 15.29 itself that refers to Mount Zion. At best, Donaldson fits Mt. 15.29-31 into his overall thesis.

(d) Donaldson interprets Mt. 24.3 within Zion categories; however 24.3 has to do with the Mount of Olives and is not Mount Zion.[129]

(e) Finally, Mt. 28.16-20 is not a mountain in relation to Jerusalem, but in Galilee.[130] This Matthean climax functions as a decisive argument against the Zion framework that he has foisted on the first Gospel. For if Zion theology were fundamental to Matthew's redaction, then he would (i) have related Jesus' final words to his disciples to a Jerusalem setting (for Zion has to do with Jerusalem, Davidic messianology) or (ii) left out the reference to Γαλιλαίας, so that his readers would at least attach such a Zion setting to Mt. 28.16-20. Even though from Mt. 16.21 events are heading towards Jerusalem, and the climax of his Zion emphasis would necessarily have been in Jerusalem (e.g. resurrection, ascension— the latter Matthew does not record), Matthew's climax is in Galilee and not in Zion. It may be argued that by deliberately bringing his Gospel to a climax on a mountain in Galilee, Matthew has chosen to oppose Mount Zion in Jerusalem, and by his choice of this Galilee-mountain, he is contrasting the true Israel with the faithless at Zion-Jerusalem.[131] In the light of these arguments, the application of Zion theology to the First Gospel must be re-considered.

129. See Donaldson, *Mountain*, pp. 157-69.
130. On Mt. 28.16-20, see Donaldson, *Mountain*, pp. 170-90.
131. See S. Freyne, *Galilee, Jesus and the Gospels* (Dublin: Gill & Macmillan, 1988), p. 189.

Chapter 7

CONFIRMATION OF THE IMPORTANCE OF THE JESUS-MOSES AND
TRANSFIGURATION MOTIFS ELSEWHERE IN THE NEW TESTAMENT

The purpose of this chapter is to show that the Moses Christology in the
First Gospel and particularly in Matthew's portrayal of the transfiguration is not a Matthean eccentricity, but also has significant parallels
elsewhere in the New Testament. The pervasive nature of the Moses
motif in first-century Judaism, bringing with it a focus on issues such as
the law, the covenant, the questions of food laws and circumcision,
continued to challenge the theological thinking of the early Christian
community. Several New Testament writers addressed this issue specifically by comparing and contrasting Jesus with Moses. Some in doing so
probably allude to the transfiguration. This chapter will look outside the
synoptic gospels, including at some of the Acts speeches, 2 Peter, the
book of Hebrews, and especially John's prologue and Paul's polemical
use of the Moses-δοξα tradition in 2 Corinthians 3.

1. *The Jesus-Moses Parallelism and Exodus Motifs in the Acts Speeches*

The Acts speeches give us insight into early Christian thought about
Jesus Christ, and in Acts 3.11-26 and 7.37 the prophet-like-Moses (Deut.
18.15-19) motif is applied to Jesus. The historicity and authenticity of the
Acts material is debated and it is beyond the scope of this section to
address that issue.[1] Whether the speeches are more or less Lukan, they

---

1.   The historicity of certain of the Acts speeches has been debated. M. Dibelius,
'The Speeches in Acts and Ancient Historiography', in his book *Studies in the Acts
of the Apostles* (trans. from Aufsätze Apostelegeschichte, 1951) (London: SCM
Press, 1956), pp. 138-85, argues that Luke's technique of inserting speeches (e.g.
pp. 168-9) indicates that he is borrowing from the literary style of the time, but at
some instances is also unique. For a critique of Dibelius, see W.W. Gasque, 'The

are still suggestive of the importance of Moses Christology in the development of early Christology.

Peter's Speech and the Prophet-like-Moses Motif in Acts 3.11-26
According to Acts 3.22-23, Moses—like Samuel (3.24; cf. 1 Sam. 13.14; 15.28; 16.13; 2 Sam. 7.12-16), and Yahweh through Abraham (3.25; cf. Gen. 12.3; 22.18; 26.4)—looked forward to Jesus' ('the prophet-like-Moses') day (3.22-23 cf. Deut. 18.15-19). Jesus is thus seen as an eschatological figure.[2] Whether the prophet-like-Moses prophecy in 3.22-23 refers to Christ's first or second coming has been debated.[3] But in view of the parousia motif in vv. 20-21, it may well be that Peter is warning the Jews of what attitude they ought to have towards the 'coming Messiah', the one whom they previously had rejected through 'ignorance' (v. 17).[4]

Jesus' (the prophet-like-Moses) words need to be taken seriously; otherwise ἐξολεθρευθήσεται ἐκ τοῦ λαοῦ (3.23 cf. Deut. 18.19). This emphasis is significantly parallel with Jesus' teaching about the seriousness of accepting his 'words' (Mt. 7.24-27; Lk. 9.26/Mk 8.38) and has, of course, an echo in the transfiguration story's call to 'listen to

Speeches of Acts: Dibelius Reconsidered', in R.N. Longenecker and M.C. Tenney (eds.), *New Dimensions in New Testament Study* (Grand Rapids: Zondervan, 1974), pp. 232-50. Also see C.J. Hermer, 'The Speeches of Acts 1–11', *TynBul* 40 (1989), pp. 77-85, 234-59, and his *The Book of Acts in the Setting of Hellenistic History* (Tübingen: Mohr [Paul Siebeck], 1989), Appendix 1, pp. 415-27. My main purpose, however, is to determine the influence of the Moses motifs in Luke–Acts.

2.   For the influence of Deut. 18.15-19 on Qumran, Samaritan literature, see ch. 3.4.

3.   See J. Munck, *The Acts of the Apostles* (Garden City: Doubleday, 1967), p. 29; E. Haenchen, *The Acts of the Apostles* (Oxford: Basil Blackwell, 1971), p. 209 assigns v. 22 to Jesus' first coming. H. Conzelmann, *Acts of the Apostles* (Philadelphia: Fortress Press, 1987), p. 29 finds the parousia reference in vv. 20-21 awkward.

4.   A reference to Davidic Christology has been inferred from the general reference to Samuel in v. 24, (cf. 1 Sam. 13.14; 15.28; 16.13; 28.17), see F.F. Bruce, *The Book of the Acts* (Grand Rapids: Eerdmans, 1989), p. 87. This view is mentioned with caution by I.H. Marshall, *Acts* (Leicester: IVP, 1980), p. 95. But see F.F. Bruce, *The Acts of the Apostles* (Grand Rapids: Eerdmans; Leicester: Apollos, 1990), p. 146, for a more general non-messianic meaning, so also K. Lake and H.J. Cadbury, *The Beginnings of Christianity*, I: *The Acts of the Apostles*, vol. 4 (London: Macmillan, 1933), pp. 38-39; H. Conzelmann, *Acts of the Apostles* (Philadelphia: Fortress Press, 1987), p.30; E. Haenchen, *The Acts of the Apostles*, p. 209. For Jewish tradition of Samuel as teacher of the prophets, see J.J.S. Perowne, *The Acts of the Apostles* (Cambridge: Cambridge University Press, 1887), p. 38.

him'. Here Luke's order αὐτοῦ ἀκούετε in Lk. 9.35 is the same in Acts 3.22 (αὐτοῦ ἀκούσεσθε) which is identical to Deut. 18.15 LXX, and it is possible that he has redactionally and theologically linked 9.35 with Acts 3.22.[5]

Exodus Motifs in the Speeches of Peter and Stephen Suggest a Moses Christology

I have previously shown that exodus traditions, though distinguishable from the Moses tradition, belong to the same world of ideas, and support my conclusions about the influence of the Moses motif and about the Moses-Jesus parallel. It is notable that some of the Jesus-Moses-exodus motifs in Acts 3 are paralleled by Moses-exodus motifs in Acts 7: (1) δίκαιον (Acts 3.14) and ἀρχηγόν (3.15), used here of Jesus are in 7.27 and 35 (ἄρχοντα καὶ δικαστήν) used of Moses. (2) The verb ἠρνήσασθε used of Jesus in 3.14 (denying the holy and righteous one) is in 7.35 used of Moses: τοῦτον τὸν Μωυσῆν, ὃν ἠρνήσαντο. (3) Jesus, though sent by the God of the Jews (3.26), was rejected (3.14,17); so Moses was sent by God (7.25) and was rejected (7.25), 'denied' by the people (7.35 ἠρνήσαντο), who also 'refused to obey him' (7.39).[6] (4) Finally, in 3.23 (Peter's speech) and in 7.37 (Stephen's speech)[7] Deut. 18.15-19 features prominently. If this has been taken from a 'testimony collection', it goes to show the importance of Moses-exodus themes applied to Jesus in the early church.[8]

So the Moses-exodus, and the prophet-like-Moses motifs are plain in the speeches of Peter and Stephen, and hence indicate that Moses Christology played an important role in the development of early Christology.

5.   This has been well set out by J.G. Davies, *He Ascended into Heaven* (London: Lutterworth, 1958); 'The Prefigurement of the Ascension in the Third Gospel', *JTS* 6 (1955) pp. 229-33; C.H. Talbert, *Literary Patterns, Theological Themes, and the Genre of Luke–Acts* (SBLMS, 20; Missoula, MT: Scholars Press, 1974), esp. pp. 51-52; D.L. Tiede, *Prophecy and History in Luke–Acts* (Philadelphia: Fortress Press, 1980), pp. 1-32.

6.   On this see R.F. Zehnle, *Peter's Pentecost Discourse* (Nashville: Abingdon Press, 1971), pp. 76-77.

7.   On this see M. Simon, *St Stephen and the Hellenists in the Primitive Church* (London: Longmans, Green & Co., 1958), esp. pp. 44-49. In Acts 3.23, Deut. 18.29 is probably combined with Lev. 23.29.

8.   K. Lake and H.J. Cadbury, *The Beginnings of Christianity*, p. 38, followed by Bruce, *The Acts of the Apostles*, p. 154; *The Book of the Acts*, p. 86 and nn. 49 and 53.

2. *The Transfiguration in 2 Peter 1.16-18*

In this thesis, at various points I have been referring to the 'independent witness' to the transfiguration found in 2 Pet.·1.16-18. In this tradition, as T. Fornberg, J.H. Neyrey, R.J. Bauckham, and others[9] have argued, the writer is speaking of Jesus' transfiguration as a guarantee of the parousia. The writer refers to the 'holy mountain' (ἐν τῷ ἀγίῳ ὄρει 1.18), and 'glory' (δόξαν 1.17), but there is no explicit Sinai parallelism. It is notable that (1) the author does not include the presence of Moses (and Elijah), and (2) he drops the words αὐτοῦ ἀκούσεσθε (Deut. 18.15). These omissions could seem problematic for this thesis, and yet they are explicable, since the portrayal of Jesus as the eschatological prophet like Moses is 'irrelevant to 2 Peter's purpose, which is to portray the transfiguration as Jesus' appointment as eschatological king and judge'.[10] On the other hand, if 2 Pet. 1.16-18 is drawn from the writers' own knowledge of Peter's preaching, or else oral tradition,[11] then it may possibly support my argument that the transfiguration contributed to Peter's elevation in the early church.

9.   See T. Fornberg, *An Early Church in a Pluralistic Society* (Lund: Gleerup, 1977), pp. 79-80; J.H. Neyrey, 'The Apologetic Use of the Transfiguration in 2 Peter 1.16-21', *CBQ* 42, (1980), pp. 504-519; Bauckham, *Jude, 2 Peter*, pp. 216-17, 221-22; J.W.C. Wand, *The General Epistle of St Peter and St Jude* (London: Methuen, 1934), pp. 158-59; G.H. Boobyer, *St Mark and the Transfiguration Story* (Edinburgh: T. & T. Clark, 1942), pp. 43-46; M. Green, *2 Peter and Jude* (London: Tyndale Press, 1968), pp. 82-83; J.N.D. Kelly, *A Commentary on the Epistles of Peter and Jude* (London: Adam & Black, 1969), p. 320; A.R.C. Leaney, *The Letters of Peter and Jude* (Cambridge: Cambridge University Press, 1967), pp. 112-15; M. Green, *The Second Epistle General of Peter and the General Epistle of Jude* (Leicester: IVP; Grand Rapids: Eerdmans, 1989), pp. 92-93, 96-97. According to C. Bigg, *A Critical and Exegetical Commentary on the Epistles of St Peter and St Jude* (Edinburgh: T. & T. Clark, 1910), p. 226, Peter uses the transfiguration not to prove the parousia, but the credibility of the apostles who preached the parousia, and for E. Käsemann, *Essays on New Testament Themes* (London: SCM Press, 1964), p. 189, the transfiguration anticipates 'participation in the divine nature'.

10.   Bauckham, *Jude, 2 Peter*, p. 207.

11.   Bauckham, *Jude, 2 Peter*, p. 210. That it stems from Peter himself: see D.F. Payne, *The Second Letter of Peter* in G.C.D. Howley, F.F. Bruce, H.C. Ellison (eds.), *The Pickering Bible Commentary for Today* (Glasgow: Pickering, 1980), p. 1647; also see B. Witherington, 'A Petrine Source in Second Peter', in K.H. Richards (ed.), *SBLSP (1985)* (Atlanta: Scholars Press, 1985), pp. 187-92.

3. *The Jesus-Moses Parallelism and the Letter to the Hebrews*

Moses Christology plays a vital role in the theology of the letter to the Hebrews and the purpose of this section is to study some of the Moses-Jesus comparisons that emerge from Heb. 3.1-6 in relation to similar themes found in Matthew's understanding of the transfiguration.

Moses and Jesus

No commentator can escape the prominent Moses motif in Hebrews, and this has been rightly highlighted by M.R. D'Angelo, W.L. Lane, D.A. Hagner and others.[12] Some of the prominent Moses passages in Hebrews are 3.1-6 and 11.23-27, with the Moses-Israel theme traced also in 3.7-19; 11.29 and other places. Hebrews 3.1-6 is of particular importance, since here (1) just as Moses was faithful 'in all God's house' (3.2 cf. Num. 12.7), Jesus was faithful to God (3.2). (2) Moses was faithful as a servant (θεράπων 3.5)[13] and Jesus was faithful as a son (υἱὸς 3.6). (3) Moses was a servant 'in' (ἐν) God's house (3.5), but Jesus is superior since he as son is 'over' (ἐπὶ) God's house (3.6).

In view of Jesus' superiority the writer could go on and say Jesus has been considered worthy of greater glory than Moses (3.3) (πλείονος γὰρ οὗτος δόξης παρὰ Μωυσῆν), in the same way that a builder (ὁ κατασκευάσας αὐτόν) necessarily has greater honour (τιμήν) than the house itself (3.3). Here the identity of the builder has been disputed, for in v. 4 (also cf. 1.2; 2.10) it is God who is the builder. According to F.F. Bruce, no distinction is to be made between Father and Son here, for God founds his own household through his Son.[14] But since in v. 3 Jesus is being compared with Moses, it could well be that the author associates Jesus with the builder, and Moses with the house.[15]

---

12. M.R. D'Angelo, *Moses in the Letter to the Hebrews* (Montana: Scholars Press, 1979), *passim*; W.L. Lane, *Hebrews: A Call to Commitment* (Peabody, MA: Hendrickson, 1988), pp. 55-71; *Hebrews 1–8* (WBC; Dallas: Word, 1991), pp. 71-80; Hagner, *Hebrews* (Peabody: Hendrickson, 1990), pp. 59-68.

13. Drawn from Num. 12.7 LXX, on this see, Hagner, *Hebrews*, p. 62; Lane, *Hebrews: A Call to Commitment*, p. 58; *Hebrews 1–8*, pp. 72-73; F.F. Bruce, *The Epistle to the Hebrews* (Grand Rapids: Eerdmans, 2nd edn, 1988), p. 56.

14. Bruce, *The Epistle to the Hebrews*, p. 57, also see n.14 for the possibility that the second clause of v. 4 means 'he who founded everything' (i.e. Christ, according to 1.2) is God (ὁ δὲ πάντα κατασκευάσας Θεός).

15. For the view that Jesus is the builder see Hagner, *Hebrews*, p. 60. For Father

Thematic Similarity in Hebrew 3.1-6 and Matthew 17.1-9

In my discussion on Mt. 17.4-5 I argued that among other things the 'voice' pointed Peter to Jesus as the true builder. This (Matthean) emphasis, along with the Jesus-Son of God motif in Mt. 17.5 (and par.) where Moses himself was present, makes for an interesting comparison with this passage in Hebrews: where Jesus is 'Son', 'builder' of his house (τοῦ οἴκου), 'the church' (cf. 3.6b οὗ οἶκός ἐσμεν ἡμεῖς and compare also οἰκοδομήσω μου τὴν ἐκκλησίαν in Mt. 16.17-19), in contrast to Moses who is θεράπων. The idea that Jesus was worthy of 'much more glory (δόξης) than Moses' (Heb. 3.3) parallels the similar stress at the transfiguration on, for example, the radiance of Jesus' face and is reminiscent of δεδόξασται (of Moses in Exod. 34.29-31 LXX, also 2 Cor. 3.7). As in Mt. 17.1-9 (and as I shall show in 2 Cor. 3.7-18, and 4.6), so in Heb. 3.1-6, Jesus' glory exceeds Moses' glory or the law's glory (which came ἐν δόξῃ 2 Cor. 3.7, 9-11).

Hence it is not inconceivable that Heb. 3.3 echoes a transfiguration tradition, particularly Matthew's, where the event was portrayed as a new and Sinai event. In view of the similarity of ideas between Heb. 3.1-6 and the transfiguration tradition, it is also tempting to connect ὃς ὢν ἀπαύγασμα τῆς δόξης (1.3) with the transfiguration seen as a manifestation of the 'radiance which bursts out of a brilliant light'.[16] However, ἀπαύγασμα also finds a parallel in *Wis.* 7.26 where wisdom (σοφια) is said to be an ἀπαύγασμα of the glory of the Almighty.[17]

The Law Motif

The phrase πᾶς γὰρ οἶκος κατασκευάζεται ὑπό τινος (Heb. 3.4) contributes to the Moses-Jesus parallelism. Guthrie has rightly pointed out that 3.4 is a generic statement which hardly needs to be made unless there are grounds for disputing it, and those grounds may have been in what was a current approach to the law.[18] But God is the originator of the law (v. 4) and not Moses; and the 'glory' of God's Son, Jesus, is far greater than that of Moses and the Mosaic law. For the writer presents

and Son as builders, see Bruce, *The Epistle to the Hebrews*, p. 57; D. Guthrie, *Hebrews* (Leicester: IVP, 1983), p. 100; B.F. Westcott, *The Epistle to the Hebrews* (London: Macmillan, 1889), p. 76, prefers God in view of v. 4.

16. Guthrie, *Hebrews*, p. 66.

17. For wisdom associations see H.W. Attridge, *The Epistle to the Hebrews* (Philadelphia: Fortress Press, 1989), pp. 42-43.

18. Guthrie, *Hebrews*, pp. 100-101.

Moses himself as looking forward to Jesus' day, and hence Moses (and the law) served in a role of preparation and not of fulfilment: εἰς μαρτύριον τῶν λαληθησομένων.[19]

So I conclude that the writer to the Hebrews displays a robust Moses Christology, for he portrays Moses positively (he is faithful), while also arguing that he was inferior (a servant) and had a preparatory role (looking forward to Jesus' day). In addition, the motifs of Jesus-glory and Jesus-Son, make for a significant comparison with similar motifs at the transfiguration.

4. *Moses-Sinai and Transfiguration Motifs in the Fourth Gospel*

The forceful presence of Jesus-Moses typology and other Moses-wilderness motifs in the Fourth Gospel has been well demonstrated by T.F. Glasson,[20] and brought out also in the writings of Bowman, Meeks, and others.[21] In this section I shall focus primarily on Jn 1.1-18 where the writer has blended together both Hellenistic and Hebrew language and thought,[22] with v. 14, as most commentators are agreed, forming the climax of the whole prologue.[23]

---

19. Guthrie, *Hebrews*, p. 101; Hagner, *Hebrews*, p. 60; Attridge, *Hebrews*, p. 111; Bruce, *The Epistle to the Hebrews*, p. 58.

20. T.F. Glasson, *Moses in the Fourth Gospel* (London: SCM Press, 1963), *passim*.

21. Meeks, *The Prophet King*, passim; Bowman, 'The Samaritan Studies', pp. 298-327; see my ch. 3.4 and works cited there, also recently Allison, *The New Moses*, pp. 89-90.

22. For a useful survey on this see C. Brown, 'Word', in *NIDNTT*, vol. 3, pp. 1081-1119; R.E. Brown, *The Gospel according to John*, vol. 1 (London: Geoffrey Chapman, 1966), esp. pp. 519-24; also R. Bultman, *The Gospel of John* (Oxford: Basil Blackwell, 1971), pp. 13-83, who however argues for a Mandaen Gnostic word-myth background. But as far as sources go, Gnostic sources are late and so inconclusive. For a recent critique of Bultmann's approach see D.A. Carson, *The Gospel according to John* (Leicester: IVP, 1991), pp. 31-33.

23. Cf. G.R. Beasley-Murray, *John* (Waco: Word, 1987), pp. 2-3; Brown, *The Gospel according to John*, vol. 1, pp. 30-35; C.K. Barrett, *The Gospel according to St John* (London: SPCK, 2nd edn, 1978), pp. 164-67; E. Haenchen, *John 1* (Philadelphia: Fortress Press, 1980), pp. 119-20; B. Lindars, *The Gospel of John* (Grand Rapids: Eerdmans; London: Marshall, Morgan & Scott, 1982), pp. 93-96. The prologue itself introduces the reader to major themes in the rest of the gospel. J.A.T. Robinson, *Twelve More New Testament Studies* (London: SCM Press, 1984), p. 68, followed by Carson, *The Gospel according to John*, p. 111, have shown the

The Moses-Jesus Contrast in John 1.16-17

In Jn 1.17 the writer contrasts Moses and the law with the coming of grace through Jesus. The previous verse (v. 16) has led up to this comparison, for if ἀντὶ[24] in the phrase καὶ χάριν ἀντὶ χάριτος (1.16) means 'instead of',[25] then the implication is that the 'grace and truth' that came through Jesus (διὰ...ἐγένετο 1.17, also 1.14) are what replace the law.[26] In other words, what vv. 16-17 imply is that the 'grace' of the old Sinai-covenant is bettered (if not replaced) by the 'grace' of the new covenant brought by the 'Word' become flesh.[27] So vv. 16-17

following links: 1.1-2/17.5; 1.4/5.26; 8.12; 1.5/3.19; 12.35; 1.9/3.19; 12.46; 1.11/ 4.44; 1.13/3.6; 8.41-42; 1.14/12.41; 1.14,18; 3.16; 1.17/14.6 and 1.18/6.46. This makes our observations about the Moses-Sinai-Law-Light vs Jesus-Word-Light-Life motifs all the more significant.

24. Cf. Brown, *The Gospel according to John*, vol. 1, pp. 15-16 for three basic views, replacement, accumulation, correspondence. Also, Arndt and Gingrich, *Lexicon*, pp. 73-74.

25. See Carson, *The Gospel according to John*, pp. 131-34.

26. Here the law itself is to be considered as an earlier display of grace.

27. The contrast in v. 17 reopens the thorny issue of Jesus and the law: The issue is (1) if ἡ χάρις καὶ ἡ ἀλήθεια διὰ Ἰησοῦ Χριστοῦ ἐγένετο is in direct contrast to the law that was given (ἐδόθη) through Moses, or (2) if there is some sort of continuity, or fulfilment idea. According to Barrett, *St John*, p. 169, it is a contrast between 'Moses and Christ', 'law and gospel'. The law in John bore witness to Christ (5.39), but Moses is primarily an accuser (5.45). C.H. Dodd, *The Interpretation of the Fourth Gospel* (Cambridge: Cambridge University Press, 1953), p. 84; Lindars, *The Gospel of John*, pp. 97-98; Brown, *The Gospel according to John*, vol. 1, p. 16; Beasley-Murray, *John*, p. 15, have seen the contrast more in terms of shadow and substance rather than direct opposition. This view also takes into consideration the writer's positive appraisal of Moses in 1.45 (Jesus, attested by Moses in the law and also the prophets), 3.14 ('as Moses lifted up the serpent'), 5.46 ('if you believed in Moses, you would have believed in me').

But certain contrasts between Jesus and Moses too may be seen. (1) For example the 'water of life' in Jn 4.13-14 may be contrasted with the Jewish understanding of the Torah as 'fountain of life' (cf. CD 3.16; 6.3-9; 19.34). (2) The teaching on 'bread of life' (Jn 6.35), 'living bread' (6.51) may be contrasted with the law-bread, and manna-Torah associations made in Jewish thinking. These passages seem to express a contrast between Jesus and the law. On the other hand, in Jn 5.46, the phrase περὶ γὰρ ἐμοῦ ἐκεῖνος ἔγραψεν perhaps could refer to a specific passage like Deut. 18.18. But vv. 46-47 may also suggest that Jesus is the fulfilment of the law, akin to Mt. 5.18, and so as the prophet-like-Moses, he also shares a continuity with and is the eschatological fulfilment of the law. If this is accepted, then just as the first redeemer brought the law, the second redeemer initiates a new exodus

emphasise the role of the Moses-Sinai motif in the prologue.

The ideas of 'fulness' (1.14; 1.16) and 'grace and truth' (1.14; 1.16) structurally (taking 1.14-18 as a unit), thematically and linguistically link Jn 1.14 with the Moses-Sinai motif (1.16-17). And it is with this Moses-Sinai theme in view that I now will comment on the Sinai themes that climax in Jn 1.14.

The Moses-Sinai Motif and John 1.14

The phrase καὶ ὁ λόγος σὰρξ ἐγένετο καὶ ἐσκήνωσεν ἐν ἡμῖν in Jn 1.14 is significant. The use of ἐσκήνωσεν has been taken variously. For example: (a) it has been argued that ὁ λόγος...ἐσκήνωσεν recalls wisdom speculation (e.g. *1 En.* 42.2; Sir. 24.6-8, 10, 23).[28] In Sir. 24.8 for example καὶ ὁ κτίσας με κατέπαυσε τὴν σκηνήν μου, and in 24.10 wisdom served God ἐν σκηνῇ ἁγίᾳ. But in Sir. 24.3, 23 'wisdom' is associated with the Sinai-Torah. So in view of the prominent Moses-Sinai-law emphasis in Jn 1.14-18, it is possible that such a Sinai-Torah theme has been taken up into ὁ λόγος of Jn 1.1. And according to this line of argument, the writer is presenting Jesus himself as the embodiment of the new Torah.

On the other hand (b), in certain Old Testament passages the verb ἐσκήνωσεν is linked with the wilderness-Sinai and tabernacle ideas. In Num. 35.34 Yahweh says to Israel 'I am the Lord tabernacling (κατασκηνῶν) in the midst of you.' In Exod. 25.9 the people were to make a tabernacle (τῆς σκηνῆς, המשכן MT), which in 33.7 is called Σκηνὴ μαρτυρίου. Since in the fourth Gospel the writer seems to present Jesus as the replacement of the tabernacle (Jn 2.19-22), it could be argued that ἐσκήνωσεν ἐν ἡμῖν suggests that Jesus is the new 'localisation of God's presence on earth'.[29] (c) A related observation is that σκηνόω (and the radicals σ κ ν) is like the Hebrew שכן in sound

characterised by ἡ χάρις καὶ ἡ ἀλήθεια διὰ Ἰησοῦ χριστοῦ (a repeated emphasis in vv. 14 and 17).

28. Cf. Lindars, *The Gospel of John*, pp. 93-96; Barrett, *St John,* pp. 164-67; R. Schnackenburg, *The Gospel according to St John* (Tunbridge Wells: Burns & Oates, 1980), p. 265; Beasley-Murray, *John*, pp. 8-10; Brown, *The Gospel according to John*, vol. 1, pp. 521-23; Haenchen, p. 119, also draws attention to 2 Cor. 5.1 (οἰκία τοῦ σκήνους) and 5.4 (σκήνει). Partially Carson, *The Gospel according to John*, 115-116, who with F.F. Bruce, *The Gospel of John* (London: Pickering & Inglis 1983), pp. 29-31 favours an Old Testament association.

29. See Bruce, *The Gospel of John*, pp. 40-41; Brown, *The Gospel according to John*, vol. 1, p. 13; Carson, *The Gospel according to John*, pp. 127-28.

and meaning; this too signifies Yahweh's dwelling with Israel (Exod. 25.8; 29.45; Zech. 2.14). It is from this root that the noun *shekinah* is derived—which in rabbinic literature was used as a periphrasis for the name of God himself (e.g. *Mishna Aboth* 3.3).[30] If ἐσκήνωσεν in 1.14 is to be given such a significance, then Jesus himself is God's *Shekinah*, who has ἐσκήνωσεν ἐν ἡμῖν.[31]

It is difficult to choose between the above views, and perhaps John had more than one Old Testament and Jewish association in the background. But one common factor is that each of these views is closely associated with the Sinai event and related motifs such as the Torah, tabernacle, cloud, and glory.

Certain other Sinai motifs feature in Jn 1.14 and so contribute to my arguments. For example (a) the phrases (i) καὶ ἐθεασάμεθα τὴν δόξαν αὐτοῦ and (ii) πλήρης χάριτος καὶ ἀληθείας suggest that the writer has Old Testament motifs in mind. For it may be argued that the phrase πλήρης χάριτος καὶ ἀληθείας especially in view of its reappearance in the Sinai setting in 1.16, recalls Exod. 34.6 and the Moses-Mount Sinai setting of Exod. 33.12–34.8, the covenant mercy of God.[32] (b) The phrase καὶ ἐθεασάμεθα τὴν δόξαν αὐτοῦ is significant, for it majors on the δόξα motif.[33] We have already seen the echo of הסד ואמת (Exod. 34.6) on χάριτος καὶ ἀληθείας (Jn 1.14). But these words, Exod. 34.6-7, were specifically spoken to Moses in the

---

30. Brown, *The Gospel according to John*, vol. 1, p. 33 who cites Targum of Deut. 12.5 which has God's *shekinah* dwell in the sanctuary rather than his name.

31. Cf. J.T. Marshall, 'Shekinah', in J. Hastings, *A Dictionary of the Bible*, vol. 4 (Edinburgh: T. & T. Clark, 1906), pp. 487-89. Also Ramsey, *The Glory of God and the Transfiguration of Christ*, pp. 59-60; L. Morris, *The Gospel according to John* (Grand Rapids: Eerdmans, 1971), pp. 104-105; Bruce, *The Gospel of John*, pp. 40-41; Carson, *The Gospel according to John*, pp.127-28.

32. Barrett, *St John*, p. 167; Lindars, *The Gospel of John*, p. 95; Beasley-Murray, *John*, p. 14; Bruce, *The Gospel of John*, pp. 41-42; Carson, *The Gospel according to John*, pp. 129-30.

33. It is well known that δόξα has been used variously in the New Testament. See G.B. Caird, *The New Testament Conception of doxa* (unpublished dissertation; Oxford, 1944); S. Aalen, 'Glory, Honour', in *NIDNTT*, vol. 2, pp. 44-48. For the influence of the Hebrew כבוד on LXX use of δόξα and the New Testament see L.H. Brockington, 'The Septuagintal Background to the New Testament use of Doxa', in D.E. Nineham, (ed.), *Studies in the Gospels* (Oxford: Basil Blackwell, 1955), pp. 1-8.

context where he wanted to see Yahweh's glory (Exod. 33.18-23).[34] So it may be argued that just as the Sinai motifs of Exod. 33.12–34.8 are echoed in χάριτος καὶ ἀληθείας (cf. Exod. 34.6) so also a Moses-Sinai-δόξα motif (cf. Exod. 33.18-23) is seen in καὶ ἐθεασάμεθα τὴν δόξαν of Jn 1.14.

Moses-Sinai Motifs Elsewhere in the Prologue
The Moses-Sinai parallel elsewhere in the prologue strengthen my arguments about Jn 1.14. (a) Moses-Sinai motifs may be echoed in v. 18. For example, Θεὸν οὐδεὶς ἑώρακεν πώποτε may be paralleled with the partial manifestation (cf. Exod. 34.20) that Moses received in Exod. 34.23.[35] And it is only out of this encounter (partial manifestation) that Moses was given the 'revelation of the law'. But now by contrast, it is μονογενὴς Θεός (or ὁ μονογενὴς Θεος)[36] who shares the nature of God and gives the true 'exegesis' (ἐξηγήσατο), the full declaration of God to humanity.[37] So in contrast to Moses' partial 'view' of God (ἑώρακεν v. 18), the point is not merely that Jesus has a fuller 'seeing' or 'view' of God, but that he shares God's nature, (cf. v. 1, καὶ ὁ λόγος ἦν πρὸς τὸν Θεόν, καὶ Θεὸς ἦν ὁ λόγος). So v. 18, like vv. 14 and 17, stresses that the Moses-Sinai motif is not merely paralleled but also is superseded by Jesus.

In addition to this, (b) in Jn 1.4, 5, 8, 9 Jesus (the Word) is associated with 'light', and in 1.4 with both 'light and life'. It is true that if 1.4 and 5 are read in the context of 1.1-3 with reference to the ἀρχῇ, the Word is related to creation and hence to creation light (Gen. 1.3); that is, the Word at creation became the light of the human race (τὸ φῶς τῶν ἀνθρώπων Jn 1.4). But it must also be borne in mind that both Wisdom and Torah are associated with life and light in the Jewish sources.[38] In

34. In the MT Exod. 33.18, Moses' request is to see Yahweh's 'glory' כבוד, but Yahweh's reply is 'I will make all my goodness (טוב) pass before you.' 33.22 however has 'when my glory shall pass by' (ἡ δόξα μου LXX). In the LXX Καὶ λέγει, ἐμφάνισόν μοι σεαυτόν, for which the answer is 'I will pass by before thee with my glory', σου τῇ δόξῃ.

35. This is in keeping with passages like Judg. 13.22, Sir. 43.27-33.

36. Both have good textual support, i.e. μονογενὴς Θεός P⁶⁶ ℵ* B C* L, and ὁ μονογενὴς Θεός P⁷⁵ ℵ 33 cop^bo. Cf. UBS, p. 322, n.18.

37. 'Sonship' is an important motif in John's Gospel, but the Son of David motif seems to be virtually absent. Jesus' Davidic descent is raised only as a matter of public speculation in 7.42.

38. See Brown, *The Gospel according to John*, vol. 1, p. 523.

Prov. 6.23 the Torah is a lamp and the teaching a light, a motif also seen in Ps. 119.105: λύχνος τοῖς ποσί μου ὁ νόμος σου LXX. *T. Levi* 14.4 speaks of 'the light of the law which was granted...for the enlightenment of every man', which makes an interesting comparison with Jn 1.9 ὃ φωτίζει πάντα ἄνθρωπον.[39] So, (i) given the Moses-Sinai-law theme in 1.16-17, also v. 14, and (ii) the Torah-light association, it is perhaps not impossible that John's portrayal of Jesus as Word-light-life was his response to Jewish speculation on the Sinai-law.

John's Gospel and the Transfiguration Motif
We have seen the unmistakable Moses-Sinai and exodus parallels in the prologue, and that, when the writer states καὶ ἐθεασάμεθα τὴν δόξαν αὐτοῦ (v. 14), he quite likely links it with the Moses-Sinai theophany. There is, however, one further question: could there be any particular event (or a series of events) in Jesus' earthly life with which this Sinai motif could be associated? It is of course well known that the δόξα motif, which is used variously in John's Gospel, is specifically associated with (a) Jesus' death (13.31-32; 17.1) and subsequent glory.[40] Note for example the use of ἐδοξάσθη in 7.39, and 12.16 (which includes the idea of the resurrection/exaltation); (b) Jesus' glory, displayed in his 'signs' (2.11; 11.4, 40). However, given the Moses-Sinai and light-law associations in the prologue, it is worth asking whether καὶ ἐθεασάμεθα τὴν δόξαν αὐτοῦ in 1.14 points to an event in Jesus' life that the early church associated with Moses-Sinai (while incorporating the general significance of the concept of 'glory' in the fourth Gospel).[41]

For example, καὶ ἐθεασάμεθα τὴν δόξαν αὐτοῦ (v. 14) may be taken as a general statement, and certainly the writer wants his readers to know that the glory of God could be seen in Jesus Christ (e.g. 2.11), that the whole ministry of Jesus was evidence of God's glory. But I suggest that the transfiguration may lie behind Jn 1.14. Certain factors could be said to favour this association:

39. Perhaps also 12.28, but this refers simply to Jesus' obedient life. In 21.19 of Peter's death.
40. Also as in Lk. 24.26; Rom. 8.17; Phil. 3.12; 2 Thess. 2.14; 1 Tim. 3.16.
41. J. Ashton, *Understanding the Fourth Gospel* (Oxford: Oxford University Press, 1993), pp. 500-501 comments: 'There is no room for a transfiguration scene in the Fourth Gospel. The Johannine Jesus carries his glory with him and his garments are always "glistening intensely white"'. But see Brown, *The Gospel according to John*, vol. 1, p. 34 'there is much to recommend the suggestion that 14c, d is an echo of the Transfiguration'.

1. The use of the first person plural ἐθεασάμεθα, in 1.14, as in 1 Jn 1.1, is plausibly taken as a reference to the apostolic witness.[42] If this is accepted, then 1.14 could well refer to the three apostolic witnesses of the transfiguration. In his version of the transfiguration, Luke makes repeated reference to the δόξα motif (9.31, 32), and makes special mention that the apostles witnessed Jesus' glory: εἶδον τὴν δόξαν αὐτοῦ (9.32), which makes an interesting comparison with καὶ ἐθεασάμεθα τὴν δόξαν αὐτοῦ of Jn 1.14, especially in view of the well-known links between Luke and John.[43]

2. 2 Pet. 1.16 may support this suggestion, since this same apostolic witness is referred to (note ἐγνωρίσαμεν, ἐπόπται v. 16), and here it is with specific reference to the transfiguration (vv. 16-18). Here too the transfiguration is described in language such as μεγαλειότητος, δόξαν, μεγαλοπρεποῦς δόξης.

3. This apostolic witness-transfiguration-δόξα hypothesis in connection with Jn 1.14 (indeed the whole prologue) may be further strengthened by recognising that, just as the prologue speaks of δόξαν ὡς μονογενοῦς παρὰ πατρός, so at the transfiguration, the heavenly voice proclaims Jesus as ὁ υἱός μου ὁ ἀγαπητός (Mt 17.5; Mk 9.7; 2 Pet. 1.17), ὁ υἱός μου ἐκλελεγμένος (Lk. 9.35).[44] Moreover, since μονογενής (Judg. 11.34) and ἀγαπητός (Gen. 22.2, 12, 16) in the LXX translate יחיד, ἀγαπητός in the transfiguration may be compared with μονογενής in Jn 1.14.[45] Another point of comparison is that just as in the apostolic witness in 2 Pet. 1.16-17, Jesus received

---

42. Brown, *The Gospel according to John*, vol. 1, p. 13, also *The Epistles of John* (London: Geoffrey Chapman, 1982), pp. 168-61.

43. On this see R. Maddox, *The Purpose of Luke–Acts* (Edinburgh: T. & T. Clark, 1985), pp. 158-76.

44. As ὁ ἐκλεκτός μου in Isa. 42.1 which compares well with ὁ ἐκλελεγμένος of Lk. 9.35 (also cf. Jn 1.34, see UBS, p. 324 n.9, *SQE*, p. 27, note on v. 34 NA[26], p. 249).

45. Other 'echoes' cited are: the echo of baptism in 1.32-34; Gethsemane agony in 12.27-30 and 18.11 (cf. Morris, *John*, p. 44). The baptism motif does not fit ἐθεασάμεθα τὴν δόξαν αὐτοῦ of Jn 1.14 since there τεθέαμαι speaks of the Baptist's exclusive experience and is not to be confused with the apostolic witness ἐθεασάμεθα of 1.14.

λαβὼν γὰρ παρὰ Θεοῦ πατρὸς τιμὴν καὶ δόξαν, so also in Jn 1.14 the 'glory' comes from God, δόξαν ὡς μονογενοῦς παρὰ πατρός.

4. Perhaps the most convincing argument in favour of this interpretation is one that is based on the Moses-Sinai-law-light typology that is evidenced in the prologue. For I have shown, with special reference to Matthew, that the one conspicuous event in the earthly life of Jesus that distinctly echoes the Sinai event is the transfiguration. It was at this Sinai-related event that the disciples, the nucleus of the new Israel, are said to ἀκούετε αὐτοῦ (Mt. 17.5; Mk 9.7; Lk. 9.35 cf. Deut. 15.18). So if in the prologue, the evangelist, among other things, is engaging in a polemic against Jewish speculations on the Sinai-law, with its attendant motifs such as light, life and the authority of Moses, then an allusion to the transfiguration of Jesus with its Moses-Sinai-Jesus parallelism could well have helped his case.

It is true, unlike the synoptics, the evangelist does not record the transfiguration event, but this is no argument against the view that he is alluding to it.[46] For it may be pointed out that other important events like the baptism, the institution of the eucharist, the agony at Gethsemane, also have been omitted, but echoes of some of these events are seen throughout the gospel. For example, John does not describe exorcisms, but sees Jesus' whole life and especially death as one big exorcism (cf. 12.31).

John 3.13 and the transfiguration: One other passage in the Fourth Gospel perhaps further strengthens my argument. The saying καὶ οὐδεὶς ἀναβέβηκεν εἰς τὸν οὐρανὸν εἰ μὴ ὁ ἐκ τοῦ οὐρανοῦ καταβάς, ὁ υἱὸς τοῦ ἀνθρώπου [ὁ ὢν ἐν τῷ οὐρανῷ] continues to puzzle scholars. Some argue that it is not a saying that could be placed within the setting of the historical ministry of Jesus but that it alludes in particular to his ascension.[47] ἀναβέβηκεν (*has* ascended) poses difficulties for

46. But see Bultmann, *The Gospel of John*, p. 428 n. 1 for the possible link between Jn 12.28 and Mk 9.7. See n. 59 below.

47. So G.C. Nicholson, *Death as Departure: The Johannine Descent-Ascent Schema* (SBLDS 63; California: Scholars Press, 1983), pp. 91-98; E. Haenchen, *John I: A Commentary on the Gospel of John Chapters 1–6* (Philadelphia: Fortress Press, 1930), p. 204; Brown, *The Gospel according to John*, vol. 1, p. 145; R. Schnackenburg, *The Gospel according to St John*, vol. 1, pp. 392-94 who also suggest that ὁ υἱὸς τοῦ ἀνθρώπου here may be linked to Dan. 7.14 (for such an

as C.K. Barrett states 'It seems to imply that the Son of Man had already at the moment of speaking ascended into heaven', had previously ascended before his descent.[48] Moreover the phrase ὁ ὢν ἐν τῷ οὐρανῷ is omitted by the two oldest manuscripts of John (P[66] and P[75]—also א B W, among others) which demonstrates the difficulty posed by ἀναβέβηκεν; and the improvements in the Syriac versions ('who *was* in heaven' and 'who is *from* heaven') were intended to remove this difficulty.[49] The descent motif (ὁ ἐκ τοῦ οὐρανοῦ καταβάς) has often been associated with the incarnation,[50] but as I have noted, the use of the perfect ἀναβέβηκεν poses problems for such a view.[51]

In view of these difficulties F.H. Borsch suggests that 'the reference here is to the liturgical and/or mythical ascent...'[52] In a similar manner others take Jn 3.13 as something that is directed against claims made by or on behalf of those apocalyptic seers (*and above all Moses*) who are supposed to have 'ascended to heaven' to receive revelations in order to make them known to people.[53]

Given the 'Jewish' setting of the entire passage, Jesus' dialogue with Nicodemus (3.1-14),[54] the mystical ascent theory—and particularly that of Moses at Sinai—has much to commend it. This point is forcefully

association for the Johannine Son of Man sayings see S.S. Smalley, 'The Johannine Son of Man Sayings', *NTS* 15 (1969), pp. 278-301).

48. Barrett, *The Gospel according to St John*, p. 213; Morris, *John*, p. 223 n. 50 notes the difficulty and observes 'There is the thought of continuing possession but the primary reference may well be spiritual rather than physical'—which is unsatisfactory.

49. See UBS, p. 329 and NA[26], p. 253 on Jn 3.13.

50. Carson, *John*, p. 201; Beasley-Murray, *John*, p. 50; Bultmann, *The Gospel of John*, pp. 150-51; J.H. Bernard, *A Critical and Exegetical Commentary on the Gospel according to St John*, vol. 1 (Edinburgh: T. & T. Clark, 1928), pp. 111-12.

51. Bultmann, *The Gospel of John*, p. 149 n. 3 argues that the perf. ἀναβέβηκεν 'in the source had the force of a present tense', also see p. 150 n. 2 and p. 151 n. 2. But on this and on the use of εἰ μή see F.H. Borsch, *The Son of Man in Myth and History* (London: SCM Press, 1967), pp. 272-75.

52. Borsch, *The Son of Man*, pp. 273-74.

53. Meeks, *The Prophet King*, pp. 295-301; Carson, *John*, p. 200; Beasley-Murray, *John*, p. 50; Bultmann, *The Gospel of John*, p. 150 n. 1; Borsch, *The Son of Man*, p. 273 and n. 3; Brown, *The Gospel according to John*, I, p. 145. On Moses' ascent see my ch. 3.

54. T.L. Brodie, *The Gospel according to John* (Oxford: Oxford University Press, 1993), p. 198: 'the conversation seems to reflect not just the meeting of Jesus and Nicodemus, but also the dialogue of the church with Judaism'.

made by G.C. Nicholson who agues that in the light of 'contemporary belief in the ascension of Moses, and in the light of the Johannine community's belief that Moses and things Mosaic have been replaced by Jesus (1.17; 5.42; 6.32) we feel justified in understanding 3.13 as a polemic against belief in a Mosaic ascent...John is opposed to this Moses mysticism, which honours Moses as God's agent among men because he has ascended to the heavens to have direct contact with God himself...'[55] This is further supported by the fact that (1) the themes of 'ascent' (ἀναβέβηκεν) and 'descent' (καταβάς) compare well with Moses' ascent (cf. ἀνέβη Exod. 24.9, 12 LXX) and descent (cf. κατέβαινε Exod. 34.29 LXX) at Sinai. Moreover (2) vv. 14-15 clearly make a Jesus-Moses comparison, which adds weight to the possible Jesus-Moses parallelism in v. 13.

So I suggest that if Jn 3.13 reflects some kind of anti-mystical and particularly anti-Moses-ascent polemic, then the use of the transfiguration tradition could very well lend itself for such polemical use.[56] For, as the text stands, (a) the themes of 'ascent' and 'descent' not only compare well with Moses' ascent and descent at Sinai but also with Jesus' ascent and descent at the mount of transfiguration—an event with which tradition also associates Moses (and Elijah). (b) Transfiguration themes such as 'the voice from heaven', 'the cloud', 'light', the Christophany, seem to lend themselves to such a polemical (mystical-ascent) understanding of Jn 3.13; where like Moses at Sinai—who was associated with the idea of mystical ascent and descent (cf. Philo *Mos.* 1.158-59; *Memar Marqua* 4.3; Ezekiel the Tragedian 68–82, *Bib. Ant.* 12.1)[57]—Jesus ascends and descends. Jesus as καταβάς did bring knowledge from above[58] and his incarnation (which involved death by means of the cross Jn 3.14-15) was confirmed by the Father's voice at the transfiguration and also in 12.28.[59]

55. Nicholson, *Death as Departure*, pp. 91-92.

56. I am thankful to Associate Professor W. Loader of Murdoch University, Perth, for alerting me to such a possibility while reading and commenting on my manuscript.

57. See my ch. 3 and recently Allison, *The New Moses*, pp. 177-78.

58. Bultmann explains the passage in terms of the gnostic myth of the descent of the redeemer but gnostic influence is generally thought to be late: see Morris, *John*, p. 223 n. 52.

59. Bultmann, *The Gospel of John*, p. 428 n. 1 suggests that if the evangelist knew the Gospel of Mark (e.g. Mk 8.34 in Jn 12.25), then perhaps he gives a counterpart to Mk 9.2-8 (which he probably knew as a resurrection story—but see my ch. 2.1) in Jn

So Jn 3.13 may well be another echo of the transfiguration tradition, and if so this view offers a fresh insight into this puzzling verse.

Summary

So I conclude the cumulative effect of my arguments could suggest that καὶ ἐθεασάμεθα τὴν δόξαν αὐτοῦ in 1.14, seen with the light-life-law and Moses-Sinai-law polemic in the prologue, is an allusion to the transfiguration which is seen by the fourth evangelist as the epitome of Jesus' ministry. In 3.13 too the evangelist could be using the transfiguration in a polemical manner. In the light of these considerations it is not surprising that there is prominent Moses-Jesus typology in this Gospel.

5. *Moses-Sinai and Transfiguration Motifs and 2 Corinthians 3.7-18 and 4.1-6*

2 Corinthians 3.7-18 (indeed 3.7–4.6) is one of the most interesting but problematic portions in Pauline writings, and literature on this passage is abundant.[60] It raises various issues[61] but for my purposes it is significant

---

12.28, the φωνὴ being a counterpart to the voice from heaven in Mk 9.7. Ashton, *Understanding the Fourth Gospel,* pp. 500-501 seems to approve of Bultman's suggestion.

60. It is full of 'problems, ambiguities and pitfalls' so: M.D. Hooker, 'Beyond the Things that are Written? St Paul's Use of Scripture', *NTS* 27 (1980–81), p. 296 (also pp. 295-309). This is echoed by all who have addressed the issues of this passage: for example, W.C. van Unnik, '"With Unveiled Face", An Exegesis of 2 Corinthians iii 12–18', *NovT* 6 (1963), pp. 153-69, 'one of the most interesting portions of the "Corpus Paulinum"' (p. 153). For comparison with *PT Exodus* 33–34 and *TJI Nm* 7.89 see M. McNamara, *The New Testament and the Palestinian Targums to the Pentateuch* (Rome: Pontifical Biblical Institute, 1966), pp. 168-88. Other articles include: J.D.G. Dunn, '2 Corinthians III.17— "The Lord is Spirit"', *JTS* 21 (1970), pp. 309-20; C.J.A. Hickling, 'The Sequence of Thought in II Corinthians, Chapter Three', *NTS* 21 (1974–75), pp. 380-95; A.T. Hanson, 'The Midrash in II Corinthians 3: a reconsideration' *JSNT* 9 (1980), pp. 2-28; J.A. Fitzmyer, 'Glory Reflected On the Face of Christ (2 Cor. 3.7–4.6) and a Palestinian Jewish Motif', *TS* 42 (1981), pp. 630-46; E. Richard, 'Polemics, Old Testament, and Theology, A Study of II Cor. III.1–IV.6', *RB* 88 (1981), pp. 340-67; J. Lambrecht, 'Transformation in 2 Cor. 3,18', *Bib* 64 (1983) pp. 243-54; N.T. Wright, 'Reflected Glory: 2 Corinthians 3.18' in L.D. Hurst and N.T. Wright (eds.), *The Glory of Christ in the New Testament* (Oxford: Clarendon Press, 1987), pp. 139-50, and F. Young and D.F. Ford, *Meaning and Truth in 2 Corinthians* (London: SPCK, 1987), pp. 90-96. For most recent treatment see Belleville, *Reflections of Glory.* Also see V.P. Furnish, *II Corinthians* (Garden City: Doubleday, 1984), pp. 173-252;

to note the following points: (1) There is a forceful portrayal of the Moses-Sinai-covenant motif in Paul's *midrash pesher* of Exodus 34 in

Martin, *2 Corinthians*, pp. 50-81; J. Murphy-O'Connor, *The Theology of the Second Letter to the Corinthians* (Cambridge: Cambridge University Press, 1991), pp. 32-33.

61. The nature of this study prevents me from going into the intricacies of the debate, but I shall note some of the key issues:

1. For example the nature of Paul's hermeneutical method, additions, have posed problems. See Hooker, *NTS* 27 (1980–81), pp. 297-98 (for whom Paul was inconsistent in his *midrash pesher* method of using Exod. 34). Also see C.H. Talbert, *Reading Corinthians* (London: SPCK, 1990, p. 144; E. Richard, 'Polemics, Old Testament and Theology', pp. 341-42, (who highlights Paul's particular use of LXX and its idiom).

2. Paul, includes a non-Old Testament idea that Moses put the veil that the Israelites may not see the 'end (τέλος) of the fading splendour' (cf. 2 Cor. 3.13, on this see A. Plummer, *The Second Epistle of Paul the Apostle to the Corinthians* (Cambridge: Cambridge University Press, 1903), pp. 33-34; Furnish, *II Corinthians*, p. 207; Martin, *2 Corinthians*, pp. 67-68). For Paul's differing (inconsistent?) use of κάλυμμα in 3.13, 14, 15, 16, 18 (ἀνακεκαλυμμένῳ) and especially 4.3 (κεκαλυμμένον τὸ εὐαγγέλιον ἡμῶν), see especially van Unnik, '"With Unveiled Face"', pp. 153-69, according to whom παρρησία taken from an Aramaic loan-word (pp. 159-62) meaning 'barefacedness', boldness, to be linked with ἀνακεκαλυμμένῳ.

3. Among others, the interpretations of ἐπιστρέψῃ πρὸς κύριον (v. 16), ὁ δὲ κύριος τὸ πνεῦμά ἐστιν· (v. 17), κύριος in the phrase καθάπερ ἀπὸ κυρίου πνεύματος (v. 18b) has been questioned. On this see Dunn, '"The Lord is Spirit"', pp. 309-20, also Hanson, 'The Midrash in II Corinthians 3', esp. pp. 19-20. Hanson's contribution to the debate on 2 Cor. 3.7-18 is that Paul in his midrash on Exodus 34 understood Moses to have seen the pre-existing Christ in the tabernacle.

4. Does κατοπτριζόμενοι in the enigmatic 3.18 mean 'beholding' or 'reflecting' or both? and what is the mirror? Wright, 'Reflected Glory' (p. 145) suggests that 'mirror' refers to *one another*, those who belong to the new covenant are being changed by the Spirit into the glory of the Lord: when they come face to face with one another they are beholding, as in a mirror, the glory itself. Perhaps a similar thought is behind van Unik's statement 'unified in likeness to one another' (p. 167), or Dunn's 'family likeness', '"The Lord is Spirit"', p. 320.

    One must also note that the mirror image occurs in 1 Cor. 13.12 βλέπομεν γὰρ ἄρτι δι' ἐσόπτρου ἐν αἰνίγματι, τότε δὲ πρόσωπον πρὸς πρόσωπον. Here (also considering that Corinth was famous for producing excellent bronze mirrors, a motif Paul may have been exploiting, see G.D. Fee, *The First Epistle to the Corinthians*, 1989, pp. 647-48) Paul is contrasting the indirect and wanting vision of God (and Christ) with the real thing that is to come. Could this 'impermanence-mirror' motif also be applied 2 Cor. 3.18? At least ἀπὸ δόξης εἰς δόξαν, and the present indicative passive μεταμορφούμεθα suggests that it is a process, and hence imperfect. But I shall show that more importantly, the *force* of τῆς δόξης τοῦ Θεοῦ ἐν προσώπῳ Χριστοῦ in 4.6 needs to be taken into consideration.

5. What is the significance of Paul's use of μεταμορφούμεθα (3.18, also Rom. 12.2 μεταμορφοῦσθε)? On etymology and comments on the term see Lambrecht, 'Transformation in 2 Cor. 3, 18', esp. pp. 251-54, also J.A. Fitzmyer, 'Glory Reflected On the Face of Christ', esp. pp. 632-33. For our purposes, its parallel with the use (μετεμορφώθη) in Mk 9.2; Mt 17.2 is of significance.

2 Cor. 3.1-18. (2) In addition to motifs such as: Moses-Sinai, old covenant/ law-glory (ἐγενήθη ἐν δόξῃ cf. 3.7; vv. 10-11), the following contrasts may be seen, some being more forceful than others: (a) between the 'new covenant' (3.6), also defined as ἡ διακονία τοῦ πνεύματος (v. 8) and ἡ διακονία τοῦ θανάτου ἐν γράμμασιν ἐντετυπωμένη λίθοις ἐγενήθη ἐν δόξῃ (v. 7); (b) between the 'ministry' of Paul and of Christians (διακόνους cf. v. 6; 4.1) and that of Moses; (c) between Israel (13-15) and believers (16-18, also v. 7 against v. 18), and (d) between Moses who was 'veiled' (v. 13, also Jews v. 14) and believers (ἡμεῖς δὲ πάντες ἀνακεκαλυμμένῳ...3.18, also ὃς ἔλαμψεν ἐν ταῖς καρδίαις ἡμῶν 4.6); perhaps also (e) in a real sense, though at a secondary level, there is a Moses-Jesus parallelism: note the contrast between the sons of Israel unable to gaze (ἀτενίσαι) at Moses' 'face', and the 'glory' of Jesus' 'face' in 4.6: ὃς ἔλαμψεν ἐν ταῖς καρδίαις ἡμῶν πρὸς φωτισμὸν τῆς γνώσεως τῆς δόξης τοῦ Θεοῦ ἐν προσώπῳ Χριστοῦ.[62] So Paul's polemical *midrash pesher* exegesis of the Moses-δοξα tradition once again demonstrates the powerful influence of the Moses-Sinai-law traditions in the first century.

That is relatively non-controversial: A more controversial conclusion is that Paul may be responding to the Jesus-transfiguration tradition and the influence it had in elevating Peter in particular. Paul's opponents may have used this against Paul to devalue his apostolic credibility. Paul, however, counters this by claiming that he and fellow Christians too have 'beheld the glory of the Lord' (3.18). My thesis at this point is, that the transfiguration narrative is to be seen as playing a part in the controversy within the church between Paul and his opponents. Paul's opponents were Judaizers who emphasised the law and Peter (compare the tradition of Matthew), and Paul was emphasising his qualification as one who had also seen the glory of the Lord.[63]

62. Scholars emphasising different parts of the text come to differing sets of contrasts. But accepting the over all argument that Paul is contrasting the character of his (new covenant) ministry with the old covenant (cf. Hickling, 'Sequence of Thought', esp. pp. 387-88; Wright, 'Reflected Glory', p. 139; Furnish, *II Corinthians*, pp. 226-27; Talbert, *Reading Corinthians*, p. 144), in varying degrees all these contrasts are seen in Paul's arguments.

63. There is some debate about who Paul's opponents were. J.L. Sumney, *Identifying Paul's Opponents* (Sheffield: JSOT Press, 1990), *passim*, tries to argue that the Judaizers are not referred to in 2 Corinthians 1–9 (p. 189), but he comes to this conclusion only after his 'method' makes him exclude 3.7-18 (p. 145, also pp. 130-47). On the other hand C.K. Barrett, *A Commentary on the Second Epistle to the*

Paul's Use of μεταμορφούμεθα *(2 Cor. 3.18)*
To begin my discussion I shall focus on the key term μεταμορφούμεθα, which naturally is reminiscent of the transfiguration account of Mk 9.2 and Mt. 17.2. Paul uses the term to describe the gradual transformation of believers (τὴν αὐτὴν εἰκόνα...ἀπὸ δόξης εἰς δόξαν...). This is supposed to take place in those who with 'unveiled face' (ἀνακεκαλυμμένῳ προσώπῳ) are 'beholding/reflecting as in a mirror the glory of the Lord' (3.18).

We have already met the verb μεταμορφόω while discussing Philo. It is rare before New Testament times, and I have already argued that its usage in Hellenistic Greek writings (especially Philo *Mos.* 1.57; 2.288-89; *Leg. Gai.* 95) brings its occurrence in Mk 9.2; Mt. 17.2; 2 Cor. 3.18; Rom. 12.2 into the context of transformation ideas; albeit the transfiguration of Jesus is to be seen within Jewish categories. But since (1) μεταμορφόω is linked to μορφή and its derivatives, and since (2), as R.P. Martin and others have shown, μορφή and its derivatives could also be associated with εἰκών and δόξα,[64] Paul's uses of μεταμορφόω in 3.18 (and Rom. 12.2), and also its usage in the transfiguration context of Mk 9.2, and Mt. 17.2 may be seen in relation to motifs such as εἰκών, δόξα.[65] Whether Paul himself was aware of the use of μεταμορφόω in a pre-synoptic Jesus-transfiguration tradition will be discussed later.

Corinthians (London: A. & C. Black, 1973), pp. 40-41 points out that the 'letters of recommendation' in 3.1 seem to have emanated from Jerusalem 'and can hardly have been unconnected with the "Pillars" Gal. 2.7' (p. 40), and that this 'establishes the opponents' Jewish and Judaizing background' (cf. 11.22)—for their apostolate was 'from men and through men' (Gal. 1.1). J. Murphy-O'Connor, *The Theology of the Second Letter to the Corinthians*, p. 32, strongly endorses the 'Judaizers' view (in 2 Cor. 3–4) by also pointing out that if Paul 'introduces the idea of "tablets of stone" (3.3) it can only be because he associated the bearers of the letters of recommendation with the Mosaic Law'.

64. Cf. Martin, *Carmen Christi*, pp. 99-133. For Pauline examples of links between δόξα and εἰκών, see Rom. 1.23; 9.29-30; 1 Cor. 11.7; 2 Cor. 3.18; 4.4. Also see Hanson, 'The Midrash in II Corinthians 3', pp. 6-7; S. Kim, *The Origin of Paul's Gospel* (Grand Rapids: Eerdmans, 1982), p. 230.

65. Luke, does not use μεταμορφώθη (τὸ εἶδος τοῦ προσώπου αὐτοῦ ἕτερον 9.29) but δόξα features prominently: vv. 31, 32 δὲ εἶδον τὴν δόξαν αὐτοῦ. It has been shown that in the LXX, εἶδος and ὁμοίωμα are synonymous (cf. Martin, *Carmen Christi*, p. 103, cf. Judg. 8.18; *Tob.* 1.13; Job 4.16; *Wis.* 18.1; Isa. 44.13; Dan. 3.19; *4 Macc.* 15.4). And hence, considering Luke's Septuagintisms, and fondness for the use of LXX, the absence of μεταμορφώθη in Lk. 9.29 is compensated by his use of εἶδος with its links with μορφή.

τῆς δόξης τοῦ Θεοῦ ἐν προσώπῳ Χριστοῦ *(2 Cor. 4.6) and the Transfiguration*

In 2.14–4.6 Paul is contrasting the character of his ministry of the new covenant with the old Mosaic-Sinai covenant,[66] but doing justice to, and holding together, the various details in the text is highly problematical.[67] In my view, while 2 Cor. 3.1-18 has received considerable scholarly attention, its relation to 4.1-6, especially the relation between 3.18 and the phrase τῆς δόξης τοῦ Θεοῦ ἐν προσώπῳ Χριστοῦ in 4.6, has not been fully exploited.[68] Before I comment on this phrase in the light of its

66. Cf. Hickling, 'II Corinthians Chapter 3', esp. pp. 387-88; Wright, 'Reflected Glory', p. 139: Furnish, *II Corinthians*, p. 226-27; Talbert, *Reading Corinthians*, p. 144.

67. For example, κατοπτριζόμενοι (3.18), 'beholding' (on the basis of linguistic evidence, Philo, *All. Int.* 3.101, also translations in Syriac, Coptic, Latin; cf. Young and Ford, *Meaning and Truth in 2 Corinthians*, p. 91) is supported by Furnish, *II Corinthians*, p. 214; P.E. Hughes, *The Second Epistle to the Corinthians* (Grand Rapids: Eerdmans, 2nd edn, 1986), pp. 117-18; also, Wright, 'Reflected Glory', p. 145, Lambrecht, 'Transformation in II Cor. 3, 18', p. 245. For 'reflecting' see Plummer, *The Second Epistle of Paul the Apostle to the Corinthians*, p. 36; Caird, 'Everything to Everyone: A Theology of the Corinthian Epistles', *Interpretation* 13 (1959), p. 392 ; van Unnik, '"With Unveiled Face"', p. 167; Hooker, 'Beyond the Things That are Written?', p. 301. But the difference is artificial, for only by beholding (gazing, e.g. use of ἀτενίσαι in 3.13) could one 'reflect', we both 'behold and reflect' and as Young and Ford, *Meaning and Truth in 2 Corinthians*, p. 92, have argued, the demand for a decision between these two meanings is perhaps 'distorting our apprehension of the meaning of the text'. In 1 Cor. 11.7 humanity is εἰκὼν καὶ δόξα Θεοῦ (the 'glory' which they had come short of καὶ ὑστεροῦνται τῆς δόξης τοῦ Θεοῦ, cf. Rom. 3.23) and it is as we see ourselves in the light of God's glory mirrored in the face of Jesus Christ (4.6) who is also the εἰκὼν τοῦ Θεοῦ (to be compared also with the use of τὴν αὐτὴν εἰκόνα of 3.18 and as noted with regards to people in 1 Cor. 11.7) that we are being transformed. Young and Ford rightly compare this idea with that in Mk 9.2-3 (we may add also Mt. 17.2, Lk 9.28) where too 'light', 'splendour', are given by God, and is a reflection of God's own glory (*Meaning and Truth in 2 Corinthians*, p. 92). The idea that one's 'face' illumi-nated by God also becomes a light (to bring knowledge to the world) is something we have already seen in relation to the Teacher of Righteousness in DSS (see section on Qumran in ch. 3.3), and it is interesting to note that Fitzmyer, in 'Glory Reflected on the Face of Christ', pp. 639-40, attests this transformation by vision and gives further examples which also apply to the covenantors. Also see Martin, *2 Corinthians*, pp. 80-81; Talbert, *Reading Corinthians*, p. 145.

68. Belleville, *Reflections of Glory,* pp. 283, 285, cites 4.6 in conjunction with 4.4 in relation to the 'gospel of the glory of Christ', but does not adequately account for

total context, it must be noted that Caird, Bruce, Hughes, Kim, recently Martin, Talbert and Dunn, have all seen 4.6 in the light of Paul's Damascus Christophany.[69] Kim, in particular, viewing v. 6 in the light of 3.7–4.6, goes on to argue that Paul interpreted his Damascus Christophany itself as a 'parallel' to the Moses-Sinai-exodus event.

Commenting on 2 Cor. 3.1-18 and 4.1-6, Kim concludes that as Moses saw God appearing in glory on Mount Sinai (3.7-11), so Paul saw Christ appearing in glory on the Damascus road, and 'just as the ministry of the old covenant came to Moses in glory, so the ministry of the new covenant came to Paul in glory' (p. 235). Nevertheless, he makes an erroneous claim that 'Paul must have been aware that other ministers did not receive their ministry of the new covenant in a theophany or Christophany which could be compared with the Sinai theophany to Moses' (p. 235).

Kim's assumption fails to consider that Paul may well have known the transfiguration tradition. For I wish to argue that (1) the transfiguration story in any version (Mk 9.2-10; Mt. 17.1-9; Lk. 9.28-36; 2 Pet. 1.16-18) tells against Kim, for it was (as described) a theophany/Christophany 'seen' quite as much as Paul's. And as I have already argued, it was very probably something that set the three disciples apart.[70] (2) Matthew's version in particular brings out the Sinai parallel and associates it with Peter's call/commission in 16.13-19. (3) Luke uses δόξα language and this makes for an interesting comparison with Paul's use of similar

---

the 'face' motif. 4.6 naturally links with the 'face' motif in 3.18 and also 3.7. Hughes, *The Second Epistle to the Corinthians*, pp. 114-15 briefly associates 2 Corinthians 3 and 4 with the transfiguration; also see Chilton, 'The Transfiguration', pp. 115-24. A.F. Segal, *Paul the Convert* (New Haven & London: Yale University Press, 1990), p. 112, compares the transfiguration tradition, but does not suggest that Paul is responding to that tradition.

69. Caird, *The New Testament Conception of doxa*, p. 209; also 'Everything to Everyone: A Theology of the Corinthian Epistles', p. 388; F.F. Bruce, *1 and 2 Corinthians* (Grand Rapids: Eerdmans; London: Marshall, Morgan & Scott, 1971), p. 196; Kim, *The Origin of Paul's Gospel*, pp. 6-8, 229-32 (who also points out that the aorist verb ἔλαμψεν 'has shone' refers back to this incident); Talbert, *Reading Corinthians*, p. 156; Martin, *2 Corinthians*, p. 80; J.D.G. Dunn, *Jesus, Paul and the Law* (London: SPCK, 1990), p. 95; Hughes, *The Second Epistle to the Corinthians*, pp. 133-34.

70. See discussion on the 'standing ones' (Mk 9.1; Mt. 16.28; Lk. 9.27) in relation to στῦλοι (Gal. 2.9) in Wenham and Moses, '"There Are Some Standing here"'.

language in 2 Corinthians 3 and 4. These points will be elaborated on below.

In the transfiguration accounts, (a) Matthew in particular presents the transfiguration in Moses-Sinai-Jesus categories (Luke has more of an exodus perspective: see Appendix). (b) Matthew (alone) describes the transfiguration as a 'vision' (τὸ ὅραμα 17.9, with its Sinai and Daniel 7 connotations). But the synoptic accounts agree that this was 'seen' by Peter, James and John (ὤφθη Mt. 17.3, Mk 9.4; εἶδον Lk. 9.32 (Mk 9.9); ἑώρακαν Lk. 9.36). (c) Luke emphasises the δόξα motif in his account of the transfiguration (9.31-32), and the three disciples εἶδον τὴν δόξαν (9.32). (d) This is also confirmed by the independent attestation of the transfiguration in 2 Pet. 1.16, according to which the apostles were ἐπόπται[71] γενηθέντες τῆς ἐκείνου μεγαλειότητος. If this passage reflects genuine Petrine tradition, it suggests that Peter himself saw the transfiguration as highly significant,[72] but even if it does not, still the writer sees Jesus' transfiguration as a high point for those there, giving them special eyewitness status. And given the important role Peter had in the early church (Mt. 16.17-19; Lk. 22.32; Jn 21.15-19), the transfiguration event enhanced his importance. The upshot of all this is that it is not only Paul who had witnessed Jesus' 'glory' but also the three disciples at the transfiguration.

Furthermore, if a Sinai-Moses-δοξα motif is to be pressed, it is more sharply attested at the transfiguration (where Moses himself is said to have appeared!) than in the Damascus road experience. So even though Kim does make a point, he has overworked it by claiming it exclusively for Paul. His assumption that Paul 'must have been aware that other ministers did not receive their ministry in a theophany or Christophany compared with Sinai theophany to Moses' is weak.[73]

Paul and the Disciples' Experience of the Transfiguration
On the other hand, it is to be noted that the overall argument of 2 Cor. 2.14–4.6 (also 2.14–6.13) is linked to the defense of the nature of Paul's

71. For the writer's emphasis on 'eyewitnesses' see Bauckham, *Jude, 2 Peter*, pp. 215-17.

72. See Bauckham, *Jude, 2 Peter*, p. 210.

73. Moreover, Kim reads too much into Paul's Damascus road experience, he argues that the Damascus Christophany was the source for Paul's conception of Christ as εἰκὼν τοῦ Θεοῦ, *The Origin of Paul's Gospel*, pp. 223-39. For a critique of Kim see Dunn, *Jesus, Paul and the Law*, pp. 95-100.

ministry. In view of this, (a) could it be that while engaging in polemical use of the Moses-δόξα tradition in 3.1-8, Paul is also answering his opponents in Corinth, who were elevating Peter, pointing among others things to his exclusive experience of the transfiguration? (b) could it be that Paul, by the phrase τῆς δόξης τοῦ Θεοῦ ἐν προσώπῳ Χριστοῦ (4.6), is in a subtle manner alluding to this transfiguration event but also hinting that his Damascus experience too matches up to such a transfiguration experience? By way of answering these questions, certain points need to be stated:

a. In 3.1 Paul has been talking about letters of recommendation: ἢ μὴ χρήζομεν ὥς τινες συστατικῶν ἐπιστολῶν πρὸς ὑμᾶς... This suggests that some of Paul's opponents did elevate other apostles above Paul and held that he needed to carry 'letters' perhaps from the Jerusalem council or the 'pillars' (στῦλοι Gal. 2.9) of the church.

b. It is clear that there was some party spirit in the early church, particularly at Corinth, with one party elevating their man above the other (1 Cor. 3.1-23). There also seems to have been a 'Cephas' party (3.22), and Paul seems sensitive to Peter's rights, perhaps due to his elevated status in 9.1-8. While it is true that James (the brother of Jesus) did take on an active leadership role, the towering figure of Peter (and John) constituting the στῦλοι cannot be minimised. It needs to be noted that if there was a single event that set Peter, John and James (the martyr, Acts 12.2) apart from the rest, it was the transfiguration of Jesus.[74]

c. This vision-call-commission motif may also be paralleled with other call visions in the Scriptures (e.g. Exodus 3, Isaiah 6; Jeremiah 1; Ezekiel 1–2, Daniel 8.15-19; 10.8-12, also visions in the New Testament, e.g. Rev. 1.9-20, 4.1-11, etc.), and due to the transfiguration-vision (τὸ ὅραμα Mt. 17.9), it is likely that Peter, James and John would have been highly esteemed in the early church.

d. As I have already pointed out, in Matthew in particular, this vision-call-commission is especially applicable to Peter for the following reasons: (i) In Matthew, Peter was the first disciple to be called (Mt. 4.18; Mk 1.16, but see Jn 1.41-42). (ii) In

---

74. See Wenham and Moses, '"There Are Some Standing here"'.

Matthew alone the early tradition of Peter's commissioning with its ἐκκλησία and βασιλεία ramifications occurs in 16.13-19. (iii) In view of these factors, it may be argued that his call was reaffirmed through the vision-call and ἀκούετε αὐτοῦ particularly addressed to Peter (Mt. 17.5; Lk. 9.35; Mk 9.7), for as I have observed, the voice from out of the clouds was prompted by Peter's suggestion to build booths, and hence specially applicable to Peter (cf. Mt. 17.5; Lk. 9.34). In view of the relation between Mt. 16.13-19 and 17.4-5 it is conceivable that the transfiguration-event could very well have elevated Peter and his words in the early church.[75]

e.   D. Wenham, following up suggestions made by J. Chapman, has argued that Paul was aware of Peter's commission (Gal. 2.7, 8) and, in this, Mt. 16.18, 19 figures prominently.[76] He also compares Mt. 16.15, 17, 18 with Gal. 1.12, 15, 16; 1.1, 12, 16 and argues that Paul speaks of his own commissioning in terms reminiscent of Mt. 16.17-19, and perhaps is drawing from this 'M' tradition. Moreover, while in Gal. 2.7, 8 Paul speaks of 'Peter', elsewhere in Galatians and in his writings he always uses Cephas. This peculiar usage seems to add weight to Paul's allusion to the Peter-tradition with its Peter/rock word play. The parallels here are quite impressive, and in the light of Paul's knowledge of the Jesus tradition, at times in its pre-synoptic form, it is conceivable that he was aware of the M tradition behind Mt. 16.18-19.[77]

---

75. See ch. 5.4 for the Peter-building motif.

76. D. Wenham, 'Paul's Use of the Jesus Tradition: Three Samples', in D. Wenham (ed.), *Gospel Perspectives*, vol. 5 (Sheffield: JSOT Press, 1984), pp. 7-37, esp. pp. 24-28.

77. 'M' material is often regarded as late, but a case could be made that some of it reflects early tradition, for example, the Peter/rock/church tradition. For the defence of this position see B.F. Meyer, *The Aims of Jesus* (London: SCM Press, 1979), pp. 185-97. For Paul's knowledge of early Jesus tradition see D. Wenham in 'Paul's Use of the Jesus Tradition', also his *The Rediscovery of Jesus' Eschatological Discourse* (Sheffield: JSOT Press, 1984); P. Richardson and P. Gooch, 'Logia of Jesus in 1 Corinthians', in D. Wenham (ed.), *Gospel Perspectives*, vol. 5 (Sheffield: JSOT Press, 1984), pp. 39-62. For the state of the debate and recent discussion on Paul's knowledge of the Jesus tradition see the collection of essays in A.J.M. Wedderburn (ed.), *Paul and Jesus: Collected Essays* (Sheffield: JSOT Press, 1989); Wenham, *Paul: Follower of Jesus or Founder of Christianity*.

Whether he was or not, the question arises as to whether Paul also was aware of a pre-synoptic transfiguration tradition? The use of the rare verb μεταμορφόω in Mk 9.2; Mt. 17.2; 2 Cor. 3.18,[78] may point us in the right direction but needs to be further supported.

A Comparison of Paul's Damascus Christophany with the Transfiguration

A possible argument is: if Paul found common points between his Damascus road experience and that of Peter, James and John, then he could have had a basis for comparing them and also theologically relating them to others' experience of Christ as in 2 Cor. 3.18. Interestingly, both in terms of form and content there are themes, words, and at points narrative sequences in common between the two events.

While keeping in mind that in the Acts' description of Paul's conversion it is Luke's vocabulary that we meet, the following comparisons could be made:

For example, (a) φῶς (Acts 9.3), φῶς ἱκανὸν (22.6), especially τὴν λαμπρότητα τοῦ ἡλίου...φῶς in 26.13—which as in Acts 22 records Paul's words—compares well with Matthew's vocabulary ὡς ὁ ἥλιος... τὸ φῶς (Mt. 17.2). (b) The 'voice' from 'heaven' Acts 9.4, 22.7, 26.14; compare Mt. 17.5; Mk 9.7; Lk. 9.35. (c) Falling on the ground πεσὼν Acts 9.4; ἔπεσά 22.7; καταπεσόντων 26.14; once again compare with Mt. 17.6 ἔπεσαν. (d) Paul's response, a 'questioning' during Christophany Acts 9.5; 22.8; 26.15, may be compared with Peter's 'question/suggestion' at the transfiguration event Mt. 17.4; Mk 9.5; Lk. 9.33. (e) The heavenly instruction to obey Christ's instruction Acts 9.6; 22.10; 26.16. In 26.16, (in Paul's address before Agrippa) a commission is given. This compares with ἀκούετε αὐτοῦ of Mt. 17.5; Mk 9.7, αὐτοῦ ἀκούετε Lk. 9.35. (f) In Acts 26.19 Paul describes it as a heavenly 'vision' ὀπτασίᾳ which compares with Matthew's (alone) τὸ ὅραμα 17.9.[79]

---

78. For comment on the use of μεταμορφόω in Rom. 12.2 see ch. 3.1; where in Philo *Quaet. in Exod.* 2.29 it is transformation of the mind, but it is Moses' mind which is in focus, and so has links with his Moses-transformation theme in *Mos.* 1.158-59, and 2.70 etc. In Rom. 12.2 however, it is difficult to see a Moses motif, or Moses polemic as in 2 Cor. 3.1-18, but speaks of a moral transformation, see J.D.G. Dunn, *Romans 9–16* (Waco: Word, 1988), p. 713.

79. It is interesting that if Paul's claim in Gal. 1.16, that God 'was pleased to reveal (ἀποκαλύψαι) his son (τὸν υἱὸν αὐτοῦ) in me' recalls his Damascus road experience (so: R.N. Longenecker, *Galatians* (Dallas: Word, 1990), pp. 31-32;

It may be hazardous to deduce much from a comparison of the three Lukan accounts of Paul's conversion with the three different synoptic accounts of the transfiguration, and yet the general point that Paul's conversion could have been seen as somehow parallel to the transfiguration—by Luke (as author of Acts and narrator of the transfiguration) at least—remains.

Parallels with Matthew 17.1-9?

The similarities leave room for thought that Paul himself could have considered his Damascus road experience comparable to Peter's or the other two apostles' witness of Jesus' transfiguration experience. It also appears that Matthew's presentation of the transfiguration has most similarities to the accounts of Paul's conversion. For example like Matthew, Paul makes an analogy with the 'sun', see point (a), and falls to the ground, see point (c). In Acts 26.16-18 Paul is given a commission, specifically with respect to the 'Gentiles.' This may be compared with Peter's commission in Mt. 16.17-19, which Paul in Gal. 2.7, 8 links with apostleship 'to the circumcision' (see further below). Finally Paul describes the Damascus road Christophany as a 'vision', so does Matthew.

This, at least, and at this stage of my argument, allows for the 'possibility' that Paul could have known of a Matthean or pre-Matthean

R.Y.K. Fung, *The Epistle to the Galatians* (Grand Rapids: Eerdmans, 1986), p. 64; also F.F. Bruce, *The Epistle to the Galatians* (Exeter: Paternoster Press, 1982), pp. 92-93), then the ἀποκαλύψαι-τὸν υἱὸν αὐτοῦ link also compares well with a similar theme at the transfiguration (Mt. 17.5; Mk 9.7; Lk. 9.34). For in Mt. 17.1-8 and par., the three disciples receive a 'revelation' (in fact the whole transfiguration event was a 'revelation'), which *also* 'included' a 'revelation' about Jesus' sonship (ὁ υἱός μου Mt. 17.5; Mk 9.7; Lk. 9.34). Furthermore, since Peter is particularly in focus in Matthew's presentation of the transfiguration, the 'revelation-sonship' in Mt. 17.5 also compares well with Mt. 16.16 (Peter's confession: ὁ υἱὸς τοῦ Θεοῦ), which according to v. 17 was 'revealed' to Peter (ἀπεκάλυψέν, compare Gal. 1.16).

So, it is instructive to compare Gal. 1.16 also with (1) Mt. 17.5 and parallels (another hint of Paul viewing his Damascus road experience as being on par with the disciples' transfiguration experience?). (2) Gal. 1.16 is also to be compared with Mt. 16.16-17—note comparable use of ἀποκαλύπτω, and Jesus-God's son themes. My suggestions on the Gal. 1.16/Mt. 16.16-17; 17.5 comparison also needs to be set in the context of the Paul-Peter (Gal. 2.8) and Paul-pillars (2.9-10) contrast. As a general argument, if Paul's polemic against his opponents in 2 Corinthians makes him also to 'boast' of ὀπτασίας καὶ ἀποκαλύψεις κυρίου, this makes an interesting comparison with the Peter-ἀπεκάλυψέν theme in Mt. 16.16-17, (and the transfiguration Mt. 17.5), perhaps made much of by Paul's opponents.

or a pre-synoptic tradition of the transfiguration, and viewed his experience as somehow analogous, especially due to the elevation that Peter and others received through their witness of it. The parallels with Matthew's portrayal of the transfiguration are important. For if Paul knew of such a Matthean or pre-Matthean tradition, then Paul's 'emphasis' especially in Acts 26 is explainable.[80] But my discussion does not end with Matthean or pre-Matthean traditions, for it will shortly be seen that Paul could also have known a pre-synoptic tradition of the transfiguration, especially represented in Luke.

Possible Textual Support for Transfiguration Parallels
It is interesting to compare the transfiguration-texts with some of the phrases and terms used in 2 Cor. 3.1-18 and 4.1-6. The relevant texts for comparison are as follows:

Mt. 17.2	καὶ μετεμορφώθη ἔμπροσθεν αὐτῶν, καὶ ἔλαμψεν τὸ προσωπον αὐτοῦ ὡς ὁ ἥλιος, τὰ δὲ ἱμάτια αὐτοῦ ἐγένετο λευκὰ ὡς τὸ φῶς.	2 Cor. 3.18	ἡμεῖς δὲ πάντες ἀνακεκαλυμμένῳ προσώπῳ τὴν δόξαν κυρίου κατοπτριζόμενοι τὴν αὐτὴν εἰκόνα μεταμορφούμεθα ἀπὸ δόξης εἰς δόξαν, καθάπερ ἀπὸ
Mk 9.2	καὶ μετεμορφώθη ἔμπροσθεν αὐτῶν...		κυρίου πνεύματος.
Lk. 9.29	τὸ εἶδος τοῦ προσώπου αὐτοῦ ἕτερον καὶ ὁ ἱματισμὸς αὐτοῦ λευκὸς ἐξαστράπτων.	2 Cor. 4.6	ὅτι ὁ Θεὸς ὁ εἰπών· ἐκ σκότους φῶς λάμψει
			ὃς ἔλαμψεν ἐν ταῖς καρδίαις ἡμῶν πρὸς φωτισμὸν τῆς
Lk. 9.32	δὲ εἶδον τὴν δόξαν αὐτοῦ καὶ τοὺς δύο ἄνδρας τοὺς συνεστῶτας αὐτῷ		γνώσεως τῆς δόξης τοῦ Θεοῦ ἐν προσώπῳ
Lk. 9.31	οἳ ὀφθέντες ἐν δόξῃ ἔλεγον τὴν ἔξοδον αὐτοῦ...		Ἰησοῦ Χριστοῦ.

---

80. On the other hand, Matthew's use of such a tradition also fits (1) his Peter emphasis, and (2) perhaps also the idea that Matthew was anti-Pauline (i.e. in the sense that he opposed those who were misrepresenting Paul's teaching on Christian liberty).

Here the following parallels may be seen: (a) There is the use of the verb μεταμορφόω in Mt. 17.2; Mk 9.2 and 2 Cor. 3.18. (b) The δόξα motif in 2 Cor. 3.18 and 4.6 may be paralleled, particularly with Luke's (alone) emphasis of the same motif (9.32 also 31). But more specifically Luke refers to Jesus' altered face in 9.29, and this associated with the Jesus-δόξα tradition in 9.31 makes a striking comparison with Paul's specific association of δόξα with Jesus' face in 2 Cor. 4.6...τῆς δόξης τοῦ Θεοῦ **ἐν προσώπῳ 'Ιησοῦ Χριστοῦ**. This δόξα-προσώπον association is highly suggestive of the transfiguration.[81]

But the Jesus-face motif also occurs in Mt. 17.2. Interestingly the verb μεταμορφόω which is associated with Jesus' face in Mt. 17.2 (also Mk 9.2) is associated with fellow-Christians in 2 Cor. 3.18, together with the idea of face. With regard to the latter, given that Paul closely associates the believer with Jesus; for example, with Jesus' death εἰ γὰρ σύμφυτοι γεγόναμεν τῷ ὁμοιώματι τοῦ θανάτου αὐτοῦ (Rom. 6.5) and resurrection, ὃς μετασχηματίσει[82]...τῷ σώματι τῆς δόξης αὐτοῦ (Phil. 3.21, Rom. 6.4-11; 1 Cor. 15), it is possible that Paul has associated the Jesus-δόξα, and transfiguration motif also with fellow-Christians in 2 Cor. 3.18. Implying, that just as he too had a transfiguration-type experience on the Damascus road, fellow Christians share in this, albeit theologically/Christologically (taking 3.18 with 4.6).

If this is accepted, then it is conceivable that in 2 Cor. 3.18 and 4.6, Paul betrays knowledge of Jesus-transfiguration traditions represented both in Lk. 9.29, 32 and Mt. 17.2. Moreover, since Matthew and his tradition contribute for example the 'μεταμορφόω...πρόσωπον' motif and Luke and his tradition the 'δόξα...πρόσωπον' associations, it is

81. In view of the Luke-Paul relation, it is plausible that the Lukan/probably Pauline church emphasised the transfiguration as a δόξα-event. If so, this makes it the more plausible to see the transfiguration in 2 Corinthians 3 and 4.

82. Interestingly, Paul does use terms signifying 'change' in several instances, but μεταμορφόω only in 2 Cor. 3.18 and Rom. 12.2. In Phil. 3.21 μετασχηματίζω is quite similar to μεταμορφόω, and means 'to remodel, transfigure, to fashion'. But in 2 Cor. 11.13, 14, 15 it is used negatively of 'false apostles'. Also see negative use of μεταλλάσσω in Rom. 1.25, 26; ἀλλάσσω is used in 1 Cor. 15.51, 52, but negatively in Rom. 1.23. In view of this range of terms, it is of interest that he uses μεταμορφόω in 2 Cor. 3.18. Given, 2 Cor. 4.6 with its distinct reference to τῆς δόξης...ἐν προσώπῳ 'Ιησοῦ Χριστοῦ, and the Moses-δόξα polemic in 3.1-18, it is not impossible that it was prompted by Jesus-transfiguration traditions associating δόξα-μεταμορφόω-προσώπον, especially those of Mt. 17.1-8 and Lk. 9.28-36 with their Moses-Sinai links.

conceivable that in a pre-synoptic Jesus-transfiguration tradition both μεταμορφόω and δόξα motifs were linked with the 'face' motif, with Paul attesting all three pre-synoptic motifs, Jesus-face, Jesus-δόξα and Jesus-μεταμορφόω motifs.

Summary

1. My line of argument suggests that (a) Paul quite probably knew the pre-synoptic Jesus-transfiguration tradition. (b) He was aware of the influence it had in elevating Peter (and John), something that his opponents may have used against him. He, however, assigns his Damascus road experience a function comparable to that of the transfiguration (from a disciple's point of view). He also relates it to the experience of fellow believers (2 Cor. 3.18) just as he relates Jesus-death-resurrection motifs to himself and fellow-believers (Rom. 6.1-11; Gal. 2.20; Phil. 3.10-11). (c) In addition, in 2 Corinthians 3-4 (among other things) he perhaps links/contrasts his Damascus Christophany (4.6) and especially his and the fellow believers' δόξα-experience (3.18) with Moses' Sinai experience, for two reasons: (i) in order to refute the Judaizers who continued to press for obedience to the Mosaic law, the old covenant with its legal requirements, and (ii) also to counter those who had elevated Peter (James and John), since they too had a Moses-Sinai type experience and hence were 'a type of Moses' whose word was made much of.

Matthew's conservative attitude towards the law, his position within the mainstream of Jewish Christianity which flowed from the earliest Jerusalem community, his Moses-Sinai-Jesus parallelism together with his Peter emphasis at the transfiguration are all things that could have been used against Paul. For Paul's opponents, the Judaizers, emphasised the law, and probably also Peter's authority—as seen in the tradition of Matthew, (Mt. 16.16-19, and at the transfiguration 17.4).[83] Paul responds by emphasising his qualification as one who has also seen the glory of the Lord.

2. It is also clear from Paul's polemical use of Exodus 34 in 2 Cor. 3.1-18 that: (a) the Moses-Sinai-law motif had a forceful influence in

---

83. For the view that the anti-Pauline element stemmed from the Jerusalem congregation, and despite the Jerusalem conference, position of the so called 'pillars' (Gal. 2.2, 6-7), it continued to plague Paul. On this see G. Luedemann, *Opposition to Paul in Jewish Christianity* (Minneapolis: Fortress Press, 1989), pp. 35-63. If this is so, it further supports my position, since Matthew probably reflects the theology of the earliest Jerusalem community, the anti-Paulinists could well have used (or misused) his 'conservative' tradition.

first-century Judaism. (b) This Moses-Sinai motif was undoubtedly a staunch rallying point to those who were arguing for the divine validity and continuity of the law, and the old covenant. But Paul turns the tables by arguing that the new covenant that has 'come' in far-exceeding splendour (3.9), far supersedes the 'splendour' of Mount Sinai, and the coming of the law ἐν δόξῃ (3.7, 10-11).[84]

3. Significantly, this is precisely what we encountered in the prologue of the Fourth Gospel. Moreover, Hooker and recently R.P. Martin[85] have rightly pointed out the common motifs in the evangelist's use of the Moses motif in the prologue and in 2 Corinthians 3–4. The evangelist, for example, begins with the light of creation and moves to the story of Moses on Sinai. Paul begins with Moses and uses Gen. 1.3 (in 2 Cor. 4.6) as a climax. Furthermore, in 2 Cor. 4.6 the 'glory of God' is to be sought not in the law of the old dispensation, but ἐν προσώπῳ Ἰησοῦ Χριστοῦ. This finds a direct parallel in Jn 1.17 'law was given through Moses, grace and truth came through Jesus Christ'; an idea also seen in Hebrews 8.

Conclusions

In this chapter I have shown that Matthew's Jesus-Moses parallelism and Christology is not an isolated and eccentric piece of theology in the development of early Christology, but is also paralleled in certain other New Testament writers, in Acts 3 and 7, Heb. 3.3-6, John's prologue, Jn 3.13, John 4 and 6, and in Paul's polemical use of the Moses-δόξα tradition in 2 Corinthians 3 and 4. I have also shown the possible echo of the transfiguration theme in John's prologue and its polemical use in 2 Corinthians 3 and 4. All this shows the vital importance of the Moses-Jesus parallelism, and the Jesus/new and greater Moses motif for the early church, and also makes a contribution towards the current interest in the Jewishness of Jesus.

---

84. This polemic against 'Mount Sinai and its law' is also seen in Gal. 4.24 (i.e. 'Mount Sinai-Hagar-children of slavery' identification, a motif also repeated in the textually disputed v. 25) cf. H.N. Ridderbos, *The Epistle of Paul to the Churches of Galatia* (Grand Rapids: Eerdmans, 1953), pp. 175-78.

85. Hooker, 'Beyond the Things that Are Written?', p. 302; Martin, *2 Corinthians*, p. 73. For the view that in 2 Corinthians 3–4 Paul presented himself as Moses' superior see Allison, *The New Moses*, pp. 110-12.

OVERALL CONCLUSIONS

In this thesis I have established that Matthew's account of the transfiguration is to be seen in the context of the first-century controversy
between Christians and Jews about Jesus and Moses, with the Jews
emphasising Moses' greatness and Matthew portraying the transfiguration as a new and greater Sinai event. The narrative is also to be seen in
the context of controversy within the church between Paul and his
opponents; with Paul's opponents being Judaizers who emphasize the
law and Peter (the tradition of Matthew), and Paul emphasising his
qualification as one who had also seen the glory of the Lord. Thus
Matthew's Jesus-Moses parallelism is not an isolated piece of theology in
the development of early Christology, but is also paralleled by other
New Testament writers, in Acts 3 and 7, Heb. 3.3-6, John's prologue, Jn
1.14; 3.13 and also in John 4 and 6.

The path taken to arrive at these conclusions and the methodological
procedure adopted were as follows:

Chapter 2: A critical review of scholarly discussion on the transfiguration pericope highlighted the great divergence of interpretations and
their weaknesses. I also concluded that scholars have shown insufficient
appreciation of the function and significance of Moses and Elijah as
portrayed by the synoptic evangelists. For example in Mark, the Elijah-
Baptist-Jesus/suffering-death parallelism (in Mk 9.9-13) functions as an
hermeneutical control on Mk 9.2-8; but this control is muted by
Matthew and is abandoned by Luke. We saw that (1) Mark by redaction
and arrangement of his tradition has probably muted the Moses-Sinai
motif found originally in his source, in order to emphasise the Jesus-
Elijah parallelism. (2) Matthew by the insertion of the facial radiance and
light motifs has reinstated the Moses-Sinai motif. (3) Luke emphasises
the new-exodus motif rather than a Moses-Sinai parallelism and this is
shown in the Appendix.

At this introductory stage of my thesis, I proposed that the transfiguration, in Matthew in particular, looks more than anything else like a new

Sinai theophany and his merging of this with Danielic motifs, his 'Son of Man' *inclusio*, also his Elijah-resurrection motifs are explained in chs. 4 and 5.

Chapter 3: In this chapter I engaged in a study of the Moses-Sinai and transfiguration motifs in Philo, Josephus, Qumran, Samaritan literature, the Apocrypha and Pseudepigrapha and rabbinic literature. This study showed the pervasive influence of the Moses-Sinai motif in first-century Judaism, and all this contributed towards the Moses 'ideology' of the time, a factor that could not be ignored by the early Christian community.

Jewish identity at the time was very much bound up with the law and hence the figure of Moses. And Pharisaic theology, to take one example, with its stress on law, was a major challenge to the thinking of the early Jewish Christian community. This intellectual and theological climate also contributed towards the controversy between the Jews and the Christians, with the scribes and the Pharisees—who sat 'on Moses' seat' (23.2)— emphasising Moses' greatness, the law (23.23 also cf. 5.20; 19.7), the law related function of the Temple (24.1; 26.61), and their interpretation and traditions around the Mosaic law (15.1-20), and the Christians emphasising Jesus' greatness, and his teachings.

Chapter 4: With the Moses propaganda as a background, in chs. 4 and 5 it was shown how Matthew responds to this challenge. In this chapter I go on to show that Matthew has portrayed his transfiguration pericope within a vision-form (τὸ ὅραμα Mt. 17.9) paralleling both Moses-Sinai (cf. Exod. 3.3 τὸ ὅραμα LXX) and Daniel 7 (ἐν ὁράματι 7.13).

I also argued that Matthew presents the transfiguration within a Danielic Son of Man *inclusio* (16.27; 16.28–17.1-8–17.9; 17.12). This hermeneutical device enables him to blend Moses-Sinai and Daniel 7 motifs; in Matthew's theology of the transfiguration Jesus is the new and greater Moses precisely because he is the Danielic Son of Man, who is also the Son of God. The resulting Jesus-Son of Man-Sinai association is not entirely novel to Matthew, for I have shown that in an interesting passage in the pre-Christian Ezekiel the Tragedian, Daniel 7 categories are applied to Moses. Matthew goes further in that he also emphasises that Jesus is the Son of God. The exegetical and theological implications of this were worked out in ch. 5.

Chapter 5: This chapter is largely exegetical and the following salient points have emerged: my exegesis and redaction-critical study of Mt. 17.1-13 confirm the arguments in ch. 4, showing that Matthew has blended both Moses-Sinai and Daniel 7 apocalyptic motifs, using categories common to both traditions such as (1) the 'coming of God', (2) the kingdom of God, and (3) glory. Through the transfiguration, Matthew demonstrates that in Jesus 'the coming of God' has a past, present and future significance. (1) The transfiguration confirms his earlier emphasis that in Jesus, God had come (cf. 1.23; 3.3; 12.28). (2) In view of Matthew's Son of Man *inclusio* and especially the influence of Mt. 16.28, Matthew's transfiguration pericope also suggests that the 'coming of God' will take place in the near future, particularly in the cross-resurrection (16.21; 17.9; 17.2-23; 26.64; 27.51-54; 28.18-20). (3) in view of Mt. 16.27 and 28, Matthew portrays the transfiguration as a prolepsis of the 'coming of God in Jesus' which also will take place at the 'close of the age' (13.40-43; 16.27; 24.29-31; 25.31-33).

At the transfiguration Matthew presents Jesus as the Son of Man who is also the Son of God, and it is precisely because of this combination that he is greater than, or is the new and greater, Moses. Jesus represents and is new-Israel, with the three disciples as its potential nucleus. Heeding Jesus' words (17.5; Deut. 18.15) means heeding God (7.24-26; 28.19), or else meeting the consequences (Deut. 18.19; Mt. 26.27). So for Matthew, the transfiguration is also a demonstration of King Jesus in his kingdom which has immediate and far reaching consequences.

Matthew displays considerable interest in the Peter motif and at the transfiguration (1) he highlights Peter positively as one with a special role in Jesus' ἐκκλησια/kingdom-building (16.16-19). But (2) Matthew also points Peter to Jesus the true builder who was to be listened to. Matthew emphasises that the command 'listen to him' was particularly addressed to Peter. Peter's role was appreciated by the early Christian community, the over-emphasis on which caused problems for people like Paul.

I have shown that Matthew, by redaction of Mk 9.2-13 and by thematic and linguistic associations, has firmly linked the transfiguration with (1) the baptism (3.13-17), particularly the baptism-voice (3.17); (2) the temptation narrative (4.1-11); (3) the interpretation of the 'weeds and the tares' (13.36-43); (4) the passion narrative (especially with 27.32-54); and also (5) Jesus' post-resurrection appearance in 28.16-20; all of which points are further developed in ch. 6.

I have also argued that the 'light' at the transfiguration may also take on a theological and missiological significance and compares with (1) Jesus as light in the 'Galilee of the Gentiles' (4.15-16), (2) disciples as lights (5.14-16), (3) 'light and kingdom' (13.43), and that it anticipates

28.18-20. In this, Matthew's interests in theological-geography—Galilee (4.17–16.20; 16.21–18.35; 26.32; 28.10, 16), the 'Galilee of the Gentiles' (4.15), and the location of the transfiguration—play a crucial part.

It is clear that Matthew has redactionally and theologically linked this new-Sinai event of the transfiguration with all the major events in Jesus life and ministry, and so Mt. 17.1-8 occupies a pivotal place in Matthew's structure and theology.

Chapter 6: In this chapter I demonstrate that Matthew has woven this Moses-Christology into his whole gospel. (1) I show that the Moses-exodus and Israel-God's Son theme are applied to Jesus in the infancy narratives (Mt. 1–2). (2) In the baptism narrative (Mt. 3.13-17) too Matthew applies Moses-exodus-Israel themes and Yahweh–new exodus motifs to Jesus. In this passage, Matthew also takes further the Jesus-Israel-God's Son identification already seen in Mt. 2.15. (3) In the temptation narratives Matthew has combined Jesus-Israel and Jesus-manna-Moses ideas and possibly has portrayed Jesus as refusing 'pseudo-Sinai' glory and kingdom motifs at the mount of temptation. Matthew has also redactionally and theologically linked 4.8 with 17.1-8 and 28.18-20. (4) The link between the transfiguration and the sermon on the mount features prominently in my thesis and I have shown that Matthew 5–7 anticipate 17.1-8.

In this discussion I have argued that Matthew is conservative in his attitude to the law (cf. 5.1-20; 15.17-20; 23.2-3). Matthew stands within the mainstream of Jewish Christianity which was probably linked to the earliest Jerusalem community. Matthew presents the continuity but also the discontinuity (in the sense of being greater than) between (1) Jesus and Moses (19.3-9/5.31-32; 5.21-48), and (2) Jesus and Israel (2.15; 3.17; 4.1-11). He portrays Jesus as founder of renewed Israel (16.18-19): the renewed Israel starts—significantly—with the 'twelve' 10.1; 19.28, Peter playing a key role (16.16-19). In this section the light–mountain motifs in 5.14-16 and the redactional links between that passage and 17.2 and 28.18-20 were explored and were found to be plausible.

(5) I have tried to show that (a) the Moses-Sinai blood covenant in Exod. 24.3-8 and (b) the theme of the messianic banquet and Sinai in Exod. 24.11 and their links with Matthew's account of the last supper (Mt. 26.17-29) heighten Matthew's Moses-Jesus typology. (6) Finally Matthew concludes his 'gospel' on a mountain not in Zion-Jerusalem but in Galilee. He has portrayed Jesus' words here as of a Moses-type (Deut. 1–34) farewell discourse, and so his gospel comes to climax in a

powerful Jesus-Moses parallelism, where once again the 'commands' of Jesus, the new Moses, are emphasised.

In this chapter we also see that even though, for Matthew, Jesus is the 'Son of David', and hence Davidic Christology is important for Matthew (cf. Mt. 1.1–2.12), he senses that that was also open to, and had acquired, misleading nationalistic and perhaps militaristic overtones. He therefore found Son of David categories inadequate as a programmatic framework for his gospel. On the other hand, since Matthew stands solidly within the mainstream of Jewish Christianity—the type represented by James, Jesus' brother and also Peter—he found Moses categories adequate, appropriate and safe to frame his gospel with.

But at the transfiguration, this new-Moses, new-Sinai theme needs to be set in perspective. For Matthew has blended Moses-Sinai and Daniel 7 motifs. It is in his capacity as 'Son of Man' with the 'authority' that it entails (Mt. 9.6; 28.18) that Jesus 'fulfils' the law, radicalises parts of it, and even renders some of it redundant. It is as the Danielic 'Son of Man' that Jesus is the new and far greater Moses. By presenting Jesus as the new and greater Moses Matthew is able to portray Jesus' continuity and discontinuity with Israel, thereby initiating new Israel.

Chapter 7: Here I have argued that Matthew's Jesus-Moses parallelism and Christology is not an isolated and eccentric piece of theology in the development of early Christology, but is also paralleled in certain other New Testament writers. (1) The prophet-like-Moses motif is applied to Jesus in Acts 3.22-23 and 7.37. (2) In Heb. 3.3-6 Jesus is worthy of 'much more glory than Moses': and it is not inconceivable that Heb. 3.3 echoes a transfiguration tradition, particularly akin to Matthew's. (3) Whether 2 Pet. 1.16-18 supports a Sinai motif is debatable, but (a) its emphasis on the glory (τιμὴν καὶ δόξαν 1.17), which Jesus receives from God his Father (1.17) and (b) its emphasis on sonship (1.17) certainly ties in with the similar theme in Heb. 3.3-6 and Mt. 17.1-8. If a Petrine tradition is behind 2 Pet. 1.16-18, then the use of this tradition perhaps also reflects Peter's elevation (precisely due to the transfiguration) in the early church.

(4) I also show that there is a very plausible echo of the transfiguration in John's prologue—καὶ ἐθεασάμεθα τὴν δόξαν αὐτοῦ—(1.14), a passage where there is also a Jesus-Moses comparison; a motif that fits in well with John's similar typology elsewhere in his gospel: for example, John 4 and the Samaritan *Taheb* concept, and John 6 with its Jesus-Moses-manna parallelism.

(5) I have also argued that it is probable that Paul considered his Damascus road experience comparable particularly to Peter's witness of the transfiguration . Through his polemical use of the Moses-doxa tradition in 2 Cor. 3.1-18; 4.1-6, (a) Paul emphasised his qualification as one who had also seen the glory of the Lord in the 'face of Jesus Christ': τῆς δόξης τοῦ Θεοῦ ἐν προσωπῳ 'Ιησοῦ Χριστοῦ (2 Cor. 4.6), and (b) just as he saw himself and the believer as incorporate in Christ (Gal. 4.19) and sharing in Christ's experiences: death (Gal. 3.20; Rom. 6.3-11), resurrection (Rom. 6.4-11; 1 Cor. 15; Phil. 3.10) and glorification (Phil. 3.21), he democratised the transfiguration motif and applied it to the believer (2 Cor. 3.18).

My thesis has shown the vital importance of the Moses-Jesus parallelism, and the Jesus/new and greater Moses motif for the early church. I have tried to show that Matthew represents the tradition that was sensitive to this aspect of early Christology. In his portrayal of the transfiguration pericope, Matthew has made a vital contribution towards this Moses-Christology. Matthew has used the transfiguration of Jesus as a polemic against the prevailing Moses, Sinai and law emphasis of the time.

So this thesis has shown that Moses-Christology was a much more important motif in the development of early Christology than has usually been recognised by contemporary scholarship. It confirms what many scholars have recently been rediscovering and reemphasising, namely that Jesus and early Christianity need to be understood in the context of first-century Judaism. This thesis is also relevant to discussion of Matthew's *Sitz im Leben*. For Matthew represents one stream of Jewish Christian tradition in which Peter and the law are especially highly regarded, and it is from this position that Matthew contends against the Pharisees with their emphasis on Moses and the law.

The thesis has also cast interesting light on early Christianity, on Paul and others. It has demystified the transfiguration and has shown its importance.

APPENDIX:

LUKE'S UNDERSTANDING OF THE TRANSFIGURATION

Introduction

Perhaps the two most pressing issues in Luke's presentation of the transfiguration are: (1) The minor agreements between Luke and Matthew against Mark, and so the issue whether Luke knew Matthew, and (2) Luke's conspicuous omission of Mk 9.11-13. Other issues include: (1) Luke's ὡσεὶ ἡμέραι ὀκτὼ (9.28) for ἡμέρας ἓξ in Mk 9.2 = Mt. 17.1 (see discussion in ch. 2). (2) He omits the term μετεμορφώθη (Mk 9.2 = Mt. 17.1). (3) He tells us that Jesus was transfigured while praying (9.29). (4) He alone gives the conversation between Jesus, Moses and Elijah: ἔλεγον τὴν ἔξοδον αὐτοῦ, ἣν ἤμελλεν πληροῦν ἐν Ἰερουσαλήμ (9.31). (5) In Luke alone Moses and Elijah are seen in glory (οἳ ὀφθέντες ἐν δόξῃ, 9.31), a motif also applied to Jesus in v. 32 τὴν δόξαν αὐτοῦ καὶ τοὺς δύο ἄνδρας τοὺς συνεστῶτας αὐτῷ. (6) He alone calls Moses and Elijah ἄνδρες δύο (9.30, 32). These points naturally raise source and redaction critical issues. In this short appendix I shall comment on the main issues, firstly the minor agreements.

1. *The Minor Agreements between Luke and Matthew against Mark*

The minor agreements in the triple tradition pose problems for Markan priorists. For recent discussion see Davies and Allison, who solve the riddle by appeal to coincidental editing, oral tradition, and textual corruption.[1] Others, while accepting Markan priority, get around the problem of minor agreements by postulating that Luke knew Matthew.[2]

This treatment of the issue can only be brief, and I am indebted in this to F. Neirynck's article 'Minor Agreements Matthew-Luke in the Transfiguration Story'.[3]

---

1.   Davies and Allison, *Saint Matthew*, I, pp. 109-114.
2.   Farrer, 'On Dispensing with Q', in Nineham (ed.), *Studies in the Gospels*, pp. 55-88; A.W. Argyle, 'Evidence for the View that St Luke Used St Matthew's Gospel', *JBL* 83 (1964), pp. 390-96; Goulder, 'On Putting Q to the Test', *NTS* 24 (1978), pp. 218-34; Gundry, *Matthew*, p. 346.
3.   F. Neirynck, 'Minor Agreements Matthew-Luke in the Transfiguration Story', in P. Hoffmann (ed.), *Orientierung an Jesus: Zur Theologie der Synoptiker* (Freiburg: Herder, 1973), pp. 253-66.

He helpfully sets out the minor agreements. I shall use his analysis without endorsing all his conclusions.[4] The following are the minor agreements:

(a)   *Mt. 17.1/Lk. 9.28:* Here both omit τὸν before Ἰάκωβον καὶ Ἰωάννην contra Mk 9.2. But Luke differs from Matthew in omitting τὸν from the names of all three disciples, and the omission may well be purely stylistic. We have noted that Matthew has τὸν before Peter (τὸν Πέτρον) probably emphasising Peter's role.[5]

(b)   *Mt. 17.2/Lk. 9.29:* Here (i) both refer to Jesus' transfigured face contra Mark. (ii) Mt./Lk. omit στίλβοντα (Mk 9.3). (iii) Mt./Lk. omit Mark's οἷα γναφεὺς . . . λευκᾶναι (Mk 9.3). Point (i) is significant, but by itself it does not suggest Luke's dependence on Matthew. We would have to explain why Luke changed Matthew's 'sun' analogy ὡς ὁ ἥλιος to simply ἕτερον. However there seem to be several words in Luke: τὸ εἶδος, ἕτερον, ἐξαστράπτων (the latter not unlike Matthew's ὡς ὁ ἥλιος) that suggest Luke's free use of Mark and/or his access to a different source (Matthew seems to follow Mark more closely: note the use of μετεμορφώθη ἔμπροσθεν αὐτοῦ . . . τὰ (δὲ) ἱμάτια αὐτοῦ ἐγένετο λευκὰ 17.2/Mk 9.3). Each minor agreement may not be significant, but the three taken together may point to a common source.

(c)   *Mt. 17.3/Lk. 9.30:* Here (i) both begin with καὶ ἰδού, (ii) both change Mark's order to Moses and Elijah, using καί instead of σύν, (iii) and both omit τῷ Ἰησοῦ. The use of καὶ ἰδού, however, is characteristic of both Matthew and Luke (note Luke's Septuagintisms), and in context also seem to bring out the theophanic and in Luke's case angelophanic motifs; for example, note the link between ἄνδρες δύο (9.30, 31) with the same use of the 'two' angels in 24.24.4; Acts 1.10. The change of Mark's order to 'Moses and Elijah' was the natural/chronological order in which they appear in the OT, and need not suggest Lukan dependence on Matthew. And yet, it may depend on early transfiguration traditions that cited them in this order.[6] The omission of τῷ Ἰησοῦ and insertion of μετ' αὐτοῦ (Mt.), αὐτῷ (Lk.), may be explained as independent and insignificant modifications of Mark.

---

4.   Neirynck dismisses sources other than Mark. This is followed by Fitzmyer, *The Gospel according to Luke*, I, pp. 791-92; Davies and Allison, *Saint Matthew*, II, p. 685.

5.   For such an emphatic use of the article see: F. Blass, *Grammar of the New Testament Greek* (London: Macmillan, 1898), pp. 162-63.

6.   At least Lk. 1.1-3 allows for many sources. That Luke has access to 'a couple of sources' in his transfiguration pericope, see Marshall, *Luke*, p. 381; also see B.O. Reid, 'Voices and Angels: What Were they Talking about at the Transfiguration? A Redaction-Critical Study of Luke 9.28-36', *Biblical Research* 34 (1989), pp. 19-31; J. Murphy-O'Connor, 'What Really Happened at the Transfiguration?', *Bible Review* 3 (1987), pp. 8-21. T.W. Manson, *The Teaching of Jesus* (Cambridge: Cambridge University Press, 1955), p. 32, makes an interesting suggestion that Lk. 10.23-24, (Mt. 10.41) belongs to the context of the transfiguration, influenced by a 'Q version of the event'.

(d) *Mt. 17.4/Lk. 9.33:* Here (i) both have εἶπεν for Mark's λέγει. But εἶπεν is widely used by both Matthew and Luke. (ii) Mark's ῥαββί is changed to κύριε (Mt.) and ἐπιστάτα (Lk.). This is hardly an agreement but reflects Matthew's and Luke's individual theological interests. For example Luke uses ἐπιστάτα (cf. 8.24, 45; 9.33, 49; 17.13), when the synoptic parallels have either διδάσκαλος (Mk 4.38; 9.38), or κύριος (Mt. 17.4). Perhaps it is also significant that Luke permits ἐπιστάτα to be used only by the disciples, or near-disciples, whereas διδάσκαλος is used by non-disciples (7.40).

(e) *Mt. 17.5/Lk. 9.34:* Here both change Mark's participle ἐπισκιάζουσα to ἐπεσκίασεν (Mt.) and ἐπεσκίαζεν (Lk.). But both are taken from Mark's ἐπισκιάζουσα and so may be taken as independent redactions of it.

(f) *Mt. 17.5/Lk. 9.35:* Both use λέγουσα absent in Mark. Some Markan manuscripts include λέγουσα (e.g. A D W Θ λ φ 33 *al* lat syᵖ) and if Matthew and Luke used such a text, then their agreement is explained. Admittedly, here the agreement is more striking than our previous examples. It may be coincidental, but allusion to a common source may not be ruled out.

Observations

Some of the minor agreements can be explained in terms of stylistic traits and redaction, with Luke displaying a freer use of Mark than Matthew, who follows Mark closely. There is no clear evidence of Lukan dependence on Matthew. On the other hand, the cumulative weight of agreements could suggest that Matthew and Luke may have had access to another source than Mark. The possibility of the influence of oral tradition and other sources on the gospel-writing process are increasingly being recognised by scholars. For while recent debate on the synoptic problem has been dominated by the two rival themes of literary dependence, the two-document and Griesbach theories, scholars have increasingly questioned theories based on simple literary dependence and 'linear solutions' to the synoptic problem.[7]

2. *Luke's Omission of Mark 9.11-13 (Mt. 17.10-13) and the 'Coming of Elijah'*

The Elijah-John and Elijah-Jesus relationship in Luke's Gospel has been much debated. H. Conzelmann disregards Luke's birth narrative and John's role in it, and concludes that John is not Elijah *redivivus* but, as in 16.16, he is last of the OT prophets.[8] A similar view (but accepting the birth narratives) is held by W. Wink, A. Hastings, and R. Zehnle.[9] According to J.A.T. Robinson,[10] Luke applies the Elijah motif to both John and Jesus, and this is due to a combination of traditions which

7.   On this see discussion in ch. 1 and works cited there.

8.   Conzelmann, *The Theology of St Luke*, pp. 18-27, 101f., 167.

9.   W. Wink, *John the Baptist in the Gospel Tradition* (Cambridge: Cambridge University Press, 1968), pp. 42-43; A. Hastings, *Prophet and Witness in Jerusalem* (Baltimore: Helicon, 1958), p. 75; R. Zehnle, *Peter's Pentecost Discourse* (Nashville: Abingdon Press, 1971), p. 58.

10.   Robinson, 'Elijah, John and Jesus', pp. 263-81.

remain in tension. For the Baptist, however, Jesus was Elijah *redivivus*. This is supported by J. Fitzmyer,[11] and E. Franklin.[12] Recently R.J. Miller tries to show that for Luke, Jesus is not Elijah (e.g. 7.27), but that the Baptist (who denies an Elijah role in Jn 1.21) attributes the eschatological role to Jesus.[13]

The debate on Luke's understanding of the Elijah-John connection goes on. It may be that Luke omits Mk 9.11-13 (Mt. 17.10-13), because, according to Luke, Elijah's 'restoration' ministry (Mal. 4.5-6) was not completely fulfilled by John, but would be fulfilled by Jesus. In Acts 3.21, Peter speaks of the anticipated 'times of restitution' (χρόνων ἀποκαταστάσεως πάντων), a phrase which not only needs to be taken with ἀποκαθιστάνεις in 1.6, but also in relation to Elijah's restoration in Mk 9.12 (ἀποκαθιστάνει and ἀποκαταστήσει Mt. 17.11), the very pericope omitted by Luke. If χρόνων ἀποκαταστάσεως πάντων is seen as an 'Elijah motif', then Luke transfers to the expected advent of Jesus language originally applied to the ministry of Elijah.[14]

Moreover, Luke does show particular interest in Jesus-Elijah typology, and attributes Elijah-type functions to Jesus: (1) In Lk. 3.16-17 the themes of 'winnowing' and 'clearing the threshing floor'—qualities of a fiery prophetic figure—fit the figure of Elijah. (2) In 4.1-2 both Elijah and Moses motifs seem to be attributed to him. (3) Moreover, in Luke alone Jesus explicitly compares himself with Elijah (and Elisha) in 4.25-27; a passage which closely follows the Nazareth manifesto (4.16-18 = Isa. 61.1-2). (4) In 7.11-16 Jesus does an Elijah-type miracle. (5) ὁ ἐρχόμενος in the Q passage of 7.18-23/Mt. 11.2-6 is interesting. It is arguable that in view of τοῦ Χριστοῦ in 11.2 (absent in Luke) Matthew's ὁ ἐρχόμενος takes the meaning of 'Messiah' here. But since Mt. 11.2 is absent in Luke, it is possible to argue that in 7.27 Jesus reverses the role attributed to him by the Baptist. If so, ὁ ἐρχόμενος in Luke could mean the Elijah of Mal. 3.1. In Lk. 9.8 (Mk 6.15), he was precisely taken to be so by the people. Other Jesus-Elijah motifs have also been seen in 9.8, 30, 51, 54-55, 61-62, perhaps 10.1-12; 12.49-53. And the 'ascension' theme in Lk. 24.51, Acts 1.9 (also ἀναλήμψεως Lk. 9.51) has been viewed in relation to the Elijah-translation theme (2 Kgs 2).[15]

11. Fitzmyer, *The Gospel According to Luke*, I, pp. 472-73.

12. E. Franklin, *Christ the Lord: A Study in the Purpose and Theology of Luke–Acts* (Philadelphia: Westminster Press, 1975), p. 200.

13. R.J. Miller, 'Elijah, John and Jesus in the Gospel of Luke', *NTS* 34 (1988), pp. 611-22.

14. For the 'restoration' idea see R.B. Rackham, *The Acts of the Apostles* (London: Methuen, 1901), pp. 53-54; W.M. Furneaux, *The Acts of the Apostles* (Oxford; Clarendon Press, 1901), p. 56; Haenchen, *The Acts of the Apostles*, p. 208; Marshall, *Luke*, p. 94.

15. Several scholars have tried to highlight this Jesus-Elijah/Elisha parallelism in Luke: see W. Wink, *John the Baptist in the Gospel Tradition*, p. 43, notes Acts 1.4-5, 9, 11 etc. Some of Wink's examples are criticised by Miller, *NTS* 34 (1988), pp. 611-22, though there is more to some of Wink's arguments than Miller would allow. See also T.L. Brodie, 'Towards Unravelling Luke's Use of the Old Testament: Luke 7.11-17 as an imitatio of 1 Kings 17.17-24', *NTS* 32 (1986), pp. 247-67; C.A. Evans, 'Luke's Use of the Elijah/Elisha Narratives and the Ethic of Election', *JBL* 106/1 (1987), pp. 75-83. For Jesus-Elisha parallels: H.J. Blair, ' "Putting One's Hand to the Plough", Luke ix.62 in the light of 1 Kings xix.19-21', *ExpTim* 79 (1967–68), pp. 342-43; D.G. Bostock, 'Jesus as the New Elisha', *ExpTim* 92 (1980–81), pp. 39-41; T.L. Brodie, 'Jesus as the New Elisha:

Observations

Thus, in view of Luke–Acts' interest in the Jesus-Elijah parallelism, Luke's omission of Mk 9.9-13 perhaps suggests that, just as he saw an Elijah-Jesus parallelism in Jesus' earthly ministry, he also gave Jesus an eschatological Elijah-type function (cf. Acts 3.21); that is, Luke was interested in an Elijah-Christology.

3. *Luke's Exodus Emphasis*

Luke's interest in the 'exodus' motif, in certain cases with its Moses-new-exodus ramifications, has been recognised by several scholars.[16] In this the exodus-Jerusalem reference in the transfiguration pericope is crucial, since Lk. 9.28-36 occupies a key position leading into Luke's 'central section' which C.F. Evans sees as parallel in structure to Deuteronomy.[17] Some of Evans' parallels are unimpressive, but, with modifications, other scholars have supported Evans' thesis about Luke's 'central section'.[18] Apart from the book of Deuteronomy itself, the 'exodus' theme has recently been emphasised by D.A.S. Ravens, who argues that Luke's positioning of the three miracles, 'feeding' (9.12-17), 'transfiguration' (9.28-36) and 'healing of the possessed boy, preceded by lack of faith' (9.38-43), recall Israel's wilderness experiences: 'manna', 'Moses on Sinai', 'golden calf'.[19] And here, he points out that the order he has suggested fits the book of Exodus rather than Deuteronomy.

Whatever the case, it is sufficiently clear that Luke is interested in the exodus theme in this part of his Gospel, and his distinctive reference at the transfiguration to τὴν ἔξοδον αὐτοῦ (9.31, which would include death/resurrection/ascension themes) betrays his interest in the Jesus-new-exodus theme.[20]

4. *Links with Other Parts of Luke–Acts*

G.B. Caird held that a satisfactory explanation of the transfiguration must recognise its connection with 'the baptism, Caesarea Philippi, Gethsamane, crucifixion, resurrection,

Cracking the Code', *ExpTim* 93 (1981), pp. 39-42; R.E. Brown, 'Jesus and Elisha', *Perspective* 12 (1971), pp. 85-104 (in John's Gospel).

16. See J. Manek, 'The New Exodus in the Books of Luke', *NovT* 2 (1958), pp. 8-23; D.P. Moessner, 'Luke 9.1-50: Luke's Preview of the Journey of the Prophet Like Moses of Deuteronomy', *JBL* 102/4 (1983), pp. 575-605; D.A.S. Ravens, 'Luke 9.7-62 and the Prophetic Role of Jesus', *NTS* 36 (1990), pp. 119-29.

17. C.F. Evans, 'The Central Section of St Luke's Gospel', in D.E. Nineham (ed.), *Studies in the Gospels* (Oxford: Basil Blackwell, 1957), pp. 37-53, and in his commentary *Saint Luke* (London: SCM Press, 1990), pp. 34-35.

18. See J. Drury, *Tradition and Design in Luke's Gospel* (London: Darton, Longman & Todd, 1976), esp. pp. 138-64; J.M. Derrett, *The Law in the New Testament* (London: Longman and Todd, 1970), esp. pp. 126-55; M.D. Goulder, *The Evangelist's Calendar* (London: SPCK, 1978), esp. pp. 95-101, also Moessner, 'Luke 9.1-50', pp. 575-605; and his earlier work: 'Jesus and the "Wilderness Generation": The Death of the Prophet Like Moses according to Luke', in K.H. Richards (ed.), *SBLSP* (Chico: Scholars Press, 1982), esp. pp. 339-40; Evans, 'The Ethic of Election', esp. pp. 82-83.

19. Ravens, 'Luke 9.7-62', pp. 119-29.

20. Especially see Manek, 'The New Exodus', pp. 8-23; Ravens, 'Luke 9.7-62', pp. 119-29.

ascension, the parousia, the persecution of the disciples and their share in the present and future glory of the risen and ascended Christ, and its own importance as a crisis in the life of Jesus'.[21] Recently Caird's position has been affirmed by A.A. Trites,[22] who in addition to Caird's list also has linked it to the 'temptation' pericope. This is not a novel view since in various ways Manek, Conzelmann, Davies[23] have linked Lk. 9.28-36 with other passages within Luke. Trites and Davies, however, have by and large neglected the figures of Moses and Elijah (see ch. 2), but in general the links suggested are quite probable.

Some conclusions

Due to the nature of this appendix my evaluation and arguments have been very condensed, but the following conclusions may be drawn: (1) At least in the transfiguration pericope, most of Luke's minor agreements with Matthew may be explained via (a) Luke's freer redaction on Mark, and (b) his possible access to other sources. In our comparison no clear evidence has emerged of Luke's dependence on Matthew. (2) Due to Luke's exodus and Elijah emphasis, it is arguable that Luke has blended together Moses-Sinai and Elijah-Sinai and Jesus-Elijah typologies. (3) Lk. 9.28-36 occupies a key position leading into his central section and it has been structurally and redactionally linked to important events in Jesus' ministry.

21. G.B. Caird, 'The Transfiguration', *ExpTim* 67 (1955–56), pp. 291-94, quote from p. 292.

22. A.A. Trites, 'Transfiguration in the Theology of Luke', in L. Hurst and N.T. Wright (ed.), *The Glory of Christ in the New Testament: Studies in Christology* (Oxford: Clarendon Press, 1987), pp. 71-81; also his earlier article 'The Transfiguration of Jesus: The Gospel in Microcosom', *EvQ* 51 (1979), pp. 67-79.

23. Cf. Manek, 'The New Exodus', pp. 8-33; Conzelmann, *The Theology of Luke*, (1961), pp. 57-59 (links the passion); J.G. Davies, 'The Prefiguration of the Ascension in the Third Gospel', *JTS* 6 (1955), pp. 229-33 also in his *He Ascended into Heaven* (London: Lutterworth, 1958) (where he links the ascension).

BIBLIOGRAPHY

Aalen, S., 'δόξα', in C. Brown (ed.), *NIDNTT*, II, pp. 44-48.

Abrahams, I., *Studies in Pharisaism and the Gospels* (Second series; Cambridge: Cambridge University Press, 1924).

Aland, K., *Synopsis Quattuor Evangeliorum* (Stuttgart: Deutsche Bibelsellschaft, 13th edn, 1984).

Aland, K. *et al.* (eds.), *The Greek New Testament* (Stuttgart: United Bible Societies, 2nd edn, 1968).

—*Novum Testamentum Graece* (Stuttgart: Deutsche Bibelsellschaft, 26th edn, 1979).

Albright, W.F., 'The Names "Nazareth" and "Nazorean"', *JBL* 65 (1946), pp. 397-401.

Albright, W.F., and C.S. Mann, *Matthew* (Garden City, NY: Doubleday, 1973).

Allan, G., 'He shall be Called a Nazarite?', *ExpTim* 95 (1983), pp. 81-82.

Allegro, J.M., *The Dead Sea Scrolls* (Harmondsworth: Penguin, 1956).

—'Further Messianic References in Qumran Literature', *JBL* 75 (1956), pp. 186-87.

Allen, W.C., *A Critical and Exegetical Commentary on the Gospel according to St. Matthew* (Edinburgh: T. & T. Clark, 1912).

Allison, D.C., 'Elijah Must Come First', *JBL* 103 (1984), pp. 256-58.

—*The End of the Ages has Come* (Philadelphia: Fortress Press, 1985).

—'Jesus and Moses (Mt. 5.1-2)', *ExpTim* 98 (1986/7), pp. 203-205.

—*The New Moses: A Matthean Typology* (Minneapolis: Fortress Press, 1993).

Alsup, J.E., *The Post-Resurrection Appearance Stories of the Gospel Tradition* (Stuttgart: Calwer Verlag; London: SPCK, 1975).

Ambrozic, A., *The Hidden Kingdom: A Redaction-Critical Study of the References to the Kingdom of God in Mark's Gospel* (Washington, DC: Catholic Biblical Association of America, 1972).

Anderson, B.W., 'Exodus Typology in Second Isaiah', in B.W. Anderson and W. Harrelson (eds.), *Israel's Prophetic Heritage* (London: SCM Press, 1962).

Anderson, H., *The Gospel of Mark* (London: Oliphants, 1976).

Argyle, A.W., *The Gospel according to Matthew* (Cambridge: Cambridge University Press, 1963).

—'Evidence for the View that St.Luke Used St. Matthew's Gospel', *JBL* 83 (1964), pp. 390-96.

Ashton, J., *Understanding the Fourth Gospel* (Oxford: Oxford University Press, 1993).

Attridge, H.W., *The Epistle to the Hebrews* (Philadelphia: Fortress Press, 1989).

Auerbach, E., *Moses* (Detroit: Wayne State University, 1975).

Aune, D., *Prophecy in Early Christianity and the Ancient Mediterranean World* (Grand Rapids: Eerdmans, 1983).

Bacon, B.W., 'The Transfiguration Story', *AJT* 6 (1902), pp. 236-65.

—'The "Five Books" of Matthew against the Jews', *Expositor* 15, (1918), pp. 56-66.

—'Jesus and the Law: A Study of the First "Book" of Matthew (Mt. 3-7)', *JBL* 47 (1928), pp. 203-31.

—*Studies in Matthew* (London: Constable, 1930).

Badcock, F.J., 'The Transfiguration', *JTS* 22 (1921), pp. 321-26.

Bailey, J.L., 'Josephus' Portrayal of the Matriarchs' in L.H. Feldman, and G. Hata, (eds.), *Josephus, the Bible and History* (Detroit: Wayne, 1989), pp. 170-71.

Bailey, K.E., *Poet and Peasant, A Literary Cultural Approach to the Parables in Luke* (Grand Rapids: Eerdmans, 1976).

Baltensweiler, H., *Die Verklärung Jesu* (Zürich: Zwingli Verlag, 1959).

Banks, R., 'Matthew's Understanding of the Law: Authenticity and Interpretation in Matthew 5.17-20', *JBL* 93 (1974), pp. 226-42.

—*Jesus and the Law in the Synoptic Tradition* (Cambridge: Cambridge University Press, 1975).

Barth, G., 'Matthew's Understanding of the Law', in G. Bornkamm, G. Barth and H.J. Held (eds.), *Tradition and Interpretation in Matthew* (London: SCM Press, 1960).

Barrett, C.K., *Jesus and the Gospel Tradition* (London: SPCK, 1967).

—*A Commentary on the Second Epistle to the Corinthians* (London: Black, 1973).

—*The Gospel according to St. John* (London: SPCK, 2nd edn, 1978).

Bassuk, D.E., *Incarnation in Hinduism and Christianity* (London: Macmillan, 1987).

Bauckham, R.J., 'The Martyrdom of Enoch and Elijah: Jewish or Christian?' *JBL* 95/3 (1976), pp. 447-58.

—'The Son of Man: "A man in my position" or "someone"?' *JSNT* 23 (1985), pp. 23-33.

—*Jude, 2 Peter* (Waco: Word, 1986).

Bauer, D.R., *The Structure of Matthew's Gospel* (Sheffield: Almond Press, 2nd edn, 1989).

Bauer, W., *A Greek–English Lexicon of the New Testament and Other Early Christian Literature* (trans. W.F. Arndt and F.W. Gingrich; rev. F.W. Gingrich and F.W. Danker; Chicago: University of Chicago Press, 2nd edn, 1979).

Beale, G.K., 'The Use of Daniel in the Synoptic Eschatological Discourse and in the Book of Daniel' in D. Wenham (ed.), *Gospel Perspectives* (6 vols.; Sheffield: JSOT Press, 1984), V, pp. 129-53.

Beare, F.W., *The Gospel according to Matthew* (Oxford: Blackwell, 1981).

Beasley-Murray, G.R., *Jesus and the Future* (London: Macmillan, 1954).

—*Jesus and the Kingdom of God* (Grand Rapids: Eerdmans/Exeter: Paternoster, 1987).

—*John* (Waco: Word, 1987).

—'Resurrection and Parousia of the Son of Man', *TynBul* 42.2 (1991), pp. 298-309.

Behm, J., 'μεταμορφω', *TDNT*, IV, p. 756.

Belleville, L.L., *Reflections of Glory: Paul's Polemical Use of the Moses-Doxa tradition in 2 Corinthians 3.1-18* (Sheffield: JSOT Press, 1991).

Bentzen, A., *King and Messiah* (London: Lutterworth, 1955).

Bernardin, J.B., 'The Transfiguration', *JBL* 52 (1933), pp. 181-89.

Best, E., *The Temptation and Passion: The Markan Soteriology* (Cambridge: Cambridge University Press, 1965).

—*Following Jesus: Discipleship in the Gospel of Mark* (JSNTSup, 4; Sheffield: JSOT Press, 1981).

—*Mark: The Gospel Story* (Edinburgh: T. & T. Clark, 1983).

Best, T.F., 'The Transfiguration: A Select Bibliography', *JETS* 24 (1981), pp. 157-61.

Betz, H.D., 'Jesus as Divine Man', in F.T. Trotter (ed.), *Jesus the Historian* (Philadelphia: Westminster Press, 1968), pp. 114-30.

Betz, O., 'Miracles in the Writings of Flavius Josephus', in L.H. Feldman and G. Hata (eds.), *Josephus, Judaism and Christianity* (Leiden: Brill, 1987), pp. 212-35.

Bigg, C., *A Critical and Exegetical Commentary on the Epistles of St. Peter and St. Jude* (Edinburgh: T. & T. Clark, 1910).

Black, M., *The Scrolls and Christian Origins: Studies in the Jewish Background of the New Testament* (New York: Scribner, 1961).

Blackburn, B.L., 'Miracle Working θEIOI ANΔPEΣ in Hellenism (and Hellenistic Judaism)', in D. Wenham and C. Blomberg (eds.), *Gospel Perspectives* (6 vols.; Sheffield: JSOT Press, 1986), VI, pp. 185-218.

Blair, E.P., *Jesus in the Gospel of Matthew* (New York: Abingdon Press, 1960).

Blair, H.J., '"Putting One's Hand to the Plough", Luke ix.62 in the Light of 1 Kings xix.19-21', *ExpTim* 79 (1967-68), pp. 342-43.

Blass, F., *Grammar of New Testament Greek* (London: Macmillan, 1898).

—and Debrunner, A., and Funk, R.W., *A Greek Grammar of the New Testament and other Early Christian Literature* (Chicago: University of Chicago Press, 1961).

Bloch, R. 'Methodological Note for the Study of Rabbinic Literature', in W.S. Green (ed.), *Approach to Ancient Judaism: Theory and Practice* (Missoula, MT: Scholars Press, 1978), pp. 51-75.

Blomberg, C.L., 'Midrash, Chiasmus, and the Outline of Luke's Central Section', in R.T. France and D. Wenham (eds.), *Gospel Perspectives. III. Studies in Midrash and Historiography* (Sheffield: JSOT Press, 1983).

Bonnard, P., *L'Evangile selon saint Matthieu* (Neuchâtel: Delachaux and Niestlé, 1963).

Boobyer, G.H., *St Mark and the Transfiguration Story* (Edinburgh: T. & T. Clark, 1942).

Borg, M.J., *Conflict, Holiness and Politics in the Teachings of Jesus* (NY & Toronto: Mellen, 1984).

Borgen, P., 'God's Agent in the Fourth Gospel', in J. Neusner, (ed.), *Religions in Antiquity* (Leiden: Brill, 1968), pp. 137-48, reprinted in *Logos was the True Light and Other Essays in the Gospel of John* (Trondheim, 1983), pp. 121-32.

—*Philo, John and Paul* (Atlanta: Scholars Press, 1987).

Bornkamm, G., 'The Authority to "Bind" and "Loose" in the Church', in G.N. Stanton (ed.), *The Interpretation of Matthew* (London: SPCK, 1983).

Borsch, F.H., *The Son of Man in Myth and History* (London: SCM Press, 1967).

Bostock, D.G., 'Jesus as the New Elisha', *ExpTim* 92 (1980-81), pp. 39-41.

Bourke, M.M., 'The Literary Genus of Matthew 1–2', *CBQ* 22 (1960), pp. 160-75.

Bowman, J., 'Early Samaritan Eschatology', *JJS* 6.2 (1955), pp. 63-72.

—'The Samaritan Studies', *BJRL* 40 (1958), pp. 298-327.

—'The Importance of Samaritan Researches', *Leeds University Oriental Society* (1960), pp. 43-54

—*The Samaritan Problem: Studies in the Relationships of Samaritanism Judaism, and Early Christianity* (originally published as *Samaritanische Probleme; Studien zum Verhaltnis von Samaritanertum, Judentum und Urchristendum*) (Pennsylvania: Pickwick, 1975).

Brady, J., 'The Rôle of Miracle-Working as Authentication of Jesus as "The Son of God" ', *Churchman*, 103.1 (1989), pp. 32-39.

Braithwaite, W.C., 'The Teaching of the Transfiguration', *ExpTim* 17 (1905–1906), pp. 372-75.

Bretscher, P.G., 'Exodus 4.22-23 and the Voice from Heaven', *JBL* 87 (1968), pp. 301-11.

Bright, J., *A History of Israel* (London: SCM Press, 1972).

Brockington, L.H., 'The Septuagintal Background to the New Testament use of δόξα', in D.E. Nineham (ed.), *Studies in the Gospels* (Oxford: Blackwell, 1955).

Brodie, T.L., 'Jesus as the New Elisha: Cracking the Code', *ExpTim* 93 (1981), pp. 39-42.

—'Towards Unravelling Luke's Use of the Old Testament: Luke 7.11-17 as an imitatio of 1 Kings 17.17-24', *NTS* 32 (1986), pp. 247-67.

—*The Gospel according to John* (Oxford: Oxford University Press, 1993).

Brooke, G.J., 'The Amos-Numbers Midrash (CD 7.13b-8.1a) and Messianic Expectation', *ZNW* 92 (1980), pp. 397-403.

Brower, K., 'Mark 9.1 Seeing the Kingdom in Power', *JSNT* 6 (1980), pp. 17-26.

Brown, C., 'Word', in *NIDNTT*, III, pp. 1081-119;

Brown, R.E., 'The Messianism of Qumran', *CBQ* 19 (1957), pp. 82-83.

—'J. Starcky's Theory of Qumran Messianic Development', *CBQ* 28 (1966), pp. 51-57.

—'The Teacher of Righteousness and the Messiah(s)', in M. Black (ed.), *The Scrolls and Christianity* (London: SPCK, 1969), pp. 37-44, 109-12.

—*The Gospel according to John*, I (2 vols.; Garden City, NY: Doubleday, 1966–71).

—'Jesus and Elisha', *Perspective* 12 (1971), pp. 85-104.

—*The Birth of the Messiah: A Commentary on the Infancy Narratives in Matthew and Luke* (London: Chapman, 1977).

—*The Epistles of John* (London: Chapman, 1982).

—'The Gospel of Peter and Canonical Gospel Priority', *NTS* 33 (1987), pp. 321-43.

Brown, S., 'The Two-fold Representation of the Mission in Matthew's Gospel', *ST* (1977), pp. 21-32.

—'The Mission to Israel in Matthew's Central Section', *ZNW* 69 (1978), pp. 73-90.

Brownlee, W.H., 'Messianic Motifs of Qumran and the New Testament', *NTS* 3 (1956–57), pp. 12-30, 195-210.

—*Ezekiel 1–19* (Waco: Word, 1986).

Bruce, F.F., *1 and 2 Corinthians* (Grand Rapids: Eerdmans; London: Marshall, Morgan & Scott, 1971).

—*The Epistle of Paul to the Galatians* (Exeter: Paternoster Press, 1982).

—*The Epistle to the Hebrews* (Grand Rapids: Eerdmans, 2nd edn, 1988).

—*The Book of the Acts* (Grand Rapids: Eerdmans, 1989).

—*The Acts of the Apostles* (Grand Rapids: Eerdmans; Leicester: Apollos, 1990).

Buchanan, G., 'Samaritan Origin of the Gospel of John', in J. Neusner (ed.), *Religions in Antiquity* (Leiden: Brill, 1968), pp. 149-75.

—'The Use of Rabbinic Literature in New Testamnent Research', *BTB* 7 (1977), pp. 110-22.

Bultmann. R., *The History of the Synoptic Tradition* (Oxford: Blackwell, 1963).

—*The Gospel of John* (Oxford: Blackwell, 1971).

Burkill, T.A., *Mysterious Revelations: An Examinationof the Philosophy of Mark* (Ithaca, NY: Cornell University Press, 1963).

Burn, A.E., 'The Transfiguration', *ExpTim* 14 (1902-3), pp. 442-47.

Burrows, M., 'The Messiah of Aaron and Israel (DSD IX, 11)', *ATR* 34 (1952), pp. 202-206.

Buse, I., 'The Markan Account of the Baptism of Jesus and Isaiah LXIII', *JTS* 7 (1956), pp. 74-75.

Caird, G.B., *The New Testament Conception of doxa* (unpublished dissertation; Oxford, 1944).

—'The Transfiguration', *ExpTim* 67 (1955–56), pp. 291-94.

—'Everything to Everyone: A Theology of the Corinthian Epistles', *Interpretation* 13 (1959), pp. 387-99.

—*Saint Luke* (Harmondsworth: Penguin, 1963).

—*Jesus and the Jewish Nation* (London: Athlone, 1965).

—*Language and Imagery of the Bible* (London: Duckworth, 2nd edn, 1988).

Caragounis, C.C., *The Son of Man: Vision and Interpretation* (Tübingen: Mohr, 1986).

Carson, D.A., 'Matthew', in F. Gaebelein (ed.), *The Expositor's Bible Commentary* (12 vols.; Grand Rapids: Zondervan, 1984), VIII, pp. 3-599.

—*The Gospel According to John* (Leicester: IVP, 1991).

Carlston, C.E., 'Transfiguration and Resurrection', *JBL* 80 (1961), pp. 233-40.

—'The Things that Defile (Mark 7.14) and the Law in Matthew and Mark', *NTS* 15, (1968–69), pp. 57-69.

Catchpole, D.R., 'The Answer of Jesus to Caiaphas (Mt. XXVI.64)', *NTS* 17 (1970/1), pp. 213-26.

Casey, M., 'Method in our Madness, and Madness in their Methods: Some Approaches to the Son of Man Problem in Recent Scholarship', *JSNT* 42 (1991), pp. 17-43.

Chavasse, C., 'Jesus: Christ and Moses', *Theology* 373.54 (1951), pp. 244-50, continued in 374.54, (1951), pp. 289-96.

—*The Servant and the Prophet*, 1972.

Charlesworth, J.H., 'The Concept of the Messiah in the Pseudepigrapha', *ANRW*, II 19.1 (1979), pp. 188-218.

—*The Old Testament Pseudepigrapha* (2 vols.; London: Darton, Longman & Todd, 1983, 1985).

—*Jesus within Judaism* (London: SPCK, 1988).

Childs, B.S., *Exodus* (London: SCM Press, 1974).

Chilton, B.D., *God in Strength* (Freistadt: Plöchl, 1977).

—'An Evangelical and Critical Approach to the Sayings of Jesus', *Themelios* 3 (1977–78), pp. 78-85.

—'The Transfiguration: Dominical Assurance and Apostolic Vision', *NTS* 27 (1980), pp. 115-24.

Clark, K.W., 'The Gentile Bias in Matthew', *JBL* 66 (1947), pp. 165-72.

Clements, R.E., *God and Temple* (Oxford: Blackwell, 1965).

—*Old Testament Theology* (London: Marshall, Morgan & Scott, 1978).

Clifford, R.J., *The Cosmic Mountain in Canaan and the Old Testament* (Cambridge, MA: Harvard University Press, 1972).

Coats, G.W., *Moses: Heroic Man, Man of God* (Sheffield: JSOT Press, 1988).

Coggins, R.J., *The Samaritans and Jews* (Oxford: Blackwells, 1975).

—'The Samaritans and Acts', *NTS* 28 (1982), pp. 423-34.

—'The Samaritans in Josephus', in L.H. Feldman and G. Hata (eds.), *Josephus, Judaism, and Christianity* (Leiden: Brill, 1987), pp. 257-73.

Combrink, H.J.B., 'The Structure of the Gospel of Matthew as Narrative', *TynBul*, 34 (1983), pp. 61-90.

Conzelmann, H., *The Theology of Saint Luke* (London: Faber and Faber, 1961).

—*Acts of the Apostles* (Philadelphia: Fortress Press, 1987).

Cowley, A.E., 'The Samaritan Liturgy, and Reading of the Law', *JJS* 8 (1894), pp. 121-40.

—'The Samaritan Doctrine of the Messiah', *Expositor*, fifth Series, 1 (1895), pp. 161-74.

—(ed.), *The Samaritan Liturgy* (2 vols.; Oxford: Clarendon Press, 1909).

Cox, G.E.P., *The Gospel of St. Matthew* (London: SCM Press, 1952).

Craigie, P.C., *The Book of Deuteronomy* (Grand Rapids: Eerdmans, 1976).

Cranfield, C.E.B., 'The Baptism of our Lord: A Study of St. Mark 1.9-11', *SJT* 8 (1955), pp. 53-63.

—'Thoughts on New Testament Eschatology', *SJT* 35 (1982), pp. 497-512.

Crown, A.D., 'Some Traces of Heterodox Theology in the Samaritan Book of Joshua', *BJRL* 50 (1967), pp. 178-98.

—*The Samaritans* (Tübingen: Mohr, 1989).

Cullmann, O., *Peter: Disciple, Apostle, Martyr* (London: SCM Press, 1952).

—*Baptism in the New Testament* (London: SCM Press, 1958).

—*The Christology of the New Testament* (London: SCM Press, 1963).

—*The Johannine Circle: Its Place in Judaism, among the Disciples of Jesus and in Early Christianity* (London: SCM Press, 1976).

Dabeck, P., '"Siehe, es erschienen Moses und Elias" (Mt. 17.3)', *Bib* 23 (1942), pp. 175-89.

Daly, R.J., 'The Soteriological Significance of the Sacrifice of Isaac', *CBQ* 39 (1977), pp. 68-71.

D'Angelo, M.R., *Moses in the Letter to the Hebrews* (Missoula, MT: Scholars, 1979).

Danby, H. (ed.), *The Mishna* (Oxford: Oxford University Press, 1933).

Daniélou, J., 'Le symbolisme eschatologigue de la Fête des Tabernacles', *Irenikon* 31 (1958), pp. 19-40.

Davies, J.G., 'The Prefiguration of the Ascension in the Third Gospel', *JTS* 6 (1955), pp. 229-33.

—*He Ascended into Heaven* (London: Lutterworth, 1958).

Davies, M., *Matthew* (Sheffield: JSOT Press, 1993).

Davies P.R., and B.D. Chilton, 'The Aqedah: A Revised Tradition History', *CBQ* 40 (1978), pp. 514-46.

Davies, W.D., *Torah in the Messianic Age and/or the Age to Come* (Philadelphia, 1952).

—'"Knowledge" in the Dead Sea Scrolls and Matthew 11.25-30', *HTR* 46 (1953), pp. 113-39.

—*Christian Origins and Judaism* (London: Darton, Longman & Todd, 1962).

—'Torah and Dogma', *HTR* 61 (1968), pp. 87-105.

—*The Setting of the Sermon on the Mount* (Cambridge: Cambridge University Press, 1974).

Davies, W.D., and D.C. Allison, *A Critical and Exegetical Commentary on the Gospel according to Saint Matthew* (2 vols.; Edinburgh: T. & T. Clark, 1988, 1991).

—'Reflections on the Sermon on the Mount', *SJT* 44.3 (1991), pp. 283-309.

Del Agua, A., 'The Narrative of the Transfiguration as a Derashic Scenification of a Faith Confession (Mark 9.2-8 PAR)', *NTS* 39 (1993), pp. 340-54.

Derrett, J.M., *The Law in the New Testament* (London: Darton, Longman & Todd, 1970).

Deutsch, C., *Hidden Wisdom and the Easy Yoke* (Sheffield: JSOT Press, 1987).

Dexinger, F., 'Limits of Tolerance in Judaism: The Samaritan Example', in E.P. Sanders, A.I. Baumgarten and A. Mendelson (eds.), *Jewish and Christian Self-Definition* (3 vols.; London: SCM Press, 1981), II, pp. 88-114.

—'Samaritan Eschatology', in A.D. Crown (ed.), *The Samaritans* (Tübingen: Mohr, 1989), pp. 276-79.

Dibelius, M., *Studies in the Acts of the Apostles* (London: SCM Press, 1956).

Dimant, D., 'Qumran Sectarian Literature', in M.E. Stone (ed.), *Jewish Writings of the Second Temple Period,* Section 2 (Assen: Van Gorcum; Philadelphia: Fortress Press, 1984).

Dobschütz, E. von, 'Matthew as Rabbi and Catechist' in G.N. Stanton, *The Interpretation of Matthew* (Philadelphia: Fortress Press; London: SPCK, 1983), pp. 19-29.

Dodd, C.H., 'The Appearance of the Risen Christ: An Essay in Form-Criticism of the Gospels', in D.E. Nineham (ed.), *Studies in the Gospels* (Oxford: Blackwell, 1955).

—*Parables of the Kingdom* (New York: Charles Scribner's Sons, 1961).

—*The Interpretation of the Fourth Gospel* (Cambridge: Cambridge University Press, 2nd edn, 1965).

Donaldson, T.L., *Jesus on the Mountain* (Sheffield: JSOT Press, 1985).

Dozeman, T.B., *God on the Mountain* (Atlanta: Scholars Press, 1989).

Dulling, D.C., 'Solomon, Exorcism, and the Son of David', *HTR* 68 (1975), pp. 235-52.

—'The Therapeutic Son of David: An Element in Matthew's Christological Apologetic', *NTS* 24 (1977/8), pp. 392-410.

Dunn, J.D.G., '2 Corinthians III.17—"The Lord is Spirit"', *JTS* 21 (1970), pp. 309-20.

—*Unity and Diversity in the New Testament* (London: SCM Press, 1977).

—*Romans* (2 vols.; Waco: Word, 1988).

—*Jesus, Paul and the Law* (London: SPCK, 1990).

Drury, J., *Tradition and Design in Luke's Gospel: A Study in Early Christian Historiography* (London: Darton, Longman & Todd, 1976).

Eccles, R.S., *Erwin Ramsdell Goodenough: A Personal Pilgrimage* (Chico: Scholars Press, 1985).

Eichrodt, W., *Theology of the Old Testament* (2 vols.; London: SCM Press, 1967).

Ellis, E.E., *The Gospel of Luke* (London: Oliphants, 1974).

—'The Composition of Luke 9 and the Sources of its Christology', in G.F. Hawthorne (ed.), *Current Issues in Biblical and Patristic Interpretation* (Grand Rapids: Eerdmans, 1975), pp. 121-27.

Epstein, I. (ed.), *The Babylonian Talmud* (18 vols.; Hindhead, Surrey: Soncino, 1961).

Evans, C.A., 'Luke's Use of the Elijah/Elisha Narratives and the Ethic of Election', *JBL* 106.1, (1987), pp. 75-83.

Evans, C.F., 'The Central Section of Luke's Gospel', in D.E. Nineham (ed.), *Studies in the Gospels* (Oxford: Blackwell, 1955), pp. 37-53.

—*Saint Luke* (London: SCM Press, 1990).

Evans, D., 'Academic Scepticism, Spiritual Reality and the Transfiguration', in D. Hurst and N.T. Wright (eds.), *The Glory of Christ in the New Testament* (Oxford: Clarendon Press, 1987), pp. 175-86.

Faierstein, M.M., 'Why do the Scribes Say that Elijah Must Come First?', *JBL* 100.1 (1981) pp. 75-86.

Farrer, A., 'On Dispensing with Q', in D.E. Nineham (ed.), *Studies in the Gospels* (Oxford: Blackwell, 1955).

Fee, G.D., *The First Epistle to the Corinthians* (Grand Rapids: Eerdmans, 1989).

Feldman, L.H., *Josephus and Modern Scholarship (1937–1980)* (Berlin: de Gruyter, 1984).

—'Editors Preface', in L.H. Feldman and G. Hata (eds.), *Josephus, Judaism, and Christianity* (Leiden: Brill, 1987), p.14.

Feldman, L.H., and G. Hata (eds.), *Josephus, the Bible, and History* (Detroit: Wayne, 1989).

Feuillet, A., 'Les perspectives propers a chaque evangeliste dans les recits de la Transfiguration', *Bib* (1958), pp. 281-301.

Filson, F.V., *A Commentary on the Gospel according to St. Matthew* (London: A. & C. Black, 1960).

Fitzmyer, J.A., 'The Use of Explicit Old Testament Quotations in Qumran Literature and in the New Testament', *NTS* 7 (1960–61), pp. 297-333.

—*Essays on the Semitic Background of the New Testament* (London: Chapman, 1971).

—'The Son of David Tradition and Mt. 22.41-46 and Parallels', *Concilium* 10.2 (1966), pp. 40-46, reprinted in *Essays on the Semitic Background of the New Testament* (London: Chapman, 1971), pp. 113-26.

—*The Dead Sea Scrolls: Major Publications and Tools for Study* (Missoula, MT: Scholars Press, 1977).

—*A Wandering Aramean* (Missoula, MT: Scholars Press, 1979).

—'Glory Reflected on the Face of Christ (2 Cor. 3.7-4.6) and a Palestinian Jewish Motif', *TS* 42 (1981), pp. 630-46.

—*The Gospel according to Luke* (I-IX) (Garden City, NY: Doubleday, 1983).

—'More about Elijah Coming First', *JBL* 104 (1985), pp. 295-96

—*The Gospel according to Luke* (X-XXIV) (Garden City, NY: Doubleday, 1986).

Ford, D., *The Abomination of Desolation in Biblical Eschatology* (Washington: University Press of America, 1979).

Fornberg, T., *An Early Church in a Pluralistic Society* (Lund: Gleerup, 1977).

France, R.T., *Jesus and the Old Testament* (London: Tyndale, 1971).

—'The Massacre of the Innocents—Fact or Fiction?', in E.A. Livingstone (ed.), *Studia Biblica*, II (Sheffield: JSOT Press, 1978), pp. 83-94.

—'Herod and the Children of Bethlehem', *NovT* 21 (1979), pp. 98-120.

—'The Formula-Quotations of Matthew 2 and the Problem of Communication', *NTS* 27 (1980/1), pp. 233-51.

—'Scripture, Tradition and History in the Infancy Narratives of Matthew', in

R.T. France and D. Wenham (eds.), *Gospel Perspectives* (6 vols.; Sheffield: JSOT Press, 1981), II, pp. 239-66.

—'The Church and the Kingdom of God: Some Hermeneutical Issues', in D.A. Carson (ed.), *Biblical Interpretation and the Church* (Exeter: Paternoster Press, 1984), pp. 30-44.

—*The Gospel according to Matthew: an Introduction and Commentary* (Leicester: IVP, 1985).

—*Matthew: Evangelist and Teacher* (Exeter: Paternoster Press, 1989).

—*Divine Government* (London: SPCK, 1990).

Franklin, E., *Christ the Lord: A Study in the Purpose and Theology of Luke–Acts* (Philadelphia: Westminster Press, 1975).

Freed, E.D., 'Did John Write his Gospel Partly to Win Samaritan Converts?', *NovT* 12, 1970, pp. 241-56.

Freedman, H., and M. Simon, *Midrash Rabbah* (10 vols.; Hindhead, Surrey: Soncino, 1937).

Freriches E.S., and J. Neusener, *Goodenough on the History of Religion and on Judaism* (Atlanta: Scholars Press, 1986).

Freyne, S.G., *Jesus and the Gospels* (Dublin: Gill & Macmillan, 1988).

Friedrich, G., 'προφήτης', in *TDNT*, VI, p. 843.

Fryer, A.T., 'The Purpose of the Transfiguration', *JTS* (1904), pp. 214-17.

Fuller, R.H., *The Foundations of New Testament Christology* (London: Collins, 1969).

Furneaux, W.M., *The Acts of the Apostles* (Oxford: Clarendon Press, 1901).

Furnish, V.P., *II Corinthians* (Garden City, NY: Doubleday, 1984).

Gaechter, P., *Das Matthäus-Evangelium: Ein kommentar* (Innsbruck: Tyrolia Verlag, 1963).

Gager, J.G., *Moses in Greco-Roman Paganism* (New York: Abingdon Press, 1972).

Garland, D.E., *Reading Matthew: A Literary and Theological Commentary on the First Gospel* (New York: Crossroad, 1993).

Gärtner, B., 'The Habakkuk Commentary (DSH) and the Gospel of Matthew', *ST* 8 (1955), pp. 1-24.

—*The Temple and the Community and the New Testament* (Cambridge: Cambridge University Press, 1965).

Gasque, W.W., 'The Speeches of Acts: Dibelius Reconsidered', in R.N. Longenecker and M.C. Tenney (eds.), *New Dimensions in New Testament Study* (Grand Rapids: Zondervan, 1974), pp. 232-50.

Gaster, M., *The Samaritans* (London: Oxford University Press, 1925).

—*The Asatir* (London: The Royal Asiatic Society, 1927).

—*Samaritan Oral Law and Ancient Traditions* (The Search: 1932).

—*The Samaritan Book of the 'Secrets of Moses'; Together with the Pitron or Samaritan Commentary and Samaritan Story of the Death of Moses* (London: The Royal Asiatic Society, 1957).

Gaster, T.H., *The Scriptures of the Dead Sea Sect* (London: Secker and Warburg, 1957).

—'Samaritans', *IDB*, IV, p. 190.

Geddert, T.J., *Watchwords: Mark 13 in Markan Eschatology* (Sheffield: JSOT Press, 1989).

Gerber, W., 'Die Metamorphose Jesu: Mk 9,2-3 par.', *TZ* 23 (1967), pp. 385-95.

Gerhardsson, B., *The Testing of God's Son* (Lund: Gleerup, 1966).

Gibbs, J.M., 'Purpose and Pattern in Matthew's use of the Title "Son of David"', *NTS* 10 (1963/4), pp. 449-50.

Ginzberg, L., 'Elijah', *JewEnc*, V.

—*The Legends of the Jews*, (7 vols.; Philadelphia: Jewish Publication Society, 1938).

Glasson, T.F., *The Second Advent* (London: Epworth, 1945).

—*Moses in the Fourth Gospel* (London: SCM Press, 1963).

—'Theophany and Parousia', *NTS* 34 (1988), pp. 259-70.

Goodenough, E.R., 'Philo's Exposition of the Law and his de vita Mosis', *HTR* 27 (1933), pp. 109-26.

—*By Light, Light—The Mystic Gospel of Hellenistic Judaism* (New Haven: Yale University Press, 1935).

—*An Introduction to Philo Judaeus* (Oxford: Oxford University Press, 2nd edn, 1962).

—*Jewish Symbols in the Greco-Roman Period*, I-XIII (New York: Pantheon, 1953–68).

Goldingay, J.E., *Daniel* (Dallas: Word, 1989).

Goldingay, J., *Approaches to Old Testament Interpretation* (Leicester: Apollos, 1990).

Goulder, M.D., 'The Chiastic Structure of the Lukan Journey', in F.L. Cross (ed.), *Studia Evangelica* (2 vols.; Berlin: Academie Verlag, 1964), II, pp. 195-202.

—*Type and History in Acts* (London: SPCK, 1964).

—*Midrash and Lection in Matthew* (London: SPCK, 1974).

—'On Putting Q to the Test,' *NTS* 24 (1978), pp. 218-34.

—*The Evangelist's Calendar* (London: SPCK, 1978).

—'Mark XVI.1-8 and Parallels', *NTS* 24 (1978), pp. 235-40.

Green, M., *2 Peter and Jude* (London: Tyndale, 1968).

Groves, W.L., 'The Significance of the Transfiguration of our Lord', *Theology* 11, (August 1925), pp. 80-92

Gruenwald, I., *Apocalyptic and Merkavah Mysticism* (Leiden: Brill, 1980).

Grundmann, W., *Das Evangelium nach Matthäus* (Berlin: Evangelische Verlagsanstalt, 1968).

Guelich, R.A., *The Sermon on the Mount* (Waco: Word, 2nd edn, 1983).

—*Mark* (2 vols.; Dallas: Word, 1989).

Gundry, R.H., *The Use of the Old Testament in St. Matthew's Gospel* (Leiden: Brill, 1975).

—*Matthew: A Commentary on his Literary and Theological Art* (Grand Rapids: Eerdmans, 1982).

—*Mark: A Commentary on his Apology for the Cross* (Grand Rapids: Eerdmans, 1993).

Guthrie, D., *Hebrews* (Leicester: IVP; Grand Rapids: Eerdmans, 1983).

Haacker, K., 'Samaritan', in *NIDNTT*, III, pp. 449-67.

Haenchen, E., *The Acts of the Apostles* (Oxford: Basil Blackwell, 1971).

—*John 1* (Philadelphia: Fortress Press, 1980).

Hagner, D.A., *Hebrews* (Peabody: Hendrickson, 1990).

—*Matthew 1–13* (Dallas: Word, 1993).

Hahn, F., *The Titles of Jesus in Christology* (London: Lutterworth, 1969).

Hammerton-Kelly, R.G., and R. Scroggs (eds.), *Jews, Greeks and Christians: Religious Cultures in Late Antiquity: Essays in Honour of W.D. Davies* (Leiden: Brill, 1976).

Hanson, A.T., 'The Midrash in II Corinthians 3: A Reconsideration', *JSNT* 9 (1980), pp. 2-28.

Hanson, P.D., *The Dawn of Apocalyptic* (Nashville: Abingdon, 1987).

—*Old Testament Apocalyptic* (Nashville: Abingdon, 1988).

Hare, D.R.A., *The Theme of Jewish Persecution of Christians in the Gospel according to Matthew* (Cambridge: Cambridge University Press, 1967).

Hartman, L., *Prophecy Interpreted: The Formation of Some Jewish Apocalyptic Texts and of the Eschatological Discourse Mark 13 Par.* (Lund: Gleerup, 1966).

Hastings, A., *Prophet and Witness in Jerusalem* (Baltimore: Helicon, 1958).

Hata, G., 'The Story of Moses Interpreted within the Context of Anti-Semitism', in L.H. Feldman and G. Hata (eds.), *Josephus, Judaism, and Christianity* (Leiden: Brill, 1987), pp. 180-97.

Hatch, E., and H.A. Redpath (eds.), *A Concordance to the Septuagint* (2 vols.; Oxford: Clarendon Press, 1897).

Hay, D.M., 'Review', in D.T. Runia (ed.), *The Studia Philonica Annual: Studies in Hellenistic Judaism* (Atlanta: Scholars Press, 1989), pp. 128-34.

Headlam, A.C., 'Theudas', in J. Hastings (ed.), *A Dictionary of the Bible* (4 vols.; Edinburgh: T. & T. Clark, 1899-1902), IV, p. 750.

Heinemann, J., 'Anti-Samaritan Polemics in the Aggadah', in *Proceedings of the Sixth World Congress of Jewish Studies* (Jerusalem: Hacohen, 1977), III, pp. 57-69.

Hengel, M., *Judaism and Hellenism: Studies in their Encounter in Palestine During Early Hellenistic Period* (2 vols.; Philadelphia: Fortress Press, 1974).

—*The Son of God* (Philadelphia: Fortress Press, 1976).

Hermer, C.J., *The Book of Acts in the Setting of Hellenistic History* (Tübingen: Mohr [Paul Siebeck], 1989).

—'The Speeches of Acts 1-11', *TynBul* 40 (1989), pp. 77-85.

Hickling, C.J.A., 'The Sequence of Thought in II Corinthians, Chapter Three', *NTS* 21 (1974-75), pp. 380-95.

Higgins, A.J.B., 'Jewish Messianic Belief in Justin Martyr's Dialogue with Trypho', *NTS* 9 (1967), pp. 298-305.

Hill, C.C., *Hellenists and Hebrews: A Reprisal* (unpublished dissertation; Oxford University, 1989).

Hill, D., *The Gospel of Matthew* (Grand Rapids: Eerdmans, 1972).

—'"Son of Man" in Psalm 80 v. 17', *NovT* 15 (1973), pp. 261-69.

—'The Figure of Jesus in Matthew's Story: a Response to Professor Kingsbury's Literary-Critical Probe', *JSNT* 6 (1980), pp. 2-16.

Holmes, R., 'The Purpose of the Transfiguration', *JTS* 4 (1903), pp. 543-47.

Holladay, C.R., 'The Portrait of Moses in Ezekiel the Tragedian', *SBLSP 1976* (Missoula, MT: Scholars Press, 1976), pp. 447-52.

—*Theios Aner in Hellenistic Judaism: A Critique of the Use of this Category in New Testament Christology* (Missoula, MT: Scholars Press, 1977).

Hooker, M.D., *The Son of Man in Mark* (London: SCM Press, 1967).

—'Beyond the Things that are Written? St Paul's Use of Scripture', *NTS*, 27 (1980-81), pp. 295-309.

—'What Doest thou Here Elijah?', in L.D. Hurst and N.T. Wright (eds.), *The Glory of Christ in the New Testament* (Oxford: Clarendon Press, 1987).

—*The Gospel according to St. Mark* (London: A. & C. Black, 1992).

Horstmann, M., *Studien zur markinischen Christologie: Mk 8, 28-9, 13 als Zugang zum Christusbild des zweiten Evangeliums* (NTAbh, 6; Münster: Aschendorff, 1969), pp. 72-103.

Huck, A., and H. Greeven (eds.), *Synopsis of the First Three Gospels* (Tübingen: Mohr, 1981).

Hughes, P.E., *A Commentary on the Epistle to the Hebrews* (Grand Rapids: Eerdmans, 1977).

—*The Second Epistle to the Corinthians* (Grand Rapids: Eerdmans, 2nd edn, 1986).

Hurtado, L.W., *One God, One Lord* (London: SCM Press, 1988).

James, M.R., *The Apocryphal New Testament* (Oxford: Clarendon Press, 1954).

Jeremias, J., *Jesus' Promise to the Nations* (London: SCM Press, 1958).

—*New Testament Theology*. I. *The Proclamation of Jesus* (London: SCM Press, 1971).

—'Ἠλείας', in *TDNT*, pp. 928-41.

—'Μωυσῆς', in *TDNT*, pp. 863-64.

Jervell, J., 'The Mighty Minority', *ST* 34 (1980), pp. 13-38.

Johnson, A.R., *Sacral Kingship in Ancient Israel* (Cardiff: University of Wales Press, 1955).

Johnson, F.S.E., *A Commentary on the Gospel according to Mark* (New York: Harper and Brothers, 1960).

Käsemann, E., *Essays on New Testament Themes* (London: SCM Press, 1964).

Kazmierski, C.R., *Jesus, the Son of God: A Study of the Markan Tradition and its Redaction by the Evangelist* (FzB, 33; Würzburg: Echter, 1979), pp. 105-26.

Keck, L.E., 'The Sermon on the Mount', in D.G. Miller and D.Y. Hadidian (eds.), *Jesus and Man's Hope* (2 vols.; Pittsburgh: Theological Seminary, 1971), II, pp. 311-22.

—'Toward the Renewal of New Testament Christology', *NTS* 32 (1986), pp. 362-77.

Kelly, J.N.D., *A Commentary on the Epistles of Peter and Jude* (London: Black, 1969).

Kennedy, H.A.A., 'The Purpose of the Transfiguration', *JTS* 4 (1903), pp. 270-73.

Kenny, A., 'The Transfiguration and the Agony in the Garden', *CBQ* 19 (1957), pp. 444-52.

Kilpatrick, G.D., *The Origins of the Gospel according to St. Matthew* (Oxford: Clarendon Press, 1946).

Kim, S., *The Origin of Paul's Gospel* (Grand Rapids: Eerdmans, 1982).

Kimelmann, R., '*Birkat ha-Minim* and the Lack of Evidence for an Anti-Christian Jewish Prayer in Late Antiquity', in E.P. Sanders (ed.), *Jewish and Christian Self-definition* (3 vols.; Philadelphia: Fortress Press, 1981), II, pp. 226-44.

Kingsbury, J.D., *Matthew: Structure, Christology, Kingdom* (Philadelphia: Fortress Press, 1975).

—'The Title "Son of David" in Matthew's Gospel', *JBL* 95.4 (1976), pp. 591-602.

—'The Figure of Jesus in Matthew's Story: a Literary-Critical Probe', *JSNT* 21 (1984), pp. 3-36.

Kirk, J.A., 'The Messianic Role of Jesus and the Temptation Narrative: A Contemporary Perspective', *EvQ* 44.1 (1972), pp. 11-29, continued in 44.2 (1972), pp. 91-102.

Klausner, J., *The Messianic Ideal from its Beginning to the Completion of the Mishna* (London: Allen & Unwin, 1956).

Klostermann, E., *Das Markusevengelium* (Tübingen: Mohr, 1950).

—*Das Matthäusevangelium* (Tübingen: Mohr, 1971).

Knibb, M.A., *The Qumran Community* (Cambridge: Cambridge University Press, 1987).

Krentz, E., 'The Extent of Matthew's Prologue', *JBL* 83 (1964), pp. 409-414.

Lagrange, M.J., *Evangile selon saint Matthieu* (EBib; Paris: Gabalda, 1923).

Lake K., and H.J. Cadbury, *The Beginnings of Christianity*. I. *The Acts of the Apostles* (4 vols.; London: Macmillan, 1933).

Lambrecht, J., 'Transformation in 2 Cor. 3, 18', *Bib* 64 (1983), pp. 243-54.

Lane, W.L., *The Gospel according to Mark* (Grand Rapids: Eerdmans, 1974).

—'Theios Aner Christology and the Gospel of Mark', in R.N. Longenecker and M.C. Tenney (eds.), *New Dimensions in New Testament Study* (Grand Rapids: Zondervan, 1974), pp. 144-61.

—*Hebrews: A Call to Commitment* (Peabody: Hendrickson, 1988).

Leaney, A.R.C., *The Rule of Qumran and its Meaning* (London: SCM Press, 1966).

—*The Letters of Peter and Jude* (Cambridge: Cambridge University Press, 1967).

Levenson, J.D., *Theology of the Program of Restoration of Ezekiel 40–48* (Missoula, MT: Scholars Press, 1976).

—*Sinai and Zion* (Minneapolis: Winston Press, 1985).

Lieberman, S., *Hellenism in Jewish Palestine* (New York: Jewish Theological Seminary, 1962).

Liefeld, W.L., 'μεταμορφοω', in *NIDNTT*, III, pp. 861-864.

—'Theological Motifs in the Transfiguration Narrative', in R.N. Longenecker and M.C. Tenney (eds.), *New Dimensions in New Testament Study* (Grand Rapids: Zondervan, 1974), pp. 162-79.

—'Luke', in F.E. Gaebelein (ed.), *The Expositor's Bible Commentary* (12 vols.; Grand Rapids: Zondervan, 1984), VIII, pp. 797-1059.

Lindars, B., *New Testament Apologetic: The Doctrinal Significance of the Old Testament Quotations* (London: SCM Press, 1961).

—*The Gospel of John* (Grand Rapids: Eerdmans; London: Marshall, Morgan & Scott, 1972).

—*Jesus Son of Man: A Fresh Examination of the Son of Man Sayings in the Gospels in the Light of Recent Research* (London: SPCK, 1983).

—'Response to Richard Bauckham: The Idiomatic Use of *Bar Enasha*', *JSNT* 23 (1985), pp. 35-41.

Lohmeyer, E., 'Die Verklärung Jesu nach dem Markusevangelium', *ZNW* 21 (1922), pp. 85-215.

—*Das Evangelium des Markus* (Göttingen: Vandenhoeck & Ruprecht, 1937).

—*Das Evangelium des Matthäus* (Göttingen: Vandenhoeck & Ruprecht, 1958).

Lohse, E., 'υἱος', in *TDNT*, VIII, pp. 362-63.

—*Die Texte Aus Qumran: hebräisch und deutsch* (München: Kösel, 1971).

Longenecker, R.N., *Galatians* (Dallas: Word, 1990).

Lowy, S., *The Principles of Samaritan Exegesis* (Leiden: Brill, 1977).

Luedemann, E., *Opposition to Paul in Jewish Christianity* (Minneapolis: Fortress Press, 1989).

Luz, U., 'The Disciples in the Gospel according to Matthew', in G.N. Stanton (ed.), *The Interpretation of Matthew* (Philadelphia: Fortress Press; London: SCM Press, 1983), pp. 98-128.

—*Matthew 1–7* (Edinburgh: T. & T. Clark, 1989).

—'Das Primatwort Matthäus 16.17-19 aus Wirkungsgeschichtlicher Sicht', *NTS* 37 (1991), pp. 415-33.

MacDonald, J., 'Comprehensive and Thematic Reading of the Law by Samaritans', *JJS* 10 (1959), pp. 67-74.

—'The Samaritan Doctrine of Moses', *SJT* 13.2 (1960), pp. 149-62,

—'The Theological Hymns of Amram Darah', *ALUOS* 2 (1961), pp. 70-72.

—*Memar Marqah (The Teaching of Marqah)* (2 vols.; BZAW, 83; Berlin: Verlag Alfred Topelmann, 1963).

—*The Theology of the Samaritans* (London: SCM Press, 1964).

—*The Samaritan Chronicle No II (or Sepher Ha-Yamin, from Joshua to Nebuchadnezzar)* (Berlin: de Gruyter, 1989).

McCown, C.C., 'The Geography of Luke's Central Section', *JBL* 57 (1938), pp. 51-66.

McCurley, F.R., '"And after Six Days" (Mark 9:2): A Semitic Literary Device', *JBL* 80 (1961), pp. 79-81.

McNamara, M., *The New Testament and the Palestinian Targums to the Pentateuch* (Rome: Pontifical Biblical Institute, 1966).

McNeile, A.H., *The Gospel according to St. Matthew* (London: Macmillan, 1955).

McGuckin, J.A., *The Transfiguration of Christ in Scripture and Tradition* (Lewiston: Mellen, 1986).

Maccoby, H., *Early Rabbinic Writings* (Cambridge: Cambridge University Press, 1988).

Maddox, R., *The Purpose of Luke–Acts* (Edinburgh: T. & T. Clark, 1985).

Maier, G., 'The Church in the Gospel of Matthew: Hermeneutical Analysis of the Current Debate', in D.A. Carson (ed.), *Biblical Interpretation and the Church* (Exeter: Paternoster Press, 1984), pp. 45-63.

Malina, B.J., *The Palestinian Manna Tradition: The Manna Tradition in the Palestinian Targums and its Relationship to the New Testament Writings* (Leiden: Brill, 1968).

—'The Literary Structure and Form of Matthew 28.16-20', *NTS* (1970/71), pp. 87-103.

Manek, J., 'The New Exodus in the Books of Luke', *NovT* 2 (1958), pp. 8-23.

Mann, C.S., 'The Organization and Institutions of the Jerusalem Church in Acts', in J. Munck, *The Acts of the Apostles* (New York: Doubleday, 1967).

Manson, T.W., 'The Old Testament in the Teaching of Jesus', *BJRL* 34 (1951/52), pp. 323-24.

—*The Teaching of Jesus* (Cambridge: Cambridge University Press, 1955).

Marsh, J., *The Fulness of Time* (London: Nisbet, 1952).

Marshall, I.H., 'Son of God or Servant of Yahweh? A Reconsideration of Mk 1.11', *NTS* 15 (1968/9), pp. 326-36.

—'Palestinian and Hellenistic Christianity: Some Critical Comments', *NTS* 19 (1973), pp. 271-87.

—*Acts* (Leicester: IVP, 1980).

—'The Hope of a new age: the Kingdom of God in the New Testament', *Themelios* 11.1 (1985), pp. 5-15.

—*The Gospel of Luke: A Commentary on the Greek Text* (Grand Rapids: Eerdmans, 1986).

Marshall, J.T., 'Shekinah', in J. Hastings (ed.), *A Dictionary of the Bible* (4 vols.; Edinburgh: T. & T. Clark, 1899-1902), IV, pp. 487-489.

Martin, R.P., *Carmen Christi* (Cambridge: Cambridge University Press, 1967).

—*2 Corinthians* (Waco: Word, 1986).

Martyn, J.L., *The Gospel of John in Christian History* (New York: Paulist Press, 1978).

Masson, C., 'La Transfiguration de Jesus (Marc 9.2-13)', *RTP* 3.14 (1964), pp. 1-14.

Mauser, U.W., *Christ in the Wilderness: The Wilderness Theme in the Second Gospel and its Basis in the Biblical Tradition* (London: SCM Press, 1963).

Meeks, W.A., *The Prophet King* (Leiden: Brill, 1967).

—'The Divine Agent and his Counterfeit in Philo and the Fourth Gospel', in E.S. Fiorenza (ed.), *Aspects of Religious Propaganda in Judaism and Early Christianity* (Notre Dame: University of Notre Dame Press, 1976), pp. 43-67.

Meier, J.P., *Law and History in Matthew's Gospel* (Rome: Pontifical Biblical Institute, 1976).

—'Two Disputed Questions in Mt 28.16-20', *JBL* 96 (1977), pp. 407-24.

—*The Vision of Matthew* (New York: Paulist Press, 1979).

Metzger, B.M., *A Textual Commentary on the Greek New Testament* (London: United Bible Societies, 1971).

Meyer, B.F., *The Aims of Jesus* (London: SCM 1979).

Meyer, H.A.W., *Kritisch-exegetischer Handbuch über das Evangelium des Matthäus* (Göttingen: Vandenhoeck, 1844).

Michaelis, D.W., *Das Evangelium nach Matthäus*, II (2 vols.; Zürich: Zwingli Verlag, 1948–49).

Michel, O., 'The Conclusion of Matthew's Gospel: a Contribution to the History of the Easter Message (1950)', in G.N. Stanton (ed.), *The Interpretation of Matthew* (Philadelphia: Fortress Press; London: SPCK, 1983), pp. 30-41.

Micklem, P.A., *St. Matthew* (London: Methuen, 1917).

Milik, J.T., 'Le Testament de Lévi en Araméen', *RB* 62 (1955), pp. 405-406.

Miller, R.J., 'Elijah, John and Jesus in the Gospel of Luke', *NTS* 34 (1988), pp. 611-22.

Moberly, R.W.L., *At the Mountain of God* (Sheffield: JSOT Press, 1983).

Moessner, D.P., 'Jesus and the "Wilderness Generation": The Death of the Prophet Like Moses according to Luke', in K.H. Richard (ed.), *SBLSP 1982* (Chico, CA: Scholars Press, 1982), pp. 339-40.

—'Luke 9.1-50: Luke's Preview of the Journey of the Prophet Like Moses of Deuteronomy', *JBL* 102.4 (1983), pp. 575-605.

Mohrlang, R., *Matthew and Paul* (Cambridge: Cambridge University Press, 1984).

Montgomery J.A., *The Samaritans, the Earliest Jewish Sect: Their History, Theology and Literature* (Philadelphia: Wiston, 1907).

Moo, D.J., 'Jesus and the Authority of the Mosaic Law', *JSNT* 20 (1984), pp. 3-49.

Moore, A.L., *The Parousia in the New Testament* (Leiden: Brill, 1966).

Moore, G.F., *Judaism in the First Century of the Christian Era* (2 vols.; Cambridge: Cambridge University Press, 1927).

Mor, M., 'The Persian, Hellenistic and Hasmonaean Period', in A.D. Crown (ed.), *The Samaritans* (Tübingen: Mohr, 1989).

Morris, L., *The Gospel according to John* (Grand Rapids: Eerdmans, 1971).

Moule, C.F.D., *An Idiom Book of the New Testament* (Cambridge: Cambridge University Press, 2nd edn, 1959).

—*The Origin of Christology* (Cambridge: Cambridge University Press, 1977).

—'St. Matthew's Gospel: Some Neglected Features', in F.L. Cross (ed.), *Studia Evangelica*, II (Berlin: Akademie-Verlag, 1964), pp. 90-99; reprinted in C.F.D. Moule, *Essays in New Testament Interpretation* (Cambridge: Cambridge University Press, 1982), pp. 67-74.

Moulton, J.H., and G. Milligan, *The Vocabulary of the New Testament Illustrated from the Papyri and Other Non-Literary Sources* (London: Hodder & Stoughton, 1914–30).

Müller, H.P., 'Die Verklärung Jesu', *ZNW* 51 (1960), pp. 56-64.

Müller, U.B., 'Die christologische Absicht des Markusevangeliums und die Verklärungsgeschichte', *ZNW* 64 (1973), pp. 59-93.

Munck, J., *The Acts of the Apostles* (Garden City, NY: Doubleday, 1967).

Murphy-O'Connor, J., 'What Really Happened at the Transfiguration?', *Bible Review* 3 (1987), pp. 8-21.

—*The Theology of the Second Letter to the Corinthians* (Cambridge: Cambridge University Press, 1991).

Neirynck, F., 'Minor Agreements Matthew–Luke in the Transfiguration Story', in P. Hoffmann (ed.), *Orientierung an Jesus: Zur Theologie der Synoptiker* (Freiburg: Herder, 1973).

Neusner, J., 'Jewish Use of Pagan Symbols after 70 CE', *JR* 43 (1963), pp. 285-94.

—*First-Century Judaism in Crisis: Yohanan ben Zakkai and the Renaissance of Torah* (Nashville: Abingdon, 1975).

—'Josephus' Pharisees: A Complete Repertoire', in L.H. Feldman and G. Hata (eds.), *Josephus, Judaism and Christianity* (Leiden: Brill, 1987), pp. 274-92.

Neyrey, J.H., 'The Apologetic Use of the Transfiguration in 2 Peter 1.16-21', *CBQ* 42 (1980), pp. 504-19.

Nicholson, G.C., *Death as Departure: The Johannine Descent-Ascent Schema* (Chico, CA: Scholars Press, 1983).

Nickelsburg, G.W.E., 'Enoch, Levi and Peter: Recipients of Revelation in Upper Galilee', *JBL* 100.4 (1981), pp. 575-600.

Nineham, D.E., *Saint Mark* (Harmondsworth: Penguin, 1963).

Nolan, B.M., *The Royal Son of God* (Göttingen: Vandenhoeck & Ruprecht, 1979).

Nolland, J., *Luke 1–9:20* (Dallas: Word, 1989).

Noth, M., *Exodus* (London: SCM Press, 1972).

Nützel, J.M., *Die Verklärungserzählung im Markusevangelium: Eine redaktionsgeschichtliche Untersuchung* (FzB, 6; Würzburg: Echter, 1973).

Obermann, J., 'Calendrical Elements in the Dead Sea Scrolls', *JBL* 75 (1956), pp. 285-97.

Orton, D., *The Understanding Scribe: Matthew and the Apocalypytic Ideal* (Sheffield: JSOT Press, 1985).

Overman, J.A., *Matthew's Gospel and Formative Judaism* (Minneapolis: Fortress Press, 1990).

Pamment, M., 'Moses and Elijah in the Story of the Transfiguration', *ExpTim* 92 (1981), pp. 338-39.

—'The Son of Man in the First Gospel', *NTS* 29 (1983), pp. 116-29.

Payne, D.F., 'The Second Letter of Peter', in G.C.D. Howley, F.F. Bruce, H.C. Ellison (eds.), *A Bible Commentary for Today* (London/Glasgow: Pickering and Inglis, 1980), pp. 1645-51.

Pedersen, S., 'Die Proklamation Jesu als des eschatologischen Offenbarungsträgers (Mt. xvii.1-13)', *NovT* 17 (1975), pp. 241-64.

Perowne, J.J.S., *The Acts of the Apostles* (Cambridge: Cambridge University Press, 1887).

Perrin, N., *The Kingdom of God in the Teaching of Jesus* (London: SCM Press; Philadelphia: Westminster Press, 1963).

Pesch, R., 'Der Gottessohn im matthäischen Evangelienprolog (Mt. 1-2): Beobachtungen zu den Zitationsformeln der Reflexionszitate', *Bib* 48 (1967), pp. 411-18.

—*Das Markusevangelium* (2 vols.; Freiburg: Herder, 1976).

Plummer, A., *The Second Epistle of Paul the Apostle to the Corinthians* (Cambridge: Cambridge University Press, 1903).

—*An Exegetical Commentary on the Gospel according to St. Matthew* (London: Robert & Scott, 1915).

Plumptre, E.A., 'The Samaritan Elements in the Gospel and Acts', *Expositor* 10 (1878), pp. 22-40.

Porter, J.R., *Moses and the Monarchy* (Oxford: Basil Blackwell, 1963).

Pummer, R., 'The Samaritan Pentateuch and the New Testament', *NTS* 22 (1982), pp. 441-43.

Rackham, R.B., *The Acts of the Apostles* (London: Methuen, 1901).

Ramsey, A.M., *The Glory of God and the Transfiguration* (London: Longmans, Green & Co., 1949).

Ramsey, M.J., *Servant and Son: Jesus in Parable and Gospel* (Atlanta: John Knox, 1981).

Ravens, D.A.S., 'Luke 9.7-62 and the Prophetic Role of Jesus', *NTS* 36 (1990), pp. 119-29.

Reid, B.O., 'Voices and Angels: What Were they Talking about at the Transfigurations? A Redaction-Critical Study of Luke 9.28-36', *Biblical Research* 34 (1989), pp. 19-31.

Rengstorf, K.F., 'Old and New Testament Traces of a Formula of this Judean Royal Ritual', *NovT* 5 (1962), pp. 241-42.

Reese, J.M., 'How Matthew Portrays the Communication of Christ's Authority', *BTB* 7 (1977), pp. 139-44.

Richard, E., 'Polemics, Old Testament, and Theology, A Study of 2 Cor. III.1-IV.6', *RB* 88 (1981), pp. 340-67.

Richardson, P., and P. Gooch, '*Logia* of Jesus in 1 Corinthians', in D. Wenham (ed.), *Gospel Perspectives* (6 vols.; Sheffield: JSOT Press, 1984), V, pp. 39-62.

Riches, J., *Jesus and the Transformation of Judaism* (London: Darton, Longman & Todd, 1980).

Ridderbos, H.N., *The Epistle of Paul to the Churches of Galatia* (Grand Rapids: Eerdmans, 1953).

Riesenfeld, H., *Jésus transfiguré: L'arrière-plan du récit évangélique de la transfiguration de Notre-Seigneur* (Copenhagen: Ejnar Munksgaard, 1947).

Ringgren, H., *The Messiah in the Old Testament* (London: SCM Press, 1961).

Roberts, J.M., 'Zion in the Theology of Davidic-Solomonic Empire' in T. Ishida, Yamakawa-Shuppansha (ed.), *Studies in the Period of David and Solomon and other Essays* (Tokyo: 1982), pp. 93-108.

Robinson, J.A.T., *Jesus and his Coming* (London: SCM Press, 1957).

—'Elijah, John, and Jesus: An Essay in Detection', *NTS* 4 (1958), pp. 263-81.

—*Twelve New Testament Studies* (London: SCM Press, 1962).

—*Twelve More New Testament Studies* (London: SCM Press, 1984).

—*Redating the New Testament* (London: SCM Press, 1985).

Robinson, J.M., 'On the Gattung of Mark (and John)', in D.G. Buttrick (ed.), *Jesus and Man's Hope* (Pittsburgh: Pittsburgh Theological Seminary, 1970), pp. 116-18.

Rowe, R.D., 'Is Daniel's "Son of Man" Messianic?', in H.H. Rowdon (ed.), *Christ the Lord* (Leicester: IVP, 1982).

Rowland, C., *The Open Heaven* (London: SPCK, 1982).

—*Christian Origins* (London: SCM Press, 1985).

Rowley, H.H., 'Sanballat and the Samaritan Temple', *BJRL* 38 (1955), pp. 66-198.

Runra, D.T., *The Studia Philonica Annual: Studies in Hellenistic Judaism*, I (Atlanta: Scholars Press, 1989).

Sabbé, M., 'La rédaction du récit de la Transfiguration', in E. Massaux (ed.), *La venue du Messie: Messianisme et eschatologie* (RechBib 6; Bruges: Brouwer, 1962), pp. 56-100 reprinted and slightly expanded in *Studia Neotestamentica: Collected Essays* (BETL, 98; Leuven: Leuven University Press, 1991), pp. 65-104,

Safrai, S. 'Oral Torah' in S. Safrai (ed.), *The Literature of the Sages* (Assen: VanGorcum; Philadelphia: Fortress Press, 1984).

Saldarini, A.J., 'The Gospel of Matthew and Jewish-Christian Conflct', in D.L. Balch (ed.), *Social History of the Matthean Community* (Minneapolis: Fortress Press, 1991).

—*Matthew's Christian-Jewish Community* (Chicago/London: Univesity of Chicago Press, 1994).

Sanders, E.P. *The Tendencies of the Synoptic Tradition* (Cambridge: Cambridge University Press, 1969).

—'The Overlaps of Mark and Q and the Synoptic Problem', *NTS* 19 (1972/3), pp. 453-65.

—*Paul and Palestinian Judaism: A Comparison of Patterns of Religion* (Philadelphia: Fortress Press, 1977).

—*Jesus and Judaism* (London: SCM Press, 1985).

Sanders, E.P. and M. Davies, *Studying the Synoptic Gospels* (London: SCM; Philadelphia: Trinity, 1989).

Sanders, J.A., 'Ναζωραῖος' in Matt. 2.23', *JBL* 84 (1965), pp. 169-72.

Sandmel, S., 'Parallelomania', *JBL* 81 (1962), pp. 1-13.

Schaeffer, S.E., 'The Guard at the Tomb (Gos. Pet. 8.28-11.49 and Matt 27.62-66; 28.2-4, 11-16): A Case of Intertextuality?', *JBL* (1991), pp. 499-507.

Schlatter, A., *Der Evangelist Matthäus* (Stuttgart: Calwer, 1963).

Schmid, J., *Das Evangelium nach Matthäus* (Regensburg: Pustet, 1965).

Schmithals, W., 'Der Markusschluss, die Verklärungsgeschichte und die Aussendung der Zwölf', *ZTK* 69 (1972), pp. 394-95.

Schnackenburg, R., *The Gospel according to St John* (Tunbridge Wells: Burns & Oates).

Schneider, J., ἔρχομαι, in *TDNT*, II, pp. 670-71.

Schniewind, J., *Das Evangelium nach Matthäus* (Göttingen: Vandenhoeck & Ruprecht, 1968).

Schnellbächer, E.L., 'ΚΑΙ ΜΕΤΑ 'ΗΜΕΡΑΣ ΕΞ (Markus 9.2)', *ZNW* 71 (1980), pp. 252-57.

Scholem, G.G., 'Kabbalah', in *JewEnc*, X, pp. 495-97.

—*Jewish Gnosticism, Merkaba Mysticism, and Talmudic Tradition* (New York: Jewish Theological Seminary of America, 1960).

Schürer, E., *The History of the Jewish People in the Age of Jesus Christ (175 BC—AD 135): A New English Version Revised and Edited* (ed. G. Vermes *et.al.*; 3 vols.; Edinburgh: T. & T. Clark, 1973).

Schweizer, E., *The Good News according to Matthew* (London: SPCK, 1975).

—'Christianity of the Circumcised and Judaism of the Uncircumcised: The Background of Matthew and Colossians', in R.G. Hammerton-Kelly and R. Scroggs (eds.), *Jews, Greeks and Christians: Religious Cultures in Late Antiquity* (Leiden: Brill, 1976), pp. 45-56.

—'Matthew's Church', in G.N. Stanton (ed.), *The Interpretation of Matthew* (Philadelphia: Fortress Press; London: SPCK, 1983).

—*The Good News according to Luke* (London: SPCK, 1984).

Scobie, C.H., 'The Origins and Development of Samaritan Christianity', *NTS* 19 (1972/3), pp. 390-414.

Scroggs, R., *The Last Adam* (Oxford: Basil Blackwell, 1966).

—'The Earliest Hellenistic Christianity', in J. Neusner (ed.), *Religions in Antiquity* (Leiden: Brill, 1968).

Seebas, H., 'Moses', in *NIDNTT*, II, pp. 635-43.

Segal, A.F., 'Paul and Ecstasy', in K.H. Richards (ed.), *SBL 1986 Seminar Papers* (Chico, CA: Scholars Press, 1986), pp. 555-80.

—*Paul the Convert* (New Haven & London: Yale University Press, 1990).

—'Matthew's Jewish Voice', in D.L. Balch (ed.), *Social History of the Matthean Community* (Minneapolis: Fortress Press, 1991).

Sheriffs, D.C.T., '"A Tale of Two Cities"—Nationalism in Zion and Babylon', *TynBul* 39 (1988), pp. 19-57.

Silberman, L., 'The Two Messiahs of the Manual of Discipline', *VT* 5 (1955), pp. 77-82.

Silver, D.J., 'Moses and the Hungry Birds', *JQR* 64 (1973-74), pp. 123-53.

Simon, M., *St Stephen and the Hellenists in the Primitive Church* (London: Longmans, Green & Co., 1958).

Smalley, S.S., 'The Johannine Son of Man Sayings', *NTS* 15 (1969), pp. 278-301.

Smallwood, E.M., 'The Date of the Dismissal of Pontius Pilate from Judaea', *JJS* 5 (1954), p. 12.

Smith, M., 'Palestinian Judaism in the First Century', in M. Davis (ed.), *Israel: Its Role in Civilization* (New York: 1956), pp. 67-81.

—'What is Implied by the Variety of Messianic Figures?', *JBL* 78 (1959), pp. 66-72.

—'A Comparison of Early Christian and Early Rabbinic Tradition', *JBL* 82 (1963), pp. 169-76.

Smolar, L., and M. Aberbach, 'The Golden Calf Episode in Post-Biblical Literature', *HUCA* 39 (1968), pp. 91-116.

Soares Prabhu, G.M., *The Formula Quotations in the Infancy Narrative of Matthew* (Rome: Biblical Institute Press, 1976).

Solodow, J.B., *The World of Ovid's Metamorphoses* (London: Chapel Hill, 1988).

Spencer, K.J., 'Was Capernaum the Home of Jesus?', *JBL* 65 (1946), pp. 131-41.

—'Nazarean and Nazareth', *JBL* 66 (1947), pp. 79-81.

Spiro, A., 'Stephen's Samaritan Background', in J. Munck, *The Acts of the Apostles* (Garden City: Doubleday, 1967), pp. 285-300.

Stanton, G.N., 'The Gospel of Matthew and Judaism', *BJRL* 66 (1984), pp. 264-84.

—'The Origin and Purpose of Matthew's Gospel: Matthean Scholarship from 1945 to 1980', in H. Temporini and W. Haase (eds.), *Aufstieg und Niedergang der römischen Welt* (Berlin: de Gruyter, 1985), pp. 1889-1951.

—'The Origin and Purpose of Matthew's Sermon on the Mount', in G.F. Hawthorne and O. Betz (eds.), *Tradition and Interpretation in the New Testament* (Grand Rapids: Eerdmans; Tübingen: Mohr, 1987), pp. 181-92.

—*A Gospel for a New People: Studies in Matthew* (Edinburgh: T. & T. Clark, 1992).

Stein, R., 'A Misplaced Resurrection-Account?', *JBL* 95 (1976), pp. 79-96.

Stendahl, K. (ed.), *The Scrolls and the New Testament* (London: SPCK, 1957).

—'Quis et Unde? An Analysis of Matthew 1-2', in W. Eltester (ed.), *Judentum,*

Urchristentum, Kirche (Berlin: Töpelmann, 1960), pp. 94-105; reprinted in G.N. Stanton (ed.), *The Interpretation of Matthew* (London: SPCK, 1983), pp. 54-66.

—'Matthew', in M. Black and H.H. Rowley (eds.), *Peake's Commentary on the Bible* (London: Nelson, 1962).

—*The School of Matthew, and its Use of the Old Testament* (Philadelphia: Fortress Press, 1968).

Strack, H.L., and P. Billerbeck, *Kommentar zum Neuen Testament aus Talmud und Midrasch* (4 vols.; München: Beck, 1951–1956).

Streeter, B.H., *The Four Gospels: A Study of Origins* (London: Macmillan, 1924).

Strickert, F.M., 'Damascus Document VII, 10-20 and Qumran Messianic Expectation', *RQ* 47.12 (Dec 1986), pp. 327-49.

Suggs, M.J., *Wisdom Christology and the Law in Matthew's Gospel* (Cambridge, MA: Harvard University Press, 1970).

Sumney, J.L., *Identifying Paul's Opponents* (Sheffield: JSOT Press, 1990).

Swartley, W.M., 'The Structural Function of the Term "Way" (*Hodos*) in Mark's Gospel', in H. Charles (ed.), *The New Way of Jesus* (Kansas: Faith & Life, 1980), pp. 73-86.

Swete, H.B., *The Gospel according to Mark* (London: Macmillan, 1913).

Swetnam, J., *Jesus and Isaac* (Rome: Pontifical Biblical Institute, 1981).

Tagawa, K., 'People and Community in the Gospel of Matthew', *NTS* 16 (1969–70), pp. 149-62.

Tal, A., 'Samaritan Literature', in A.D. Crown (ed.), *The Samaritans* (Tübingen: Mohr, 1989).

Talbert, C.H., *Literary Patterns, Theological Themes, and the Genre of Luke–Acts* (Missoula, MT: Scholars Press, 1974).

—*Reading Corinthians* (London: SPCK, 1990).

Taylor, A.B., 'Decision in the Desert: The Temptation of Jesus in the Light of Deuteronomy', *Int* 14 (1960), pp. 300-309.

Taylor, J., 'The Prayer Motif in Luke–Acts', in C.H. Talbert (ed.), *Perspectives on Luke–Acts* (Macon, GA: Mercer University Press, 1978), pp. 168-86.

—'The Coming of Elijah, Mt 17,10-13 and Mk 9,11-13. The Development of texts', *RB* 97 (1991), pp. 107-19.

Taylor, V., *The Gospel according to St. Mark* (London: Macmillan; New York: St Martin's, 1966).

Teeple, H.M., *The Mosaic Eschatological Prophet* (SBLMS, 10; Philadelphia: Society of Biblical Literature, 1957).

Thrall, M.E., 'Elijah and Moses in Mark's Account of the Transfiguration', *NTS* 16 (1969-70), pp. 305-17.

Thurston, R.W., 'Midrash and "Magnet" Words in the New Testament', *EvQ* 51 (1979), pp. 22-39.

—'Philo and the Epistle to the Hebrews', *EvQ* 58 (1986), pp. 133-43.

Tiede, D.L., *Charismatic Figure as Miracle Worker* (Missoula, MT: Scholars Press, 1972).

—*Prophecy and History in Luke–Acts* (Philadelphia: Fortress Press, 1980).

Tödt, H.E., *The Son of Man in the Synoptic Tradition* (London: SCM Press, 1965).

Tolbert, M.A., *Sowing the Gospel: Mark's World in Literary-Historical Perspective* (Minneapolis: Fortress Press, 1989).

Tov, E., 'Proto-Samaritan Texts and the Samaritan Pentateuch', in A.D. Crown (ed.), *Samaritans* (Tübingen: Mohr, 1989), pp. 397-407.

Trilling, W., *Das Wahre Israel: Studien zur Theologie des Matthäus-Evangeliums* (München: Kösel, 3rd edn, 1964).

—*The Gospel according to St. Matthew* (2 vols.; London: Burns & Oates, 1969).

Trites, A.A., 'The Transfiguration of Jesus: The Gospel in Microcosom', *EvQ* 51 (1979), pp. 67-79.

—'Transfiguration in the Theology of Luke', in L.D. Hurst and N.T. Wright (eds.), *Glory of Christ in the New Testament: Studies in Christology* (Oxford: Clarendon Press, 1987), pp. 71-81.

Turner, C.H., 'Ο ΥΙΟΣ ΜΟΥ Ο ΑΓΑΠΗΤΟΣ', *JTS* 27 (1926), pp. 113-29.

Twelftree, G.H., 'Jesus in Jewish Traditions', in D. Wenham (ed.), *Gospel Perspectives* (6 vols.; Sheffield: JSOT Press, 1985), V, pp. 289-341.

Unnik, W.C. van, '"With Unveiled Face": An Exegesis of 2 Corinthians iii 12-18', *NovT* 6 (1963), pp. 153-69.

Verhoef, P.A., *The Books of Haggai and Malachi* (Grand Rapids: Eerdmans, 1987).

Vermes, G., 'La Figure de Moïse au Tournant des Deux Testaments', in H. Cazelles (ed.), *Moise, l'homme de l'alliance* (Paris: Desclée, 1955), pp. 78-89.

—*Scripture and Tradition* (Leiden: Brill, 1973).

—*The Dead Sea Scrolls: Qumran in Perspective* (London: SCM Press, 2nd edn, 1982).

—*Jesus the Jew* (London: SCM Press, 3rd edn, 1989).

Verseput, D.J., 'The Role and Meaning of the "Son of God" Title in Matthew's Gospel', *NTS* 33 (1987), pp. 532-56.

Viviano, B.T., 'Where was the Gospel according to St. Matthew Written?', *CBQ* 41 (1979), pp. 533-36.

—'Matthew', in R.E. Brown, J.A. Fitzmyer and R.E. Murphy (eds.), *The New Jerome Bible Commentary* (Englewood Cliffs, NJ: Prentice Hall, 1990), pp. 630-74.

Wacholder, B.Z., *The Dawn of Qumran: The Sectarian Torah and the Teacher of Righteousness* (Cincinnati: Hebrew Union College, 1983).

—'The «Sealed» Torah versus the «Revealed» Torah: An Exegesis of Damascus Covenant V, 1-6 and Jeremiah 32,10-14', *RQ* 47.12, (1986), pp. 351-68.

Wade, G.W., *The Book of the Prophet Isaiah* (London: Methuen, 1911).

Wand, J.W.C., *The General Epistle of St. Peter and St. Jude* (London: Methuen, 1934).

Watts, J.D.W., *Isaiah 34–60* (Waco: Word, 1987).

Webb, R.L., *John the Baptist and the Prophet* (Sheffield: JSOT Press, 1991).

Wedderburn, A.J.M., (ed.), *Paul and Jesus: Collected Essays* (Sheffield: JSOT Press, 1989).

Weeden, T.J., *Mark—Traditions in Conflict* (Philadelphia: Fortress Press, 1971).

Weider, N., 'The "Law-Interpreter" of the Sect of the Dead Sea Scrolls: The Second Moses', *JJS* 4 (1953), pp. 158-75.

Weiss, B., *Das Matthäus-Evangelium* (Göttingen: Vandenhoeck & Ruprecht, 1898).

Wellhausen, J., *Das Evangelium Marci* (Berlin: G. Reimer, 1909).

Wenham, D., 'Jesus and the Law: An Exegesis on Matthew 5.17-20', *Themelios*, 4.3 (1979), pp. 92-99.

—'"This Generation will Not Pass..." A Study of Jesus' Future Expectation in Mark 13', in H.H. Rowdon (ed.), *Christ the Lord* (Leicester: IVP, 1982).

—'Paul's Use of the Jesus Tradition: Three Samples', in D. Wenham (ed.), *Gospel Perspectives* (6 vols.; Sheffield, JSOT Press, 1984), V, pp. 7-37.

—*The Rediscovery of Jesus' Eschatological Discourse* (Sheffield: JSOT Press, 1984).

—'The Kingdom of God and Daniel', *ExpTim* 98 (1986–87), pp. 132-34.

Wenham, D., and A.D.A. Moses, '"There are Some Standing Here...": Did they Become the "Reputed Pillars" of the Jerusalem Church? Some Reflections on Mark 9.1, Galatians 2.9 and the Transfiguration', *NovT* 36.2 (1994), pp. 146-63.

—*Paul: Follower of Jesus or Founder of Christianity?* (Grand Rapids: Eerdmans, 1995).

Westcott, B.F., *The Epistle to the Hebrews* (London: Macmillan, 1889).

Wessel, W.W., 'Ebionites', in *ISBE*, pp. 9-10.

—'Mark', in F.E. Gaebelein, *The Expositor's Bible Commentary* (12 vols.; Grand Rapids: Zondervan, 1984), VIII, pp. 603-793.

Whybray, R.N., *Isaiah 40–66* (London: Oliphants, 1975).

Wiener, A., *The Prophet Elijah in the Development of Judaism: A Depth-Psychological Study* (London: Routledge & Kegan Paul, 1978).

Wifall, W., 'Son of Man—A Pre Davidic Social class?', *CBQ* 37 (1975), pp. 331-40.

Wilkins, M.J., *The Concept of Disciple in Matthew's Gospel* (Leiden: Brill, 1988).

Williamson, R., *Philo and the Epistle to the Hebrews* (Leiden: Brill, 1970).

Wink, W., *John the Baptist in the Gospel Tradition* (Cambridge: Cambridge University Press, 1968).

Winter, P., 'Jewish Folklore in the Matthean Birth Story', *HeyJ* 53 (1954), pp. 34-42.

Wolfson, H.A., *Philo: Foundations of Religious Philosophy in Judaism, Christianity, and Islam* (Cambridge, MA: Harvard University Press, 1948).

Wood, J.E., 'Isaac Typology and the New Testament', *NTS* 14 (1967/68), pp. 583-89.

Wright, N.T., 'Jesus, Israel and the Cross', in K.H. Richards (ed.), *SBLSP* (Atlanta: Scholars Press, 1985), pp. 75-95.

—'Reflected Glory: 2 Corinthians 3.18', in L.D. Hurst and N.T. Wright (eds.), *The Glory of Christ in the New Testament* (Oxford: Clarendon Press, 1987), pp. 139-50.

—*The New Testament and the People of God* (Minneapolis: Fortress Press, 1992).

Whybray, R.N., *Isaiah 40–66* (London: Oliphants, 1975).

Young, F., and D.F. Ford, *Meaning and Truth in 2 Corinthians* (London: SPCK, 1987).

Young, J., *The Book of Isaiah* (3 vols.; Grand Rapids: Eerdmans, 1981).

Zehnle, R., *Peter's Pentecost Discourse* (Nashville: Abingdon, 1971).

Ziesler, J.A., 'The Transfiguration Story and the Marcan Soteriology', *ExpTim* 81 (1970), pp. 263-68.

Zimmerli. W., and J. Jeremias, *The Servant of God* (SBT, 20; London: SCM Press, 1957).

INDEXES

INDEX OF REFERENCES

OLD TESTAMENT

Reference	Page	Reference	Page	Reference	Page
Genesis		2.15-22	53	18.12	186
1.1-2	56	2.15	165, 166	19–35	111
1.3-31	54	3	79, 81, 103,	19–34	45, 89, 112,
1.3	218, 238		129, 231		129, 130,
1.27	121	3.1–4.17	112		136, 203
6.2	148	3.1-2	44	19–24	45
6.4	148	3.3-6	149	19–20	103, 104
7.19	118	3.3	91, 103,	19	157
7.20	118		149, 240	19.1-25	103
12.3	195, 209	3.6	47, 149	19.3	109, 176
18.2	128	3.24-34	44	19.5-6	111
18.18	195	4.10	147	19.5	105, 130
22	142-44, 147	4.16	74	19.7	75
22.2	34, 140,	4.19	165	19.9	105, 112,
	143, 147,	4.22	34, 142,		137
	205, 220		143, 148,	19.10	107
22.12	140, 143,		205	19.11-12	109
	220	6.12	145	19.11	103, 105
22.16	140, 143,	7–12	162	19.12	176
	220	7.1-11	74	19.13	176
22.18	195, 209	7.2	190	19.14	107, 109,
26.4	195, 209	7.14–12.42	103		110
28.13	128	12	185-87	19.16-17	111
31.46	186	12.41	165	19.16	107, 137,
31.54	186	13.17-22	103		169
32.24	87	13.21-22	21	19.18-19	109
35.13	87	14.1–15.21	103	19.18	103, 105,
37	82	14.19-20	21		169
49.10	193	14.31	50, 147	19.19	107, 110
		15	106	19.20	103, 105
Exodus		15.17-18	106	19.21	105
1–15	81	15.18	105, 106,	20.12-16	47
1.15-22	165		110	20.12	47
1.15	194	15.27	81	20.17	71
2.1-10	165	16.4-5	172	20.18	149, 169

20.21	74	33–34	45	20.9	47
20.25-26	53	33.7-11	134	23.29	210
21	52	33.7	216	23.43	30
21.16	47	33.11	149		
21.20	150	33.12–34.8	217, 218	*Numbers*	
23.20	167	33.18-23	218	6.3	57
24–31	45	33.18-19	79	9.15-23	21
24	43, 44, 82,	33.18	74, 111, 218	12.7-8	147
	186	33.19-23	107	12.7	212
24.1-8	187	33.22	111, 218	12.8	121
24.1-2	186	34	62, 78, 85,	20.12	175
24.1	43		103, 120,	24.17	194
24.2	109		129, 174,	27.12-14	174
24.3-8	185, 186,		225, 237	35.34	216
	242	34.5	107, 137		
24.8	186	34.6-7	217	*Deuteronomy*	
24.9-11	186	34.6	74, 217, 218	1–34	187, 242
24.9	43, 109, 223	34.8	110, 149	1.2	104
24.11	186, 242	34.11-17	173, 174	1.3	190
24.12-14	187	34.20	218	1.26	190
24.12	176, 223	34.23	218	1.43	190
24.13	43, 176	34.28-35	62	3.22-23	209
24.14	59	34.28-29	52	3.23-28	174
24.15-18	45, 111,	34.28	172, 206	3.24	147, 209
	115, 136	34.29-35	62, 75, 105,	3.25	209
24.15-16	48		126	4.2	190
24.15	137	34.29-31	213	4.13	190
24.16-18	111	34.29-30	48, 109, 123	4.34	74
24.16-17	43	34.29	43, 110,	4.40	190
24.16	43, 45, 53,		121, 122,	5.16-20	47
	54, 56, 137		128, 223	5.19-24	89
24.17	169	34.30	44, 46, 121,	5.22	21
24.18	52, 75, 137		149, 150	5.26-27	71
24.28	75	34.31-32	150	5.28-29	64
25.7-8	53	34.35	48, 121	5.29	190
25.8	217	34.40	56	5.31	190
25.9	216	34.45	128	6–18	171
25.10–31.18	134	35–40	132	6–8	171, 172
25.10–31.11	45	40.34-38	48, 136	6.1	75, 190
29.35	190	40.34-35	43	6.2	190
29.45	217	40.34	111, 137	6.5	46
31.18	75	40.35	137	6.13-15	174
32–34	45	40.38	137	6.13	171, 173
32	109, 110,	44.22-23	140	6.14	174
	120, 130,			6.16	171
	174	*Leviticus*		6.17	174, 190
32.9-10	173	10.1-8	40	6.25	190
32.15	75	19.18	46	7.9	190

7.11	190	30.11	190	6.20-21	87
8.1-10	172	31.9-13	63	8.18	227
8.1	190	32.5-6	148	9.1-6	166
8.2	171, 190	32.5	109, 110,	11.34	143, 220
8.3	171		120, 175	13.4-5	57
8.5	171	32.6	54	13.7	164
8.6	190	32.8	148	13.22	218
8.11	190	32.15	106	16.7	164
9.9	172, 176,	32.20	109, 110,		
	206		120, 175	*1 Samuel*	
9.11	75	32.48-52	174	13.14	209
9.18	172, 206	33	106, 191	15.28	209
9.23	190	33.1-29	190	16.13	209
10.13	190	33.1-5	105	28.17	209
11.1	190	33.1-2	106		
11.8	190	33.2	169	*2 Samuel*	
11.13	190	33.4	106	5.2	194, 195
12.5	217	33.5	106	5.8	199
14.1	54	33.26	106	7.12-16	209
15.16	146	34	189	7.14	34, 148
15.18	221	34.1-4	174		
17.14-15	60	34.1	190	*1 Kings*	
17.20	190	34.5	40, 147	10.1-13	195
18	34, 145, 148	34.10	42, 149	11.40	166
18.5	145			18.36-40	130
18.15-22	191	*Joshua*		19	44, 103
18.15-20	184	1.1-9	191	19.2-10	156
18.15-19	50, 64, 122,	1.1	147	19.5-8	173
	123, 145,	1.2	147	19.7-18	104, 203
	146, 208-10	1.7	147	19.8-18	130
18.15-18	59, 70, 71,	1.13	147	19.8	172, 206
	198, 201	1.15	147	22.19	88, 112
18.15-16	111	2.4	147		
18.15	26, 40, 46-	8.31	147	*2 Kings*	
	48, 65, 71,	8.33	147	2	248
	145, 159,	9.24	147	2.11-12	129
	210	11.12	147	2.11	40, 88
18.16	145	11.15	147	10.1-11	166
18.18-22	71	12.6	147	11.1-2	166
18.18-19	130	13.8	147	18.12	147
18.18	40, 41, 69,	14.7	147		
	70, 74, 145,	18.7	147	*1 Chronicles*	
	146, 215	22.2	147	6.3-14	193
18.19	130, 159	22.5	147	6.49	147
18.29	210			24.9	147
24.12	74	*Judges*			
27.15-26	162	5.4-5	104	*2 Chronicles*	
28.16-17	162	5.31	124	1.3	147

15.10-13	63	132.11-18	202	53.10	185
21.2-4	166	132.11-13	202	53.12	185
24.6	147	133.3	118	58.12	133
28.11	145	147	82	59.1-9	126
		1926-27	148	60.3	195
Ezra				61.1-2	248
7.6	50	*Proverbs*		63.19	168, 169
		6.23	219	64	104
Nehemiah				64.1-2	169
1.8	50	*Isaiah*		64.1	169, 170
		2.2-4	206	64.2	169
Job		2.2-3	133, 202,	64.3	169
4.16	121, 227		203		
42.17	38	4.5-6	136	*Jeremiah*	
		4.5	137	1	231
Psalms		6	231	1.11-19	138
2	142, 205	6.1-13	112	4.23-25	133
2.6	118, 202	6.1-8	138	6.26	140
2.7	32-34, 140-	6.1-2	88	6.27	143
	43, 145, 148	6.7	101	8.19	118
8	90, 199	9.1-2	127	22.28-30	194
8.2	199	10.16-17	127	26.21	166
8.4	199	11.12	107	31.1-25	202
8.5-8	199	14.13	118	31.20	148
17	121	15.24	127	31.31-34	185, 206
29.1	148	24.23	202, 203	31.31	62, 64, 65
29.6	118	25.6	186	35.6	57
33.1	121	27.13	107		
42.6	118	28.4	118	*Ezekiel*	
48.2	118	29.6-8	202	1–2	112, 117,
50.3	203	29.8	202		231
68.7-8	104	30.26	124	1	83, 118
68.15-18	202	40.3	157, 167,	1.1	168
68.17-18	104		168, 170	1.3	88
72.8-11	195	42	158	1.4-28	138
77.16	104	42.1-2	142	1.4-5	117
78.12-16	203	42.1	34, 140,	1.4	89, 128
78.67-71	202		141, 144,	1.22-23	88
80	90		146, 147,	1.22	88
89.7	148		205, 220	1.24	82
89.12	118	43.16-20	170	1.26	82, 83
96.13	41, 108	44.13	227	1.28	101, 149
97.2	136	49.22	107	2.1	90, 98, 149,
110.1	200, 201	51.9-10	104, 105		158
110.2	202	52.7	203	8.1-2	88
110.4	193	52.13–53.11	186	8.10	88
118.22-23	134	53	66	10.3-4	21
119.105	219	53.3	156	17.22-24	132, 203

17.22	133		188, 191,	8.3	168
20.11	75		201, 240,	8.15-19	231
20.33-44	202		243	8.17-18	101
20.33	203	7.1	136	8.17	98, 101, 149
20.40	203	7.2-12	91, 105	8.18	110, 112,
30.3	136	7.2	136		149, 150
34.9	131	7.9-12	109	8.19	102
34.23-31	203	7.9-10	82, 88, 93,	9	104
37.27	131		106, 109,	10.5-21	101
39.17-20	186		111	10.5-6	88, 112
40–48	104, 149,	7.9	101	10.5	102
	202	7.10	110	10.6-21	102
40	118	7.11	110	10.6	87, 89, 102,
40.2	117	7.12	90		120
43.1-5	117	7.13-18	91, 99, 100,	10.7-9	149
43.1-2	112		113	10.8-12	231
43.7	131	7.13-14	82, 91-93,	10.9	102
			97, 100,	10.10-11	102
Daniel			102, 109,	10.10	102, 150
2	158		111, 123,	10.12	102, 110,
2.37	174		189		150
2.44	106, 111	7.13	48, 83, 90,	10.15-19	149
3.19	227		91, 99, 102,	10.16	150
3.25	148		107-109,	10.18	150
4.3	111		117, 128,	10.19	102
4.14	189		136, 157,	12	155
4.17	106, 111		159, 240	12.2-3	98, 101
4.22	189	7.14	106, 107,	12.3	53, 87, 91,
4.25-26	106, 111		174, 188,		122-24,
4.29	189		189, 221		126, 157
4.31	138, 168	7.15-28	100, 102	7.13	109
4.32	111	7.15	90, 91, 136,		
4.34-35	106		149	*Hosea*	
4.34	111	7.16-27	91	2.15	54
4.37	106	7.16-17	100	6.6	182
5.12	111	7.16	91	11.1	56, 134,
5.21-23	106	7.18	99, 110		143, 148
5.21	189	7.19-28	100	11.18-19	148
7	48, 49, 80-	7.19	91	12.14	50
	85, 90-92,	7.21-22	105, 156		
	98-103,	7.21	99, 112	*Joel*	
	105-109,	7.22	106, 110	3.9-21	202
	112, 113,	7.26	111		
	117, 118,	7.27	106, 110,	*Amos*	
	123, 129,		189	2.12	57
	137, 155,	7.28	91, 100,	8.10	140, 143
	158, 160,		110, 149	9.11	133
	163, 187,	8.1-18	149		

Micah			14.16	30	*Ecclesiasticus*	
1.3	41, 108				4.10	148, 196
3.12–4.2	202		*Malachi*		24.3	216
4.6-7	203		1.11	145	24.6-8	216
4.11-13	202		3.1-2	168	24.10	216
5.2-4	203		3.1	128, 167	24.23-24	75
5.2	70, 194		3.7	130	24.23	216
			3.22-24	129, 130	43.27-33	218
Habakkuk			4.2	124	44.23–45.5	74, 103, 148
3.1-5	104		4.4-6	42, 129,	44.23	74
				130, 133	45.1	74, 84, 147
Zephaniah			4.5-6	168, 248	45.2-3	74
1.15	136		4.5	154	45.2	129, 147
			9.9-10	150	45.4	147
Zechariah			9.11-13	150	45.5-6	74
2.10-11	131				45.5	84
2.14	217		*Tobit*		48.1-12	42, 129
8.3	131		1.13	227	48.2	129
8.8	131				49.16	79
8.23	133		*Wisdom of Solomon*			
9.9	155		2.16	196	*1 Maccabees*	
12.10	143		2.17-18	148	2.58	129
14.4	118		2.18	196		
14.6-9	131		5.5	196	*2 Maccabees*	
14.8-11	203		7.26	213	2.8	136, 137
14.16-19	33		18.1	227		

NEW TESTAMENT

Matthew			1.18-25	196	2.5-6	70, 164,
1–2	163, 170,		1.18-21	165		166, 182
	194, 201,		1.18	195	2.6	195
	242		1.20	127, 145,	2.9	126
1.1–2.12	243			194, 195	2.12	56, 194
1.1-17	163, 164,		1.21	194, 196	2.13-23	120
	166, 194		1.22-23	166, 182,	2.13-15	166
1.1	145, 164,			195	2.13	127, 166
	193, 195,		1.22	180	2.15-16	182
	198		1.23	101, 113,	2.15	54-56, 134,
1.6-11	193			157, 187,		143, 148,
1.6	145, 193			241		166, 170,
1.12-16	193		1.25	164, 195		171, 196,
1.12	194		2	166		242
1.13-23	100, 113		2.1-12	164	2.17-18	164, 182
1.16	164, 194,		2.1	127	2.17	166
	195, 198		2.2-18	165	2.18	166
1.17	145, 164		2.2	127, 194	2.19-20	165
1.18–2.23	163, 164				2.19	127

2.20	164, 166		187, 189,	5.19	182
2.21-23	148		205, 206,	5.20-48	177
2.22-23	124, 165		242	5.20	178, 240
2.23-24	182	4.9	173	5.21-48	179, 181-
2.23	164, 166	4.10	124, 171,		83, 242
3.1	124, 167		173, 174	5.23-24	47
3.3-4	101	4.11	173	5.31-32	242
3.3	157, 167,	4.14-16	182	5.32	182
	168, 170,	4.14	124	6.1-6	178
	241	4.15-16	159, 241	6.1	178
3.7	124	4.15	19, 160,	6.7	201
3.11-12	134		201, 204,	6.10	188
3.13-17	167, 170,		242	6.16-18	178
	171, 241,	4.16	126, 127	6.19	57
	242	4.17	133	6.20	57
3.13	124	4.18-22	138	6.32	201
3.15	178	4.18-20	159	6.33	178
3.16	126, 168,	4.18-19	132	7.1-13	85
	170	4.18	131, 231	7.12-27	177
3.17	27, 31, 54,	4.21	116	7.12	57
	55, 124,	4.23	146	7.15-23	182
	137-39,	5-7	126, 163,	7.17	183
	142, 144,		175-78,	7.21-27	65, 122, 134
	145, 147,		184, 191,	7.21	131, 183,
	159, 168,		242		184, 196
	196, 197,	5	176	7.23-29	183
	205, 242	5.1-20	242	7.23	178
4	163	5.1	117, 176,	7.24-29	191
4.1-11	134, 159,		177, 187,	7.24-27	110, 135,
	170, 172,		189, 205,		146, 178,
	174, 187,		206		182, 184,
	241, 242	5.3-11	162		209
4.1	171	5.6	57, 178, 186	7.24-26	159, 241
4.2	206	5.10-12	178	7.24	184, 188
4.3-6	197	5.10	178	7.28-29	182
4.3	54, 55, 148,	5.11	99, 178	7.28	162, 183,
	171, 173,	5.12-14	182		184
	174, 196	5.14-16	126, 127,	7.29	184
4.4	171		160, 205,	8-9	162
4.5	171		242	8.1	117
4.6	54, 55, 148,	5.14-15	175	8.2	131
	151, 173,	5.14	117	8.4	47, 151
	174, 196	5.17-20	178, 179,	8.5-13	19
4.7	171		182, 183	8.6	131
4.8-11	174	5.17-19	179	8.10-13	134
4.8-10	173, 175	5.17-18	181	8.11	38, 186
4.8-9	174	5.18-20	177	8.15	173
4.8	117, 172,	5.18	180, 215	8.17	182

Reference	Pages
8.21	153
8.24-27	112
9.3	101
9.6	243
9.9	117, 119
9.10-13	178
9.10	127
9.18	127, 135
9.27	145, 197
9.30	151
9.32	127
9.35	146, 197
9.36–10.42	176
10.1	242
10.2	116
10.3	117, 119
10.5-6	132, 133
10.6	19
10.24-25	153
10.32-33	55, 92, 93, 196
10.40	196
10.42	153
11.1	162, 183
11.2-6	197, 248
11.5	198
11.10-15	168
11.10	128, 167, 168, 170
11.11	153, 167
11.13	177, 183
11.14	128
11.16-24	134
11.18	155
11.19	178, 191
11.25-30	178, 181, 183, 184, 191
11.25	198
11.27	174, 188
11.28-30	65, 110, 182
12.1-8	181-83
12.1-4	177, 178
12.6	148, 158
12.9-14	181-83
12.16	151
12.17-21	182
12.18	141, 144
12.22-23	197
12.23	145
12.28	115, 157, 241
12.38-45	110, 134
12.39	175
12.41-42	55, 148
12.46	127, 135
12.50	55, 196
13.19	146
13.24-30	93, 124, 125, 205
13.27	131
13.30	125
13.34	53
13.35	182
13.36-43	124-26, 133, 137, 205, 241
13.37	92, 125
13.38-43	97
13.38	123, 125, 126
13.40-43	241
13.40-42	125
13.41-43	93, 98, 189
13.41	56, 100, 125, 179
13.43	87, 101, 122-26, 157, 158, 160
13.46	126, 127
13.53	162, 183
13.54	182
14.3-12	37
14.13-21	172
14.15-21	163, 173
14.22	173
14.23	117, 176, 206
14.26	172
14.27	149, 150
14.28-33	131, 159
14.28-31	27
14.31	153
14.33	54, 139, 148, 153, 196
15.1-20	177, 240
15.4	47, 151, 190
15.13	55, 196
15.15	27
15.17-20	178, 242
15.17	180
15.21-39	19, 133, 159, 201
15.22	131, 145, 197
15.24	133, 196
15.29-31	206, 207
15.29	117, 176, 177, 205-207
15.30-31	197
15.32-39	163, 173
16.1-12	133, 159
16.4	134
16.6-12	177
16.12	182
16.13–17.13	114, 115
16.13–17.8	134
16.13-20	116, 120, 132, 138, 159
16.13-19	229, 232
16.13-14	119
16.13	30, 92, 115, 139
16.14	37, 38
16.16-20	48
16.16-19	105, 115, 116, 131, 132, 134, 159, 190, 237, 241
16.16	27, 31, 54, 115, 135, 139, 148, 234
16.17-20	110, 119, 135
16.17-19	27, 213, 234
16.17	50, 139, 196

16.18-19	133, 205, 242	17.2	43, 46, 48, 56, 80, 87, 89, 91, 98, 101	19.7	151, 190, 240
16.18	119, 132, 145, 146, 159, 181	17.3	21, 46	19.8-9	151
				19.9	182
16.20	151	17.4	31, 45, 48	19.11-12	57
16.21–18.35	191	17.5	27, 31, 41, 48, 54, 55, 65, 100, 101, 124, 183	19.12	99
16.21-28	147, 184			19.17	131
16.21-26	115			19.18	47
16.21-23	30			19.21	131
16.21	99, 115, 143, 180, 207, 241	17.6-8	91	19.23-30	133
		17.6-7	44	19.23-28	184
				19.27-30	159
16.22-23	115, 116, 131, 134	17.6	101	19.27	133, 204
		17.9-13	36, 39, 91	19.28	56, 92, 97, 100, 133, 175, 189, 242
16.22	153, 204	17.9-12	98		
16.23	124	17.9	23, 91, 92, 98-100, 191		
16.24-28	112			20.20-28	133
16.24	131	17.10-13	25, 38, 100	20.23	196
16.25	99	17.11	38	20.30-31	131, 197
16.27-28	91, 97, 103, 106, 115, 152, 175, 189	17.12-13	37	20.30	145
		17.12	91, 92, 98, 99	20.31	145
		17.14-20	120	21.1	117
16.27	92-94, 98-101, 107, 125, 137, 157, 158, 240, 241	17.17	109, 120, 134, 175	21.2	155
				21.4-5	56, 182
		17.18	109	21.4	180
		17.20	117, 120	21.7	155
		17.21	55	21.9	145, 166, 198, 201
16.28	39, 56, 92-94, 97-101, 105, 107, 125, 137, 146, 157, 158, 229, 240, 241	17.22–18.35	176	21.11	198, 201
		17.22-27	184	21.14-15	197
		17.22-23	99, 147	21.14	198, 199
		17.23	143, 180	21.15-16	197
		17.24-27	27, 47, 159	21.15	145, 166
		17.26	124	21.16	199
		18.1-35	184	21.21	117
17	83	18.10	196	21.23–23.39	198
17.1-13	16, 20, 37, 46, 49, 77, 80, 99, 100	18.12	117	21.23	146
		18.14	196	21.30	131
		18.15-16	145	21.32	155, 178
17.1-9	14, 36, 45, 90, 100, 101	18.17	145	21.33-46	196
		18.19	196	21.33-43	134
17.1-8	13, 56, 63, 91, 99	18.21	27	21.37	148
		18.35	196	21.42-46	198
17.1	26, 43, 44, 53, 54, 58	19.1	162, 183	21.42	134
		19.3-12	163, 184	21.43	127, 133
17.2-8	54	19.3-9	177, 242	22.1-10	186
17.2-5	91			22.1	131

22.29	200	24.42-44	155	27.11	139
22.31	47	25.20	131	27.32-54	241
22.41-46	193, 199, 200	25.31-46	125, 137, 189	27.43	197
				27.47	38
22.41-45	145, 197	25.31-33	158, 241	27.51-54	241
22.42	200	25.31-32	92, 97, 133, 175	27.52-53	98, 180
22.46	200			27.53	171
23–25	176	25.31	56, 100, 101, 107	27.54	54, 139, 143, 148, 196
23.1-36	182		
23.1-9	181	25.32-33	179
23.1-2	183	25.33-40	158	27.56	116
23.2-3	177, 182, 242	25.34	56, 196	28.5	131
		25.41-46	158	28.8-10	187
23.2	163, 177, 178, 240	25.41	39	28.10	160, 204
		25.44	173	28.11	127
23.3	180	25.46b	158	28.16-20	113, 149, 159, 160, 163, 174, 175, 187-89, 191, 207
23.4-22	183	26.1	162, 183		
23.5-22	182	26.2	92		
23.9	196	26.17-29	163, 185, 242		
23.13-33	162				
23.14	134	26.25	131	28.16	117, 160, 175, 190, 204, 205
23.23	182, 183, 240	26.27-28	186		
		26.27	241		
23.28	178	26.28	66	28.17	149, 153
23.29-36	134	26.29	98, 146, 186, 187, 196	28.18-20	19, 110, 157, 160, 182, 190, 201, 241, 242
23.33	124				
23.38	204				
23.39	98	26.30	117		
24.1–25.46	184	26.32	160		
24.1	240	26.39	197	28.18	56, 100, 101, 113, 149, 180, 184, 188, 189, 191, 243
24.2	204	26.42	196, 197		
24.3-4	177	26.47	127, 135, 198		
24.3	59, 117, 205, 207	26.49	131		
		26.50-56	153		
24.12	178	26.53	196	28.19-20	98
24.14	133	26.54-56	180	28.19	127, 133, 159, 196, 241
24.15-28	204	26.55	146		
24.16	117	26.61	240		
24.27	59	26.63	196, 201	28.20-68	162
24.29-31	158, 241	26.64	54, 92, 98, 101, 105, 136, 139, 157, 175, 180, 188, 189, 201, 241	28.20	65, 112, 122, 134, 135, 146, 174, 178, 183, 184, 188, 189, 191
24.30-31	107, 108, 175, 189				
24.30	39, 92, 100, 101, 136				
24.34	180				
24.35	146				
24.37	59				
24.39	59	27.9-10	182		

Mark				
1.2	23	9.2-10	40, 47, 229	9.25	109
1.6	23	9.2-9	45	9.2a	114
1.10	168	9.2-8	13, 25, 27,	9.31	28
1.11	27, 138,		36, 37, 43,	9.32-33	32
	140, 142		46, 63, 115,	9.38	247
1.12-13	29		223, 239	10.3-9	47
1.13	172, 173	9.2-3	43, 120, 228	10.4	151
1.16	231	9.2	28, 43, 44,	10.32	28
1.44	47		53, 54, 58,	10.39	96
2.14	117, 119		225, 227,	10.47	197
3.31	135		233, 235,	12.10	36, 37
4.1-23	124		236, 245,	12.25-27	38
4.26-29	124		246	12.26	47
4.36	28	9.3	46, 48, 89,	12.29-31	46
4.38	247		118, 246	12.32-34	200
5.21	135	9.4	21, 46, 230	12.34	200
5.40	28	9.5	27, 31, 45,	12.35-37	199
6.15	38, 248		46, 130,	13.21-22	38
6.35-43	173		135, 149,	13.24-27	94
6.45	173		205	13.26	21, 105, 136
7.10	47	9.6	28, 44, 136,	13.27	38
7.18-23	178		148, 152	13.30-31	94
7.18-20	182	9.7	27, 31, 38,	13.30	94
7.19	180		41, 43, 44,	14.24	186
7.25	197		46, 48, 54,	14.26	28
8.1-10	173		135-38,	14.33	28
8.27–9.13	27		143, 144,	14.36	28, 96, 197
8.27–9.1	27		156, 220,	14.40	28
8.27	30		221, 232,	14.62	21, 91, 94,
8.28	38		234		105, 136
8.29	27, 139	9.8	117, 150	15.35-36	38
8.31–9.1	26	9.9-13	36, 37, 39,	15.37-39	93
8.31-33	30, 37		49, 91, 152,	15.40	116
8.31-32	26, 29		239, 249	16.5	120
8.31	96	9.9-10	151	16.12	121
8.32	27	9.9	23, 230	8,38	27
8.34-38	36	9.10-13	24	9.2-8	95
8.34-37	37, 96	9.10-11	23, 46		
8.34	223	9.10	152	*Luke*	
8.38	25, 37, 92-	9.11-13	38, 47, 154,	1.1-3	246
	94, 105, 209		155, 245,	1.27	193
9.1-13	25, 128		247, 248	1.31	194
9.1	25, 27, 28,	9.11-12	152	1.32	193
	39, 40, 92-	9.11	153, 156	1.35	136
	97, 99, 115,	9.12	38, 98, 156,	1.36	194
	125, 229		157	1.69	193
9.2-13	20, 23, 49	9.13	156	1.75	178
		9.19	109	2.4	193

Reference	Pages
2.11	193
3.12	24
3.16-17	248
3.21-22	171
3.21	168
3.22	27, 31, 138, 140, 142, 145
4.1-2	248
4.2	172
4.3	171
4.9-12	173
4.9	171
4.16-18	248
4.25-27	248
5.14	47
5.27	117, 119
6.20-49	184
6.22	99
6.46	183
7.11-17	248
7.11-16	248
7.12	143
7.18-23	248
7.27	248
7.40	247
8.24	247
8.42	143
8.45	247
9.8	38, 248
9.12-17	173, 249
9.18	27
9.19	38
9.20	27, 31, 139
9.22	30
9.26	92, 209
9.27	93, 99, 229
9.28-36	13, 24, 36, 63, 229, 236, 249, 250
9.28	228, 245, 246
9.29-32	245
9.29-31	246
9.29	43, 46, 89, 102, 227, 235
9.30	24, 46, 248
9.31-32	25, 220, 227, 235, 236, 230, 249
9.31	24, 40, 230
9.32	247
9.33-35	31, 45, 131, 205, 247
9.33	44, 54, 136, 137, 148, 232, 234
9.34	31, 41, 54, 138, 140, 142, 144, 210, 220, 221, 232
9.35	230
9.36	24
9.37-43	249
9.38-43	143
9.38	109
9.41	109
9.42	247
9.49	24, 248
9.51	70
9.52-53	248
9.54-55	248
9.61-62	248
10.1-12	120
10.18	246
10.23-24	70
10.33-37	246
10.41	120
11.36	92, 93
12.8-9	248
12.49-53	186
13.28-29	186
13.29	24
13.34	181
16.116-17	247
16.16	180
16.17	145
16.29	145
16.31	70
17.11-18	247
17.13	120
17.24	47
18.20	47
18.24-30	133
18.38	197
20.27	199
20.37	47
20.41-44	199
21.27	136
22.28-30	133
22.30	133
22.32	230
22.42	197
23.34	24
24.4	25, 120, 128
24.26	219
24.51	248

John

Reference	Pages
1	238, 239
1.1-18	214
1.1-11	184
1.1-3	218
1.1-2	215
1.1	216, 218
1.4-5	218
1.4	215
1.5	215
1.6	219
1.8-9	218
1.9	215
1.11	215
1.13	215
1.14-18	216
1.14	137, 215-21, 224, 239, 243
1.16-17	215, 219
1.16	216, 217
1.17	215, 223, 238
1.18	55, 215, 218
1.21	70, 129, 248
1.29	144
1.34	140, 141
1.41-42	231
1.45	215
2.11	219
2.19-22	216
3.1-14	222
3.6	215

3.13	221-24, 238, 239	12.28	219, 221, 223			210, 238, 239
3.14-15	223	12.31	221	7.16	71	
3.14	215	12.35	215	7.25	210	
3.16	143, 144, 215	12.41	215	7.27	210	
		12.46	215	7.31	91, 103	
3.19	215	13.31-32	219	7.35	210	
4	67, 69-71, 74, 238, 239, 243	13.34	161	7.37	70, 71, 74, 145, 208, 243
		14.2	132			
		14.6	215			
4.9	70	16.8	178	7.39	210	
4.13-14	215	16.10	178	7.52	24	
4.22	69, 70	17.1	219	7.59-60	24	
4.25	69, 145	17.5	215	8.3	19	
4.28-30	70	18.11	220	8.4-25	70	
4.44	215	20.26	31	9.1-2	19	
5.25	145	21.15-19	230	9.3	120, 233	
5.26	215	21.19	219	9.4	101, 233	
5.42	223			9.12	89	
5.46	215	*Acts*		9.13-14	19	
6	238, 239, 243	1.4-5	248	9.21	19	
		1.6	39, 132, 133, 204	10.3	89	
6.5-14	173			10.17	89	
6.14-15	173	1.9	21, 248	10.19	89	
6.14	70, 198	1.10	24, 120, 128, 246	11.5	89	
6.31-32	173			12.2	116, 231	
6.31	60	1.11	248	12.9	89	
6.32	223	1.18-19	24	13.22-23	193	
6.35	215	1.18	24	13.33	205	
6.46	55, 215	2	94	15.13	116	
6.51	215	2.29-36	193	15.16-17	133	
7	30	2.37	24	16.9	89	
7.1-2	29	3	238, 239	17.9	233	
7.39	219	3.11-26	208, 209	21.38	172	
7.40	70	3.13	24	22	233	
7.41-42	70	3.14	210	22.3-5	19	
7.42	218	3.15	210	22.6	120, 233	
8.12	215	3.17	210	22.7	101, 233	
8.41-42	215	3.19-21	39, 133	22.10	233	
8.47	145	3.21	248, 249	22.19	19	
8.52	96	3.22-23	145, 243	26	235	
8.56	144	3.22	210	26.4	101	
11.4	219	3.23	210	26.9-11	19	
11.40	219	4.11	134	26.13	233	
12.16	219	5.15	137	26.14	233	
12.25	223	5.36-37	171	26.16-18	234	
12.27-30	220	5.36	60	26.16	233	
		7	67, 69-71,	26.19	233	

28.28   145

Romans
1.3   193, 205
1.4   93
1.23   227, 236
1.25-26   236
2.20   121
3.23   228
6.1-11   237
6.3-11   244
6.4-11   236
6.5   236
8.17   219
8.32   144
9.29-30   227
12.2   53, 56, 121, 225, 227, 233, 236

1 Corinthians
3.1-23   231
3.18   228
3.22   231
4.6   228
9.1-8   231
10.1-5   170
10.1-4   38, 50
11.7   121, 227, 228
13.12   225
15   144, 236, 244
15.9   19
15.23   59, 125
15.51-52   236

2 Corinthians
1–9   226
2.14–6.13   230
2.14–4.6   228, 230
3–4   16, 227, 230, 236-38
3   208
3.1–4.6   50
3.1-18   226, 228, 229, 233, 235-37, 244

3.1-8   231
3.1   227, 231
3.3   227
3.7–4.6   229
3.7-18   213, 224, 225
3.7   213, 238
3.9   238
3.10-11   238
3.13-16   225
3.13   225
3.18   56, 121, 225, 227, 228, 233, 235-37, 244
4.1-6   224, 228, 229, 235, 244
4.3   225
4.6   213, 225, 226, 228, 229, 231, 235-38, 244
9.29   236
11.13-15   236
12.9   137

Galatians
1.1   227
1.12   232
1.13   19
1.15-16   232
1.16   234
2.2   237
2.6-7   237
2.7-8   232, 234
2.7   227
2.9-10   234
2.9   96, 116, 121, 229, 231
2.20   237
3.16   144
3.20   244
4.19   121, 244
6.2   161

Ephesians
1.21   188

Philippians
2.6-7   121
2.9-10   188
3.5-6   19
3.10-11   237
3.10   244
3.12   219
3.21   236, 244

Colossians
1.16-21   188
3.16   184

1 Thessalonians
2.13-16   19
2.19   59
3.13   59
4.13-18   107
4.15   59
4.16   107
4.17   21, 136
5.23   59

2 Thessalonians
1.7-8   39
2.1-12   107
2.1   59
2.8   39, 59
2.14   219

1 Timothy
1.13   19
3.16   219

2 Timothy
2.8   193
3.5   121

Hebrews
1.1   184
1.2   212
1.3-14   33
1.3   213
1.5   205
2.9   96

2.10	212	1.16-18	25, 26, 47,	2.26-28	205
3.1-6	55, 212, 213		86, 138,	3.4-5	120
3.3-6	238, 239,		211, 220,	4.1-11	231
	243		229, 243	4.4	87
3.3	159	1.16-17	22, 39	4.5	107
3.7-16	212	1.16	59, 93, 220,	5.1-12	33
5.5	205		230	5.5	193
7.11-17	193	1.17	142, 144	6.2	120
7.28	205	3.4	59	7.9-12	33
8	238			7.15	137
9.8-21	186	*1 John*		10.1	123, 124
11	38	1.1	220	10.4	138, 168
11.17	143	2.28	59	11.3	129
11.23-27	212	4.9	144	11.12	21, 138, 168
11.29	212			11.19	87
12.2	38	*Jude*		12.1	87, 124
		14	128	12.3	87
James				12.5	205
2.20	144	*Revelation*		14.13	138
		1.1	101	14.14	168
1 Peter		1.9-20	231	19.9	186
1.11	38	1.12-20	149	19.11	128
1.19	144	1.12-17	33	19.13	184
1.23-25	184	1.12-16	101	19.15	205
2.4	134	1.12	101	20.11	120
2.7	134	1.14	87	21.3	131
		1.16	123, 124	21.10	118
2 Peter		1.17	101	22.16	193
1.4	86	2.17	120, 186		

PSEUDEPIGRAPHA

1 Enoch		39.4-8	132	93.8	154
13.7-10	119	39.7	53, 88		
13.8	138, 168	41.2	132	*2 Baruch*	
14.11	89	42.2	216	4.1-7	84
14.17	89	50.1	55	13.1	138, 168
14.20-21	89	52.1	88	22.1	138, 168
14.20	53, 55, 87,	54.2	87	29.4	186
	112, 123,	62.14	186	40.1-4	203
	124	62.15-16	88	50.10	55, 87
17.9	88	62.15	123	51.3	87, 123
18.8-9	88	65.4	138, 168	51.5	87, 123
18.18	118	70.2	88	51.10	87, 113, 123
25.3	88	71	88	51.12	87
37–71	90	71.1	88, 123	53.1-12	136
38.4	55, 87, 123	71.11	53	59.3	108
39.3	88	71.16	132	59.4-12	75, 103

2 Enoch
1.5   123
3.1   88
11   124
22.8-9   53, 88
42.5   186
61.23   132

3 Enoch
7   89
15   89
15.1-2   79, 123
19.2   89
19.4   89
26.4   89
48C   89
48D   75

4 Ezra
3.18-19   75, 81
6.25-26   39, 40
6.26   96
6.49-50   186
7.97   55, 87, 88
7.109   154
13   203
13.3   136

4 Maccabees
15.4   227

Apoc. Elij.
4.7-12   154

Aristob.
2.3   75
2.6   75
2.12-17   80, 84
2.13-16   81, 84

Ass. Mos.
1.14   148
1.15   75
1.57   78, 84
1.158-59   84
2.70   84
2.280   84
2.288-89   84
2.292   78
12.6   148

Eupol.
26.1   75

Ezek. Trag.
1-31   81
32-38   81
39-67   81
66-82   108
68-89   81, 148
68-82   84, 117, 157, 165, 223
68   81, 82, 106
70-76   83
70   83
74-76   82
76   83
79   82
85   82
86   82
87-89   82
90-192   81
96-100   78, 84
96   83
100   83, 147
101   83

Gk. Apoc. Ezra
6.5-13   147

Jub.
1.1-2   75, 103
1.2-4   75
1.4-5   76, 82
1.4   148
1.24-25   148
1.27-29   118
2-4   75
23.32   75

Liv. Proph.
2.8   76
2.11   76
2.14-15   41, 77, 84, 108, 147, 148
2.15   76
3.12   76
21.1-15   129
21.2   129

Odes
11.13   124

Ps.-Philo
11.5   103
12.1   122, 148
15.5-6   103
19.16   129

Pss. Sol.
2.2   201
2.19-25   201
7.1-3   201
8.23   201
13.8   196
17–18   201
17.13-15   201
17.21-33   201
17.23-51   203
17.23-24   205
17.36   201
18.5   201
18.7   201

Sib. Or.
2.185-95   154, 155, 160
2.220-50   155
3.256   75

T. Abr.
12   87, 113
12.4-5   53, 88
20.14   132

T. Adam
1.11   124

T. Jac.
7.3   75

T. Jud.		14.4	219	4.2-6	77
24	80, 84			10.1-12	77
24.1	194	*T. Mos.*		12.3	77
		1.8-9	77	12.4-5	77
T. Levi		1.14-15	148	12.7-13	77
2–7	119	1.14	84, 147	12.7	77
2.3-5	119	3.9	77	12.8	77
8.11-12	80, 84	3.11-12	77		

QUMRAN

1QH		*1QpHab*		8.21	64
4.5-6	62-65, 123	2.2	65	15.5-11	63
4.24-28	64	2.3	62, 64, 65	19.34	215
4.27-29	62, 63	2.7-8	64, 65	20.12	64
5.11-12	63	2.8	65	119.33	64
5.11	64, 65	7.4	64, 65		
5.29-32	63, 65, 123	8.1	66	Targums	
7.23-25	62, 65			*Targ. Ps.-J.*	
16.9	62	*4QFlor*		1.15	165
16.19	65	1.2	63		
		1.12	63	Mishnah	
1QM		1.15	63	*Ab.*	
2.5	66	1.19	63	1.1	84
		1.18–2.1	205	3.3	217
1QS					
1.3	42	*4QpPs*		*B. Bat.*	
2.19-25	63	37	186	75a	133
2.22-23	63				
4.5	62	*CD*		*B. Meṣ.*	
5.6	66	1.11	64, 65	1.8	42
5.7-9	62, 65	3.10-14	64	2.8	42
5.8-9	64	3.16	65, 215	3.4	42
5.8	62	4.4	64		
8.15	42, 63	4.11	64	*'Ed.*	
8.4-10	66	5.1	62	8.7	84
9.4-5	66	5.21b–6.1a	42		
9.11	65	6.2-11	64	*Pe'ah*	
9.19	63	6.2-10	65	2.6	78, 84
		6.2-3	63	186	133
1QSa		6.3-9	215		
1.2-3	64	6.19	62, 64, 65	*Soṭ.*	
1.3	66	7.18-19	194	9.15	154
1.4-5	63	8.12-15	64	9.18	160

TALMUDS

b. Ber.		*b. Pes.*		*t. Šab.*	
4b	78	13a	42, 154	3c	155
17a	78	20b	154		
				t. Sanh.	
b. B. Meṣ.		*b. Šab.*		113a	155
114a	42	61b	78		
		108a	42, 154	*t. Soṭ.*	
b. 'Erub.		145b-46a	78	49a	176
4a	78				
43b	154	*b. Sanh.*		Midrash	
97a	78	38b	75	*Deut. R.*	
				3.17	41, 76, 129
b. Ḥag.		*b. Ta'an.*		11.17-18	154
3b	78	3a	78		
				Exod. R.	
b. Meg		*b. Yeb.*		1.18	165
14a	195	103a	78	2.4	195
19b	78, 129, 130				
		t. B. Meṣ.		*Gen. R.*	
b. Men.		114a	129	21.5	39, 40
63a	42, 154				
		t. Meg.		*Tanḥ.*	
b. Ned.		21a	176	1.139	80
37b	78, 84				

PHILO

Conf. Ling.		*Fug.*		3.144	55
95–97	55	139	57	3.147	55
146	53-56, 147	147	56	3.173	55
Congr.		*Gig.*		*Leg. Gai.*	
170	56	47–48	55	4.147	53
		53–54	52	95	227
Dec.		53	55		
11	78			*Migr. Abr.*	
18	55	*Leg. All.*		14	55
		1.4	147	23	55
Deus Imm.		1.43	53-55	44–45	55
109-10	55	2.87	55	151	56
		2.93	55		
Ebr.		3.43	56	*Mut. Nom.*	
92	55	3.45	55	2.67-71	52
94	55	3.131	55	2.70	52
		3.140	55	2.74-76	52

7	52
25–26	55
103	56
125	56

Omn. Prob. Lib.
| 75–91 | 57 |

Poster. C.
| 28 | 55 |
| 173 | 55 |

Praem. Poen.
| 56 | 55, 56 |
| 104 | 57 |

Quaest. in Exod.
1.86	129
2.29	53, 233
2.37	53, 55
2.44	55, 103
2.45	53, 57, 59
2.46-47	53, 54, 84
2.46	42, 56
2.51-52	53, 54
2.54	55
2.87-88	55
2.108	55
2.117	55

Quaest. in Gen.
1.86	56
2.33	55
2.59	55
2.64	55
2.81	55
3.5	55
3.21	55
4.137	55

Rer. Div. Her.
| 21 | 55 |
| 301 | 55 |

Sacr.
9	55, 147
50	55
130	55

Somn.
| 1.193-94 | 55 |
| 2.189 | 56 |

Spec. Leg.
| 2.104 | 55 |

Virt.
| 177 | 60 |
| 75 | 55 |

Vit. Mos.
1.1	55, 165
1.8-9	165
1.8	55
1.12	165
1.18-32	165
1.18-31	55
1.32	55
1.48	55, 165
1.57	56, 121, 227
1.60	56
1.148-62	56
1.152	56
1.155-56	56
1.156-57	55
1.158-59	52, 56, 57, 223, 233
1.158	55, 165
1.162	55
1.249	56
1.328	56
2.4	55
2.5	56
2.66-186	56
2.70	57, 233
2.187-291	42, 56
2.280	53, 57
2.288-89	54, 57, 227
2.288	56, 121, 147

Josephus
Ant.
1.18-26	59
1.19	59
1.25	59
2.145	59
2.151-54	59

2.168-71	59
2.205-209	165
2.205-206	165
2.210-16	165
2.217-27	165
2.234	165
2.238-39	58
2.264-65	53, 58
2.283-84	58
2.291	58
2.323	58
2.327	42
2.349	58
3.1-62	58
3.11-12	58
3.26-27	59
3.63	60
3.75-76	58
3.76	58
3.77	58
3.80	55, 59, 61, 81, 84, 103
3.82-83	58, 84
3.87	59
3.93	59
3.94	59
3.99	58
3.180	60, 147
3.188-92	60
3.212	60
3.286	59
3.287	59
3.320	59
4.8.48	75
4.28	60
4.79	60
4.117	58
4.159	58
4.165	42
4.176-77	58
4.198	59
4.223-24	60
4.223	60
4.320	42
5.1	59
5.39-40	59
5.91	59
5.96	59

5.117	59
5.126-27	59
6.133	59
6.86	59
6.88	59
6.93	59
7.4.1	29
7.7	129, 130
7.13	129, 130
7.45-49	193, 197
8.4.5	29
8.13.7	44
9.288-91	58
9.302-303	58
10.184	58
10.210	158
10.276	158
11.84-88	58
11.345-47	68
11.346-47	58
12.10	58
12.36-37	59
12.257-64	58
13.13.3	29
13.74-75	58
15.3.3	29
18.85-86	68, 70, 71, 74, 84
18.85	68
20	171
20.167-72	204
20.200	60
20.268	59
97	171

Apion
| 1.250 | 58 |
| 2.170 | 59 |

War
4.3	119
4.54-55	118
2.573	118
6.285-88	204

Jewish Authors
Asatir
| 9.22 | 72, 122 |

Bib. Ant.
11.5	75, 81
11.14	75
12.1-2	75
12.1	78, 84, 223
12.2-10	75
13.1-10	75
15.5-6	75
19.2-29	84
19.2-9	75
23.10	75
32.7-8	75

Hekhalot Rabbati
| 3.4 | 87, 88 |

Memar Marqah
1.1-2	103
1.1	71, 72
1.2	72
1.9	68
2.2-3	79
2.8	68
3	68
4.3	72, 84, 103, 223
4.6	84
4.8	73, 122
4.12	73
5.2	73
5.3	73, 84
5.4	73
6.3	72
6.8	72
6.9	72, 122

Orphica
| 30-41 | 84 |

Pes. R.
| 4.2 | 129 |

Similitudes of Enoch
32.3	88
36-71	88
39.3	88
40.8	88
40.23	88
67.3	88

Tehillim
| 179 | 80 |
| 21 | 80 |

Christian Authors
Apoc. Pet.
| 15-17 | 22 |

Justin
Dial.
| 8.4 | 154 |
| 49.1 | 154 |

Classical
Corp. Herm.
| 1.1-2 | 86 |

Hom. Dem.
| 233-34 | 86 |

Metamorphoses
1.551-52	86
10.235-42	86
11.291-95	86
11.410-748	86
14.576-80	86
14.757-58	86
2.508-31	86
4.264-70	86
6.374-76	86
6.378	86
6.732-45	86

Other
Bhagavad Gita
| 11.12 | 86 |

INDEX OF AUTHORS

Abrahams, I. 33
Aland, K. 28
Allison, D.C. 13, 17-19, 23, 42, 43
Alsup, J.E. 21, 22
Ambrozic, A. 39
Anderson, H. 44
Argyle, A.W. 17

Bacon, B.W. 21, 40, 43
Badcock, F.J. 30
Baltensweiler, H. 29, 30, 32-34, 44, 45
Barth, K. 25
Bassuk, D.E. 13
Bauckham, R.J. 21, 22, 25
Beare, F.W. 21
Beasley-Murray, G. 27, 29
Bernardin, J.B. 21
Best, E. 27
Best, T.F. 13
Betz, H.D. 21, 35
Bonnard, P. 30, 44
Boobyer, G.H. 21, 22, 25, 26, 32, 38, 39, 41
Bowker, J.W. 29
Braithwaite, W.C. 42, 44
Bretscher, P.G. 34
Brooks, S.H. 18
Brower, K. 28
Brown, R.E. 21
Bultmann, R. 20, 21, 43
Burkill, T.A. 27
Burn, A.E. 24, 41, 44

Caird, G.B. 24, 43
Carlston, C.E. 20, 21
Carson, D.A. 40
Chilton, B.D. 39, 40
Clark, K.W. 18
Cranfield, C.E.B. 25

Creed, J.M. 31
Cullmann, O. 34

Dabeck, P. 43
Daniélou, J. 30, 31, 33, 34
Davies, G.J. 23, 24
Davies, M. 17, 27, 37
Davies, W.D. 17-19, 42, 43
Dobschütz, E. von 17
Dodd, C.H. 22
Donaldson, T.L. 32, 33
Dungan, D.L. 16
Dunn, J.D.G. 17

Ellis, E.E. 31
Evans, D. 13

Faierstein, M.M. 23
Farrer, A. 17, 30
Fenton, J.C. 41
Feuillet, A. 37, 43
Filson, F.V. 41
Fitzmyer, J.A. 23
France, R.T. 15, 17, 18
Fryer, A.T. 42
Fuller, R.H. 34

Garland, D.E. 22
Gerber, W. 35
Ginzberg, L. 42, 44
Glasson, T.F. 33, 41
Goulder, M.D. 17
Groves, W.L. 32
Grundmann, W. 31
Gundry, R.H. 13, 17, 19, 21, 25, 40-42

Hagner, D.A. 17-19
Hahn, F. 30
Hengel, M. 19, 35

Hill, D. 34
Holladay, C.R. 35
Holmes, R. 23
Hooker, M.D. 13, 26, 36, 37, 44
Horstmann, M. 33
Hunter, A.M. 27
Hurst, D. 13

James, M.R. 22
Jeremias, J. 34
Johnson, A.R. 32, 42, 44

Kazmierski, C.R. 28, 33, 34
Keck, L.E. 15, 19
Kennedy, H.A.A. 23
Kenny, A. 28, 29, 31
Kilpatrick, G.D. 17, 19
Kimelmann, R. 19, 21, 42, 43

Lane, W.L. 25, 35, 43
Lenski, R.C.H. 45
Lieberman, S. 19
Liefeld, W. 31, 40, 41
Lohmeyer, E. 30, 35

Manek, J. 23, 24
Mann, C.M. 21
Manson, T.W. 34
Marshall, I.H. 19, 31
Masson, C. 22
Mauser, U.W. 22, 41, 42, 44
McCurley, F.R. 21, 43, 45
McGuckin, J.A. 22
Mckenzie, A.D.F. 32
Meier, J.P. 18, 41
Moore, A. 25
Morris, L. 17, 18, 22, 26, 41
Moses, A.D.A. 13, 40
Moule, C.F.D. 18
Mowinckel, S. 32, 33
Müller, U.B. 35, 36

Neyrey, J.H. 22, 25
Nineham, D.E. 27, 41, 43
Nützel, J.M. 13, 22, 35

Overman, J.A. 18

Pamment, M. 37

Pedersen, S. 33
Plummer, A. 45

Ramsey, A.M. 26, 30
Ravens, D.A.S. 27
Riches, J. 19
Riesenfeld, H. 32-36, 44, 45
Ringgren, H. 33
Robinson, J.A.T. 17
Robinson, J.M. 21
Rowland, C. 22
Rylaarsdam, J.C. 33

Sabbé, M. 13, 33, 35
Saldarini, A.J. 18
Sanders, E.P. 16, 17
Schaeffer, S.E. 21
Schmithals, W. 21
Schnellbächer, E.L. 26, 44
Schweizer, E. 26, 28
Segal, A.F. 18
Segbroeck, F. van 16
Stanton, G. 18
Stein, R. 21, 22
Stendahl, K. 15, 30
Swete, H.B. 30

Tagawa, K. 17
Talbert, C.H. 23
Taylor, J. 23, 27
Thrall, M.H. 22, 38, 44
Tolbert, M.A. 27
Trilling, W. 41
Trites, A.A. 13, 24, 26, 31
Turner, C.H. 30, 34

Vaux, R. de 30, 31, 33
Vermes, G. 34
Viviano, B.T. 15, 19

Watson, F. 20, 21
Weeden, T.J. 20, 21, 25
Weiss, E. 31
Wellhausen, J. 20
Wenham, D. 13, 40
Wiener, A. 42
Wright, N.T. 13, 18

Ziesler, J.A. 33